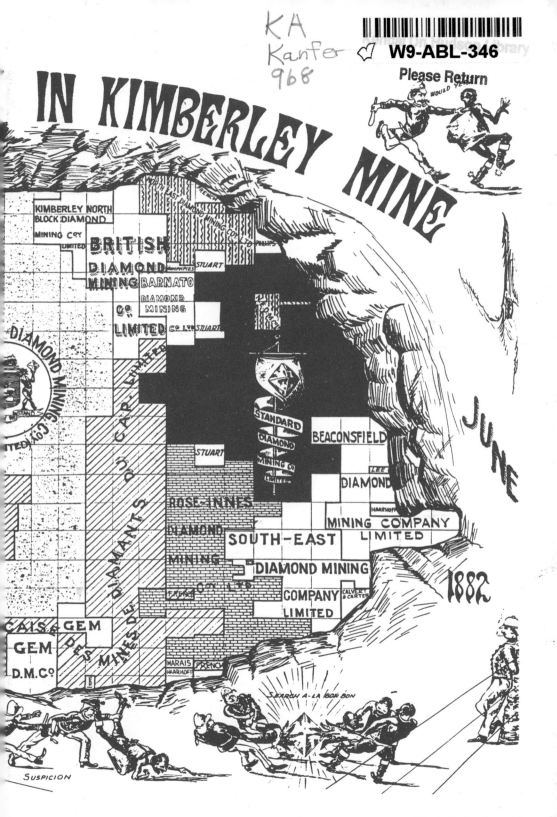

IN KIMBERLEY MINE

JUNE

1882

Africa Collection, Johannesburg

THE LAST
EMPIRE

ALSO BY STEFAN KANFER

A Summer World
A Journal of the Plague Years
The Eighth Sin
Fear Itself
The International Garage Sale

THE LAST
EMPIRE

DE BEERS, DIAMONDS, AND

THE WORLD

STEFAN
KANFER

FARRAR STRAUS GIROUX

NEW YORK

LIBRARY OF CONGRESS CATALOGING-IN-PUBLICATION DATA
Kanfer, Stefan.
The last empire : De Beers, Diamonds, and the World
/ Stefan Kanfer.—1st ed.
p.   cm.
Includes bibliographical references and index.
1. South Africa—History—1836–1909. 2. South Africa—
History—1909–1961. 3. South Africa—History—1961- .   4. Diamond
mines and mining—South Africa—History. 5. De Beers Consolidated
Mines—History. I. Title.
DT1888.K36 1993   968—dc20   92-35976 CIP

FOR LEA PAGE CASTLE
WITH LOVE AND WONDER

ACKNOWLEDGMENTS

If the diamond is the hardest substance to scratch, De Beers must be the second hardest. Some of the company's recent history resides in plain view, but much of it is kept out of sight in private files, obscure transcripts and letters, nearly impenetrable company documents, and in the memories of witnesses who, when they are willing to talk at all, will do so only off the record. Accounts of De Beers's earlier years have to be winnowed from yellowed newspapers and journals, private correspondence, court records, and out-of-print volumes.

At the same time it must be acknowledged that De Beers officials can be surprisingly courteous and helpful. In part this is because, after years of being maligned as "South Africa Inc.," they are anxious to promote their message. W. J. Lear, Director of Corporate Communications for De Beers's Central Selling Organization, wants the world to know that his employers use "a unified wage system—people are paid according to their abilities, not their sex, color or creed." As this book details, it was not always so. Still, that spokesman continues, the Oppenheimer organization has "long had an extensive social investment program aimed at redressing some of the imbalances in South Africa, particularly in education and housing. Together with our sister company, Anglo-American, our spending in this area runs at about five per cent of dividends, comparing very favorably with best practice internationally."

Having said that, the managers of De Beers and Anglo could well have shut and bolted their doors against the curious foreigner. Those executives were no doubt wary of my investigations; nonetheless, without any *quid pro quo* they made room and time for me in Kimberley, Johannesburg, and London. I am particularly grateful to Harry Oppenheimer for letting me use his magnificent library of Africana at Brenthurst, and to Nicholas Oppenheimer for his amiable conversation. In Kimberley, Barbara Kidde guided me through and around the sites of the nineteenth-century diamond rush, and pointed me toward valuable troves of material. Mrs. Muriel Macey, librarian of the Kimberley Public Library, and Ms. H. Norton of the McGregor Museum in Kimberley provided copies of letters, photographs, and long-forgotten memoirs. In the Johannesburg Library, Hillary Bruce spent many hours tracking down relevant material; she remained cheerful and indefatigable throughout. Dr. Moonyean Buys of De Beers Consolidated Mines allowed access to certain data.

One person outside the diamond business was as curious and helpful as those in it: Dr. Ruben Scher of Johannesburg, a selfless physician and friend whose work is helping to change South Africa from a foreboding land into an arena of hope and promise. He and his wife, Jean, were of immeasurable aid.

Sej Motau, now Division Manager of Corporate Communications in Johannesburg, was my guide to De Beers in London, where Robin Walker went through the oddities and rewards of diamond hunting, and where I observed the labor-intensive process of sorting the glistening high-priced pebbles. In more recent times Andrew Lamont, Press Officer and Deputy Manager of Corporate Communications, has been good enough to supply needed materials.

In New York, Lloyd Jaffe, Chairman of the American Diamond Industry Association, offered entrée to the Diamond Club on 47th Street in New York City, one of the world's most exotic organizations. Another book could be written about the traders who give it the aura of a nineteenth-century Middle Eastern bazaar under the light of TV screens and the whir of fax machines.

The most comprehensive collection of Africana outside Johannesburg can be found at the Sterling Library of Yale University in New Haven, Connecticut. Its curator of Africana, Mr. J.M.D. Crossey, helped me sift through sheaves of material and pointed me to relevant Ph.D. theses and to aspects of the superb works of William Worger, Charles Van Onselen, Geoffrey Wheatcroft, Brian Roberts, and many others. He remained a steadfast advisor from beginning to end. This book could not have been written without his patience and counsel. I am also indebted to his knowledgeable and untiring assistant, John Bennett, and to Nancy Lyon, curator of Yale's Manuscripts and Archives, who had her own pertinent suggestions.

Many obscure points were clarified by experts on the various topics of South Africa, the Oppenheimer family, the history of diamond and gold mining, and the complicated fields of finance. I am especially grateful to Joseph Lelyveld, Professor Frank Roosevelt, Marshall Loeb, Mervyn Susser, Louis Gregg, Nigel Bruce, Scott McGregor, as well as those who prefer to remain nameless.

From my earliest days of investigation, two researchers gave me vital support. Villette Harris confidently threaded her way through libraries in New York and at Yale, finding books, making illuminating suggestions, and locating sources, pictures, and maps with unfailing humor and forbearance. Jessie Wallen, a wizard of information retrieval, ransacked all sorts of obscure foreign and domestic journals and financial reports until she ran the facts to earth. When other book dealers assured me that what I wanted was impossible to get, I turned once again to Frank Scioscia, proprietor of the most unusual and most reasonable used bookstore in America—riverrun, in Hastings-on-Hudson, New York. He answered practically every request within a week.

The early encouragement by Elie Wiesel, John Bartholomew Tucker, and the late Jose Ferrer was invaluable.

Sara Bershtel was not only the line editor, she was the shaper of *The Last Empire*. She restores my faith in that battered institution, the New York publishing house. Kathy Robbins is both a counselor and a friend, and deserves a lot more than 15 percent of my gratitude. My family always seems to wind up last in the list of acknowledgments, but they know that they are first in my heart. Thanks once again to Lili and Andy and the little dedicatee, to Nate, and, for far more than 37 reasons, to May.

CONTENTS

THE LAST
EMPIRE

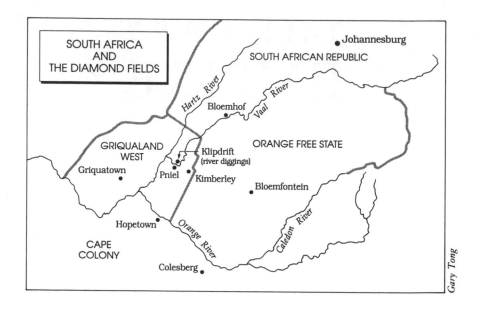

SOUTH AFRICA
AND
THE DIAMOND FIELDS

SOUTH AFRICAN REPUBLIC

• Johannesburg

Hartz River

Bloemhof
•

Vaal River

GRIQUALAND
WEST

ORANGE FREE STATE

Klipdrift
(river diggings)

Griquatown
•

Pniel
•

Kimberley

Bloemfontein
•

Hopetown
•

Orange River

Caledon River

CAPE
COLONY

Colesberg
•

Gary Tong

MERE CARBON,
AFTER ALL

ON THE FOURTH FLOOR of a modern glass-and-stone structure in the heart of London, a number of brown cardboard boxes are quietly handed out. The recipients are some fifty prosperous men seated at a very long mahogany table. The containers are just big enough to contain a pair of Adidas. But inside each package are items of greater value than running shoes. To the untrained eye they resemble bright, shiny pebbles of varying sizes: something you might find on a beach when the tide begins to recede. The gentlemen at 17 Charterhouse Street know better. In each box are rough-cut diamonds worth a minimum of $8 million.

The place is the syndicate building and the event is called a "sight." Every fifth Monday of the year the world's greatest diamond dealers are summoned here to examine the merchandise before they buy it. Once the deal is consummated, the precious stones are shipped to the buyer. He conveys them to cutters and polishers, experts who fashion glittering jewels from unglamorous rocks. The diamonds will then be sold again, this time to other, smaller dealers (all other dealers are smaller) or to individual customers like Prince Charles or Barbra Streisand.

The fifty men could refuse what they are handed; but they never do. Not after the experience of Harry Winston, the biggest name in jewelry until his death in 1978. Winston disliked this high-handed manner of diamond disposal (after all, didn't his clients include the Duke and Duchess of Windsor? the Arab emirates?).

At one sight he handed back his box, walked out, and attempted to go around the syndicate, negotiating to buy rough diamonds from an independent firm in Angola, then a Portuguese possession. One phone call was made, from a British Cabinet member to a high official in Portugal. The Crown, the member said drily, would regard a deal between the colony and Mr. Winston as "an unfriendly act." Winston got the message. He never refused a box again.

This is the way of the diamond syndicate: no threats, no tantrums, merely a discreet show of muscle at the highest levels. It sponsors sights; it detests scenes. Here in London its executives are soft-spoken Oxford men outfitted by Savile Row. They act with the utmost discretion. But they can exhibit the cold will of Mafia dons when the occasion warrants.

There was, for example, the day in 1979 when the syndicate moved its British headquarters up the street from number 2 to number 17. The dealers were "advised" to pay their respects. The gesture would consist of a gift to beautify the interior of the new building. Art works, they were told, might not agree with the taste of the designer; as for furniture, the selections had already been made. It was suggested that the dealers might wish to donate money instead. More than ten thousand dollars would be considered vulgar, less than five thousand, paltry. The amount of cash these dealers were forced to contribute was, of course, a tiny fraction of their earnings. And the syndicate was certainly able to afford any decor it chose. The ritual was simply a show of power, a display of homage to the diamond godfathers.

Many labels adhere to the syndicate—the Central Selling Organization, the Diamond Trading Company, the Anglo-American Trust. These are only names, however, part of a vast and mysterious organization. Some of it is located in London, where the rough specimens are bought wholesale. Some of it is in Tel Aviv and Antwerp and New York, where the diamonds are cut and polished and retailed. But the center of the web is in South Africa. There it is known by the more familiar name of De Beers Consolidated Mines Inc.

The word "empire" is used indiscriminately by financial newsletters to describe any large business concern: OPEC is an "oil empire"; Time Warner is a "communications empire"; Unilever is a "conglomerate empire." In fact none of these establishments fulfill Webster's definition of "an extensive social or economic organization under the control of a single person or family." De Beers, along with its younger sibling, Anglo-American, exactly fits the dictionary description. Each company is the other's largest shareholder, a maneuver that hides wealth, reduces taxes, and prevents even the thought of a hostile takeover. The extensive organization presides over 1,300 businesses, 90 percent of the world's diamonds, and much of its gold. Every one of the corporations can be traced to the Oppenheimers, a family whose style speaks of grander times and simpler moral choices, when imperialism was a profession and not a curse. The times, in short, of Cecil Rhodes, the politician-plutocrat and founder of De Beers, who took giant steps through Africa and presented his Queen with gifts of land and diamonds.

Rhodes's spirit is palpable at 36 Stockdale Street in Kimberley, South Africa. Here, four times a year, the eighteen directors of De Beers gather around a leather-topped teak table in the ground-floor board-room. The place is airy and light, with large windows and French doors leading onto a courtyard filled with trees and flowering shrubs. Voices are never raised in these precincts; the men listen with close attention to Nicholas Oppenheimer. The 46-year-old director of De Beers is a bearded, affable figure, South African by birth, educated at Oxford. The amiability is calculated. Asked what he would like to be noted for someday, Nicholas replies, "Oh, not for any particular thing. Perhaps for having lived a worthwhile life, for not being boring." Nicholas will not be boring; he is the Prince of Diamonds, heir apparent to his father the King.

That royal personage is Harry Frederick Oppenheimer, son of the late Sir Ernest Oppenheimer, the man who brought De Beers into the twentieth century. The 84-year-old retains the pleasant demeanor of a character actor, but one used to playing roles of authority: a prime minister, say, or a master spy. The pleasant wrinkles have good reason to be there. Although Harry has officially retired, his presence is still felt around the world. For one thing, Harry Oppenheimer is the richest man in South Africa, which is to say one of the richest men on earth. (*Fortune* magazine puts him in the top 20 and adds that "Harry O's companies control 54 percent of the Johannesburg Stock Exchange listings, which represents one-fourth of South Africa's wealth.") It is no wonder that when the African National Congress leader Nelson Mandela was released after 31 years in jail, "HFO" was one of the first white men he wanted to see.

Harry's 15-acre suburban estate is of course palatial. He breeds Arabian racehorses. His library of first editions and rare Africana is protected by a technical system of humidity control, dust filters, and sophisticated lighting equaled only by the new wing of the Library of Congress. His collection of Impressionist paintings is worthy of any major museum. Yet these appurtenances have only soothed his eyes; they have never clouded his vision. To Harry, acquisition without authority is meaningless. "I'm not in the least interested in controlling something just for the sake of controlling it," he says. "But I do want the power to do big, difficult things."

One of those things is administrating the amorphous, sometimes hysterical world of diamontiers. That world is in a panic just now; these are the worst times since the Great Depression, and De Beers is faced with a dilemma. Japan and America, two of its biggest outlets, are suffering from severe recessions, and the demand for baubles has dropped precipitously. There are too many diamonds at the wholesale level. In order to keep the cartel intact De Beers must buy up the surplus, and that surplus grows larger all the time. Post-colonial Angola has been torn by internal strife, and large parts of the country are virtually ungoverned. Illicit Angolan diamonds are being dumped onto the market.

To keep prices from collapsing, De Beers will have to spend at least $500 million buying up the oversupply of diamonds, even as it lays out $150 million on advertising. For only the second time in its postwar history, De Beers has slashed its dividend; in the summer of 1992, the mining giant's stock plunged from $28 a share to about $21.

A chill wind is blowing, and many will wither before its blast. Not De Beers; not Harry. He has never known a year without some kind of emergency, and he lives in South Africa, a nation in permanent crisis, disfigured by years of apartheid and threatened with social dissolution. One way or another he has prevailed, keeping the lowest possible profile while exerting the maximum possible strength, worldwide. And all the while he has kept that strength within his family.

From Johannesburg the King's authority is refracted through his companies, like the light through one of their products. (Harry himself does not wear a diamond ring or stickpin. "I belong to a generation whose men did not wear jewelry," he explains. "Things have changed." The smile lines appear. "I'm not against that change.") If sales in the United States and Japan have fallen off, they have toppled from record highs. And Harry was the one responsible for those phenomenal sales. In the United States the profits could be traced to his famous campaign, "A Diamond Is Forever." Less well known are his gratifying efforts to sell diamonds in Asia and Europe. Until the end of World War II, fewer than 1 percent of Japanese wore diamond wedding rings. Then came a guileful and relentless De Beers promotion, maintained until almost 70 percent of new brides carried a diamond on their left hands. West Germans were another group susceptible to advertising. German brides used to be satisfied with a wedding ring composed of two gold bands—until 1967, when De Beers introduced the concept of a *triset*, the third band studded with diamonds. Germany became the third largest diamond-consuming nation.

But these are merely the most obvious examples of influence. The black nations of Namibia, Botswana, Zaire, Lesotho, and Tanzania all have diamond mines. And every one of them passes its diamonds through De Beers's white hands. "We stride across Africa in a very satisfactory way in all sorts of very strange places," says one of Harry's executives. "Part of the secret is that we respect confidences. We don't talk much. And we have been able to convince governments that the system works, and that it is in their interest and ours that it continue to work."

It continues to work even though the process of mining and sorting has always been under attack as a business of unspoken segregation: dirt miners for the most part black; processors and sorters of smaller stones, colored (that is, of mixed racial ancestry); processors and sorters of large stones, white.

For decades critics have branded the managers of De Beers and Anglo as hypocrites; and the empire has gone about its business, making the system function. Its executives know exactly how to balance the use of cheap native labor and the official company policy against racial discrimination. They also know precisely how to phrase their speeches about a free market—and how to bolster the value of jewels by controlling the flow to the wholesalers. According to the company line, to go against the empire is, in the end, self-defeating. "Whether our control amounts to a monopoly I would not know," says Harry Oppenheimer. "But if it does it is certainly a monopoly of a most unusual kind. There is no one concerned with diamonds, whether as producer, dealer, cutter, jeweler, or customer, who does not benefit from it."

In the last decades, the empire has reached out to six continents, investing in financial houses and automobile assembly plants, explosives factories, paper manufacturers, breweries, uranium and platinum and copper and coal mines, travel agencies, farms. For all this diversity, however, the empire's main strengths lie where they always have: in diamonds and gold. Anglo remains the West's largest gold producer, mining 11,000 tons in the last 60 years—10 percent of the known gold in the world. As for diamonds, wherever they are unearthed, in Africa, Australia, or Russia, De Beers controls more than 90 percent of the precious stones. Theoretically, every part of the Oppenheimer holdings is equally important, but Harry has never pretended to be impartial. Diamonds may be in trouble, but they were the cornerstones of empire, and for him they retain a special luster. "People buy diamonds out of vanity," he once noted, "and they buy gold because they're too stupid to think of any other monetary system which will work—and I think vanity is probably a more attractive motive than stupidity."

He neglected to mention certain other motives. Greed, for example, and jealousy, and cruelty, and ravenous ambition. These are hardly the warmest human attributes. But they have accompanied diamonds for more than 5,000 years. The story of those stones is older than De Beers, older than South Africa, and nearly as old as avarice.

◆   ◆   ◆

FOR CENTURIES diamonds have appeared in royal treasuries and commoners' imaginations. Adventurers have journeyed thousands of miles to hunt them. Men and women have killed for them. Countries have flourished and regimes have fallen because of them. Diamonds have always been far more than jewels; they are history twinkling on the skin.

The gemstones appear in the Bible ("Etched is Judah's sin with iron pen, with diamond point engraved on the plaque of their heart. . .").

Pliny the Elder speaks about the miraculous power of diamonds to heal diseases. Others describe diamonds that render the wearer invisible. But it is not until the *Arabian Nights* that writers begin romancing the stone.

In the Second Voyage, Sinbad recalls his descent into the Valley of Diamonds. The scene has been copied by filmmakers from Cecil B. de Mille to Steven Spielberg: "The soil was of diamonds but swarmed with mighty snakes from which I sought refuge in a cave. Within was another serpent, brooding her eggs. I passed the night with her, in great fear. Staggering in the morning with hunger, terror, and fatigue, I ventured forth, and a big piece of meat dropped before me. Now, I had heard that diamond merchants cast freshly flayed sheep into the valley of diamonds; the meat being sticky, jewels cling to it; then vultures and eagles swoop and carry the meat to the mountain tops, where the merchants scare them away and collect the jewels.

"Therefore I quickly filled my clothes with diamonds, tied the meat across my chest, and lay on my back. An eagle lifted me to the mountains, where a man, shouting, drove him off; but the man himself was startled when he beheld me there. I gave him some of the diamonds and told my tale."

H. Rider Haggard imitated the scene in *King Solomon's Mines*, and so did John Buchan, author of *The 39 Steps*. (Both writers were veterans of the diamond fields.) "The whole of my stones I sold to De Beers," says the adventurous hero of *Prester John*, "for if I had placed them on the open market I should have upset the delicate equipoise of diamond values. When I came finally to cast up my accounts, I found that I had secured a fortune of a trifle over a quarter of a million pounds.

"The wealth did not dazzle so much as it solemnised me. I had no impulse to spend any part of it in a riot of folly. . . . It had been bought with men's blood. . . ."

In *The Moonstone*, England's first detective story, Wilkie Collins speaks of an enormous yellow diamond, plucked from the forehead of a Hindu deity and possessed by a series of unfortunate owners from India to Britain and back again. "This jewel that you could hold between your finger and thumb seemed unfathomable as the heavens themselves. We set it in the sun, and then shut the light out of the room, and it shone awfully out of the depths of its own brightness.

. . . No wonder Miss Rachel was fascinated; no wonder her cousins screamed. . . . The only one of us who kept his senses was Mr. Godfrey. He put an arm around each of his sisters' waists, and, looking compassionately backwards and forwards between the Diamond and me, said, 'Carbon, Betteridge! mere carbon, my good friend, after all.' "

Mere carbon; mere fiction. The truth about diamonds is much more exotic. The Koh-I-Noor, for example, was found on a riverbank in India. It was acquired by a ruling family and passed down the generations until one of the kings had it inserted into the design of the Peacock Throne. When the Persian conqueror Nadir Shah seized that chair in 1793, he found that the jewel was gone. The dethroned ruler, Mohammed, had plucked out the diamond and secreted it in his turban.

The Persian was a careful man; he knew better than to attack Mohammed and precipitate a revolution. Instead he offered to return the land he had taken and, as a gesture of friendship, abruptly suggested, "Let us exchange our headdresses in celebration of our treaty of friendship." Before witnesses, Mohammed could not refuse. He handed over his headgear. As soon as Nadir was alone he unwound the garment and shook out the gemstone. It was so large that he shouted "Koh-I-Noor," Mountain of Light.

Nadir took it back to Persia, where he was assassinated. His grandson, Shah Runk, got hold of it, but he was captured by raiders. The price of the ransom: the Koh-I-Noor, paid to one Ahmed Shah, whose family kept it for two more generations. Then Ahmed's grandson Zaman was deposed by his brother Shuja, imprisoned, and—when he refused to tell the whereabouts of the stone—blinded. Presently Shuja was driven from *his* throne and sought refuge with a leader known as Lion of the Punjab. The fee for safety, of course, was the Koh-I-Noor. The Lion's successor was murdered. The diamond did not lose its curse until the British annexed the Punjab and seized the Mountain of Light. In 1850 it was presented to Queen Victoria. Her Majesty let it be known that the stone would look a lot better if it were recut. The final product weighed 108.93 carats. It has adorned Queens ever since. Alexandra wore the Koh-I-Noor to the coronation of King Edward VII; Elizabeth II took it to her coronation. In between state occasions it can be viewed reposing with the other Crown Jewels in the Tower of London.

Other diamonds have equally bizarre histories. The story of the Orloff begins with a French soldier's visit to an Indian temple. There he spies an immense diamond flashing in the eye of yet another idol. For months he befriends the Hindu priests, and when at last they leave him alone he pries out the stone and heads for Madras. There he sells it to a ship's captain who, in turn, sells it to Count Orloff in 1775. The Russian aristocrat uses it to get back into the good graces of Catherine the Great; but after pocketing the jewel she throws him over for Potemkin.

The Regent presents another case of greed, murder, and remorse. Like the others, it is discovered in India. A slave steals the diamond and conceals it in a self-inflicted wound. He flees to the seacoast and divulges his secret to a mariner, in return for passage to a free country. En route he is thrown overboard. The mariner sells the stone, squanders the proceeds on women and liquor, and in a fit of delirium tremens, hangs himself. The diamond passes through many hands, including those of Marie Antoinette, who pins it to her black velvet hat. The Regent disappears during the French Revolution and surfaces afterward in a Paris garret. In 1797 it is pledged for money to help Napoleon in his rise to power. He has it mounted in the hilt of his sword and wears it to his coronation in 1804. When Bonaparte goes into exile at Elba, the Regent becomes part of France's crown jewels, permanently housed at the Louvre.

All of these gems—and many more, equally romantic—originated in India. For centuries that country was thought to be the sole source of diamonds. They were mined by laborers who earned about a penny a day for their efforts. A visitor recalled seeing "close upon 60,000 persons . . . the men digging . . . the women and children carrying earth."

Then, just as the Indian mines gave out, a new supply was discovered in Brazil. When Richard Burton arrived there in 1867, he visited a mine. The explorer found "no trace of crane and pulley, no rail, no knowledge of that simplest contrivance of a tackle; the negro was the only implement." Brazil's diamondiferous soil was quickly exhausted. But, as it turned out, there were plenty of stones and more than enough "implements" in the faraway land of South Africa.

PART ONE

ROMANCING THE STONE

The Victorians were lame giants; the strongest of them walked on one leg a little shorter than the other. Those that are only uncommon men are perverts and sowers of pestilence. But somehow the great Victorian man was more and less than this. He was at once a giant and a dwarf.

G. K. CHESTERTON

1

A FOCUS OF HUMAN
PASSION

DE BEERS'S STAID OFFICES and quiet Oxonian executives suggest old money and immemorial power. In fact, the history of the empire is a modern saga. Then again, so is the story of its home country. Next to South Africa, the upstart nations of Australia and the United States seem to be ancient civilizations: Sydney was founded in 1788, and Cincinnati was incorporated as a city in 1819. Kimberley, where De Beers began, mushroomed up in the 1870s. Johannesburg, home of Anglo-American, was born ten years later.

Until then, the sunstruck country lay sleeping in the Middle Ages. It had no navigable rivers, no significant railroad line, no telegraph. Transportation was by ox wagon, communication by horse and rider. The land was so sere it took six thousand acres to nourish a herd of cattle. Boats of the Dutch East India Company had once used the southernmost city, Cape Town, as a place to take on supplies before heading out to India and China. But those fleets had not been a factor for a hundred years. The one site of lingering value, the seaport at the Cape of Good Hope, was about to be rendered obsolete. Ships to the East would cut through the continent at the new Suez Canal.

After Waterloo, the British had annexed much of the territory to keep the French from getting a toehold. But in the post-Napoleonic era the occupation seemed to be a blunder. It diverted men and equipment from more important posts, and it produced no income. Historian Sir John Robert Seely spoke for many of his countrymen when he concluded that England had gained its South African possession "in a fit of absence of mind." A Victorian globe-trotter added his own withering assessment: "Her Majesty possesses not, in all her empire, another strip of land so unlovely."

Britain's competitors took much the same view, and from the late eighteenth century to the middle of the nineteenth, the imperial scramble took place north of the Limpopo River, at the very edge of South Africa. It was as if marauders had broken into a house, systematically ransacked it for linens, heirlooms, and furniture—and neglected to look downstairs, where a cache of jewels lay unguarded.

In 1867 it was accidentally pried open by a farm boy relaxing under a tree near the banks of the Orange River, northwest of Hope Town. The territory in and around the Transvaal has not altered appreciably since the time of Erasmus Stephanus Jacobs. Occasional clusters of buildings make little impression on the basic topography. Then as now the river was muddy and meandering; the earth on either side was a grayish-yellow powder, uninterrupted by vegetation except for stands of silvery grass and the incidental, umbrella-shaped thorn tree.

So it is not hard to imagine the 15-year-old on that epochal afternoon. According to Jacobs's account, given when he was in his eighties, he noticed "in the glare of the strong sun a glittering pebble some yards away. . . . I, of course, had no idea that the stone was of value. I was at the time wearing a corduroy suit, and simply put the pebble in my pocket. I did not feel at all excited at finding such a beautiful stone. . . . After reaching home I handed the *mooi klip* (pretty pebble) to my youngest sister, who simply placed it among her playthings."

A month later the Jacobses were playing a traditional game called Five Stones. One of the pieces was the *mooi klip*, the others ordinary river rocks. A neighbor, Schalk van Niekerk, "arrived during the game and greatly admired the stone, and tried to scratch a windowpane with it. My mother noticed that Mr. van Niekerk had taken quite a fancy to this 'white stone'; so she gave it to him."

◆   ◆   ◆

Like the Jacobses, Schalk van Niekerk was a member of that nomadic white tribe whose ancestors had come from the Netherlands two hundred years before. They were the only people to have brought slaves *to* Africa—mostly Javanese, acquired during the seventeenth century when the Dutch were a dominant force in the East.

The Boers (the Dutch word for farmers) were a robust folk whose clothes were homespun and generously cut and whose moral opinions were based on a literal interpretation of the Bible. The man who was to become their greatest leader, Paul Kruger, believed the earth was flat; no one ever thought to contradict him. According to Boer teachings, slave-owning was not merely condoned, it was encouraged in the Old Testament. Thus the local blacks of Africa were considered heaven-sent for the white man's use. The farmers captured as many as they could and put them to work. Among these natives were an indigenous people who called themselves the Khoikhoi. The Dutch had another name. They thought the natives sounded as if they were stammering and stuttering—*hateren en tateren*. The phrase was shortened to Hottentot. Another local people, the Bantu, were called Kaffirs. That was neither a black nor a European word; it derived from the unflattering Arabic *Qafir*—-infidel, unbeliever. Those of mixed black and white ancestry went by the name of *Bastaards*, a label that was later changed to the less offensive term, Griquas.

A visiting aristocrat, Lady Anne Barnard, came to South Africa in the late eighteenth century and made notes. She found that in the company of strangers these transplanted Dutch could be "sulky and ill-affected." Yet she had to admit that the men were fine looking, "six feet high and upwards," and she was told that on the frontier some "even reach seven feet." Lady Anne provides a striking portrait of the white Africans out for a stroll "in blue cloth jackets and very flat hats. . . . They struck me as overdressed, but the Hottentot servant who crept behind each, carrying his master's umbrella [was] underdressed . . . a piece of leather round his waist and a sheepskin round his shoulders: one or two had a scarlet handkerchief tied round his head, sometimes an old hat ornamented with ostrich feathers." She found Boer women attractive but overplump; after the age of thirty few of them weighed less than 180 pounds. This may have been the result of having children early. Too early, she thought, and was corrected by an official: "Not at all madam. They come at exactly the proper time, but the marriages took place a little late."

With the succor of Holy Writ and the aid of subjugated blacks, Boer families stolidly worked the land in the southernmost part of South Africa, raising cattle for food and sheep for wool. Despite the work of developers, the Cape Town region has changed very little from the days of the Dutchmen. Back from the wide silvery beaches the land rises steeply into the Drakensburg Mountain range. It catches the rain and turns the valleys of Stellenbosch and Drakenstein into lush farmland. As in the distant past, the soil supports crops of cotton, corn, beans, and grapes for excellent wines and a raw brandy called Cape Smoke. Beyond the valleys the land abruptly gives way to a plateau. Here the earth is cracked and powdery. Farming becomes impossible without irrigation, and the vegetable fields are replaced by vast stretches of grazing land. It is hardly enough for the demands of an industrial society. But it suited the Boers until the early nineteenth century, when two factors combined to push them on. First was the shortage of acreage to support a suddenly expanding population: the Boers, who felt crowded if they could hear the sounds of a neighbor chopping wood, were being undone by their own fertility. Second was the lack of sympathy from their British overlords.

These Englishmen had possessed *de facto* authority since the Napoleonic era. They had *de jure* control after 1815, when the Netherlands transferred its territory to Britain in exchange for some £6 million. Boer and Briton eyed each other uneasily, but there were certain calm occasions. One had come early on, in 1809, when administrators of William IV imposed the first Pass Law. It was as if the English King had read the Boers' minds and granted them their fondest wish. From now on every black had to have a "fixed place of abode." In order to move he required a pass from his master or from a local official. Failure to obey meant a fine or jail.

From London, the antislavery movement looked on and vowed to end this iniquity. Dr. David Livingstone gave expression to its deepest feelings. In Africa, he recalled, "The strangest disease I have seen seems really to be broken-heartedness, and it attacks free men who have been captured and made slaves." After five years of incessant lobbying the government gave way. In 1814 the Pass Law was revoked and a commission appointed to investigate the cruel usage of blacks.

Boer tradition has it that South African slavery was essentially a benign patriarchal system, far gentler than the one in America. The truth is that it was arbitrary, violent, and inhuman. Cape Town's Slave Lodge had been turned into a brothel, open one hour a night for the pleasure of sailors on leave; and male slaves were treated with the full harshness of the age. For disobedience they could be broken on the wheel, flogged, or tied hand and foot, sewed into sacks, and thrown in the bay. One offender was ordered to be "bound on a cross, his right hand shall be cut off, his body pinched in six places by red-hot irons, his legs and arms broken to pieces, after that to be impaled before the Town House on the Square, his dead body afterwards to be thrown outside the town at the usual place and left to be a prey to the birds in the air." For most farmers, human property was too valuable to be treated with such barbarism. But the threat was always there, and if rural slaves were seldom broken on the wheel, none of them were ever free of terror.

When the English revoked the Pass Law some sixty defiant Boers rose in armed protest. Five of them were hunted down, and in 1815 they were sentenced to death at a place called Slachter's Nek. The hangings were particularly horrific. Four times the rope broke and the condemned men were hurtled to the ground, still alive. The crowd saw this as a sign from heaven and pleaded for mercy. The officer in charge turned his back, and the men were hanged until they swung lifeless against the South African sky. It was a bitter and unforgivable day, and Slachter's Nek was turned into the first of many Boer shrines.

The final blow fell in 1833 when all South African slaves were declared freemen by order of His Majesty. The farmers valued their human property at £3 million; the Crown offered £1.2 million in compensation, payable only in London. This was the ultimate gesture of contempt. The Boers could hardly afford round-trip passage to England, and they were forced to accept sums handed down through a hierarchy of agents and lawyers. By the time the checks were cashed the owners received a mere fraction of their entitlements. Some got nothing at all. The black workers abandoned the farms, aimlessly roaming the countryside or squatting outside the small towns. Quite a few supported themselves by stealing.

Now it was the Boers who were chained to the land. Without a work force their farm economy was ruined. In 1837, ten thousand of them packed their cumbrous ox wagons, left the hated British, and headed north and east on their Great Trek. Kipling imagined the trekker at this time:

His neighbor's smoke shall vex his eyes, their voices
break his rest.
He shall go forth till south is north, sullen
and dispossessed.

One of the dispossessed, Anna Steenkamp, candidly explained to
relatives that it was "not so much the freeing of our slaves which drove
us to such length, as their being placed on an equal footing with
Christians, contrary to the laws of God. . . ."

Her 54-year-old uncle, Pieter Retief, added a warning: "We leave
this country with a desire to enjoy a quieter life. . . . We will not
molest any people, nor deprive them of the smallest property, but if
attacked we shall consider ourselves justified in defending our persons
and effects to the utmost of our ability against the enemy."

The quieter life eluded them on the road as it had on their farms.
Wherever they rode they were subject to attacks by the most feared
soldiers in the region, Zulus under their chief Dingaan. For several
centuries these people had been patriarchal and nomadic. Their economy centered on the possession of cattle, an animal so important to
them that while English has barely a dozen words for cows, bulls, and
calves, the Zulu tongue has over three hundred. Then had come a
chief named Shaka. He developed a new form of warfare: instead of
the old hit-and-retreat tactics, Shaka's Zulus formed highly disciplined
and ruthless regiments—*indunas*—that almost never knew defeat.
Zulu territory expanded from 1,200 square miles to a region twelve
times as large, ranging from the east coast several hundred miles into
the interior.

From 1815 to 1828, the years of Shaka's rule, black South Africa
experienced a cataclysmic *mfecane*—a great crushing. Shaka decimated
or drove out rival tribes and dissident chiefs. Shaka had absolute power,
and he terrified everyone in his court; a mere wave of his hand was
enough to have a man clubbed to death by guards. But in the thirteenth
year of his rule, Shaka's hand grew unsteady and too many advisors
were put to death. His half-brother Dingaan knew it was only a matter
of time before he became a target, and in September 1828 he and two
fellow conspirators stabbed their leader to death and took control of

the Zulu tribe. The assassination brought no change in policy; under Dingaan the raids went on as before.

Dispatches arriving in the United States several months later were read without surprise; any American who had made the journey west through Indian territory already knew how the drama would unfold. In Act One the white invaders are driven back by local tribes; in Act Two the foreigners' technology brings them victory after victory until the final surrender. This is interpreted as a sign of divine approval. Act Three shows "native policy," put in place by the new rulers.

The curtain rose on Zulus assuming their feathered headdresses, shields, and deadly short spears. They raided every Boer wagon they could find. Whole families were annihilated in minutes. Retief himself was betrayed one February afternoon in 1838 when he and some seventy fellow trekkers came to a clearing at Dingaan's invitation. The chief offered them a peace treaty and invited his visitors to witness a ritual dance. As the Boers made themselves comfortable, the warriors rose up on a prearranged signal, dragged the men to a place of execution, and cracked their skulls. The Zulus then went on to other encampments. Nearly five hundred more Boers were slain in the following days, most of them women and children.

The same year, on the sixteenth of December, Dingaan's men massed for one more battle. Their target was a group of wagons camped near the Ncome River, about 300 miles north of the Cape Colony. This time the Boers were prepared. The night before a dynamic young commander, Andries Pretorius, ordered the drivers to circle their wagons in a defensive *laager*. According to Boer tradition he clambered onto a gun carriage and asked his men to join him in a vow. If they triumphed, they "would note the date . . . to make it known even to our latest posterity in order that it might be celebrated to the honour of God."

In the morning the defenders trained their artillery and elephant guns on the open fields and waited for the mist to disperse. The raiders came in suicidal waves. Before nightfall three thousand black men lay dead; spears were no match for shells and grapeshot. The Boers suffered three casualties. Pretorius had been severely cut in the hand, and two other farmers were superficially wounded. Gazing at the bodies piled three-deep outside the wagons, a Dutch Reform minister concluded, "The word of the Lord was fulfilled. 'By one way shall your enemies come, but by the blessing of the Lord they shall fly before your face.'" The Ncome ran red and was renamed Blood River. This became, and remains, the greatest of all Boer shrines, the place where the savages died and the martyrs were avenged.

Similarities between the Great Trek and the biblical Exodus were preached in pulpits of the Dutch Reform Churches and discussed at meetings. Trekkers saw themselves as the new Chosen People, unwilling to trust those outside the circle, particularly the British and the blacks. Their very language seemed as exclusive as Hebrew. Called Afrikaans, a Dutch dialect including Malay and Portuguese idioms picked up from eastern trade and domestic slaves, it was spoken nowhere else in the world.

Britain sensed that these fractious and insular people could not be ruled as easily as the blacks. His Majesty's representatives had no appetite for a war among white men. In the early 1850s, British troops withdrew, and the Boers were allowed to establish their own independent governments, free of English law and language. Two separate Afrikaaner republics were set up: the Orange Free State and the Transvaal; in each the *laager* mentality prevailed. North of the Vaal river, leaders determined that there would be "no equality in church and state" between the races. And no "bastards"—meaning any person of mixed Caucasian and Negro blood "down to the tenth degree"—were to participate in the legislature.

Nothing like these laws had ever been passed under the British administration. Yet no official voice of criticism was to be heard from Whitehall. For one thing, despite the increasing number of anti-slavery agitators, not all British citizens believed in the idea of equality. Some, like the explorer Richard Burton, regarded the black African as genial but incapable of improvement: "He seems to belong to one of those childish races which, never rising to man's estate, fall like worn-out links from the great chain of animated nature."

Samuel Baker, the wealthy adventurer who had discovered Lake Albert in 1864, was harsher. "I wish the black sympathizers in England could see Africa's inmost heart as I do," he wrote in his diary. "Human nature viewed in its crude state as pictured amongst African savages is quite on a level with that of the brute, and not to be compared with the noble character of the dog. There is neither gratitude, pity, love, nor self-denial; no idea of duty; no religion; but covetousness, ingratitude, selfishness and cruelty. All are thieves, idle, envious, and ready to plunder and enslave their weaker neighbors."

Still, the crucial reason for indifference and rancor was the subcontinent itself. It was more trouble than it was worth, especially for England. In *The Story of an African Farm*, Olive Schreiner describes the uninviting country in the drought year of 1862: "From end to end of the land the earth cried for water. Man and beast turned their eyes to the pitiless sky. . . . On the farm, day after day, month after month, the water in the dams fell lower and lower; the sheep died in the fields; the cattle, scarcely able to crawl, tottered as they moved from spot to spot in search of food. Week after week, month after month, the sun looked down from the cloudless sky, till the karoo bushes were leafless sticks, broken into the earth, and the earth itself was naked and bare; and only the milk-bushes, like old hags, pointed their shrivelled fingers heavenwards, praying for the rain that never came."

Why argue over dirt that could barely sustain herds of sheep? Let the Boers and the Bantus have their turf wars; it had nothing to do with the imperialists of Europe. South Africa went on withering in the sun until the fateful occasion of Mrs. Jacobs's presentation to her fellow Boer, Schalk van Niekerk.

♦   ♦   ♦

EVEN THE ROUGHEST DIAMOND, with pieces of dirt still clinging to it, has unique properties. It is the hardest natural substance in the world. Dip it in water and it emerges dry. Rub it against cloth and it assumes a positive electrostatic charge. Expose it to sunlight and it will glow that night with an eerie phosphorescence.

Van Niekerk considered all this, and yet he could not be sure the stone in his hand was the real thing. He tried to scratch a glass with it, but the results were inconclusive. Perhaps he pressed too hard, or not hard enough. In any case he was unsure of what he had. Impatient and hungry, van Niekerk sold his treasure for a few pounds. The buyer was an itinerant trader named Jack O'Reilly, and he was also uncertain about the value of the stone. O'Reilly shopped it around in

Hope Town, where he became a local source of amusement. Every merchant dismissed the specimen as worthless, and one of them bet "a dozen of beer" that it was not a genuine diamond.

In the neighboring village of Colesburg O'Reilly met with more derision—from everyone except the Acting Civil Commissioner, Lorenzo Boyes. The official scratched a windowpane with it and thought O'Reilly might have something after all. He sent the stone to an amateur mineralogist, Dr. W. Guybon Atherstone of Grahamstown. Atherstone holds two places in his country's history. He was the first of its surgeons to use anesthesia; and he was the first authority to recognize that the "rounded, apparently water-worn river stone" was a genuine homegrown jewel. In the first flush of excitement he ran to the house of his next-door neighbor, a local Catholic priest. Father James Ricards celebrated the find by scratching the initials J.R. on *his* window. That pane was to remain in place for decades, a reminder that the opening page of South Africa's new history was written on glass.

News of the diamond was all over town the next day. O'Reilly's stone measured 21¼ carats, and Atherstone speculated, "Where that came from there are lots more." His statement scarcely caused a ripple. The Colesburg *Advertiser* observed for the record that "Stranger things have come to pass in the world than the Discovery of Diamonds in South Africa"—and went on to the pressing matters of a local cattle sale and a forthcoming dance.

Atherstone mailed the stone to the Colonial Secretary in Cape Town. Richard Southey was a man of quick perceptions. He packed O'Reilly's treasure in a government dispatch bag and sent it off to London. There it was examined by the grand old firm of Garrards, jewelers to the Crown. Their experts decided that the "Cape Diamond" was legitimate. Even so, they wanted no part of it. The company directors were convinced that the South African earth had been "salted" in order to precipitate a land rush. The Director of the Museum of Practical Geology went further. Without directly accusing anyone of cheating, he reported that since the rock formations in that part of the world were nothing like those in Brazil and India, there could be no authentic diamonds in South Africa. He would stake his reputation on it.

In the next year, other diamonds were discovered near the Vaal river. They were small and insignificant, and the doubts continued. Hope

Town's Civil Commissioner, William Chalmers, thought he knew the reason why. In a letter to Southey in March 1868, he grumbled, "if a proper search were made, or rather if mining were carried on, by persons who understand the work, a great many Diamonds would have been found. . . . The Colony complains about hard times; but it deserves to be hard up when it quietly hears about the richest of all gems in one of its Districts, and takes no steps whatever to open up the vast wealth which these gems would produce."

Lorenzo Boyes decided to make a "proper search." Twice he went out prospecting, twice he came back empty, but nothing could shake his conviction that gemstones lay out there in the baked land. What the country needed, he felt, was a professional mineralogist, a kind of diamond detective to go over the evidence. Three months later that man appeared. James R. Gregory had been sent by a London diamond merchant named Harry Emmanuel. Within a day the expert announced that South Africa held absolutely no promise. If any diamonds were found in the vicinity, they must have been carried there in the gizzards of wandering ostriches.

Ostriches? When Commissioner Chalmers heard the judgment, he exploded. "My suspicions were at once aroused," he was to recall. "I felt perfectly convinced that [Gregory] had been engaged by some person or company . . . to come out here for no other purpose than to *cry down* the South African diamonds, in order to keep up the market prices of their own diamonds."

Gregory was not finished with South Africa. Back in London the mineralogist expressed even greater disdain. "I made a very lengthy examination of the districts where diamonds are said to be found," he wrote in *The Geological Magazine*, "but saw no indication that would suggest the finding of diamonds or diamond bearing deposits in any of these localities." Then came the historic declaration that would make his name—although not in the way he would have chosen: "The geological character of that part of the country renders it impossible . . . that any could have been discovered there."

This was like evaluating the contents of a bank safe by examining its door, its combination lock, its color—everything irrelevant to the main question. As geologists have since discovered, topography yields very little in the way of clues for prospectors. Diamonds have been unearthed in lands as disparate as China, Arkansas, South Africa, Brazil, and India. What unites these territories is volcanic activity that occurred ten million years ago, 60 miles below the soil.

Under incalculable pressure and heat, deposits of pure carbon were mixed with liquid rock and gases and forced upward. As the mixture rose it began to cool. The carbon crystallized into hard, clear stones. The surrounding liquid formed into large tubes, widening as they approached the surface of the earth. A cross-section would show a tornado of diamonds with a mile-wide top, winding its way downward several thousand feet. Some of the mixture broke through the surface, but instead of pouring out like lava, it cooled quickly and set into hard mounds. As the aeons passed, those mounds broke up. Land shifts, winds, and rivers scattered the uppermost diamonds far from their origin. These so-called alluvial stones were what Erasmus Jacobs and the others had found. No one knew about the phenomenally rich pipes underground.

So Gregory's opinion seemed authoritative and final. Protests from South Africa consisted of a few angry letters, printed in *The Geological Magazine*. Atherstone tried to redeem his countrymen's honor: "The parties concerned were—a farmer's child, a Dutch Boer, Mr. L. Boyes, a Government official, myself. . . . Which of these parties is the fraudulent imposter, getting up a land-jobbing speculation?" O'Reilly offered his own theory: Gregory was making false judgments so that he could sneak back to the Cape and dig up all the diamonds for himself.

These opinions and counter-accusations might soon have died out except for the efforts of a Griqua shepherd. He had heard people speak of a Boer who was paying big money for "special" pebbles. Swartbooi had acquired one of those stones. He wanted a fortune for it, and van Niekerk met his price: 500 sheep, 10 oxen, and a horse. Diamond in hand, the buyer headed back to Cape Town, and this time he was not greeted with laughter. A jeweler, Gustav Lilienfeld, immediately judged the stone to be a fine white gem of 83½ carats and made an opening offer of £11,200—well over a quarter of a million dollars in today's terms. Van Niekerk grabbed it without haggling. He was, a rival bidder sulked, "a lazy man."

Lilienfeld's labeled their newest acquisition the Star of South Africa and put it on exhibit in Cape Town. Nearly every official history of the country speaks of the Colonial Secretary, Richard Southey, borrowing the Star, showing it to the Cape Assembly, and making his dramatic prediction, "Gentlemen, this is the rock upon which the future of South Africa will be built." Like the tale of the Boers praying for victory before the battle of Blood River, it was written after the fact and grows grander with each retelling. Actually, the diamond was shipped to London aboard the H.M.S. *Celt* before the South African Parliament was convened on June 23, 1869.

In London Lilienfeld's had the Star of South Africa cut and polished. They soon found an aristocratic buyer: the Earl of Dudley, who paid £30,000 for the stone. Newspapers covered the transaction, and within a month the news was out in England, Europe, and the United States. There was a brief pause while the imperialists and fortune hunters scratched their heads. Diamonds in South Africa, the blasted heath of Dutchmen and natives? The place where summer arrived in December and snow came in July? Impossible. They confirmed their opinions by rereading Gregory's findings. Then they took another look at the price the Earl had paid. Well, they decided, perhaps it *was* worth a look around. They checked maritime schedules and packed their rough clothing and broad-brimmed hats for a season in the sun.

◆ ◆ ◆

THEY WERE LATE. In the Orange Free State and the Transvaal, ambitious men had already put down their plows and pencils and hurried to Hope Town. Civil servants throughout the Cape put in so many requests for leave that the Colonial Secretary was forced to rubber stamp his refusal. "Otherwise," he concluded, "all would go."

The second wave occurred in slow motion. From the harbor in Cape Town the immigrants proceeded north. It was at least a month's hard travel to the valley of diamonds, on the banks of the Vaal River. George Beet, nineteen when he made the trip from England, remembered the roadless journey. "At times we travelers all became so thoroughly shaken up on the way as to doubt whether we were human beings or medicine bottles. . . . It rained in torrents and thundered and lightened as it can only in South Africa."

At intervals Beet ran into long-faced prospectors returning home. "Most of these men gravely advised us not to proceed farther, as fellows at the various 'rushes' were dying in scores from fever and other diseases. The place, they said, had already earned the lugubrious so-briquet of 'the young man's graveyard.' "

But Beet and his fellow passengers had not come across two oceans to turn back at the last minute. The caravans continued to creak and groan over rocks and hillocks. The sun cracked the earth and blistered skins. Occasionally an ox or horse succumbed to the heat and strain. Hyenas and buzzards materialized and quarreled over the carrion. The riders felt the chill of death, and their voices grew a little too hearty and their jokes a little too frantic. The wagons pushed on.

On the evening of the forty-second day they completed their trek. Beet had expected a community of quiet, solitary workers. He found a frantic social hum. Zulus, Xhosas, and Bechuanas, enticed from their lands by promises of high wages, boomed out their chants of love and battle. The white tribes were composed of Englishmen, Boers, Germans, French, and Americans, most of them veterans of the recent Civil War. At night they all sat around drinking and singing and boasting in various languages. Occasionally a rifle shot sounded; someone had fired off a round just to hear the noise. Banjos and harmonicas harmonized in the background. Hundreds of dogs, ducks, pigs, and chickens added their own calls to the general chatter. "Talk about Roaring Camps!" exclaimed Beet. "If my reading of Messieurs Bret Harte and Company is correct, the hullabaloo . . . would make the roaring of any California mining camp sound like the twitterings of a dove-cot."

The American and English diggers agreed with him. The Yukon had been lethally cold, and the Alaskan prospectors had turned out to be an insular and surly bunch. California was still notorious for its claim jumpers and trigger-happy gunmen. The gold rush Down Under had been short and nasty. But here, one of the diggers commented, was "nothing . . . of Australian brutality; the rowdy element does not exist."

Optimism led them on: the diggers named their outposts Delport's Hope, Cawood's Hope, Good Hope, Last Hope. At the start, those aspirations centered on Cornelius du Plooy's sprawling farm. Diamonds had been found there, in the small hills the Boers called *kopjes* ("cop-pies" to the Americans) and at the edge of a little reservoir called a "pan."

News of the diamond strike reached Lilienfeld's, and Gustav dispatched his brother Leopold to the scene. The Cape Town jeweler made a generous offer, but he was too late. That very morning du Plooy had sold his fields to a speculator. Lilienfeld tried a new tactic. When did the transaction take place? Today? On a Sunday? The Lord's Day? Surely business should not be conducted during such holy hours. . . . The pious Boer agreed and canceled the sale. The next day Lilienfeld moved in and closed his deal. "The Jews have got ahead of us again," a prospector grumbled.

Similar protests were to follow. The Colonial Secretary received a letter complaining, "The jews of course work into each others hands & I am sure that . . . Lilienfeld have made a splendid bargain." A British trading company noted that "Diamonds are turning up every day and Jews are moving heaven and earth to keep the trade in their own hands." A Hope Town firm received a letter stating "Diamonds are cropping up fast and the trade in these Gems is now a firm fact; but the Jews up here are making . . . efforts to keep the trade in their Hands." These are the earliest recorded instances of anti-Jewish sentiment; the volume would soon increase.

Diggers fanned out from the confluence of the Vaal and Orange Rivers. Few of them had ever seen a diamond in the rough. Quartz crystals got confused with the real thing. Potential jewels were knocked into shards because the diggers mistakenly believed that diamonds could not be shattered by a hammer. Sometimes a precious stone lay just beneath the surface, and a man's fingers could scratch it from the soil. More often, pounds of yellow dirt had to be dug up and water poured over them. The sludge was then shaken and jiggled through three sieves. This diamond field "cradle" served to separate the small stones from the large ones. They were then scattered on a board covered with grease. The worthless rocks fell away; the diamonds clung there just as Sinbad had described.

In the early rush, land around the Vaal was covered with cradles and tents, and life in what one visitor called "A Canvas London" was like a holiday from school. The windy air was dry, game was plentiful, the sun brightened the diggers' work. Diamond-field humor was primitive but seldom malicious. Mistakes were exuberantly called "Gregories" in honor of the geologist who declared that there could be no

diamonds in South Africa. An American inventor, Jerome Babe, constructed a machine that made sifting easier; he was immediately dubbed
the only babe who rocked his own cradle. Complainers received the
sarcastic reply: "You're just lazy. Give me ten kaffirs and I'll do it
myself."

The informal brotherhood saw to it that no one went hungry. "A
mutual regard for each other manifested itself all through the camps,"
a digger recalled. "The unlucky shared in the luck of his neighbors.
. . . No man was long without money; some came forward and set
him on his legs again."

"To us," a digger remembered, "a diamond stood rather for crystallized romance than for a form of carbon worth so much per carat.
It stood for the making of history, for Empire, and for unbounded
wealth. We knew that wars had been waged for the possession of such
gems, that neither blackest crime nor oceans of blood could dim their
piercing lustre. We felt that every celebrated stone, whether shining
on the breast of a lovely woman or blazing in the scepter of a king,
was a symbol of power, a nucleus of tragedy, a focus of human passion."

But enchantment slowly evaporated in the sun and wind. A constant
breeze parched the nose and throat. No one could keep a pocket watch
in working order; within a month tiny grains of soil worked their way
into the gears. The nights were close to freezing, and the days could
surpass 100 degrees Fahrenheit. When the ground shimmered with
heat there was no place to hide; the shade trees had been cut down
for lumber. In the rainy season, floods were prodigious. Afterward the
men foundered in acres of mud. "Fancy sleeping in a puddle!" one of
them exclaimed. The diet of meat and eggs was not as salubrious as
it seemed. "For six months at least," a prospector wrote, he and his
colleagues "had not an ounce of vegetable diet of any sort, and then,
upon privations of all sorts, fever set in." Sanitation was primitive;
latrines drained into the rivers where the diggers bathed. Medicine
was scarce, and it took four days' ride to reach a doctor. The ill, a
correspondent reported, "slept on the ground with nothing to lie on
but a rug. I don't believe that out of the six thousand first arrivals
twenty had a mattress."

Before 1870 wound down some £300,000-worth of rough jewels
had been taken from the ground. This was not a sign of prosperity.

Given the number of diggers at the Vaal river, the gross profits worked out to about £60 each. London shopkeepers earned more and had an easier time of it. An informal brotherhood of diamond hunters still existed, but it was no longer possible to know every face or to trust every stranger. For the first time, there was petty robbery on the fields.

Further signs of civilization—policemen—appeared on both banks of the river. Men of the Frontier Armed and Mounted patrolled the Transvaal side, turned out in uniforms of dark brown corduroy with peaked leather helmets. Appearances could be deceptive: there were, a digger complained, "a good many scamps and ne'er do wells among them." The constabulary put in long hours, and any serious misdemeanor was severely punished. One witness saw two men, "convicted of a trifling theft, tied up to a wagon wheel to receive each four dozen lashes with the 'cat' laid on vigorously by a black executioner—a most degrading and painful punishment, and, I should think, a salutary caution."

On the opposite bank, constables of the Orange Free State wore whatever they pleased. The group was composed of "drunken, dissipated, seedy-looking reprobates, in garments of every shade, cut and pattern, but in dirt and dilapidation generally resembling those of the typical British scarecrow." They dispensed swift, unsubtle justice. Perpetrators—and those suspected of crimes—were put in the stocks, lashed, or intimidated with blunt instruments. No restraints were placed on the constabulary; with few exceptions the judges were straight out of a Rowlandson cartoon. A contemporary portrait of one couple is eloquent: "The Magistrate's wife on the Klipdrift side was going the rounds of the camp with a loaded revolver in her pocket to shoot anyone whom she considered offensive, and his worship her husband, who sat in robes on the Bench, went for knocking men down with his fist as a preliminary to having them locked up."

Through the early 1870s, life became more and more brutish. The conditions did nothing to discourage new prospectors; they came by the hundreds and then the thousands, from Europe, Australia, and America, attracted by the mystique of diamonds and the chance at quick riches. Two small towns sprang up around them, Pniel and Klipdrift. In sheet-metal buildings the diggers bought vegetables and alcohol at high prices, exchanged gossip, and read the two rival newspapers, *The Diamond News* and *The Diamond Field*. The region's first hotel arose, kept by a Mrs. Jardine. A few prostitutes had appeared around the camps, but the middle-aged owner was no madam. The sentimental diggers called her "Mother" and sat politely at her home-cooked dinners of roast and boiled beef, anxious for kind words and tidings of home.

With a mix of restlessness and curiosity several diggers meandered north, far from the crowded river. Twenty miles away they reached a farm called Dutoitspan, owned by Adriaan Van Wyk. The Boer thought himself shrewd when he charged the diggers seven shillings sixpence, plus 25 percent of what they found, in order to work his land. Each claim measured 30 square feet—or, as the diggers had it, "ten times the size of your grave." After several false starts the prospectors hit a lode. In one week 100 diamonds were discovered.

The men tried to keep their finds to themselves, but no secrets could be contained in that rumor-hungry region. *The Friend*, a new paper in the Free State, said that 17 "veritable gems" had been found in the mud walls of Van Wyk's homestead and corral. Other groups drifted up from the Vaal to see for themselves. En route they heard stories of a farm called *Vooruitzigt*—Foresight—where a lone explorer had unearthed some perfect diamonds. They headed there and opened negotiations with the owner's son-in-law. He was, one of them complained, "a most offensive and objectionable fellow. However we were too wise to take offense and ultimately he gave us each permission to peg out a claim, 30 ft. by 30 on the 25 per cent arrangement, and also permitted us to peg for some friends we had by the river."

They rode back to their camp and rounded up the friends. As their eight wagons pulled out, hundreds of heads curiously looked up. "Before we were out of sight," one of the drivers noted, "the majority of tents were down and oxen were being inspanned to chase after us. They forced the pace and we only managed to keep the lead, I being first wagon, the mob pretty close behind."

In the summer of 1871 the mob was joined by the free-spirited son of a Colesburg magistrate. Fleetwood Rawstone had come to the diggings on a lark, along with a party of carefree friends and an alcoholic black servant named Damon. They called themselves the Red Cap Party, dressed accordingly, and drank and gambled away the few stones they found. Then, on a July evening, Damon became disorderly and Fleetwood threw him out.

Sometime later Damon returned and poked his face into the tent: "Fleet, I want to see you."

"All right," Rawstone replied. "Come inside. We are all friends here. What do you want?"

Damon replied by opening his fist. Rough diamonds glittered in his palm. He had dug them up a few hundred yards away. "The effect on us all," said a Red Cap, "was electrical." The group tumbled out into the evening and followed Damon to a hillock about 20 feet high. It was decided that each man in the group would be allotted two claims, except for Fleetwood. As "discoverer" he was granted four. Gratefully he placed a shovel in the earth and christened the place "Colesburg kopje" after his hometown. The other Red Caps joined in, working quietly under the moonlight. This was to be their secret.

But when morning came they were no longer alone. The shouts of celebration had been too loud, and the word had passed down the line: this stone-clotted field was the richest in the world. By noon scores of men combed the fields of Vooruitzigt. Hundreds more came along a day later. The little settlements of Pniel and Klipdrift collapsed into ghost towns. Along the Vaal and Orange Rivers, diamond hunters "sick of standing knee-deep in water, cradling, and being wet all the week round," moved with all their belongings. The newspapers with their presses and types, the canteen-keepers with their barrels and bottles, the smith with bellows and anvil, the shoemaker with lapstone and hammer, the clock and watchmaker, the chemist and druggist, marched off in long processions for the new diggings."

Within weeks 800 claims were cut out of Colesburg kopje, some of them subdivided into half and quarter shares. By midsummer the 30' × 30' lots were going for £500 each. *The Friend* of August 17, 1871 reported that Colesburg possessed "the richest diggings on these fields . . . many workers would not take less than three or four thousand pounds sterling for their respective claims."

This was the New Rush, and it had a different character from the one by the river. Water in the "dry diggings" was at a premium. Wood was impossible to procure. Labor was also in short supply; the "kaffirs" demanded higher wages. All kinds of money could be made here, not only beneath the earth but above it—retailing hardware, dry goods, liquids, and produce; wholesaling sheet metal to make dwellings and stores.

A new kind of adventurer appeared. The open-faced greenhorn was on his way out, along with his frontier wardrobe and his innocence. The fresh arrivals had harder eyes and sadder experience with their fellow creatures. A local litterateur held them at arm's length: "Rabbis, rebels, rogues and roués from Russia and the Riviera, transports from Tasmania, convicts from Caledonia, ex-prisoners from Portland, brigands from Bulgaria, and choicest pickings of dirtiest street-corners in all Europe. . . . They all came here to escape grinding poverty or in many cases punishment of their crimes. Unfrocked clergymen with the air of saints and souls of sinners, who had never known the strain of work; broken, stalwart soldiers with fair moustaches and freckled faces, caring for nothing but billiards and brandy. . . . It was a horde that increased and multiplied, and would have made a fine haul for the Devil."

The owner of Vooruitzigt felt much the same way. In the opinion of Johannes Nicholaas De Beer, his son-in-law had made a great mistake. Once a fine life had been lived here. A man and his family supported themselves and communicated with the Lord in safety and solitude. Then these new claimants came and ruined it all with their spades and their cradles and their avarice. De Beer wanted no part of them.

In October 1871, his farm was sold to a group of investors from Port Elizabeth for 6,000 guineas. It was not much more than half the price of The Star of Africa. Some time afterward, the seller reflected on that fateful day. He had been desperately unhappy, he told his wife. Still, "we should have asked six million and not six thousand."

"But what would we have done with all that money?" she asked. "There are only two of us. . . ."

"We could have a new wagon."

"We have enough to buy twenty new wagons. . . . What have we to trouble about? We have enough."

The De Beers left their name but not their outlook. It had no place at New Rush. In the matter of diamonds, there would never be enough.

2

DEEPER INTO THE EARTH

ORGANIZED DIGGING at the De Beers farm started in May 1871. Perhaps a mile away another and even richer pipe was being explored: the Kimberley mine, where so many claimants dug up the dry yellow earth that it was soon known as the Big Hole. About three miles southwest two lesser mines, Bulfontein and Dutoitspan, also attracted prospectors.

The town of New Rush tried to keep up with its burgeoning population. By December the diggers could buy Christmas presents in stores along the main roads. Sheets of corrugated iron were hauled up from the Cape to build a series of new hotels and canteens. With the arrival of families the canvas and metal town of New Rush spread out, and before spring some fifty thousand souls were working and living within its precincts. Prospectors could expect to eat a diet of red meat and little else. Local sheep and cattle supplied steaks and mutton at the cost of about four pennies a pound; a handful of onions or a small cabbage went for as much as sixty pence. In the first of the diggings most of the available trees had been cut down for fuel, and haulers charged £3 for a load of firewood hauled up from the banks of the Vaal. The price was beyond the reach of many diggers, who contrived to make their fires of dried bullocks' dung—"buffalo chips," the Americans called it.

Auctions always seemed to be the most popular device for buying and selling food and supplies. An old South African hand recalled the scene: "Criers swinging bells rang up the drowsy camps for the early morning market. . . . Gatherings of bidders and lookers-on formed one of the liveliest camp scenes, especially on Saturday, when thousands of whites and blacks flocked to the auctions, surrounding the stands with dense masses of jovial bargainers. How strange and curious to the newcomer's eye was the market show."

Carcasses of shaggy wildebeests dangled on a line with sides of beef; antelopes with slender legs were stretched out alongside slaughtered sheep and lambs. The carcasses of long-legged hares, red-wing partridges, ducks, geese, and other wildfowl mingled with poultry from country farmyards. There was even an occasional leopard, hunted down by packs of dogs.

Sales of tents, miners' tools, guns, and hardware took place in a carnival atmosphere. As the auctioneers entertained bids, amateur minstrels juggled and clowned. Nearby, a merry-go-round was set up for laughing children. The inevitable fortune-tellers and wizards worked the crowd, promising that for a fee they could see through the earth to the diamonds below.

Credulous diggers waited in line to part with their money. In his memoirs Gardner Williams, De Beers's first general manager, speaks of one woman who made £30 a day, mostly from Boers. She told a digger that his claim was worthless and thereafter he could not be persuaded to pick up his shovel. Others were informed that their claims were loaded with precious stones. If the prediction worked out she was showered with coins. If no diamonds turned up, she shrugged and replied, "The niggers must have stolen them." Claimholders would then pounce on their Kaffirs and haul them to the "tronk," the camp's police station, and stand by while the blacks were thoroughly searched. "Sometimes the wizard guessed right, for diamond stealing was common, and precious stones would be brought to light with joy to the owners and credit to the fortune teller."

Originally native laborers were a minority at the diggings. By the mid-1870s black men were swarming in to do manual labor, enticed by white recruiters or forced to the fields by the collapse of their agricultural economies. None of them earned more than a few shillings per week, but that pittance was enough. Droughts had impoverished many tribes, and prospective bridegrooms needed hard cash, no matter how little, to buy hunting rifles, ammunition, and *lobola*, a traditional marriage payment made to the bride's father.

First came the Griquas and the Basutos from the south, followed by the Pedi, Tsonga, Sotho, and men from tribes ranging east to the Indian Ocean, far northwest into the Namaqua and Bechuana lands, and northeast into Matabeleland and the regions beyond the Limpopo and the Zambesi Rivers. "There was every shade of dusky color in this throng," says a mining engineer of the period, "from livid and tawny yellow to jet black." They arrived in antelope skins and leopard skins and jackal skins and bare skins, and they decorated themselves with white oxtails and black crane plumes and gorgeous feathers. They danced sober or with the aid of Cape Smoke, and they spoke in dialects full of tongue clicks and glottal stops.

In town the natives continued the ways of the veldt. They dug small holes in the ground, filled them with tobacco leaves, started a fire, and sucked at the smoke through a hollow stick. Or they puffed cigars, holding the lit end in their mouths. They entreated butchers for the entrails of sheep or bullocks, and wore them festooned around their necks. In warm weather they slept on the ground; in winter they retired to makeshift huts and huddled in dirty sheepskins.

The white diggers regarded all this with amused condescension, but in their own way they were just as gaudy and eccentric. As soon as women made their appearance, the males began to sport plumage. Corduroy trousers and collarless flannel shirts were still de rigeur. So were the old broad leather belts with pockets for diamonds and money. But the felt hat gave way to the pith helmet, and bright colors were substituted for the familiar clay and earth tones. A fashion reporter noted that "large ostrich feathers are frequently to be seen curling gracefully round the slouched felt hat of some stalwart young farmer. . . . I have seen a broad strip of . . . a silver jackal, or some other animal, going right round the crown of a hat." Further effects were produced by a vibrant mix of "red sashes . . . as well as green veils, blue veils, red and white puggarees [turbans] . . . suits of brown or yellow cords, with 'white ducks' here and there."

The females who prompted this display were diggers' wives or whores; there was not much middle ground. Reputable women, looking up from their housework, must have been grateful for any notice. Even the lower-middle-class Victorian household had a live-in servant or two; here in the camp the wives were on their own. Nostalgic for the old life, a Mrs. Alice Stockdale hired the "raw Kaffir" Master Jim as her laundryman. She came home to find him in the yard, doubled over with laughter; the source of hilarity was her underclothing. "The boy," she was distressed to find, "was holding up one of my garments and letting the wind blow it into shape. I rushed at him, pulled it out of his hands and told him, he was to wash the things but not look at them."

The ladies of the evening could also be found in the daytime. The black ones, according to a client, were identifiable "by their bolder and richer apparel, their constant promenading about the camp, and their impudent looks." The more demure white prostitutes worked as barmaids in boldly named canteens: The Scarlet Bar, The Perfect Cure, The Old Cock, The Red Light; or as "hostesses" at the rough new racetrack between Bulfontein mine and the neighboring Dutoitspan.

Most flamboyant of all the demimondaines was a lady called Sa Singularite. Before a raucous crowd at Graybittel's canteen, some in evening dress for the occasion, she climbed aboard a champagne case and auctioned herself off to the highest bidder. Offers began at five pounds. "Ultimately," an eyewitness remembered, "the erring one was knocked down, after a keen and heated competition, to Mr. John Swaebe for twenty-five pounds and three cases of champagne. With a soul on fire Johnny departed with his bargain, to the envy and disappointment of many of his rivals." After half an hour the rivals grew too curious to stay at the bar. Swaebe lived in a canvas dwelling, it was summer, and " 'the boys' got round the tent and carried it bodily away, thus exposing to view the amorous pair—and the honeymoon was over."

Sex was not the only diversion; it was not even the main one. There were nowhere near enough women to go around, and the majority of diggers gambled their money away. They wagered on anything: cards, coin tosses, horse races, informal boxing matches between men who did battle as "The Ladies Pet" or "Cockney Bill." More exotic combats consumed the late hours, with posted odds on eight-legged favorites and contenders. A digger's wife shuddered to remember "the only pet we disagreed upon . . . an immense, ugly, hairy thing with a spotted body and malevolent black eyes that used to glare at me through the glass top of its cage. It was a fighting spider and for a long time was the champion in that part of the country where spider fights roused as much interest and won or lost as much money as cockfights. William used to drive miles to enter the horrid thing in mortal combat with some rival spider whose owners had issued a formal challenge, and after a successful battle it was hard to decide who was the more pleased with himself, William or his cannibalistic pet."

For those with more traditional tastes, croupiers were always available to take diggers' money at the roulette wheel. One night a young Londoner stepped into Dodds canteen and edged over to its gambling table. Nothing about David Harris seemed prepossessing. The middle-sized Jewish cockney had black, curly hair and a weedy moustache. As a digger he had managed to unearth little more than dirt and disappointment. As he stood idly watching the wheel spin, a winner ordered drinks all around. Harris later recalled that "just as I had finished my glass of champagne one of the proprietors remarked significantly that some men only visited the rooms for the purpose of getting free drinks. This remark aroused my ire . . . so purely out of pique, I put a sovereign on number thirteen with the intention of losing it and clearing out." Number thirteen payed 35 to 1. Harris let his winnings ride, and ended the evening £1,400 richer. He could have gone back to the fields and bought himself a stake; instead he returned to London. There he told his cousins Henry and Barnett Isaacs of his adventures in New Rush. Beguiled, the brothers scraped together enough for the voyage. They were to become the country's greatest gamblers, in sports, in diamonds, and in the history of South Africa itself.

But this was still several years away; in 1872 David Harris was only a high roller, his cousins mere street toughs, and New Rush just another frontier town, with its overcrowding and racial antagonisms, its illusion of effortless wealth and hectic confidence men. "The over-and-under tables were there in galore," a visitor noted. "Thimble rigging and three-card tricksters were vigorously prosecuting their devices to swindle an easily-gulled public." Fly Loo was the classic game. It could be played indoors and out, day or night. Sugar cubes were placed on a surface, one for each player. The owner of the first cube to attract a fly won the pot. At times sugar was at a premium; insects, never.

Even after the introduction of families, sanitation remained a fairly primitive business. Latrines were little more than open ditches; water, hauled from questionable wells, stagnated in the sun. When Dr.

Atherstone visited the place in 1871 he could only shake his head. "Just fancy," he wrote, "the organic debris of [thousands] with their belongings, canine, equine, asinine, and bovine deposited on the edge of a pan without outlet."

The flies came after the carrion, and the diseases came with the flies. Men and women succumbed to dysentery, typhus, and a malarial "camp fever." Eventually town leaders built a rudimentary hospital, and three doctors signed on. But this part of South Africa was still no more than an outpost of civilization, and a Conradian horror hovered close by. The corpse of one digger never received an autopsy. It was placed in a mortuary tent where, the next morning, a physician discovered "merely the trunk of the poor fellow's body left; the prowling, ravenous dogs having devoured the poor man's limbs, which they had torn in pieces from his body."

Survival on the diamond fields would always demand a strong constitution and psychological stability. Most of the diggers had these attributes, but they would gladly have traded them away for the most elusive blessing of all: luck. The camps were depressingly full of stories about men who dug and dug without finding a single stone, sold their share for a pittance, and watched the next owner stumble upon a treasure. The digger who started it all, Fleetwood Rawstone, was one of these unfortunates. Less than 100 feet from his own claims a latecomer paid £50 for a piece of turf, plucked out £20,000-worth of diamonds in ten months, then sold out to a man who found 657 more stones. Fleetwood, genial as ever, kept on digging. But all he ever turned up was dirt.

A diarist recorded some of the diamond field quirks:

A Dutchman buys an old claim for ten shillings; before dinner that day he finds a diamond of 14 carats.

An English gentleman having worked . . . for six months and found nothing, went home disgusted, giving away his claim. The man who got it, found on the same day a fine diamond of 29½ carats before he had gone six inches deeper than his predecessor. I believe he was offered £2,500 for it.

Four English gentlemen lately set off to tramp down to the coast, penniless, hoping to work their passage back to England. "Hard lines!" And there are plenty of broken-down loafers about the camp. But then of course it is all a lottery; so says every one.

Late in 1873 *The Digger's Gazette*, a new journal, amused its readers with an account of misfortune. The diggings at Kimberley had begun in a wide circle, with everyone's territory clearly marked. But as the shovels ventured deeper into the earth, the roadways between claims grew thinner and thinner and finally collapsed. Now the diggings resembled a bowl thousands of feet across and 80 feet deep at the center. It was impossible for miners to climb up every time they found a promising shovelful, so they worked out an elaborate system of ladders and pulleys. Sometimes the earth was hauled up in a bucket; sometimes the digger climbed up, rung by rung, on a device precariously balanced on a man-made ledge.

One morning, reported the *Gazette*, a miner "discovered a large diamond, estimated at from 50 to 60 carats' weight. He put it into his mouth, and proceeded to ascend the ladder out of the depths. While doing so a nigger at the top happened to shake the machine. Perfectly naturally, and according to the usual custom of the fields, the gentleman spake sharply with his tongue, and favored our colored brother with a few of those flowers of language for which the diggings are achieving a reputation. Alas, as he made these *cursory* observations the diamond escaped from between his lips, fell into the adjoining claim, and was seen no more of men. We have heard of ladies dropping pearls as they spoke, but we have a still rarer instance of a man cursing diamonds!"

The incident could very well have been fanciful; local newspapers seldom had scruples about printing fiction if it was colorful enough. What is instructive here is the *journalistic* use of the word "nigger." The Boers and British were hardly models of tolerance, but when they referred to blacks they used terms like Bantu, Kaffir, Hottentot. Nigger was an American term, brought over from the War Between the States and readily absorbed into the common vocabulary. It reflected the mounting dislike and distrust of the native population.

Newcomers expected that the several hundred claims would be

owned by whites. Yet more than forty were held by men of mixed
blood, partly white, partly Hottentot or Zulu or Xhosa or any one of
a dozen other tribes. These Griquas or "Cape Coloreds" were not
looked upon kindly by the Europeans. "It would be almost impossible
for white men to compete . . . as diggers," argued *The Diamond News*.
"The differences between the general wants, necessities, character and
position of the two races utterly forbid it." Given this sentiment, it
was only a matter of time before Jim Crow moved onto the fields.

The turning point came early in 1872, when a group of claimholders
drew up a list of demands and presented it to the local commissioners.
There were thirteen demands in all, and every one was aimed at the
black population.

From here on, no "Kaffir or colored person" was to hold a digging
license. Those with licenses would lose them, unless they were supported by 50 white claimholders—an event about as likely as finding
a 500 carat stone.

Employees could be searched at the whim of their masters. Any
"native or colored person" holding a diamond for which he could not
"satisfactorily account" would be liable to at least fifty lashes.

Anyone, other than claimholders, convicted of purchasing a diamond
from a "native or colored servant" was to receive fifty lashes in public,
have his property confiscated, and be banished from the fields.

No native would be allowed to move about the camp after 8:00 p.m.

Except for its language, the memorandum seemed reasonable to the
Colonial Office. Britain's officially colorblind policies would not permit
open bias on the fields. References to "natives" and "colored persons"
were quietly expunged and the word "servant" substituted throughout.
Once that was done, the demands became law. In July a Servant's
Registry Office was opened, and there black laborers obtained temporary passes. Once they made their mark on a contract, usually for
a minimum of three months, they received another piece of official
paper. This pass had to be carried at all times and shown "to anyone
who may demand it."

South African history turns on this decision. Nowhere in the country
was it morally or legally possible to identify black men as slaves. But
there is no way to regard their situation on the diamond fields except

as slavery. They could no longer wander freely in their own land. They were forbidden to leave their jobs for any reason. Their employers' word was absolute law, and if arrested for any reason they were considered guilty until proved innocent.

In the first year of the revived Pass Law, the Magistrate's Court dealt with nearly 5,000 cases, the most common by far being "desertion of employment" by black workers. A prisoner known only as Sunday was typical. He was convicted of leaving his job without permission and received twelve lashes. Prisoners Jacob and Buffalo were sentenced to eleven lashes for the same offense. Jimmy, Hans, Jim, and Boy were lesser offenders: for the crime of being in camp without a pass, each was allowed the choice of a fine or three strokes of the whip. These sentences were dispensed without the formality of a trial, on the oath of the arresting officer.

A German sailor administered the lashings; he had rendered the same service aboard a man-o'-war. On land he gave a theatrical performance, walking up and down the rank of trembling prisoners as he drew the pliant leathers through his hand. A correspondent for *Harper's Magazine* followed him down the line: "The blacks, on the whole, displayed much firmness and fortitude under punishment, and but few yelled and screamed, as some notorious garroters did when being flogged in London a few years ago."

The journalist saw one prisoner receive thirty-five lashes. "He stood up bravely, while strips of flesh hung down from his back and great drops of blood coursed down his legs. Whir, whir, the cat crossed his shoulders until his large eyes were blood-shot, his lips quivering, his hands working in agony; but he kept silence until the thirtieth time the lash descended, when, with a deep groan, full of the misery of physical torture, he fainted." At such scenes, the writer went on, black spectators grew restive. "They would grind their teeth, and with menacing looks gaze upon the officers of justice. I often thought they only waited for some favorable opportunity to wreak vengeance on their masters."

The vengeance often took the form of illicit diamond buying, always referred to by its initials: to give the whole name was to pronounce the unspeakable. Beneath the parasol of I.D.B. every aspect of theft was covered, from the laborer purloining a stone right under his master's nose, to armed robbery, to the furtive peddling of diamonds to "fences," middlemen who conveyed stolen diamonds to legitimate dealers.

At the top of the list were the white perpetrators, some of them well-mannered Englishmen like John William Harding, who spied an unattended window at the Kimberley post office, grabbed a mailbag, and spirited it away. The envelopes contained a total of 2,381 diamonds. Police finally caught up with him aboard an outgoing ship. Recovering all the diamonds proved more difficult, until an investigator thought to look down the barrel of Harding's hunting rifle. The gems lay there twinkling, all in a row. The white thief received a fair trial; the same could not be said of men with darker cast.

Scarcely a month after Harding's arrest, an Indian merchant was accused of I.D.B. A group of diggers surrounded his tent and barged in. They found incriminating diamonds, stripped their victim, flogged him, and turned him out of the camp. But even this was not enough to cool the vigilante fever. The next night four thousand men rampaged through the town, knocking down tents and setting fire to canteens.

A squad of mounted police galloped up too late. The crowd was uncontrollable. Under the eyes of constables, tents were defiantly torched for no other reason than to see the flames. An innocent butcher was forced to stand by while his shop burned to the ground, and a mother and child only escaped injury when one of the mob shouted, "Save the female." An inspector tried to calm the crowd; he was taken hold of and, reported *The Diamond News*, "threatened with closer proximity to the flames than appeared pleasant." After that, "the gallant officer retired."

For native workers, the treatment could be far worse. The first recorded death of a black on the fields came about because of I.D.B. A digger, "indignant and disgusted at the laziness" of his man, punished him with kicks. When a diamond dropped from the Zulu's loincloth, the digger tied him to a pole and left. Many hours later he found the laborer lying dead of heat prostration at the bottom of the claim. There was no prosecution.

Six months later another white digger was brought before the magistrate's court for flogging two of his black employees and leaving them bound and naked through the freezing night. One had died of exposure.

This time the case came to trial, and the defendant was found guilty of common assault, committed under "great provocation." He was bound over for only six months, and even this was thought to be excessive. An editorial in *The Diamond Field* suggested that the sentence had "done more to defeat the ends of justice than uphold the dignity of the law."

◆   ◆   ◆

EARLY IN 1873 a veteran digger gazed down at the Kimberley mine. "This time last year," he reflected, "there were roads leading across the vast abyss and connecting . . . with each other. Carts and horses and men crossed and recrossed daily. Now the roads have gone." He congratulated himself on his courage. "It needs a firm nerve to stand upon the brink alone where I am now standing, and look through the running gear—the great network of ropes that cover the face of the koppie. . . . I have seen strong men tremble . . . whilst they looked into this great human ant-hill . . . the giddy heights, the noise, the bustle, the elbowing, are sufficient to bewilder anyone. . . ."

What had happened was easy for the miners to understand, but difficult for them to accept. Late in 1872 they had run out of earth. The soft yellow ground disappeared after about 80 feet, and a hard blue material lay underneath. It was unpredictable, and when it caved in more than tools were lost. The old life was swallowed up with them. At Kimberley and De Beers, a different kind of mining began.

Rough timber platforms were set around the mouth of the pit. Ropes and pulleys lowered buckets down to the black laborers. They filled them with dirt and raised them to the top, where the diggers—in name only, for they no longer handled the picks and shovels—sifted the ground for gemstones. Buckets were made of rawhide because it would not dent or rust, and ropes were constructed of iron and steel because hemp frayed with the constant rising and falling. Effort had to be exerted only one way; the force of gravity took the buckets back to the claims.

This arrangement was not only practical, it also provided a great pageant. "Never has any eye seen such a marvelous show of mining as was given in this grand amphitheater," wrote a contemporary observer, with only a touch of hyperbole. Deep in the earth thousands of laborers, "grimy, sweating and odorous," swarmed around, groaning, shoveling, raising up loads of diamond ground on the shuttles of a monstrous loom. The wires twanged in dissonant keys, the men shouted in various dialects, and the noise of rattling wheels and falling dirt added to the din.

All this disappeared with the sun. At night the unsightly Babel quieted down, and the camp fires and lanterns of New Rush glowed under the Southern Cross like the tail of a fallen comet. On certain evenings the Big Hole seemed to be covered with an enormous cobweb whose strands gleamed in the moonlight, and then it became a favored trysting place for the miners' teenage daughters. A De Beers miner remembered "the solemn stillness and romance of night—and such romance! It was amusing on occasion to see some lovelorn maid sliding gingerly from some unguarded portion of the roadway into a fairly shallow claim hole, there to make great moan till some gallant and fearless young digger arrived just in time to rescue her from a horrible death. O yes, the dear, sweet things were just as artful then as they are now, and ever will be! Bless 'em!"

Back in London, the government grew increasingly aware of New Rush and its sudden wealth. The Secretary of State for the Colonies, Lord Kimberley, realized that there were distinct possibilities in the forsaken land of South Africa. Memoranda were exchanged, a constitution planned, measures taken to forbid gambling houses, especially those run by Americans. Above all, said His Lordship, the localities "must receive decent and intelligible names." It was understood that he "declined to be in any way connected with such a vulgarism as New Rush." As as for Vooruitzigt, he could neither spell it nor pronounce it. A subordinate offered what he hoped was an appropriate suggestion. What if New Rush were to be named after the Secretary himself? A splendid notion, thought His Lordship, and by official declaration of July 5, 1873, New Rush disappeared from the maps. Henceforth the city would be known as Kimberley. It still is.

But changing a town's name has never done much to alter its reputation. Despite the threats of jail, beating, and even death, I.D.B. continued to flourish in every corner of Kimberley. The rewards were worth the risks. All a laborer had to do was come across a stone, conceal it from the owner, and peddle it through a white intermediary who, in turn, would sell the diamond for hard cash to one of the *"kopje wallopers"*—small-time operators whose shacks could be found on almost every street.

Wallopers provided a bridge between the diggers and the big retailers in Cape Town. Some were scrupulous and fair; others accepted diamonds from any source with no questions asked. A disproportionate number of them were Jewish, inheritors of ghetto tradition: in medieval Europe, the Jewelers Guild was one of the very few organizations to admit Hebrew members and taught them the difficult trade of cutting and polishing. But diamonds played a far more important role in ghetto life. During the years of the Inquisition, Spanish Jews hastily fled across the Pyrenees to the Low Countries. It was impossible to travel with furniture or heavy valuables, and impractical to carry currency. Jewels, on the other hand, were precious and portable; a fortune could be concealed in the heel of a shoe. An almost mystical belief in the power of diamonds had possessed the Jews ever since. It had gone with them to Antwerp and Amsterdam and Berlin, and now it was about to be proclaimed in Kimberley.

The majority of diamond-field Jews had fled from the anti-Semitic policies of Germany and Eastern Europe. They were content to dig quietly and worship unobtrusively. The nearest synagogue was several hundred miles distant, and only twice a year could they afford a round-trip fare for the Cape Town rabbi; he took the wagon north to lead the Kimberley parishioners in observance of Rosh Hashana and Yom Kippur. But in the small crowd of unremarkable Jews were a handful of extravagant figures. Ikey Sonnenberg had emigrated from Germany to America in the 1850s. He often spoke about his early days in the States, where he "started as a timber merchant in a small way" (he sold wooden matches on street corners). Ikey participated in the gold rush without success and the Civil War without distinction. Then came Kimberley with its new promise of overnight wealth. After a brief and disastrous career as a digger, he married a Jewish girl from the Cape, started a passenger cart service, imported English mining tools, bought diamonds, wool, ivory, ostrich feathers, and anything else that could bring a profit.

To most of the town Sonnenberg seemed an agreeable sort, tall and gangly, with huge feet, a quick smile, and a ready handout for miners down on their luck. An amused bystander recalled that "all of the dogs around the Dutoitspan mine wagged their tails as Ikey slouched by." Not all of the folk agreed with the dogs. Although no one was brazen enough to accuse Ikey of cheating at cards, it was known that he could manipulate a cold deck. His specialty, however, was the *spiel*: hustling the "heavy, credulous Boers" into an agreement before they could change their minds. Many men swore they had been there the day Sonnenberg tossed aside a wool merchant's Ready Reckoner—a kind of elementary calculator. The Boer had added up the many bolts of yarn and presented his arithmetic. The sum was much lower than Sonnenberg's bill. In an inspired moment Ikey burst out: "Good God, man, you have last year's reckoner, it's worthless this year." He got his price.

Alfred Augustus Rothschild was another example of the bunco artist, South African style. He called himself The Baron, implying a nonexistent relationship with the great banking family, cultivated an international manner—he spoke French, German, English, and Dutch—and took great pride in what he called his "strongly marked oriental features." These were exaggerated by black, heavily greased hair and a thick beard. His Saturday afternoon routines were spellbinding; miners and their families would stand out in the sun for hours just to hear him dilate on his "diamondiferous" inventory. Customarily the Baron placed himself on a chair or an ox-wagon where he could beguile his listeners with promises of success by contagion. An ordinary appliance became "the identical sieve in which the 93 carat was found last week"; a worn implement was transformed into "a nice little pick, a diamondiferous pick—it picked out a 40 carat stone two days ago, and is warranted to do the same again."

On one occasion he advertised an estimable stallion with only two minor drawbacks. The price was bid up to £20, and after the new owner had taken possession he asked about the faults. "He is apt to break out of hand and is difficult to catch," the Baron loudly replied, "and secondly, when caught he is not much good." In fact the horse was first rate; Rothschild was just having his little joke. For all his palaver the auctioneer was a generous salesman and a forgetful lender. Periodically he issued whimsical broadsides to those who had borrowed money:

One man paid ROTHSCHILD 3s. 6d.

Owing for THREE YEARS! If you wish HEALTH
entirely restored, please follow the example
and pay, Yours respectfully, A. A. Rothschild.

These men were retailers first and showmen second. Henry Isaacs
reversed the order. He, his younger brother Barnett, and their three
sisters were raised in a crowded apartment over the family's secondhand
clothing store. It was located in the Whitechapel district, known to
Victorians as "the most dangerous thieves' den in London." Youths
got street-hardened early; Isaac Isaacs taught his boys how to box as
soon as they could walk. Like most of their companions, they dropped
out of school at 14 and hung around the streets of Aldgate, restless,
bored, and stagestruck.

For several years Harry, as he preferred to be called, served as bar-
tender and bouncer at the "King of Prussia" public house owned by Joel
Joel, husband of his sister Kate. But this was only a pastime; every spare
hour was spent before a mirror, practicing sleight of hand and improv-
ing a line of patter. In the early 1870s he convinced some East End music
halls to put him on the bill as The Wizard. Harry's brother Barnett—
known as Barney on the streets—joined the act. They were billed as the
Barnato Brothers, a surname from the night Harry took too many bows
and a stagehand jeered "Barney, too." The catcall stuck; "Barney too"
followed them wherever they appeared. It evolved into Barneyto and
then Barneto and finally assumed its Italianate form. Mama and Papa
approved: to a family with an Isaac Isaacs and a Joel Joel, there was
something appropriate about a Barney Barnato.

The brothers might have gone on to a mediocre local fame, but early
in 1872 their cousin David Harris arrived in London displaying fistfuls
of cash. True, he had made his money in a gambling hall and not by
digging diamonds, but that was beside the point. You could make
money a dozen ways in South Africa. Harris planned to return at the
earliest opportunity. There was no prejudice down there, he claimed,
no social restrictions, no ceiling over the heads of Jews. All you needed
was enterprise and energy. And—here was the irresistible enticement—everyone spoke English.

That fall The Wizard disappeared from London. He surfaced on October 29, 1872 on the stage of St. James Hall in Dutoitspan. Harry Barnato looked the part: he had a great handlebar moustache, a dark-eyed, piercing stare, and a strong whiff of the romantic Neapolitan. A reviewer judged The Wizard's sleight-of-hand tricks "as old and verdant as the hills." Still, the journalist had to admit that Barnato did bring forth "eggs from nowhere, cards from anywhere, and goldfish in glass dishes from the region of his coat-tails—value for money indeed! The night I attended the show the 'Seggnor' in the course of his amazing feats borrowed from me, as one of the audience, a sovereign which he duly returned. Now that was truly marvelous!"

Harry Barnato's popularity crested two months later when he gave a "Grand Christmas Festival" featuring "His Great Feat of *Aerial Suspension of a Human Being*, Sleeping in Mid Air! (Must be seen to be believed)." The act eventually palled, audiences stopped coming, and a Christy Minstrel Troupe took his place. A few days later Harry could be seen for free in Market Square, giving sparring exhibitions with a retired policeman. Then, like many marginal performers, he forsook show business entirely for the promise of a regular income. His new employer was a diamond dealer in Dutoitspan.

Yet the Wizard could never escape his reputation. After one notorious and well-publicized theft, *The Diamond News* received a letter implying that I.D.B. might also be a Barnato sideline. "If anybody wants to steal a parcel of diamonds," it said, "he must be quick of hand as (the) Signor." Harry replied in print: "Fully appreciating the compliment intended to be conveyed, I . . . find it liable to misconstruction by some overimaginative individuals who, in my capacity as a diamond buyer, fear that I might combine the attributes of the 'Wizard.' Allow me this opportunity of assuring them that I keep the two callings distinct, the only approach to 'magic' in the former business being the astoundingly high prices I am always prepared to give for good stones."

Very few were reassured; his own cousin, David Harris, was wary about taking him on as a partner. Harry was too ebullient to care. He wrote a letter home describing the many possibilities for a young man and advising his brother to come on down. Barney was intoxicated by the idea. He had taken over Harry's position at the "King of Prussia" and put aside a few pence; he even stopped smoking in order to save for the one-way passage. When he announced his departure, a group of friends gave him a gold watch, and his brother-in-law Joel donated 40 boxes of cheap cigars. They were to be the foundation for an import-export business. In July of 1873 the youth patted the roll of £100 he had scrimped, boarded the Union Steamship Company's *Anglia*, and set sail for Cape Town.

The ship docked 27 days later, and then the real trip began. Barney happily recalled his long journey north to the diamond fields: "It occupied nearly two months, one of the jolliest times I have ever had. The accommodation consisted of permission to walk alongside a wagon when it moved, and to sleep under it when it stopped. I made my first acquaintance with mealie porridge and biltong [corn cakes and sun-dried antelope] and have a keen relish for both still. I had not been very well or bright for some months before leaving England, but the wagon journey, or rather tramp over the veld, put me right and I marched into Dutoitspan fit for anything."

Barney searched the grounds for his brother. He found him lying in a hut, discouraged, lonely, and hungry. Harry had not struck it rich in South Africa. With a gesture that was to become typical, Barney assumed a cheery air and treated Harry to an expensive dinner. All right, he decided, diamonds were not the road to wealth. What of it? A smart Jewish boy had other means. Within a week he found a job at Paynes, a touring circus, challenging its professional boxing champion, a large Portuguese. In the ring Barney wore his loudest London jacket, narrow trousers, a bowler hat, and glasses. He removed the spectacles, pranced around to the amusement of the onlookers—and then decked the champion. The crowd loved it. The next week Barney tried stand-up routines, billing himself as the "World Famous Comedian." He lasted four days.

No matter; Barney was a human cork. He bobbed up as a peddler, selling notebooks and pencils. From some amused diggers he bought the right to give their discarded ground a second washing. Perhaps there would be small, overlooked stones in the dirt. He watched a native drawing on a piece of paper. Barney, resourceful as ever, hired him to haul water and paid him off in pencils. Only a few diamonds came into the Londoner's hands that season, but they were enough to convince him that he had come to the right country. The short, near-sighted, vulgar, theatrical, volatile, unlikely Barney Barnato was getting ready to alter the destiny of South Africa.

3

THE BOY-MEN

OUTSIDE OF SOUTH AFRICA Barney Barnato is a lost celebrity, a man swallowed up by the events he helped to create. Inside the country he remains a presence. He stares out from the walls of De Beers's boardrooms with a contemporary look of impatience: the executive who will be with you in just a minute. On the streets and in the pubs of Kimberley, where he made his first fortune, men still debate about Barney's end—was he murdered or destroyed by his own hand?—as if he had passed away last week instead of a century ago.

In many ways Barney Barnato is a caricature of the nineteenth-century "Jew d'esprit," the self-mocking, self-promoting arriviste, stooping to pick up the small change on his way to the treasury. After his lessons at the Hebrew Free School in London, Barney dipped into only one book. It was not the Bible, merely a popular novel that someone had recommended. And with all his later wealth he bought only one painting, a landscape with a sad-faced sheep. "It resembles me," he explained.

And yet Barney refuses to be pigeonholed. Put him in one category and he leaps into another. The ignoramus turns out to have a quick intelligence. He is a demon at games from dominoes to boxing to billiards, but he plays fair and when he loses he does so with panache, bowing to the victor and paying up immediately. The pennypincher is extremely generous to local and national charities, as well as to countless miners down on their luck. The whoremaster, once married, becomes intensely loyal to his wife and children. And the egomaniacal capitalist regards his stockholders as family who deserve protection and profit even when the costs eat into his personal fortune.

Louis Cohen, Barnato's first partner, gives a typically divided appraisal. Barnato was "decidedly unscrupulous," and his name would have vanished after his death, "were it not for the incredible harm he did in his life." Having said all that, Cohen turns around and admits that his former associate "had a grain of gold in his character."

The two men got acquainted at the crowded Scarlet Bar in Dutoitspan. Cohen looked up to see "a strongly built young fellow" elbowing aside a couple of diggers. "It rather interested me to see the way in which he beamed on everybody in general and nobody in particular, without taking the slightest notice of the frowns and muttered curses of the two foreigners he had separated." Cohen noticed that the stranger "wore a pair of spectacles on his uninviting dust-stained face, and had the ugliest snub nose you could imagine, but as good a pair of large gray blue eyes as ever flashed through a pair of glasses." A moment later, Barney gave a galvanic twitch, spattered his soup in a wide radius, and smiled at his neighbor. "You'll excuse me," he explained, "but a fly fell on my nose."

Louis Cohen was something of a local character himself, born in Liverpool of an Irish mother and a Jewish father, and educated, or so he claimed, on the Continent. By his mid-twenties he was a playwright, theater critic, versifier, journalist, inventor of tall stories (which he mixed with his reportage), and *kopje* walloper. This last occupation was all that interested the semiliterate Barney. His sneeze prompted a conversation, and that led to an experimental friendship. Several weeks later the two young men decided to pool their resources and become diamond buyers.

Sixty pounds was Cohen's contribution. Barney offered £30, his 40 boxes of third-rate cigars growing staler by the day, and a manic energy. The two men worked and slept in their "office," a 9′ × 6′ iron shanty next to Maloney's Bar on the main road. To Louis the guinea-a-day rent seemed prohibitive. Barney argued that thirsty diggers would line up to trade their diamonds for liquor money. "If you can make two pounds a day out of it," he reasoned, "it ain't dear."

A photograph of Cohen at twenty shows that at least one of his recollections was totally reliable. "I was," he says, "a good looking boy." His cordial manner and ready wit made him a natural for the role of negotiator. He was the one who flattered the customers and sealed the bargain with a Barnato cigar. Barney could seldom be found at headquarters. He was too busy making his rounds of the diggings, palavering with miners, paying as little as he could for the best rocks he could find. Mistakes were made in the beginning: he bought a jewel in the rough for £5, only to discover that it was quartz crystal. But Barney was a quick study. Within weeks he learned how to appraise an uncut diamond and how much to offer for it. His greatest trouble was not in purchasing. It was in finding diggers who were willing to sell at the right price. Then one afternoon Barney found a solution. He bought a spavined old horse for £27, 10 shillings—almost a month's rent.

This was no ordinary nag. Its previous owner, a prosperous walloper, was about to leave Dutoitspan for Europe. He had jealously guarded the names and locations of the men who sold cheap, no doubt because he planned to return some day. For once Barney paid the asking price; he guessed that if a horse follows a route long enough it may learn it by heart. The animal did not disappoint him. A tug on the reins and it clopped automatically from one old client to the next. As a bonus, Cohen recalled, the horse provided "introduction enough to get into conversation with the Boers, and we made much money out of Barney's inspiration."

The raffish atmosphere of the diggings was pure oxygen to the Barnatos. They were there to make a reputation—any reputation, as long as it led to riches. For a time the brothers pursued separate careers. Barney was the upstart retailer; Harry abandoned his disappointing diamond adventures for a position as proprietor of the London Hotel. It housed some theatrical clientele, a gambling room, and a goodly number of petty criminals. Local police made it a part of their rounds, and whenever they appeared, Cohen was amused to note, "some of the most eminent customers would scatter like rats that had seen a cat."

Harry was a staid bourgeois compared with his younger brother. Everyone had a Barney story, including Barney. Cohen's favorite concerned the night he and his partner visited a pair of prostitutes. Each woman had a separate room lit by a single candle. Louis was uncertain of the price. "When I heard the words 'Five pounds' muttered," he recalled, "I figured it was time to trot. But Barney hopped into the other apartment, and I had time to see him show the damsel a five pound note, when the candle went out." Louis waited outside the house. Presently Barney appeared, out of breath and urging his partner to run. An outraged wail sounded in the dark. "I showed her a five pound note," Barnato puffed, "but had a piece of paper in the other hand, and when the light went out gave her that instead."

Barney would listen to such tales with hearty amusement and then top them with his own recollection of a dinner party. He had watched silently as another guest furtively stuffed a silver soup spoon in his shoe. Over coffee and brandy Barney volunteered to entertain the guests with a little sleight of hand. He chose a matching soup spoon, made some theatrical gestures, and presto! the utensil vanished. Then he instructed a servant to "look in that gentleman's boot over there." The spoon was pulled out, and Barney bowed to general applause. Other raconteurs would have ended their story at the moment of triumph. Barney added: "And I went home with the other spoon."

Barney never denied any tale in which he played the central role. For him every knock was a boost, every shred of gossip a means of registering the Barnato name in a new world. Whatever he said was calculated to bring attention, and everything he wore was designed to be noticed, from the loud checked suit and the bright buttonhole carnation to the pince-nez and the waxed moustache. When an amateur theater company was established, Barney naturally talked himself into the job of stage manager. Before long he was on the boards playing character parts. Villains were his specialty; he was featured as Fagin in *Oliver Twist* and Iago in *Othello*. Cohen reviewed Barney in a contemporary play called *The Bells*. The impresario and actor Sir Henry Irving had played it in London; Barney had seen the performance many times. He copied every gesture and intonation but, wrote Cohen, the cockney accent ruined the effect. Barney's "Ow the dogs do 'owl" was "a monstrous inexactitude considering the animals were as absent as his h's."

Bad notices never bothered Barney. Reviewers could say whatever they wanted as long as they spelled his name right. Audiences were another matter. During a recitation from *Othello*, an actor boomed his soliloquy to increasing catcalls. When he came to the line "Haply that I am black . . ." a heckler advised, "Then go and wash your face." The performer petulantly quit the stage, to be replaced in a few minutes by Barney in blackface. He marched to the footlights and announced that he would summarily "deal with" anyone who dared to interrupt *his* recitation. The noise continued, and when the curtain was rung down he ran into the orchestra, collared the ringleader, and gave him a sound thrashing.

A reviewer for the *Independent* newspaper watched it all. "We can fully sympathise with Mr Barnato being publicly ridiculed," he sniffed, "but no one can overlook so great a want of decency as daring to threaten individuals who have paid their fees of admission, when no agreement is made beforehand whether they are to laugh or cry." He turned to Barney the Shakespearean: "We will deal with the rendering of the character as mildly as possible, by stating that it was simply fearful."

For a short and difficult period, Barney's diamond dealings were as ungainly as his performances. Despite the cigars, the horse, and the vigor, he was forced to sell out to Cohen. To save expenses he moved into a small bedroom in his brother's hotel. Prospects did not look good for either of the Barnatos until 1874. Prior to that year the law forbade diggers to own more than two claims. By the time the Barnatos had pooled their savings of £3,000 in 1876, the limit had gone up to ten claims. As a last, desperate gamble they bought four in the Kimberley mine.

It seemed the worst possible time to acquire land. By now nearly all the yellow earth had been shaken and sifted away. Below it lay hard blue ground. The diggers believed that diamonds had been carried to the region in some prehistoric flood, coming to rest in the first hundred feet of pliable soil. To them the stuff that dented their shovels signaled the end of the great diamond days. Barney thought otherwise. He told a listener that "the diamonds come from below through what was once a sort of tube in the earth." This was pure guesswork on his part, and it was the making of his fortune. Before long, every cubic foot of blue ground would yield stones worth thousands of pounds sterling.

While he was guessing, Barney ventured that the diamond fields would never last in their present form. At the Kimberley, De Beers, Dutoitspan, and Bulfontein mines, mindless exploitation had made life extremely hazardous. Walls kept caving in, burying men and animals. Competition drove up the price of labor and equipment. Gemstones flooded the market, and as a result prices plunged to new lows. If the business were to survive, the production of diamonds would have to be regulated by some central authority. But who would that be? Given the chaos of wills and egos, it would be impossible to elect a leader. The man who wanted to control the business would have to acquire the most valuable claims, then dominate the lesser holders. Barney set out to be that man.

He was not alone. Two years before, the 18-year-old Cecil Rhodes had come to South Africa, like Barney on the advice of an older brother. A prominent mining engineer knew both men and frequently compared them. "Externally," says Gardner Williams, "two young men could scarcely be more unlike than the little, chunky, bullet-headed, near-sighted, mercurial Hebrew, taking a hand in current sport or traffic, and the tall, thoughtful, young overseer, sitting moodily on a bucket, deaf to the chatter and rattle about him, and fixing his blue eyes intently on his work, or on some fabric of his brain."

Williams found, however, that with all their disparities Rhodes and Barnato were nearly identical in their "keen foresight, and extraordinary comprehension of great financial undertakings." Both craved riches, Barney "for the sheer satisfaction of moneymaking, of unfolding great schemes of production and flotation, of proving to the world that he was a master of finance"; Cecil "as a means to reach ends of Imperial scope, to throw the searchlights of civilization into every cranny of the Dark Continent . . . to create a Greater Britain than the most daring fancy before him had conceived, and stretch the hand of his Queen over a realm transcending the farthest sweep of the Macedonian or the Roman."

In a few years that fancy was to make Rhodes the most admired, feared, and execrated white man in nineteenth-century Africa. His friend Rudyard Kipling called him "an immense and brooding spirit." Mark Twain had other ideas. Late in Rhodes's career, when he was famous throughout Europe and America, he and Twain met in South Africa. "I admire him, I frankly confess it," the American wrote in

Following the Equator. "And when his time comes I shall buy a piece of the rope for a keepsake." In the 1930s, during an African voyage, Evelyn Waugh reflected on Rhodes: "There is a connexion between celibacy and 'vision' both at the lowest—Hitler—and the highest—the contemplative. Rhodes inhabited a world somewhere between. It is the childless who plan for posterity." A decade later Hannah Arendt pronounced Rhodes to be a forerunner of totalitarianism, a "vulgar megalomaniac" with "an appetite for self-glorification." Since Rhodes was "insane enough to say he could indeed 'do nothing wrong,' what he did became right. It was his duty to do what he wanted. He felt himself a god—nothing less.' "

More than twenty biographies and innumerable books and theses have been written about the man who dominated South Africa for decades, building fortunes and destroying the men and companies who dared to oppose him. The person who emerges is not savory. Rhodes could be kind to natives, but they were never more than a means to further acquisitions. "I prefer land to niggers," he impatiently declared, and dreamed of an Africa, from the Cape to Cairo, placed under British domination. He lived to see part of that grand fantasy come true. Rhodes's adroit maneuvering brought two countries within the Crown's control, and both were named for him: Rhodesia (now Zimbabwe) and Northern Rhodesia (Zambia). He expected to be remembered for four thousand years; he has already been cursed for one hundred of them.

For all the dissections of Rhodes's personality and motives he remains an elusive character whose real genius, like that of his Oxford contemporary Oscar Wilde, seems to have been most evident in conversation. All that one can detect in his early writings is an agitation that amounts to madness. For years he shuttles from England to Africa, sketching plans for a pan-British millennium in which Canada, Australia, and the United States rejoin the empire and a *Pax Britannica* covers the globe. He makes and remakes his will, a feverish and dreamy document that rarely connects with reality. He woolgathers on the diamond fields and, during one reverie, forgets to prime a water pump; it explodes.

But there is never a question of his ability to concentrate when the subject is the accumulation of capital. On the fields his surname prompts admirers to call him the Colossus. It is a continuation of the leadership he shows even in childhood, when his large and bizarre family refer to him as "long-headed Cecil," the boy with a brain to match his gangling size.

Rhodes was born on July 5, 1853 (exactly a year before Barney Barnato), the fifth son of the Rev. Francis Rhodes, vicar of St. Michael's Church in Hertfordshire. Francis married twice and fathered twelve children. Not one appears to have been a specimen of Victorian security or happiness. That may be the result of a phenomenon Samuel Butler noted in *The Way of All Flesh*: "One great reason why clergymen's households are generally unhappy is because the clergyman is so much at home and close about the house." Of the dozen children only one of the five sons and one of the seven sisters ever married. Cecil's favorite sister favored men's clothing, and his own sex life has been a matter of speculation for five generations.

He had been a sickly and wistful child. His ambition to attend Oxford was at this stage thwarted by lackluster achievements in school and by the Reverend's small income. When Herbert Rhodes left home to try cotton planting in South Africa, his young brother looked on with envy and longing. Presently letters started to arrive describing the healthy atmosphere of Herbert's new home and asking if Cecil could help with the harvest. Rhodes begged permission to go, and ultimately his parents gave in. "Aflame with excitement," he studied a map until sunrise, "by which time . . . Africa possessed my bones."

Once there, Cecil was practically handed the plantation while Herbert went off to investigate possibilities in New Rush. The adolescent responded with astonishing maturity. "I am left in charge here," he wrote his mother, "and have about 30 Kaffirs to manage, and feel quite a big man with so many black attendants." He and his staff brought in the cotton and sold it at a small profit. As Cecil made plans for a new crop, Herbert sent bulletins from the fields: he had purchased three claims at Colesburg, near the original De Beers diggings. Cecil amplified his brother's enthusiasm in letters home: "You cannot understand what an awful enticement the diamonds are . . . any day you may find a diamond that will astonish the world. Many fellows have found small fortunes just as they were giving up in despair."

In the fall of 1871 Cecil set out for the diamond fields, probably on horseback, probably leading an ox cart, probably taking with him two favorite volumes, Plutarch's *Lives* and a Greek lexicon. The reason for the uncertainty is Rhodes himself. As one of his friends commented, now and again the Colossus would reminisce, embellishing all the way. But "it was never an easy matter to get Rhodes to talk about any part of his life that was past—he lived entirely in the present and future."

Cecil made an immediate impression. No one guessed his true age. Time spent on the cotton fields had given him a new authority and physical presence. He was over six feet tall, "fair and blue-eyed, and with somewhat aquiline features, wearing flannels of the school playing field, somewhat shrunken with strenuous rather than effectual washing, that still left the color of the red veldt dust." The public Rhodes was a young man of serious mien, making long strides across the town, ordering his Kaffirs with authority and stopping now and then to stare off into space at some private vision. This was the Rhodes who would cultivate a moustache to disguise a large and melancholy mouth, who would grow heavy and prematurely gray, and who would be pleased to hear men refer to him as The Old Man before he was out of his twenties. But there was another Rhodes on the fields, an immature and petulant soul who would toy with the idea of a secret society to dominate the world, who hungered for land in order to play the great game of British imperialism, and who in a rare moment of self-analysis declared, "I am a boy! Of course I shall never grow old."

Nor would so many outstanding members of his generation. The Victorians' most revealing trait was not voracious sexual appetite but emotional immaturity. Thomas Carlyle and John Ruskin never consummated their marriages. Lewis Carroll and Edward Lear made much of childhood's estate because they never could find its exit. Benjamin Disraeli, the Prime Minister who oversaw so much land-grabbing, foppishly danced around his "Faerie Queen," proffering countries like a juvenile seeking favor from his governess. Kipling, bard of imperialism, was at his happiest writing of prepubescent adventurers like Kim and Mowgli. Rhodes's friend Baden-Powell, founder of the Boy Scouts—who was endlessly fascinated with executions and who in his old age praised *Mein Kampf*—was called The Boy-Man by his biographer. That title could fit many of his contemporaries. The list is very long and culminates in the apotheosis of child-worship, produced in 1904. "Long after writing Peter Pan its true meaning came to me," wrote James M. Barrie, "desperate to grow up, but can't."

For those desperate men who couldn't grow up, the diamond fields provided an ideal playground. Finding treasure was simply a matter of hide and seek. Cecil wrote to his mother in the tones of Alice on the other side of the looking glass. The ground at the De Beers mine, he told her, "works just like Stilton cheese, and is as like the composition of Stilton cheese as anything I can compare it to. . . . They have been able to find no bottom yet."

After two months of digging, he sent another note to England: "I average about £100 per week. Yrs. C. Rhodes."—this at a time when a servant's annual wage was about £40. But neither brother was satisfied with such returns. Herbert's restless nature pushed him north, where there were rumors of gold discoveries. Left alone once more, Cecil made the first of many brilliant intuitive moves: he took on Charles Rudd as a partner. The well-born Rudd had been a champion athlete at Oxford, but now he was a fortune hunter like the rest. Together the men tried a series of ancillary schemes, among them the manufacture of ice cream and the pumping of water. In time, these ventures would harden Rhodes's view of business, and of mankind in general.

There was, for example, the nasty business of the February flood at the Kimberley mine. Unusually heavy rains had inundated the diggings, and a rival company had been hired to pump them out. An overseer testified that one Cecil Rhodes had offered him a bribe of £300 to sabotage the machinery. Rhodes indignantly denied the charge. Rudd had powerful friends, and payoffs may have been made. In any case, the plaintiffs abruptly grew silent, the matter was never brought to court, and Rhodes and Rudd won a new contract to pump out De Beers. There was a catch: they had to do it within 30 days or forfeit a £100 bond. Rhodes spoke with bland assurance, and the miners believed him. It was all bluff. Only one pump could be brought to the fields in time, and that was owned by a farmer named Devenish. He lived eight days' drive south of the diamond country.

Rhodes hired a cart and a team of mules and never looked back. When he arrived he was refused outright; Devenish had no intention of leasing his valuable pump to some flute-voiced stranger. Day after day Rhodes tried to persuade him. Day after day the farmer refused.

Rhodes turned his attention to Mrs. Devenish. He was an honest, hardworking Englishman, jobs were at stake, he would pay an exorbitant sum—he projected an image of charm and total sincerity, and she believed him. Together they set to work on her husband. In the end the exhausted Devenish surrendered. Rhodes wrote him a check for £1,000 and another £120 for transportation costs. To save £100 he had spent £1,120. For Rhodes it was worth every penny. He had proven to clients that his word was his bond, and he had found a motto to live by: "Every man has his price." It was to become his favorite phrase. From now on the trick would be to find that price, whether it was money, status, or women, and meet it.

Throughout 1873 Rhodes spent a lot of time considering his destiny. With his last £1,500 he had purchased claims in the De Beers mine, and they had yielded a bucket of diamonds. Profit from the stones, in turn, had paid for additional claims. He was flourishing in South Africa; according to the young man's calculations, his De Beers claims were already worth £10,000. Should he stay in a foreign country amid rough strangers? Or was it time to go home, to settle down on the land where he could trace his ancestry back to the Elizabethan era? While he pondered he kept a pile of books by his side, studying in the glaring African sun. One day he announced his decision. Fellow diggers teased him: "Going up to Oxford, soon, to learn how to grow diamonds?"

Rhodes answered tolerantly: "Very true, you chaps. The educational system of Oxford seems rather unpractical but look around and everywhere in England you will find Oxford men on top!" In the middle of the year he took his first step to the top: he sailed home. The 20-year-old traveled alone. No one on board suspected that his pockets were crammed with diamonds. The passengers would not learn it from Rhodes. His shirts and jackets were ostentatiously tattered and stained, and his only pair of trousers were so threadbare they had to be mended by the ship's sailmaker.

At first his classmates were similarly deceived—not that any of them would have been impressed by displays of precious stones. The Oxford of the 1870s was a place of dreaming spires and God-haunted students. It still reverberated from the shocks of the 1840s, when John Henry Newman had left the Church of England for the Church of Rome, taking with him scores of brilliant students. Religious debate greeted young Rhodes as he entered Oriel College; but the parson's son wanted no part of it.

During his first term he confessed to a family friend: "Whether I become the village parson which you sometimes imagined me as, remains to be proved. I am afraid my constitution received rather too much of what they call the lust of the flesh at the Diamond Fields to render that result possible." He elaborated no further on his idea of lust; as for God, he had already made up his mind. There was a "Fifty-fifty chance that He exists." Much was made of this statement later; it was the only case in which Rhodes did not demand controlling interest.

Rhodes was never more than a desultory student. He announced plans to become a barrister, but nothing came of them. His primary concern was to acquire the panache and polish of that highest form of life, the English gentleman. "I shall pass," he predicted defensively, "which is all I wish to do." He squandered time at horse races and clubs, and at least once when a lecturer bored him he pulled out a box of gems and displayed them to nearby students. When the lecturer looked up and inquired about what was going on he was told, "It is only Rhodes and his diamonds." Nevertheless one don managed to catch Cecil's attention. In an inaugural address at Oxford, the new Slade Professor, John Ruskin, became the grand apologist of British imperialism.

"There is a destiny before us," he proclaimed in his ringing contralto, "the highest ever set before a nation to be accepted or refused. We are still undegenerate in race; a race mingled of the best northern blood. We are not yet dissolute in temper, but still have the firmness to govern and the grace to obey." England "must found colonies as fast and as far as she is able, formed of her most energetic and worthiest men; seizing every piece of fruitful waste ground she can set her foot on."

In the next century fascism would amplify these notions of racial superiority, of firm government and graceful obedience. In the late Victorian era it was merely intoxicating stuff for an undergraduate to dream on. More intoxication came from a volume published in 1872; Conan Doyle was sufficiently impressed with the work to make it part of Sherlock Holmes's library. "Let me recommend this book—one of the most remarkable ever penned," says the detective to Dr. Watson in *The Sign of the Four*. "It is Winwood Reade's *Martyrdom of Man*." Reade, a traveler, historian, and social Darwinist, argued that history was a process of escalation driven by anguish. "In each generation the human race has been tortured that their children might profit by their woes," he maintained. Now, at the price of pain, religion must go, although its structures might still be useful. "A season of mental anguish is at hand, and through this we must pass in order that our posterity may rise. The soul must be sacrificed, the hope of immortality must die." Accomplishments had to be in the here and now.

Reade was a philosopher Rhodes could follow from Oxford to Africa. He gave atheism a good name (thereby rejecting the life and work of the Rev. Francis Rhodes), and he believed that the future belonged to the bold. In Rhodes's view that meant Englishmen with solid incomes and imperial ambitions. Years later he remembered *Martyrdom* as "a creepy book. I read it . . . fresh from my father's Parsonage, and you may imagine the impression which it produced upon me. . . . That book has made me what I am."

Beyond all these influences there lay the feeling that he did not have much time to accomplish his aims. At the age of 19 Rhodes had suffered a mild heart attack in South Africa; the climate helped him recover quickly. Then, shortly after he entered Oxford, his mother died. He was shattered, and several months later fell seriously ill with lung disease. On the advice of a specialist Cecil returned, wholly demoralized, to South Africa. A doctor gave him six months to live.

The estimate was off by 28 years. Rhodes recovered, but he was never free of circulatory and heart problems. Convinced that his time was short, he wrote a strange will in the form of a "Private Confession" on June 2, 1877.

"It often strikes a man," he began, "to inquire what is the chief good in life. To one the thought comes that it is a happy marriage, to another great wealth, to a third travel, and so on, and as each seizes the idea, he more or less works for its attainment for the rest of his existence." The influence of Ruskin appears: "To myself, thinking over the same question, the wish came to make myself useful to my country. . . . I contend that we are the first race in the world, and that the more of the world we inhabit, the better it is for the human race. I contend that every acre added to our territory provides for the birth of more of the English race, who otherwise would not be brought into existence. Added to which the absorption of the greater portion of the world under our rule simply means the end of all wars."

The end of all wars: no wonder British civil servants were one day to define Rhodes as the High Priest of Optimism. His will subscribes to Reade's central insight: dogmas of organized religions are obsolete, but their forms could be retained. "[When] I read the story of the Jesuits I see what they were able to do in a bad cause . . . why should we not form a secret society with but one object, the furtherance of the British Empire, and the bringing of the whole uncivilized world under British rule?" And why not start with Africa? The entire country is "still lying ready for us, it is our duty to take it."

Rhodes's greatest admirers have recoiled from the juvenile quality of this "Confession." All he seems to have omitted is a secret handshake and a decoding ring. "Pathetic," "childish," and "naive" are the mildest of the critical epithets. This places too great a burden on the 24-year-old who wrote them. No doubt he was a permanent adolescent. No doubt he substituted fantasies for those ideals he could not embrace: family and faith. Yet he could not have realized those fantasies without the support of the Victorians themselves. For all his excesses, Rhodes was merely acting out the national fantasy of foreign lands as Her Majesty's properties and foreigners as her possessions.

4

"WE HAD BETTER JOIN HANDS"

IN HIS OLD AGE Joseph Benjamin Robinson hired a journalist to eulogize him. *Men, Mines and Millions* dutifully recalls the young "J.B.R." as "a robust, well-built man, alert, pugnacious, full of energy, with florid features, strong jaw and keen blue eyes, which pierced you like a diamond drill." As far as it goes the physical account is accurate; until his marriage in 1877 Robinson was considered one of Kimberley's most attractive bachelors. But "pugnacious" cannot begin to describe the autocrat whose favorite weapons were the horsewhip and the lawsuit. To Louis Cohen, Barney Barnato's old partner, Robinson was "sour-faced and green with spleen like a leek." The man had "no personality, no magnetism, but resembled a mortal who had a tombstone on his soul."

This was the gentlest of the appraisals. When Robinson died in 1929 at the age of 90 he had outlived most of his contemporaries (although not Louis Cohen), but he could not escape the judgment of *The Cape Times.* The paper noted that Robinson's will omitted any gifts to charity, and cursed him beyond the grave: "His immunity against any impulse of generosity, private or public, was so notorious that the name of J. B. Robinson became during his lifetime proverbial for stinginess. . . . The evil which the dead man thus speaks of himself is terrible to contemplate."

Unlike the other diamond magnates, J.B.R. was born in South Africa. On the family's Cape Town farm the boy was educated by itinerant schoolmasters and left to his own devices. The sixth child of a farmer had to fight with his brothers for attention, and he clamored for it the rest of his life. His adolescence was difficult and full of belligerence. By the age of 16 the oversized youth had outfought every boy in the neighborhood. Early on he set himself up as a wool merchant, farmer, and trader in the Orange Free State. This put him in an ideal position to swoop down on the Vaal at the earliest rumor of diamond discoveries. In 1868 he and his farmhands appeared at the riverside. "I brought up all my boys, Basutos," he recalled, and "showed them the diamonds which they quickly began to detect. In six weeks they had found about 30 diamonds worth £10,000."

Robinson realized that the future lay in New Rush and relocated there as a first-class "Diamond Merchant . . . now prepared to give the HIGHEST PRICES." He turned out to be a natural self-publicist, affecting a military posture and adding several inches to his height by wearing a white pith helmet indoors and out. Diggers dubbed him the Buccaneer, but they showed a wary respect for the dealer who was always sober, who stayed away from raffish elements and, as one paper had it, did "his duty in that state of life which it hath pleased God to call him like a Christian and a gentleman. He . . . hands over his cheque promptly . . . to all his customers."

So much for J.B.R.'s assets. His liabilities included an abiding contempt for colleagues as well as natives, and an ungovernable temper. Like Barney Barnato he savored a good fight. But he had none of Barney's alleviating humor or his sense of fair play. The confrontation with Ernest Moses was a case in point. Like many professional men at Kimberley, the dapper little dentist kept his fingers in several enterprises. Among them was a small diamond buying concern. Moses also fancied himself a wit and wrote a gossip column for one of the local papers. On one occasion he sold Robinson a second-rate diamond, on another he ridiculed him in print. Then Moses made a third mistake: he strolled unguarded on the street. J.B.R. spotted the dentist and dashed out of his office furiously, weapon in hand. "The pliant whip," wrote an eyewitness, "came down one, two, three, fitting the plump shoulders of Mr Moses as though it had been made for them . . . Mr Moses took the one, two, three, and then tried to run off, but Mr. Robinson is swift of foot, as well as smart of hand . . . and down came the pliant whip again, one, two, three across the Mosaic buttocks."

At first the newspaper editorials backed Robinson. But after a few weeks the editors changed their minds. Moses was half the size of his opponent. What need was there for eighteenth-century behavior in a civilized community? Robinson should have chosen legal methods of retribution. These days the horsewhip had other uses. It was an inappropriate instrument for settling arguments between white men.

To give the Buccaneer his due, he could never be mistaken for a fool. Like Barnato and Rhodes, he sensed that the haphazard days of diamond mining were coming to a close. In 1876 the ten-claim restriction was abolished. A group of diggers, backed by a London syndicate, tried to amalgamate their holdings at Kimberley. They immediately ran into trouble. Certain valuable claims stood in the way, and Robinson owned them all. Naturally he refused to relinquish a single one; amalgamation was a splendid idea as far as Robinson was concerned, but it was *his* idea.

Within a month J.B.R. made his countermove. He published a notice inviting "such claimholders as might be inclined to join [me] in amalgamating their ground for the purpose of working upon co-operative principles"—principles, it goes without saying, to be controlled by the writer. Now it was the turn of the London-backed group. If they could not win at the fields, then neither would J.B.R. *The Independent* put it succinctly: "Mr. Robinson found that the ground . . . could not be connected, owing to some claims intervening. . . . As it was essential, in order to establish a company upon the basis proposed by Mr Robinson, that the ground should be in one block, he abandoned the scheme." But only to gather strength for his next move. The fight for diamond monopoly had begun.

♦   ♦   ♦

"Mr. Whittlestaff, I must tell you that you are unreasonable."
"No doubt. I am a poor miserable man who does not know the world.
I have never been to the diamond fields."

ANTHONY TROLLOPE HAD. His last completed novel, *An Old Man's Love*, looked back to the fall of 1877 when he paid a visit to South Africa. His popularity had declined, and ideas no longer came with their former ease. Still the consummate professional ground out his forty pages a day, rain or shine, summer or winter. A travel book, he reasoned, might be just the thing to revive his reputation.

"To 'do' South Africa," Trollope told his readers, "had for years past been on my mind, till at last there was growing on me the consciousness that I was becoming too old for any more such 'doing.' Then, suddenly, the newspapers became full of the Transvaal Republic." Their stories concerned the events of May 24, 1877, Queen Victoria's birthday, when a troop of British police annexed the Transvaal on orders from London. The Boer flag was hauled down, and the Union Jack raised up by a young British official named H. Rider Haggard. Not a shot was fired in protest, but the Boers' eyes burned when they looked up at the British flag. On this day their countdown began.

For now, however, the territory was in the hands of Her Majesty's officials, and Trollope was keen to inspect it. As soon as he announced his plans, warnings flooded in: the trip was long and arduous, South Africa had a harsh climate, and even if he remained healthy, dangerous objects could block his path: commercial hustlers, armed men, Jews. The seasoned traveler had answers for these objections. His constitution remained vigorous, "the Bay of Biscay as I have felt it is not much rougher than other seas. No one ever attempted to gouge me in Kentucky or drew a revolver on me in California." Furthermore, "I have invariably found Jews to be more liberal than other men."

He arrived at Kimberley in October, the beginning of another long, dry summer. At 62 he was what James Russell Lowell called "a big red-faced, rather underbred Englishman of the bald-with-spectacles type." With greater indulgence a friend characterized him as "crusty, quarrelsome, wrong-headed, prejudiced, obstinate, kind-hearted and thoroughly honest old Tony Trollope." Yet the harrumphing author could be placid enough when he was investigating a story, and Kimberley surrounded him with plenty of plots and characters.

Just then manual labor was in great demand, and wages were higher than ever. So were the walls around the black laborers. Some were metaphorical—curfew laws that forced them off the streets by 10 p.m., for example, or capricious floggings. One Englishman saw a neighbor one morning "whipping every one of his boys as they started work, and, in reply to my question as to his reason, he said, 'If they don't want it now, they will!'"

Other walls were solid enough, and extremely confining. The blacks were segregated into "compounds," where they were required to live until the end of their contracts. Each enclosure was "unroofed, but covered with wire netting to prevent anything being thrown out of them over the walls, and with a subterranean entrance to the adjoining mine. . . . Round the interior of the wall there are built sheds or huts in which the natives live and sleep when not working." A miscellany of tribes was represented in the compounds: Zulus, Basutos, Matabeles, Bechuanas, men from the Portuguese territories and from both sides of the Zambesi, "a living ethnological collection such as can be examined nowhere else in South Africa." Food, clothing, medicine, or any other supplies could only be purchased at the company store; no spirits were allowed to enter, and neither were visitors, black or white.

With all these precautions, I.D.B. stubbornly went on. Guards reported instances of natives swallowing precious stones and disgorging them later. Inspectors found stones in the natives' hair, ears, navels, eyelids, anuses. Every available orifice was used. The more ingenious smugglers cut themselves and hid jewels in the wounds. Sometimes diamonds were fed to dogs, who could be killed and dissected at leisure.

White men not only encouraged I.D.B., they participated in it. In one notorious case, a dealer bought stolen diamonds from some native miners, submitted to a body search, and then ran off. Suspicious, a posse of policemen pursued him until he crossed over into the Orange Free State where they had no jurisdiction. Before their eyes he shot his horse and slit open its stomach to recover a sack of diamonds. After that, visitors to the town of Kimberley were treated to frequent chases on horseback as some thief headed for the border, followed by a posse of shouting policemen. Bets were taken on the cops and the robber, and quite often the odds were against the police. A popular song put it in rhyme: "Over the Free State Line/Whatever is yours is mine."

News of the compounds renewed the charges of *de facto* slavery. These were furiously rebutted: claimholders pointed out that real slaves had been indentured for life, bought and sold at their masters' whim—whereas these natives signed legal agreements to work for a specific term. It ranged from a few months to a year, and during that time they received good wages. Working the dirt, processing the rock, a man could earn ten shillings a week, plus meals and shelter. It was more than many English farmhands were making. If the black laborers fell ill they would be hospitalized and given medical care without charge. As a further benefit, during the time of their incarceration they were kept from the houses of alcohol and prostitution and gambling. Once they had fulfilled their agreement, they could live and wander as they pleased—as long as it was outside Kimberley and the diamond fields.

Unmentioned were the salaries of white workers: between £3 and £6 a week—never less than 400 percent more than the blacks. Nor did anyone refer to the coercive tactics of the government, which worked hand in glove with the claimowners. Short of help, an employer wrote to the administration: "Could not the police put a little gentle pressure on these gentlemen to oblige them to enter service?" The gentlemen were natives without contracts, and the following Sunday an inspector responded with a pass raid on natives who were "hanging about" the town. The arrested men were soon locked in compounds when they were not on the fields. As for those hospital facilities, even the official reports found them "dilapidated" and "filthy," "in defiance of all sanitary laws." Eventually, the death rate for Kimberley blacks exceeded that of Calcutta, said to be the Empire's most afflicted city.

Blacks outnumbered whites by four to one in Kimberley. Many came from tribes with long histories of pride and self-sufficiency. Others were descendants of great warriors. Some tribes owned guns. Why did they submit to harsh treatment with such docility? Part of the answer lay in the land itself. The game animals had been wiped out five years before, shot and consumed by diggers and armed tribesmen. Drought continued to burn out the crops. For the first time in their history, blacks had to purchase meat and vegetables, and the only way to earn money was in the diamond mines.

Economic factors damaged the tribes; their views of the white man did them in entirely. Early in the nineteenth century, a young Xhosa woman had a dream of Africa without Europeans. She persuaded her people that one morning the sun would rise blood red. On that day dead rulers would spring to life, and kraals would overflow with cattle. The earth would yield enormous harvests. All whites would be blown into the sea; it was the only way to get rid of them. To effect this change all livestock had to be destroyed, as well as all grain and produce. British administrators and missionaries got wind of the plan and attempted to forestall it. But they were powerless to stop the destruction. The tribe killed its animals and burned its vegetables. Famine and desolation followed, and the Xhosas dispersed, victims of a self-inflicted wound. By the time of the diamond rush they were at the mercy of the mine owners.

Almost every tribe suffered from damaging superstitions. One of J. B. Robinson's executives, a young British Jew named Lionel Phillips, kept notes on the early diamond days. He recalled that in the seventies black laborers were "real savages in all respects, with tremendous respect for the white man, who, in their eyes, could do everything except tie up the sun! . . . The poor benighted creatures had an inordinate respect for us and were quite abject in attitude, an inherited legacy, perhaps, from the slave days."

White diggers were quick to take advantage of these delusions. One warned of "too much kindness or familiarity" with blacks. It would lead to misery and social chaos. "They will ask for higher pay, lose all respect . . . be insolent and disobedient, and finally run away. . . ." Strict adherence to a code was the only rational policy. "A nigger is all very well as long as he is kept in his proper place, that is, 'kept down'; to treat him in the 'man and brother' style of . . . philanthropists, is only to spoil him and injure yourself."

Phillips anticipated the protests of do-gooders: "New-comers to the colonies find this difficult to realize, thinking that kind treatment *must* succeed, but they soon get woefully undeceived. Of course I don't mean you should ill-use Kaffirs, but keep them in their places; punish them when naughty, and never be familiar or laugh with them."

At the time of Trollope's visit hardly anything had been written about the racial climate of Kimberley, so the British author could observe it without preconceptions. His sixty-fourth book, *South Africa*, is a classic expression of Victorian liberalism. He holds that Africans are merely dawdlers in the great march of progress; by and by the natives will catch up. "Those dusky troops of laborers," Trollope reflects, "who ten years since were living in the wildest state of unalloyed savagery, whose only occupation was the slaughter of each other in tribal wars, each of whom was the slave of his Chief, who were subject to the dominion of the most brutalizing and cruel superstitions, have already put themselves on the path towards civilization." He peers into the Kimberley mine, acknowledges that "the simple teaching of religion has never brought large numbers of Natives to live in European habits," but has "no doubt that European habits will bring about religion." That being the case, "gazing down upon four thousand black laborers,—although each of them would willingly have stolen a diamond if the occasion came,—I have felt that I was looking at three or four thousand growing Christians."

Still, Trollope is not so optimistic that he overlooks malaise on the diamond fields. His is the first literary portrait of Kimberley, and remains the most irascible. Despite the kindness of some locals, he says, "the place itself was distasteful to me in the extreme . . . the meat was bad, the butter uneatable, vegetables a rarity." Corrugated iron, Kimberley's main building material, is "the most hideous that has yet come into man's hands."

Irritants lie in his path and fly all around him. During the daylight hours his thermometer registers 160 degrees Fahrenheit in the sun. He seeks relief in the shade; that turns out to be a cooler 97°. Trollope had grown famous by describing the climate and tempo of English country towns, and he admits to all the liabilities of a tourist. "Perhaps having been in such personal discomfort, I am not a fair judge of the place. But an atmosphere composed of flies and dust cannot be pleasant,—of dust so thick that the sufferer fears to remove it lest the raising of it may aggravate the evil, and of flies so numerous that one hardly dares to slaughter them by the ordinary means lest their dead bodies should be noisome."

The surrounding territory presents no relief. "I do not think there is a tree to be seen within five miles of the town. . . . I doubt whether there was a blade of grass within twenty miles. . . . Everything was brown, as though the dusty dry uncovered ugly earth never knew the blessing of verdure." Avarice is everywhere. Diggers' families are obsessed with the notion that "dirt thrice turned may yet be turned a fourth time with some hope of profit. Consequently, ladies, and children, do turn dirt, instead of making pretty needle-work, or wholesome mud-pies." It is all shame-making, Trollope grumbles; I would "almost sooner have seen my own wife or my own girl with a broom at a street crossing."

But he does say "almost"; try as he might to turn away, the eminent Victorian succumbs to a touch of diamond fever. In the struggle between curiosity and revulsion, curiosity wins every time. Trollope wanders ravenously over every part of the Kimberley mine, now the largest man-made excavation in the world, asking questions and taking notes. The pit amounts to a scooped-out, 12-acre bowl. At the very bottom, diggers pluck diamonds 230 feet from the earth's surface. The 3,500 black workers appear to be so many ants, "working with all the usual energy of the ant-tribe."

Originally Kaffirs hauled the buckets up and down; but in 1877 horses do the job, walking round and round whims, devices that pull at wires and haul the diamondiferous earth. Trollope likens those wires to "the strings of some wonderful harp,—aerial or perhaps infernal, —from which the beholder expects a louder twang to be heard." The bowl is divided into 408 claims, but this is a deceptive number. A majority of the claims are subdivided, and these portions continually change hands. Dutoitspan is even more tumultuous. There, 1,441 claims are held by 214 men. Bulfontein is divided into 1,026 claims held by 153. In every mine the claimants blast away on different levels and dig at varying speeds.

The scene suggests a Piranesi etching. "It was as if some diabolically ingenious architect had contrived a house of 500 rooms, not one of which should be on the same floor, and to and from none of which should there be a pair of stairs or a door or a window." Furthermore, "it must be imagined that the architect had omitted the roof in order that the wires of the harp . . . might be brought into every chamber. The house has then been furnished with picks, shovels, planks, and a few barrels, populated with its black legions, and it is there for you to look at."

For Trollope, the most diverting sight of all occurs at 6 p.m.: quitting time. Then the black men "come as flies come up a wall, only capering as flies never caper,—and shouting as they come." He is amused by their costumes, "in which a jacket is never absent, but of which a pair of trowsers rarely forms a portion. A soldier's red jacket or a soldier's blue jacket has more charms than any other vestment." Like many Victorian liberals he is in favor of extending the franchise to blacks on some unspecified day. But, he decides, it would not be "so grand a thing if one addresses them as the free and independent electors of Kimberley before they have got trowsers to cover their nakedness."

In time the patronizing tone fades from his text. Trollope has seen more than rocks and men; he has witnessed a brute system based on hypocrisy and money-hunger. From this he cannot turn away and smile behind his hand. "The stranger in South Africa will constantly be told that the colored man will not work," he writes, "and that this is the one insuperable cause by which the progress of the country will be impeded. . . . And yet during his whole sojourn in the country he will see all the work of the world around him done by the hands of colored people. . . . When he gets to the Diamond Fields he will find the mines swarming with black labor. And yet he will be told that the 'nigger' will not work!" The sight of flogging forces a stronger protest. "The 'iron rod' is to me abominable. It means always some other treatment for the colored man than that which is given to the white man. There can be no good done till the two stand before the law exactly on the same ground."

Today, thanks to the Barchester novels, Trollope is remembered as an accomplished raconteur of upper-middle-class intrigues. But the most discerning chapters of his travel book demonstrate that he was also a thinker and something of a prophet. As if he could see De Beers afar off, he finds it odd that the diamond mines "could contain the operations of a large number of separate speculators. It is so completely one that you are driven at first to think that it must be the property of one firm." He concludes with a long look around him. South Africa, he believes, "is a black country and not a white one . . . the important person is the Kafir and the Zulu, the Bechuana and the Hottentot;— not the Dutchman or the Englishman."

No wonder old Tony Trollope had seemed so crusty, quarrelsome, wrong-headed, prejudiced, obstinate, kind-hearted, and thoroughly honest. He had to be. He was running ahead of history.

◆　　◆　　◆

TROLLOPE'S ONE SHORTCOMING was a failure to spend enough time with Kimberley's rising young diamond men. Then again, the interviews might not have been a success. Robinson would have been rude, Rhodes never had any use for novelists, and Trollope would surely have overlooked Alfred Beit. Almost everyone did.

Barely five feet tall, with a large head and stooped shoulders, the little German could be disregarded in a crowd and sometimes in a room. He had few social graces, no athletic abilities, no skill at cards —when he was forced to sit in on a game he chose the role of banker. In mixed company he suffered from tics and twitches. His eyes bulged, his chin receded, and his moustache was insignificant. With less charity than accuracy one woman remarked that he was "less a Beit than a nibble."

Beit was born in Germany in 1853, six months after Barnato and six months before Rhodes. "I was one of the poor Beits of Hamburg," he was to say in later life. "My father found it difficult even to pay for my schooling." This was another case of a plutocrat inventing his deprived childhood. The Beit family had fled Portugal in the sixteenth century, settled in northern Germany, and eased themselves into the middle class as refiners of precious metals. Alfred's unconventional father, Siegfried, was the first of the family to break with tradition. Shortly after his marriage he quit the refinery to found his own silk-importing firm; and he and his new wife joined the Lutheran Church. They found many Hebrews in adjoining pews.

In those days the recommended antidote for *Judenhetze*—Jew hatred—was baptism. No less a personage than Theodor Herzl, the founder of Zionism, considered the idea. "I am in favor of conversion," he admitted. "For me the matter is closed but it bothers me greatly for my son Hans. I ask myself if I have the right to sour and blacken his life as mine has been soured and blackened. . . . Therefore one must baptise Jewish boys before they must account for themselves, before they are able to act against it and before conversion can be construed as weakness on their part. They must disappear into the crowd."

Alfred did exactly that. His academic work was so undistinguished that Siegfried pulled him out of school. At Papa's insistence, an Amsterdam diamond importer took the boy on as a clerk. Only Mama

Beit continued to believe in little Alfred. She would always believe in him, and Alfred would reciprocate. There would be no other woman in his life.

In Amsterdam he vanished into the background. "I just did my work," he remembered, "and wasted my spare time, like other young men." The critical moment came in 1875 when the company sent him to Kimberley. It was as if Alfred had burst from a chrysalis. Suddenly everything he touched, every venture he tried, showed a talent for finance. He simply could not lose money.

First he discovered that South African diamond dealers were a witless bunch. "I saw at once," he later commented, "that some of the . . . stones were as good as any in the world, and I saw, too, that the buyers protected themselves against their own ignorance by offering generally one-tenth part of what each stone was worth in Europe. It was plain that if one had a little money there was a fortune to be made."

No doubt with the lobbying of Mama Beit, Siegfried advanced his son £2,000, and Alfred went into business for himself. Claims could cost as much as £5,000 cash, so he used the money to buy real estate and property: "Twelve or thirteen offices, corrugated iron shanties, of which I kept one. . . . I got eighteen hundred pounds a month for them." Beit sold the land some years later for £260,000. "I got something for the dwellings, too, I think," he recollected, smiling. "Not a bad speculation!"

With his first profits Alfred set up as a diamond buyer. His own shanty resembled every other buyer's office except for one item, a large bag of silver. Metal currency was always in short supply and the diggers needed coins to pay their native workers. Diggers were allowed to leave their pound notes on the counter, reach into the bag, and make their own change on the honor system. Beit's gesture was from the heart, but it was also good advertising. Word about this trusting German got around.

Alfred had a genuine sweetness of character, and his beneficence grew along with his business. An assistant remembered the day a young girl came in with a letter from her mother. Beit read it, made a few inquiries, and impulsively handed her a check. Curious, the assistant read the note; it was from a woman whose husband had recently died, leaving her with a large family to raise. She wanted to buy a small shop. A piece of paper and the girl's answers were enough for Alfred. He donated £250 on the spot.

Such quixotic gestures, coupled with neurasthenia, would have bankrupted other men. They became Beit's most significant assets. For Alfred knew he was a psychological cripple, and he searched out those who would compensate for his weaknesses. As with money and jewels, his instincts about people were infallible.

Julius Wernher was the representative of a Parisian diamond buying concern when Beit persuaded him to become a partner. They seemed an odd match at first. On one side was the shy little free lance; on the other was the handsome and assured executive from an old Christian family in Hesse. It turned out to be an ideal marriage. Lionel Phillips left J.B.R. and joined the new firm of Wernher, Beit. "Of all the men I had become acquainted with at Kimberley," he says in his memoirs, "none was more genial and kind, none more brilliant in capacity, more bold in enterprise, or more genuinely respected and admired than Alfred Beit. His intelligence was keen and his power of decision great as it was rapid. He and his partner, Julius Wernher, were, as businessmen, a unique combination. Beit had the gift of quite unusual insight . . . while Wernher had a calmer, colder and safer judgement." The new firm of Wernher, Beit immediately prospered.

It was inevitable that Alfred Beit and Cecil Rhodes should meet and find much to admire in each other. Their first conversation is so classic that one feels that the dialogue was cut and polished many times before they went public with it. One evening in the early 1880s Rhodes was on his way home. He passed Beit's office and saw the light on. "Do you never take a rest?" he asked. "Not often," Alfred replied. "Well, what's your game?" Beit was succinct: "I intend to control the whole diamond output before I am much older." At this reply Robinson would have bristled; Barnato might have laughed or put up his fists. Rhodes knew better. "That's funny," he is supposed to have said. "I have made up my mind to do the same; we had better join hands."

Beit needed no persuasion. He had watched Rhodes buying up diamond properties and talking up his imperial vision; to Beit the Englishman seemed "a commercial Viking." Alfred and Cecil John became a common sight in town, the tall man taking big steps, his companion trotting hard to keep up. Once in a while they could be seen at a Bachelors' Ball, Rhodes whirling with the wallflowers, Beit deliberately choosing the tallest young women in the room. Beit always listened closely to Rhodes's grandiose visions; Rhodes customarily deferred to Beit's financial advice. Questions about money were met with the standard reply, "Ask little Alfred."

Rhodes kept a large account with Beit's firm, and together the finances of the two men grew faster than Kimberley. South Africa's diamond business began to receive close attention from British journalists. Most of them came to regard these new millionaires as part of Africa's natural wonders, and they wanted to see them firsthand. Generally, they sent in awed reports.

In between his notorious sexual adventures Frank Harris decided to tour Kimberley, where he made a special point of looking up Rhodes and Beit. Unlike his colleagues, he refused to be dazzled by wealth and reputation. In *My Life and Loves* he describes Beit's "little body and small limbs" and his "well-shaped" head, "the forehead very broad, and high-domed to [indicate] reverence and idealism, like a poet's." The rest of the face was "not so good; the nose fairly large, but slightly beaked, not noticeably fleshy—a good rudder; the chin rather weak than strong—no great courage or resolution anywhere."

Other than the forehead, Harris goes on, "the eyes and mouth were the two noteworthy features: the mouth coarse and ill-cut, the lower lip particularly heavy. It reminded me of Rhodes's face; but Rhodes's mouth was coarser and more cruel than Beit's; his nose, too, larger and more beaked; his chin and jaw more massive—altogether a stronger face, though not so intellectually alert."

Rhodes would have agreed with the appraisal. He made a point of choosing strength over intellect. An acquaintance once told him of plans to become a writer. The Colossus frowned: "Shouldn't do that. It is not a man's work—mere loafing." He told another friend how he spent his leisure at Kimberley: "I often go and sit at the edge of the De Beers mine and look at the blue diamondiferous ground, reaching from the surface . . . and I reckon up the value of the diamonds in the blue and the power conferred by them. In fact, every foot of blue ground means so much power." Power: that was the key. With it, he decided, one could dominate all the intellect in South Africa. In London. In the world.

5

A VEHICLE FOR
PLUNDER

ON A BRIGHT NOVEMBER MORNING in 1878, the citizens of Kimberley awoke to find blue and white ribbons fluttering all over Ward Five. Everyone recognized these as the colors of Barney Barnato's racehorses. But that fall they proclaimed another form of competition: Barney was entering politics.

He and Harry had risen mightily in the five years since their arrival. The raffish London Hotel, the days of boxing and magic, the kopje walloping were all behind them. Under the name Barnato Bros. their claims had become famous throughout Kimberley for yielding stones of the highest quality. The elder brother, anxious to be recognized as a financier, assumed his original name of Harry Isaacs. In Barney's case, however, success did not produce a corresponding dignity. He maintained his familiar bantam style, complete with plumage, and he continued to drop his h's like a man scattering coins to the multitude. When the editors of *The Diamond News* heard that Barney was running for a position on the Town Council, they broke into derisive laughter. He was pictured as a clown nominated "for the mere sake of bringing the whole Municipal Council into contempt." But Barney was in earnest, sending his representatives through the ward with the promise of free drinks and pocket money. Much too late, the *News* fulminated against "bribery in its most direct and objectionable form." On election morning Barney's opponent, a middle-aged teetotaler named George Bottomley, took the early lead. "After a little while, however," a reporter noted, "a file of ten men appeared, and in answer to the usual question [how do you vote?] replied 'Plump for Barney.' " By noon

81

Barnato was in front, and as more drunks and stooges appeared the lead lengthened. Long before the polls closed, his opponent conceded. Bottomley had not been defeated by a man or a party; he had lost to a purse.

Almost to spite the press, Barney turned out to be a hardworking and effective councillor. Public health was his first and most formidable task. According to a sanitary inspector the Kimberley cesspits were "fermenting and bubbling up," an invitation to plague. In three black cemeteries the dead were buried in shallow graves without coffins, and the "putrefying mass" had seeped into the ground water. Causes of native deaths went unmarked, but they were probably similar to those recorded for whites who perished in 1878. Of these, remittent fever and dysentery had killed 51; 36 had died from bronchitis, pneumonia, phthisis, and pleurisy. All these diseases could be traced to Kimberley's earth, air, and water. Barney, along with others, argued for better sanitary conditions and different methods of burial, and he got his way.

When the politician was not lobbying for a cleaner city he was out promoting its local retailers—always collecting a little baksheesh for his efforts. "An edifying spectacle may be observed on the Market every morning," the *News* sarcastically reported. "A full fledged Town Councillor, clad in check trousers etc., touting for the assistant Market master, holding up cabbages and other vegetables to the gaze of an admiring public, and finally returning home with a cabbage under each arm, a pocket full of carrots, or some other presents contributed by grateful sellers, who seem to appreciate the efforts of this worthy controller of our roads and morals to get them the highest prices for their products."

If journalists were the first to criticize Barnato, J. B. Robinson was the first to copy him. At the age of 37, J.B.R. was as rich as Barney, better spoken and dressed, and even more of a womanizer. Most afternoons he could be seen lounging in his doorway, ogling young females as they strolled by the office. "Although he looked as cold as a fish," claims an envious contemporary, "there was no denying his admiration for the fair sex . . . and wasn't he a Don Juan . . . he did run after the petticoats."

In the fall of 1878 J.B.R. stopped running. With unaccustomed calm he announced his engagement to Rebecca Ferguson, the respectable daughter of a diamond field pioneer. A few months later the Robinsons went off to Europe. The groom seemed to be transformed, at peace with himself and the world. Even J.B.R.'s long list of enemies smiled on the couple. All the Buccaneer had needed, went the theory, was a good woman behind him.

And then he returned. A second look showed that the only thing new about Robinson was his chin: he had grown a thick black beard. Otherwise nothing had changed. The omnipresent pith helmet sat on his head at least sixteen hours a day—some said he wore it to bed. He was as stingy as before; J.B.R. still refused to enter a bar except to conclude a business deal, and even then he peeked in first to make sure there was no worthless acquaintance who might cadge a free drink. He was as litigious as ever, and more envious. What Barnato could accomplish, he told anyone who would listen, Robinson could do better and bigger. He announced his candidacy for Mayor. The election was close and challenged in the courts. Robinson won on appeal. Once his victory was official, he concentrated on prestige and propaganda. J.B.R.'s pulpit was the Mayor's office, his mouthpiece *The Diamond Field Independent*, a daily he had once owned outright and still controlled.

Through the paper J.B.R. made his opinions known on every subject, from the pricing of diamonds to the race question. "I am no Negrophilist," he stated, as if there was any doubt, "though I am in favor of the natives being treated with justice and humanity." In his view, "the desirable object is not incompatible with humane and firm treatment, and one of the first lessons to be instilled into them will be to respect the laws of *meum* and *teum* [mine and yours]. The Diamond Fields have, in my opinion, done much to accomplish this."

Fascinated, Cecil Rhodes watched and took notes. Power was his only goal, and there were two routes to it. From Barney Barnato he learned the value of politics; from J. B. Robinson he came to understand the uses of journalism. After his fellow magnates secured their offices, Rhodes eyed the Cape Parliament. He ran for representative of an essentially rural territory, Barklay West. A large group of his constituents were Boers, and one of them told off the candidate: "In the first place, you are too young; in the second, you look so damnably like an Englishman."

Rhodes listened. He could do nothing about his age, but he assumed rough clothing, walked and rode in the fields like a farmer, and assured his listeners, "My ancestors were keepers of cows." Encouraged by the new Rhodes, some of the Afrikaaners changed their minds about the damned Englishman. That was the first stage of his campaign. The second was more expensive. This thinly populated district had no secret ballot, and because of sloth, rather than liberalism, it had never got around to denying natives the franchise. Rhodes saw to it that payments were distributed in the right places; on election day 250 blacks showed up to cast their votes. He won, and continued to hold that seat in periods of triumph, in times of disgrace and depression, until the day he died.

All through the campaign he was encouraged by a new friend, Dr. Leander Starr Jameson. The 25-year-old Scotsman was headed for a brilliant London career when he suddenly changed directions and sailed off to South Africa. The move was not as whimsical as it seemed. Like Rhodes and Barnato, Jameson had been preceded by an older brother who had sent home an uncut gem from South Africa. The young doctor immediately recognized it as his ticket to the easy life.

The roustabout atmosphere of the diamond fields was congenial to Jameson; so was the company of Cecil Rhodes. "From the day of my arrival at Kimberley, when I fell in with him," the doctor remembered, "we grew closely together and quickly became great friends. . . . We were young men together then, and naturally saw a great deal of each other. We shared a quiet little bachelor establishment together, walked and rode out together, shared our meals, exchanged our views on men and things, and discussed his big schemes, which even then filled me with admiration. I soon admitted to myself that for sheer natural power I had never met a man to come near Cecil Rhodes."

In 1879 Jameson was appointed town medical officer. The position, according to Louis Cohen's salacious memoir, allowed the doctor to indulge his appetite for the opposite sex. Jameson was short and bright, with Napoleonic energy and a devious charm. "I knew a chap once," Cohen says, "who had been very successful in life, and whose only trouble was that his wife had not presented him with a tiny image of himself. He confided in me, and on my initiative he consulted with Dr. Jim with the result that, hey presto! before the year was out, and on the first of April too, he became the proud pater of bouncing twins. The Doctor was, indeed, a life giver."

There were times when he was a life-taker, and those were not treated with such amusement. In the early 1880s a group of laborers brought smallpox into town with them. Jameson and his medical colleagues made an examination and decided not to make the results public. "If word about smallpox got out," one of the physicians later admitted, "a quarantine would have been called, the result being that the comparatively large population, mostly niggers and others, would be thrown out of work." He concluded, "Needless to say we pronounced it chicken-pox, otherwise it might have led to serious trouble."

Because of the cover-up, smallpox raged unacknowledged for almost two years. During that time some 2,300 people caught the disease; 51 whites and uncounted hundreds of blacks died of it. The observation of a Rhodes biographer seems inarguable: "Jameson, a well trained surgeon, could have had no doubts about the correct diagnosis. That he (and his medical colleagues) tried to avoid the obvious conclusion speaks to their fundamental lack of integrity." Throughout his long stay in South Africa Jameson continued to carry a moral taint, and those who came too close would be infected and in some instances destroyed.

♦   ♦   ♦

IN THE LATE 1870s a series of minor wars and rebellions broke out among various tribes. Her Majesty's troops were called upon to keep the peace. Since there were not enough of them to go around, volunteer regiments had to be raised. David Harris was one of the leaders, riding into the veld with the Diamond Field cavalry. In old age he could recall every moment of a skirmish in the Perie Bush, north of Kimberley. He had taken command after two superior officers were slain. "The natives directed their fire on the officers, whom they recognized on account of the fact that they did not carry rifles. Fortunately, however, I was armed with a carbine. Our formidable opponents endeavored to overwhelm us by sheer weight of numbers, and their head warriors goaded them on with shouts of 'We've killed the Chiefs; now wipe out the soldiers.' But our men were as steady as the proverbial rock, and maintained a well-directed fire . . . whenever it was possible to see them through the trees and bushes . . . we inflicted much damage on the enemy."

For a young man whose previous notion of combat had been sparring with his cousins Barney and Harry Barnato, these were heady days. Shootouts with the natives took on the rare and exotic quality of a stage melodrama, and the volunteer responded with stagy courage. Harris's conduct brought him to the attention of the General Staff, and eventually of the Queen herself. Of all the London cavalrymen he rose the highest; at the end of his career, the Jewish boy from the London ghetto would be addressed as Colonel Sir David Harris.

Louis Cohen also volunteered for service. But his military career ended a few months later when he fell off a cart and cracked some ribs. The wounded veteran headed for Kimberley, lured once again by the diamond fields. Always literary and self-dramatizing, Cohen saw himself as a South African Rip van Winkle, wandering back to a town where things were "strangely altered. . . . The old time digger, the farmer-digger, the gentleman-digger had almost disappeared." In their place had sprung up "a mushroom breed of financiers," men destined "to put their hands deep in the pockets of the British public."

Julius Porges was one of the most ruthless of this breed. France's leading diamond merchant had impeccable connections: he had been brought to South Africa by Julius Wernher, partner of Alfred Beit. In 1880, he learned about the plans of two successful immigrants, Isaac Lewis and Sammy Marks, and arranged to meet them. Self-made men were the envy of the world, he told them. What a remarkable climb they had made, advancing from shtetl poverty in Lithuania to prominence and wealth on the diamond fields. He offered to aid them in their attempt to take over the French Company, one of the largest claimholders in the region.

Those who imagined a vast Jewish conspiracy in South Africa were disabused the following year, when Porges ruthlessly collected enough votes to force his co-religionists off the board of their own company. Having seized their portion of the French, Porges then tried to get control of the entire Kimberley mine. At least ten other predators had the same goal in mind, and every time he bid for a holding, no matter how small, his competitors followed suit, merging claims, forming companies overnight. Shares in those companies doubled and tripled in a matter of weeks, and a new diamond rush began. This time it consisted of investors with checkbooks rather than shovels, attempting to buy shares of anything Porges was pursuing. Offices grew so crowded that checks were shoved in through the windows. The hysterical capitalism came to a brief halt in February 1881, when Kimberley's greatest need was finally satisfied: a stock exchange was officially established.

The fever then resumed in a more orderly manner. "It was astonishing how the mania seized on all classes in Kimberley," says an eyewitness, "how every one, doctors and lawyers, masters and servants, shop-keepers and workmen, men of the pen and men of the sword, magistrates and I.D.B.'s, Englishmen and foreigners, rushed wildly into the wonderful game of speculation."

In order to profit from the boom, more companies were formed, many of them without capital and some without claims. Pieces of earth were salted with diamonds before investors came by—and sometimes as they entered the diggings. In one notorious bit of mistiming, a potential backer came too early. He found himself in a hailstorm of little diamonds showered from above. Confidence men thought they could play their games for another year or two, but the Kimberley bankers knew better. In mid-1881 they had seen enough; loans were closely examined, and denied if the company was dubious. One after another collapsed for insufficient funds. The day of the little fish was over; Kimberley had entered the age of the sharks. It was only a question of which predator would remain alive at the end of the feeding frenzy.

Cecil Rhodes was a leading candidate. On April 1, 1880, he had created the De Beers Company, a major concern with assets of £200,000. It was aptly named, since Rhodes and his investors now owned a major portion of the De Beers mine. The Colossus had big plans for his infant concern. "There is every chance of our property lasting," he wrote an associate. "The old fear of the mines working out is rapidly fading . . . what I want to impress on you is the fact that this is now the richest community in the world for its size and that it shows every sign of permanency. The present proved depths of our mines alone would take at our present rate of working a hundred years to work out, and of course we cannot tell how much deeper they may go."

But there was another capital schemer in the region: Barney Barnato. He could not be laughed away this time. De Beers's position was nowhere as strong as Barnato Bros.'s. That company's assets were greater, its appetite keener, its methods more unscrupulous. Could it have been mere coincidence, for example, that the largest and finest stones kept turning up on Barnato territory? Rhodes didn't think so, and neither did any of the other diamond magnates. Rumors circulated about I.D.B. It was recalled that some of the most infamous white dealers used to hang around Harry's old London Hotel, and that Barney had always been a hustler and a bunco artist. A tourist must have had the Barnatos in mind when he observed, "As for the moneyed men on the Fields, is it a libel to say that most of them owe their wealth . . . to illicit diamond buying? . . . Some of the most prominent men of the place were yesterday selling umbrellas in the streets of London, or catching birds on Hampstead Heath. And yet, although everybody knows all this, everybody winks at it."

Winking was about all they could do. A diamond stolen from one claim could easily be dropped into another, and who would be the wiser? Of course thieves were constantly being hauled before the judges and punished with flogging or jail or fines. But everyone knew that half the stones in town were the result of I.D.B. A British investigator saw what was happening. He told officials that thievery had a great future in Kimberley because "only the small ones are caught here and the large ones escape."

They escaped with an ease that suggested musical comedy. First the illicit diamonds were stolen by laborers and sold to fences and middlemen. From there the rough stones were peddled to dealers who were also claimholders. Finally the gems were conveyed back to the fields, where they were "discovered" all over again. Years later one of Harry Barnato's enemies described the routine. "Kaffirs were bribed to swallow the 'booty,' " he wrote, "a meeting place was arranged, but in what circumstances they passed on the 'precious' stones to the purchaser of stolen property history leaves us to conjecture. It would not be incorrect to assume that many of the sparkling ornaments which at this moment adorn the neck of a beauty have been subjected to this procedure. If they could speak! Aye, if they could speak. . . . This would clear the air as lightning clears the skies of foul atmosphere."

I.D.B. impudently continued. An irate J. B. Robinson took the lead, and on June 18, 1881 he and his colleagues formed The Diamond Mining Protection Society. It hired a private detective force and issued a series of recommendations about security. "Compounding of natives in barracks," said its first report, was "the only absolute remedy." No objections were recorded, and the absolute remedy was put in place. During the last ten days of their contracts, black laborers were kept nude except for leather mittens padlocked to their hands. Two days before their release all were heavily purged and the stool examined for any diamonds that might have been swallowed earlier. In the final hours of the contract, missionaries were the only white men permitted—indeed, encouraged—to visit the compounds. Religious leaders, commented a mining engineer of the period, "are enjoined to impress upon the native mind two simple Christian precepts—the virtue of obedience and the dignity of labour. Thus the natives receive religion in moderate doses, and in like manner their allowance of Kaffir beer is regulated on strictly reasonable lines. . . . Strange to say, the Kaffir does not object to this humiliating process." Once again the silence of the blacks was mistaken for compliance, and the fuse burned on.

The authorities next turned their attention to the white workers. Mine owners wanted them searched as well. The result was the region's first major strike, and it set the tone for South Africa's next hundred years. For the collision of labor and management had nothing to do with workmen's compensation, hours, or benefits. It was all about racial privilege.

The De Beers Company received a petition from supervisors stating that whites should be exempt from examinations in the nude: "It would be a disgraceful and degrading thing if they should be compelled to disrobe in the searching house, and so lowered in the sight of the natives." White miners formed an Association for Protection of men who refused "to be searched like a common Kaffir." A Sympathizing Wife of Once a Claimholder wrote to the *Independent*, "Only put it to yourself, the ill effects it would have on our children to see their father, who has always been held up to them as an example of honesty, to have him placed on a level with the natives, who, as a rule, do not consider stealing to be a sin—in fact their only sin in this respect is being found out. Then why place a white man on a level with a black?"

At a rally, the leader of the white miners shouted that he "would not submit to being searched, although he thought he was to be shot the next minute; he would rather say 'Shoot me in my clothes' (loud and prolonged applause)." He was more prophetic than he knew. In late April a work stoppage was called, and for several days not a single diamond was mined. The strikers fatally misinterpreted the signs; unarmed, they marched on various operations within the De Beers mine. They shut down the unarmed Victoria Mining Company and then went on to the Kimberley Central Company where private constables stood guard. A labor leader called, "Don't fire on us. We are not come here to do any harm. Allow me to speak." He was silenced with a shot in the head. A 17-year-old was slain as he bent to the ground looking for a rock to throw. Before the firing ceased four other strikers had been killed.

Days of outrage followed, along with avowals never to "bow and cringe to a man simply because he was an employer of labor." But this was empty bravado. The demonstrations subsided within a week. Strike leaders were arrested; constables who had fired the fatal shots were exonerated. A local court of inquest found that the demonstrators had been killed "while engaged in unlawful and riotous behavior." In Cape Town Cecil Rhodes did his part. Some members of parliament wanted their own inquiry. He argued against it; the protest had been carried on by "white men supported by natives in a struggle against whites," and therefore an internal matter to be settled by diamond men. There was no investigation. The miners got the message. In the second week of May new searching procedures were accepted by the whites, and they quietly returned to work. For the first time in a month the owners could relax. Labor was back where it belonged, obediently turning over earth in the mines.

Other white men—some of them highly placed—were suspected of I.D.B. but never accused. In public, the Barnato Bros. attributed the rumors to envy and kept on their profitable route. In the early 1880s Barney and Harry had every right to feel immune from criticism; they were making money while they slept. Even acts of charity turned a profit. When their sister Kate's 15-year-old son showed up unannounced, they merely smiled at his *chutzpah*; young Woolf Joel reminded the uncles of themselves at that age. They quickly put him to work, and the gesture paid huge dividends. For all his youth, Woolf possessed something neither Barnato had: a passion for order. He straightened out their offices, kept the company books, and won them some badly needed friends. "I doubt if any young fellow was better liked on the Diamond Fields than equable, amiable Woolfie in his youth," says Cohen. "It was a pleasure to do business with this bright-hearted boy." The Barnatos were quick to realize the asset they had acquired. Woolf was given a salary of £50 a week, at a time when skilled mechanics earned £8 weekly—about three times what the same job paid in Britain.

On one of the Barnatos' frequent trips to London, Barney asked Kate to send along her other sons, Solly and Isaac. One can imagine Woolf in the kitchen, flashing big bills and dazzling the brothers with his new wardrobe, while Barney struts around the sitting room, telling his sister about the chances for a young Ebrew in South Hafrica. Kate agreed at last, worn down by her brother's arguments. Solly, who had Barney's love of glitter, developed into a first-rate judge of diamonds. Isaac, eldest of the three, had a talent for finance; but he also exhibited some of Barney's less appealing tendencies. These would have serious and enduring consequences.

There was, for example, the confrontation with Dr. William Murphy. During one of his bursts of euphoria Barney had put the doctor-financier on the board of Barnato Bros. It seemed a whimsical and self-destructive act. The town knew Murphy as a brutal man "who, in his life had been known to serve only two masters—Satan and J. B. Robinson." He had publicly beaten up Africans and attacked an elderly member of the Kimberley Club, the town's one exclusive social organization. On another occasion Murphy had abused his wife until she ran screaming into the street. As if these credentials were not enough, he was also violently anti-Semitic. During a board of directors' meeting he snapped at Barnatos' supporters, "Are you not the tribe, the chosen tribe?" David Harris blandly replied, "We are not here to discuss religious matters" and moved on. But just then Kimberley was experiencing a new wave of Jew-hatred, and the remark was neither forgotten nor forgiven.

To those down on their luck, or suspicious of foreigners, or who hated Barney Barnato and "the chosen tribe," Illicit Diamond Buying had become a racial characteristic. The half-Jewish Louis Cohen amused himself by referring to I.D.B.ers as the "scum of Germany and Whitechapel." And he pointed out that *gonivas*, a Yiddish word for stolen goods, was the accepted slang for illegal diamonds. The gentile critics took a harsher tone. The General Manager of the Standard Bank thought that "the departure of hordes of hook-nosed Polish and Lithuanian Jews whose evil countenances now peer from every little shanty and cigar divan would be a distinct gain to the community. Under cover of keeping a 'winkel' [store] they at present flock to Kimberley from afar, like asvogels to a dead ox, and their villainous faces enable one easily to understand the depth of hatred borne to them in Russia and elsewhere."

All this was grist for Murphy. In January 1884 he ran for a seat in the Cape Assembly. One of his speeches brimmed with contempt for Jews. The next day he was badly beaten twice: by the voters and by Isaac Joel, who assaulted him in the street. Murphy quickly pressed charges—then, just as suddenly, dropped them. The doctor had conceived a better idea of vengeance, one which would not involve him directly. That way he could humiliate the family and keep making money with Barney at the same time.

In March, while Harry and Barney were taking care of business in England, two detectives called at Isaac Joel's diamond trading office in the Barnato Building. According to their information the 22-year-old was in violation of the Diamond Trade Laws. Under the tough new statutes a dealer had to produce papers showing the origin of every stone in his possession. A search turned up four unexplained diamonds. Was this proof of I.D.B.? The head of detectives, John Fry, thought so. He placed Isaac Joel under arrest.

Woolf supplied the £4,000 bail for his brother and hired lawyers to defend him. They delayed as long as they could; witnesses happened to fall ill, technicalities were found, until just as the court was about to lose patience, the Barnatos returned. Barney rushed off to see J. B.

Robinson, recently elected chairman of the Diamond Mining Protection Society. The brothers had sent the wrong Barnato. Harry might have made a convincing appeal; Barney was all hysteria.

"He explained the whole matter to me," Robinson recalled, "and told me, or led me to believe, that he looked upon this action against his nephew as a kind of prosecution against himself, or his firm, and that there was a conspiracy against him. . . . The interview between Barnato and myself took nearly two hours; Barnato was crying most bitterly most of the time. . . . He told me that he was suffering a great deal, tore open his shirt to show me eruptions on his body, and said he could not sleep. It was a most painful scene. . . . He . . . said he would give £5,000–£10,000, if he could get his nephew clear . . . I said to him, 'Do you mean to offer money to me?' and he said 'I would give £10,000–I would give it today—to get my nephew free. My nephew is worth £30,000, and can well afford to pay £10,000 to get free.' The man was so upset that it was impossible to reason with him."

Nevertheless, Robinson felt some obligation to his fellow magnate, and he did pay a call on John Fry. The detective coldly informed him that the case against Isaac Joel was airtight, and that he was personally looking forward to the trial. When Barney heard this something in him cracked permanently. He arranged a private meeting with Fry and offered to buy the detective's diamond stickpin for £5,000. Both men knew the pin was worth about £200. When the bribery attempt failed, Barney bared his arm and exhibited his inflammations. Unimpressed, Fry told Barney to show them to the Crown Prosecutor.

But there would be no need for that. Three days later the Isaac Joel case came up for hearing in the Special Court—minus Isaac Joel. He had jumped bail and kept on running until he reached London. Escape seems to have been part one of Barney's plan. Retaliation was part two. With a vindictive spirit and unlimited funds he set out to destroy the detective who refused to be bought. The press and the politicians were all that Barney needed. He financed a newspaper, *The Diamond Times*, whose primary function was to lambaste the Detective Department. It thundered about overspending, inefficiency, careless arrests, or no arrests at all—anything that remotely smacked of impropriety. This was overkill, but once Barney brought in his ordnance there was no cease-fire. As the attack grew in heat and stridence, powerful officials were reached in Cape Town. Nothing in Fry's record indicated the slightest taint of corruption, so a charge was trumped up: he had been negligent in keeping the Detective Department's books. It sufficed. In February 1885, John Fry was dismissed and the *Times* stopped its attacks on the Department. A Cape politician wrote that the detective was "absolutely penniless with a large family" and had "been sacrificed to gratify some of the lowest wretches in the colony."

It amounted to an obituary. Three years later, at the age of 51, Fry was dead. Of natural causes, the doctors wrote; but friends attributed the end to that notorious nineteenth-century ailment, a broken heart. There was no arguing with the self-appraisal Barney had uttered when the two men met after Fry's dismissal: "I am a good friend," he allowed, "but a bitter enemy."

◆   ◆   ◆

IN 1885 KIMBERLEY BECAME the first town in South Africa to be lit by electricity. Dirt and shacks had been replaced by houses, churches, synagogues, stores, a railroad line. These signs indicated a thriving economy. But the prosperity was all on the surface. During the same period carat prices plummeted because the individual claimowners, anxious for short-term profit, kept glutting the market with stones. At Bulfontein some of the largest companies were forced to suspend operations. Miners were suddenly thrown out of work, and dealers faced bankruptcy.

Despair settled in with the autumn weather. Almost every week the newspapers printed the obituary of some prominent businessman who had taken his own life. Ministers and rabbis preached against the sin of self-murder. Newspapers took a tough-minded view. "The fact is that this mania for suicide taints the whole moral atmosphere," said *The Diamond Times*, "and it is questionable whether it is good for the safety and morality of Society that such acts be recorded with tenderness." It exhorted its readers not to lose heart. "There is never a hero without a struggle and a battle, and the battle of life is worth fighting, though a man may sometimes have to fight against desperate odds."

In this melancholy atmosphere, diamond magnates ruthlessly jostled for position. Charles Darwin—he had died only three years before—

was invoked as their patron saint. An investor saw the leaders "rushing on to ruin, each one imagining that he will have the field to himself and will be the fittest that survives." The fittest would need foreign investment; no one in South Africa had enough money to buy out all of his rivals. Although there were perhaps twenty major capitalists in Kimberley, only four seemed able to summon the capital for amalgamation: Robinson, Barnato, and Rhodes, with his *éminence grise*, Alfred Beit. As it turned out, only two were fit enough for combat.

Robinson was all fulminations and swagger. The ups and downs of diamond prices had depleted his finances, and the walls of his mines —the Standard in the big Kimberley hole and the Griqualand West at Dutoitspan—had collapsed, costing him dearly. The situation was so desperate that J.B.R. did the unthinkable: he resigned from public office. Increasing deafness, he told his colleagues, was forcing him back into private life. The move had nothing to do with his physical well-being; it was his financial health that was precarious. All his energies would be devoted to shoring up his properties and reputation. J.B.R.'s name was still impressive enough to persuade the banks to lend him money. But he was heavily in debt, with no prospects of a bailout.

With Robinson incapacitated, the idea of amalgamation took a step backward. Then, early in 1886, a Cape politician named J. X. Merriman took up the amalgamation cause, promoting it directly to Cecil Rhodes. He found the Colossus "as queer as ever, so suspicious" but "quite aware of [amalgamation's] importance and the value of it to him personally."

Encouraged, Merriman made the mistake common to many others: he trusted Rhodes. Several weeks later the Kimberley newspapers carried Rhodes's advertisement inviting the major companies to exchange shares with each other at a commonly accepted level of value. All the mines would thus be owned jointly, and South African diamond prices could be stabilized forever. When the owners responded positively, Rhodes took full credit for the new scheme.

Wounded, Merriman complained that "Rhodes is the same in business and politics, tricky, unstable and headstrong. . . . I have felt both in politics and now in business the effect of this curious fashion of lukewarm agreement. Actually as an opponent he would do far less harm than he does as a sort of half-and-half friend."

Across town Barney Barnato was busy with his own amalgamations. Early in 1886, four publicly held companies dominated the Kimberley mine: the Standard, the French, the Central, and Barnato. Barney maneuvered to acquire dominant holdings in all of them, buying up blocks of shares whenever they became available. First the Standard came under his control, then the Central. By now profits distributed among the Barnato family members had made them unimaginably wealthy. Young Woolf Joel was a millionaire before he reached his majority, and Barney assured his nephew that this was only the beginning. In July 1887, with their customary blend of vulgarity and panache, the Barnatos announced their confidence in the future by detonating explosions all around the Kimberley mine. The noise, said the *Diamond Field Advertiser*, was as if "the Transvaal Navy had suddenly appeared and were bombarding dear old Kimberley. Hundreds of people rushed towards the mine, where the cannon, that is the dynamite shots, were being fired all round the edge, while the Companies' flags were seen waving from the Central and Standard Companies works. It was an 'Amalgamation Salute' and it sounded quite gay and joyful, but nervous persons did not like it at first."

The most nervous of them all took off to seek financial backers in England. Rhodes had conceived the astonishing notion of fighting Jews with Jews—the Rothschilds versus the Barnatos. Citizens of Kimberley, the ultimate company town, sat back in the sun waiting to see who would lose and who would be crowned the King of Diamonds.

6

VANITY
AND DEPRAVITY

In London, family and friends remarked that Rhodes had filled out since his last visit. The observation could not have been entirely flattering. He looked ten years older than his actual age of 35, and he tended to walk as if he were moving under water. A colleague of the time describes him "rolling in his chair like a whale in deep seas." In repose the fleshy face assumed an air of profound melancholy. Partly this was because of delicate health: the stress of competition weighed literally upon his heart. But there were other complicating factors. Rhodes had recently suffered a series of personal sorrows, and he had fallen in love. That episode had been the saddest of all.

The string of tragedies began in 1879 when his brother perished in a peculiar incident. Herbert Rhodes, who had enticed Cecil to South Africa in the first place, was the family's compulsive wanderer. No sooner had he put in a cotton crop than he was off to Kimberley to look for diamonds. Once the jewels were unearthed he abandoned Cecil once more, this time to investigate reports of gold strikes in the interior. Since then he had prospected in the eastern Transvaal, run guns from Delgoa Bay to the Pedi tribe, and roved northward to the areas known today as Mozambique and Malawi. In every region he searched for gold; he was hunting for it when he stopped at the village of a Kololo chief. During the evening a demijohn of rum caught on fire, exploded a yard away, and killed him. He was 34. Herbert's death was reported to Cecil as "a mystery, whether killed [by African thieves] and then burned or burned accidentally."

Rhodes betrayed no emotion when he heard the news. Only in a letter to his aunt did he comment. He could not bear going into detail: "What a sad affair Herbert's death is! I send you the paper with the account of it." It took some twenty years before Cecil could deal with the fact of Herbert's demise: then he had a marble statue erected on the bank of the Shire River, where it still stands.

The next loss occurred six years later. The eminent Victorian Major General Charles George "Chinese" Gordon visited Rhodes in 1881. Lytton Strachey's acid portrait introduces the General as a believer in biblical revelation, and throughout his life the undersized figure fearlessly strolled through danger illuminated by a "spark of the god head." By contrast the gallumphing Rhodes was an agnostic and a severely practical man, with no room for worship on his schedule.

Yet in certain ways the men were cut of the same British twill. Each believed that he could deal with the natives through the force of his personality. Rhodes, the old Africa hand, would bargain, threaten, cajole. Gordon was certain "that he possessed what some described as a mesmeric power over primitive peoples and he himself called the faculty of getting into their skins." Both men nourished the idea of a secret society composed of idealistic young Britons. And both were isolates with no use for women.

Rhodes and Gordon immediately got on. They went on long walks, discussing, among other things, the future of Africa. Gordon prevailed on his new friend to leave Kimberley for Basutoland, where the General was to solve the problem of native uprisings. "Stay with me," he insisted. "We can work together." Rhodes resisted. He liked Gordon, but he thought the man was a bit too righteous for his own good— to say nothing of England's. Rhodes was appalled, for instance, when the General spoke of the time he subdued the Tai-Ping rebellion in China. A grateful government had offered him a roomful of gold as his reward.

"And what did you do?" demanded the listener.

"Refused it, of course. What would you have done?"

"I'd have taken it," said Rhodes, "and as many more roomfuls as they offered me; it is no use having big ideas if you have not the cash to carry them out."

After several more entreaties to join him, Gordon gave up. There were "very few men in the world to whom I would make such an offer," he declared petulantly. "Very few men, I can tell you; but . . . you *will* have your own way. I never met a man so strong for his own opinion; you think your views are always right."

The General went off on his own. He and Rhodes never met again, but neither man forgot the other. Two years later Gordon headed to the Sudan, attempting to suppress the Madhi, a charismatic and violent Moslem leader. Once more Gordon entreated his fellow Victorian by cable: together they might still bring peace and work wonders. It was a serious temptation. Gordon was threatening to "smash the Madhi," and Rhodes knew this was a mistake. Instead of smashing him, the Colossus would find the Madhi's price and make a deal. Alas, he noted, Cape Parliament was meeting, and there was no time to venture north; Rhodes cabled his regrets. Had he agreed, he would surely have ended as the General did only a few months later—slain in Khartoum, his head mounted on a pikestaff and paraded around the conquered city. Still, when the news of Gordon's death came to him, Rhodes acted like a grieving relative. "I am sorry I was not with him," he lamented from the safety of Kimberley, "I am sorry I was not with him."

The third loss was too severe for posturing. Early in the 1880s Neville Pickering entered Rhodes's orbit. Contemporaries found the blond young man to be "frank," "sunny-tempered," "beloved by men and women alike." Rhodes was immediately taken with Pickering and hired him as De Beers's first secretary. Next to the Colossus, Pickering—called Pickling by his intimates—seemed no more than a gregarious young South African with average intelligence and few ambitions. But Rhodes was smitten. The two men moved into a corrugated iron house opposite a cricket ground. The Imperial Secretary of Cape Town described their friendship at that time as "absolutely lover-like," and a number of whispers attended this new living arrangement. No scandal ever surfaced, however, and their association may well have been platonic. In any case Rhodes was powerfully affected. He became easier to talk to, more sociable and focused. In a matter of months he altered his will, leaving his entire fortune to his great friend.

"My dear Pickering," read the covering note. "Open the enclosed after my death. There is an old will of mine . . . whose conditions are very curious, and can only be carried out by a trustworthy person, and

I consider you one." Curious is an understatement; the paper Rhodes called his "Confession" concluded that Anglo-Saxons were "the finest race in the world." Therefore, "the more of the world we inhabit the better it is for the human race." With the help of Rhodes's enormous financial legacy, the English would elevate such lands as South Africa, "at present inhabited by the most despicable specimens of human beings."

Young Pickling would be charged with the repossession of Canada and the United States; the coopting of Asia, South America, and, it goes without saying, Africa from the Cape to Cairo. But it would not all be imperial drudgery. Rhodes's message went on: "You fully understand you are to use the interest of money as you like during your lifetime."

That great transfer of wealth and power never occurred. An absurd accident took place in 1884, and it changed the lives of everyone concerned. Neville Pickering suffered a minor spill from his horse. It seemed more nuisance than catastrophe: a few bruises and some sores where thornbushes had pierced his legs. But there were all sorts of exotic bacilli on the fields; an infection took hold and never let go. For four years Pickering oscillated from extremely ill to almost well, only to relapse each time. During that period, word came of gold strikes in the Witwatersrand, the White Water Ridge in the Northeast, some 200 miles from Kimberley. Ultimately the territory would prove to hold the largest deposit of gold in the world. J. B. Robinson went there and quickly reestablished his fortunes; Barney Barnato had a look, and so did Alfred Beit and many other diamond magnates. Rhodes was one of the latecomers, totally ignorant of what lay beneath his feet. Ask him about precious stones and he supplied a dozen answers; of precious metal he knew only that if one were given a roomful of it, one should not walk away empty-handed.

Research had hardly begun when someone gave Rhodes bad news about his beloved Pickling. Against the advice of doctors the invalid had gone to Kimberley, and there his condition suddenly deteriorated. He was not expected to last more than a few days. Rhodes appeared to be in shock. He told an associate that he would leave by the next coach: "Buy a seat from someone who has already booked . . . get a special coach—anything." No one was willing to give up his seat—

not even for the Colossus—and no special coach could be hired. Undeterred, Rhodes clambered on top of a coach and sat on a pile of mailbags. For fifteen hours he bounced painfully and silently until the vehicle pulled up at Kimberley.

Rhodes rushed to Pickering's bedside and stayed there, "careless of anything but the wants and comforts of his friend." On October 16, 1886, three weeks after the jolting ride south, Pickering muttered, "You have been father, mother, brother, and sister to me," and died in his friend's arms. Much of Kimberley turned out for the funeral. Barney Barnato wept; Rhodes, hiding his face in a large handkerchief, alternated between high-pitched, hysterical laughter and tears. Afterward, Rhodes sat at a table with Pickering's brother. Both men cried and pushed the deceased's gold watch back and forth. "No, you are his brother," came one voice. "No, you are his greatest friend," argued the other.

The head of De Beers was never to show such tenderness again. From here on Rhodes evidenced a new and bitter cynicism, along with a stronger need to dominate men and events. In time he would grow closer to Jameson, and a parade of young men known as Rhodes's lambs would serve as his secretaries. But no one truly replaced Pickering in his affections. That October, the Rhodes who was not ashamed to display warmth, affection, and human vulnerability perished along with his companion.

♦   ♦   ♦

FOR VENTURE CAPITALISTS, gaining entry to the House of Rothschild could be notoriously difficult. Not for the Colossus; a servant showed him straight in. Two men had smoothed the way. Alfred Beit, whose financial skills had drawn the attention of the Rothschilds, provided a letter of introduction. The great banking family also knew Gardner Williams, an American mining engineer with vast experience in the gold and silver mine fields of California and Nevada. Rhodes had met him in South Africa, checked his credentials, and offered him a large salary. Williams, who had intended to take the next boat back to the United States, signed on to become the general manager of De Beers.

At the beginning negotiations were frosty, but Lord Nathan Rothschild gradually warmed to Rhodes's proposal. In order for the amalgamation scheme to work, one man would have to sit atop the pyramid of diamond companies. That man would be either Barney Barnato, who controlled most of the Kimberley Mine, or Cecil Rhodes, who controlled the neighboring De Beers Mine. The stock of one major firm was still outstanding, the French Company in the Kimberley Mine. Rhodes needed that foothold in enemy territory before he made his move.

As the interview ended, the financier spoke up. "Well, Mr. Rhodes, you go to Paris and see what you can do in reference to the purchase of the French Company's property, and in the meantime I will see if I can raise the £1,000,000 which you desire."

Rothschild's "if" was enough to change the world. A few weeks later, a De Beers executive noted that the chief was back in town "looking as fit as ever. He has just returned from Paris after his *coup d'état*. The French Company that was is now practically in our hands and the Rothschilds have at last arranged to finance for us." He and Rhodes expressed delight to "have the Kimberley crowd by the throat."

Unfortunately for De Beers, Barney Barnato was not part of the crowd. He owned one fifth of the French Company's shares and, like Rhodes, he wanted it all. Barnato Bros. was prepared to offer £1,700,000 cash to the French—£300,000 more than Rhodes's opening offer. Rhodes nodded. Very well, he countered, "You can go and offer £300,000 more than we do for the French, but we will offer another £300,000 on that; you can go on and bid for the benefit of the French shareholders *ad infinitum*, because we shall have it in the end."

Barney refused to budge. He knew that De Beers's threat was backed with borrowed money. Barney was using his own. So he cannot have been surprised when Rhodes gave way in the autumn of 1887. The "surrender" was part of a grand design, imperceptible to those who were up too close to see it.

With Barnato's permission, Rhodes proposed to buy the French Company outright. He would then sell it to Barnato's Central Company for the bargain price of £300,000 cash—plus 70,000 Central shares. That way he would apparently save face, and Barney would save money. To onlookers Barney appeared to have scored a complete triumph. He came away the owner of most of the Central and all of the French.

Actually, the victory was Rhodes's; he had traded his way into Barney's territory. By the time the deal was settled he owned one fifth of the Central. Now he showed his teeth. Brokers were instructed to bid on the Central's outstanding shares. It would take £2,000,000 to get them all, and once again Rhodes had to ask for outside help. Beit knew a winner when he saw one; again he joined hands with the Colossus, "We will get the money if only we can get the shares."

Those shares did not come cheap, but Rhodes got them. In the middle of February 1888 a Central share was listed on the London and Kimberley exchanges at £14. Barney thought his friends and colleagues would remain steadfast. But he found—if he did not already know—that money creates its own loyalties. "I'll tell you what you will find out presently," Rhodes warned him. "Here you have your leading shareholders patting you on the back and backing you up, but selling out around the corner all the time." He was right. Share by share, day by day, Barnato lost control of his own company. The stock price rose to £20, then £30, and finally the high 40s. By March Rhodes had acquired three fifths of the Central.

Now it was Barney who needed cash. Prompted by desperation, he announced an outrageous plan. He would take what he owned of the Kimberley Mine, consolidate it, and make it a public company. He would then sell shares of that company in London at £1 per share. Perhaps this was a bluff; Barnato was surely aware that such a move would reduce the value of *all* diamond shares, and inevitably of diamonds themselves. It would be an act of financial suicide. Still, there was always something self-destructive about Barnato, and Rhodes could take no chances. He stalled for time with what was to become known as "the historic trick."

Rhodes planted stories that he was still short of cash. To raise money he was going to sell a large selection of De Beers's surplus diamonds. Several prospective buyers came around, including Barney who stalled, grumbled, and ultimately agreed to pay Rhodes his price for the stones. To the astonishment of Kimberley, the deal went through, even though Barney was being given a very dangerous weapon: with these new diamonds he could flood the market. It might damage Barnato Bros., but it would ruin De Beers. Then, moments before Barney took possession, Rhodes pulled his stunt. It was unworthy of him, the prank

of a fretful child. But it had very grownup consequences. He tilted
the stand that held the diamonds, and they cascaded into a large bucket.
"It took Barnato's experts six weeks' hard labor to re-sort them into
their proper classes," according to an onlooker. "This gave the European market a breathing spell." Barney proved to be a good sport.
In later years he recalled the incident indulgently: "Rhodes only beat
me once. Over those diamonds in that bucket of his. But I didn't
mind—it pleased him."

If Barney was telling the truth, if he really didn't mind, then the
denouement may well have been stage-managed. Certainly the diamond world watched it with all the intensity of playgoers; and Rhodes
and Barnato did everything but sell tickets. All of one day and night
four men gathered in Jameson's cottage to hammer out a final agreement: Cecil John Rhodes, Alfred Beit, Barney Barnato, and (since Harry
was in England attending to business) their nephew Woolf Joel. The
argument raged on past midnight, with Rhodes holding the floor most
of the time. He spoke of managing the diamond industry, and by
extension, the Africa that lay waiting to be taken. At one point Woolf
Joel asked, "Aren't those just dreams of the future? Dreams don't pay
dividends."

"No, my friend," Rhodes pointed out, "they're not dreams, they're
plans. There's a difference."

Barney seemed the most difficult to persuade. Rhodes wanted the
Central Company; without it amalgamation would be impossible. Barnato refused to sell it, even for shares in De Beers. Rhodes threw in
all sorts of emoluments: he would get Barney a membership in the
snobbish Kimberley Club ("I propose to make a gentleman of you").
He guaranteed him a Life Directorship of De Beers, a company "worth
as much as the balance of Africa." He promised Barney a seat in the
legislative assembly. At four in the morning Barnato finally succumbed.
"Some people have a fancy for *this* thing," he wearily concluded, "and
some for *that; you* have a fancy for making an Empire. Well, I suppose
I must give it to you."

Various tales grew up around this surrender, most of them false.
The Kimberley Club, for example, already had several Jewish members
and not a few vulgarians. Barney's inclusion would break no new
ground. As for joining the legislature, offices could be bought by anyone

with the means, and the Barnatos certainly had the means. A story circulated that after shoehorning Barney into the Club, Rhodes made a request. "You've had your whim. I'd like to have mine. I have always wanted to see a bucketful of diamonds; will you produce one?" And so Barney is said to have placed every available stone in a pail and allowed his old adversary to lift out "handfuls of the glittering gems and luxuriously let them back through his fingers like water." No doubt this is the Rhodes "trick" retold and distorted until the legend worked its way into the history books. The fact is that the founder of the De Beers fortune would have had no trouble getting his hands on thousands of diamonds; he might have taken a bath in them anytime he pleased.

Remove the myths and there remains a salient biographical detail: Barney Barnato was first, last, and always an actor. For all his devious schemes, he may never have been sincere about taking control of the industry. By holding out, posturing, frowning, menacing—and then capitulating with a sigh, he gained power without responsibility and wealth without industry. As one revisionist puts it, "If anybody laughed all the way to the bank at the time it was Barnato Brothers . . . thereafter the firm made handsome profits as a major shareholder."

In March 1888, the amalgamation was made official when Rhodes formed De Beers Consolidated Mines, incorporating all of his holdings. The new power only seemed to increase his appetite. The Colossus turned his attention to what he called the "poorer mines" of Bulfontein and Dutoitspan. He would make the owners of those mines "fair offers," he told the De Beers stockholders. Understandably there would be "a period of antagonism," Rhodes accurately predicted, "but we are bound to win."

There were a few obstacles on the way to total victory. In August 1888 a group of Central stockholders appeared before the Supreme Court of the Cape Colony. They could see that Barney had sold them out; instead of being essential parts of South Africa's mining industry, they were to become obedient and faceless pawns in Rhodes's grand design. Rhodes had made no secret of his aims; he had listed them in a paper available to the court. They included plans to trade in precious stones and metals, to construct railways, factories, and canals, to operate banks, to acquire "tracts of country," and even to pacify and administrate territories where "arrangements" could be made with native rulers.

The Central stockholders' counsel had no trouble proving that the new De Beers had no intention of remaining a mere diamond company. He argued that it stood to become a dangerous new entity responsible to no one but itself. Under Rhodes's direction, he pointed out, De Beers "can do anything and everything, my lord. I suppose, since the time of the East India Company, no company has had such power as this. . . . If they obtain a Charter in accordance with their trust deed from the Secretary of State, they would be empowered to annex a portion of territory in Central Africa, raise and maintain a standing army, and undertake warlike operations."

The plaintiffs had a strong case. The idea of a chartered company had begun in the administration of Prime Minister Gladstone. He allowed private enterprise to extend the Empire with the official backing of (and at very little cost to) the British government. A chartered company thus amounted to a small state, with immense and flexible powers. Theoretically it reported to British authority; except for major diplomatic decisions, it was responsible chiefly to itself.

After pondering all this the Chief Justice decided in favor of the dissidents. But he was manifestly uncomfortable. In his summation he hinted at a way to preserve the amalgamation. Rhodes took the suggestion and ran with it. He and Barnato owned a preponderance of shares in the Central Company; the dissidents held less than a tenth. It was decided to put the Central into voluntary liquidation. De Beers could then pick up the pieces, and the minority stockholders would be absolutely helpless to stop them. On January 29, 1889 the Central was formally put to sleep; on July 18, 1889, De Beers bought its scattered assets for £5,338,650, the largest check yet written. The amount dazzled the world. For years tourists bought replicas of it in the souvenir shops of Kimberley, and the original still hangs on the wall of the De Beers boardroom.

Objections resounded in London and South Africa. The financial press of England interpreted the maneuver as a sellout of stockholders, which indeed it was. Barney enjoyed every minute. He regarded all publicity as inherently good and decided to run for a seat in the Legislature. During his campaign he outdid himself, sporting a silver-gray coat with brightly colored lapels and a pale gray top hat. He was taken everywhere in a gilded carriage, drawn by four dappled horses and accompanied by riders in gold lace and jockey caps. But this time he found his speeches interrupted by miners and merchants apprehensive about De Beers's plans to cut production and mechanize the mines. In Cape Town, J. X. Merriman commented that "Men are being put forward for election who, if returned, would be a disgrace to any society." The objection did no good; an old Barney-hater looked at the election results and moaned, "I see Barnato heads the poll at Kimberley. *O tempora! O mores!*"

The criticism widened to include Rhodes. After the Central shut down, he saw no reason to carry so many employees on the payroll and ordered a wholesale dismissal of workers. In response a group of white miners, accompanied by some black men playing guitars, marched a half mile from Dutoitspan to Kimberley. In town they burned an effigy of the Colossus. One of the protestors read a dedication:

"We will now commit to the flames the last mortal remains of Cecil John Rhodes, Amalgamator General, Diamond King and Monarch of De Beers. . . . And in doing so let us not forget to give three cheers for a traitor to his adopted country, a panderer to the selfish greed of a few purse-proud speculators, and a public pest. May the Lord perish him. Amen."

Several days later a new march took place in Dutoitspan. In the market place, effigies of Barney Barnato and Alfred Beit met a similar end. It was a futile gesture. The protestors spoke boldly, but they were so wary of De Beers's new power that they wore masks.

Within a year the laborers' worst fears were confirmed. De Beers acquired the outstanding portions of the Dutoitspan and Bulfontein mines. Now Rhodes could do whatever he wanted with the diamond industry, and what he wanted was to cut the payrolls. Widespread unemployment had begun earlier, with the collapse of mine walls, and with a horrific fire that took the lives of at least 24 white men and 178 natives. But this was mere prelude. De Beers officially claimed that a reduction of the working force was necessary to save the diamond business—and besides, according to an officer, "the reduction was not quite 200." This is at odds with the known statistics. Some 25 percent of the white working force became redundant, and almost 50 percent of the black workers found themselves jobless. Rhodes personally dismissed nearly 1,000 more. Resentment rose so high that for a time he traveled with a police escort.

But after the marches and bonfires, protests quietly died away. This time no threats were necessary, no company policemen had to intimidate the populace with nightsticks and barbed wire. From the official start of amalgamation early in 1889, everyone in the diamond industry sensed that he would be dependent on De Beers for his very existence. In Kimberley, fear took the place of rage.

A measure of digger dependence can be seen in the legacies of those who died in the fire. Only four survivors left any property, and the combined total of their estates added up to £337. They carried no insurance, no workmen's compensation; the families of the other men had to live on handouts from their employer. De Beers made much of its charitable works: "The fact is worthy of mention," says the official history, "that the widows and children affected by the disaster were all provided for by the Company, the pension list remaining open for many years."

Yet the philanthropy had its dark side. All diamond laborers in Kimberley now served at the pleasure of De Beers. One learned not to complain about the size of the payments, or the conditions in which one was forced to live. To cause the Company any further distress would be more than ill-advised; it would be catastrophic. Such was the fate of the whites. After the initial shakeouts, black laborers found plenty of backbreaking work in the mines. They were always cheaper and more easily managed than the whites, and now every one of them was placed in De Beers's "monastery of labor," as *The Times* of London approvingly called it. There every black was "stripped perfectly naked and compelled to leap over bars, and their hair, mouth, ears, etc., carefully examined—not a particularly pleasant duty for the searchers when the thermometer stands at perhaps 100 Fahrenheit in the shade."

♦ ♦ ♦

THE STORIES OF GOLD STRIKES up north, coupled with the ascendancy of De Beers, renewed South Africa's appeal to the English tourist. Photographs of the period show a series of men in field jackets and women in long skirts squinting into the sun. Mines are used as back-drops for entourages of servants, ox drivers, and the mandatory white hunters. The most prominent of these visitors is the former Chancellor of the Exchequer, Lord Randolph Churchill. Having just seen his young son Winston into Sandhurst, he arrives in Africa in the spring of 1891 to have a look around and, possibly, to do a little investing. The cantankerous Lord Randolph makes Kimberley one of his main stops, and his dispatches to *The Daily Graphic* show a mixture of intrigue and revulsion.

Telephones have arrived, and new buildings go up every month. All this is of no concern to the Englishman. Although he is the guest of Alfred Beit and therefore surrounded by luxuries and servants, "nothing in the external appearance" of the place "suggests either its fame or its wealth . . . the amalgamation of the mines has restricted employment and checked immigration, and the town still preserves, and probably always will preserve, its transitory and rough-and-ready appearance." As might be expected of an aristocrat, he approves of the Kimberley Club and the racetrack; he also finds Cecil Rhodes "a public man of the first order."

Churchill is an acute observer of routine. He gets lowered to a spot 900 feet below the earth's surface to witness the extraction of stones, sees the blue ground pulverized ("at this stage of the work, the winning of the diamonds assumes more the nature of farming than of mining"), watches the "pulsator," a machine that separates the pebbles into four different sizes, then admires the sorting "done on tables, first while wet by white men, and then dry by natives."

Lord Randolph cannot keep his eyes from the searching process. The blacks "have to strip off all their clothes . . . stark naked, they then proceed to the searching room, where their mouths, their hair, their toes, their armpits, and every portion of their body are subjected to an elaborate examination." White men, he speculates, "would never submit to such a process, but the native sustains the indignity with cheerful equanimity, considering only the high wages which he earns."

Only once does Lord Randolph lose his complacency, when he learns that the legal principle of presumed innocence has no place in South Africa. If a man—even a British gentleman—walking the streets or the precincts of Kimberley "were to find a diamond and were not immediately to take it to the registrar, restore it to him, and to have the fact of its restoration registered, he would be liable to a punishment of fifteen years' penal servitude." As Churchill sees it, this reversal of justice has come about because of diamonds, extracted from the ground "solely for the wealthy classes" (of which Churchill hoped to be an outstanding member after he invested in some gold fields). Females were ultimately responsible; they displayed a "lust for personal adornment essentially barbaric if not altogether savage." If only the diamonds "adorned the beautiful, the virtuous and the young, but this, unhappily, is far from being the case, and a review of the South African diamond mines brings me coldly to the conclusion that, whatever may be the origin of man, woman is descended from an ape."

Back in London, Lord Randolph's dispatch became notorious. Male editors branded him the worst kind of misogynist. He went right on with his diatribes, and it took the wife of a De Beers official to put him in his place. On an official tour Churchill disdainfully looked down at the vast array of miners and sorters and supervisors. "All for the vanity of woman," he intoned. "And," she reminded him, "for the depravity of man."

The Knights of Labor agreed about depravity, but as far as they were concerned, "man" meant only one man: Cecil John Rhodes. The workmen's group could no longer stand silent as their city fell. Since the amalgamation Kimberley's population had dwindled along with opportunities. Shopkeepers who catered to natives were going bankrupt; their clientele, locked in compounds, had to buy their goods from Company stores. In the past, three judges had sat in the local court; in 1890 only one presided. According to the Knights, all of Kimberley's troubles originated with "the existence and domination of one great monopoly, one giant corporation, as well as the overweening greed and ambition of one wealthy, over-estimated, disappointing politician."

No need to name this villain; by the early nineties, throughout Africa—and much of Europe—Rhodes loomed as one of the greatest of all Victorians. As a member of parliament in the Cape Colony he had steadily worked to win advocates. Meanwhile, the Prime Minister of the Cape Colony, Sir Gordon Sprigg, was being accused of getting too cozy with railroad magnates, pledging taxpayers' money for new tracks that nobody needed. When his government fell in the summer of 1890, Rhodes connived for the job, making promises, collecting political debts, shrewdly piecing together a coalition of Afrikaaners and liberals, as well as his fellow imperialists. Once the scheme was accomplished, however, he tried to convince the world that it had all happened by accident. "Events hurried on faster than I expected," he told a Kimberley audience, "and before I knew where I was, I saw it would be forced upon me to take the responsibility of the government of this country."

Now the Colossus had two fonts of power. He controlled the source of 90 percent of the world's diamonds; he also held the highest office in the land. Was this a conflict of interest? The Prime Minister didn't think so. Looking back a few months later, Rhodes was certain that the destinies of De Beers and South Africa had always been identical: "one position could be worked with the other, and each to the benefit of all. At any rate I had the courage to undertake it, and I may say that . . . I have not regretted it."

The affair of the Wesselton mine gave him an early reason for self-congratulation. As the nineties began, a new diamond find occurred on a place called Wessels farm, about four miles from the center of Kimberley. The owner had left the district some time before, leasing the mineral rights to Henry A. Ward, a veteran prospector. As before, word of spectacular strikes could not be kept secret, and in February 1891 the farm was overrun with carts and pedestrians. Within two days 800 claims had been staked out. Here at last was the cure for the malady of unemployment. "The excitement," said *The Independent*, "reminded old residents of the early days when 'rushes' were frequent, and many are in hopes that the new mines will be the means of supporting a large digging community."

De Beers could hardly be expected to share in these hopes. The new diamond mine, privately owned and publicly explored, constituted the greatest threat to amalgamation since the days of Barney's holdout. The directors approached Ward with a large offer. Despite efforts to keep the negotiations secret, word got out and labor leaders organized a protest rally. Over two thousand men attended, making impromptu speeches and shouting slogans. A resolution calling De Beers employees "born slaves" and decrying the malign "influence of powerful mo-nopolists" passed unanimously.

The following day a deputation left for the Cape, to present the case for keeping the Company's hands off "Wesselton." Back in town the argument for free enterprise could be read in a letter signed by someone calling himself "Americus" and printed in *The Independent*. Karl Marx had died only a few years before, and Americus had obviously absorbed the lessons of *Das Kapital*. Up until now the South African debate was seen as a skirmish between the rich and the poor. Americus was the first to define it as a class war. He warned that the "heartless combination of capital" could only aggravate "the struggle between capital and labor." Left unchecked, it would "eventually lead to revolution."

The counterargument found its place in the *Diamond Field Advertiser*, signed "Argus." "It is contended," said the letter, "that the opening of the new mine would give employment to hundreds at present idle. No doubt it would, but would the employment last? I doubt it."

Argus reminded the reader that before amalgamation, overproduction had pushed the diamond business to the edge of chaos. Since De Beers took over, prices were controlled and economies stabilized. Now Wesselton had come into the picture. If this new mine were allowed to operate unchecked, precious stones would be overproduced once more. The inevitable result: flooded international markets, tumbling prices, and still more unemployed. "There are scores of men talking gleefully of the possible downfall of De Beers if the new mine is opened. Do they stop to consider the results? De Beers would only be effaced to make way for a foreign syndicate, which would mean such ruin and disorder to South Africa as is really appalling to contemplate."

Kimberley was torn; both Argus and Americus had their points. Rhodes set up a Special Committee to look into the matter. Asked to examine the chicken coop, his foxes decided in favor of De Beers. The idea of competition on the diamond fields effectively expired in December 1891, when the Wesselton Mine was purchased by De Beers. The company agreed to give Henry Ward rights to carry out five million loads of yellow ground over a period of five years. In grateful response, Ward suggested that the mine might take a different and more appropriate name. What about "The Premier," he inquired, in honor of Mr. Rhodes? A fine idea, responded the Colossus; and it was done.

For Cecil Rhodes, persuasion had been elevated from a craft to an art. The man who once asked a beleaguered Catholic, "Can't you square the Pope?" had proved again that anyone could be bought. Sometimes diamonds were the instrument, sometimes money or flattery. Whatever it took, Rhodes was ready. Perhaps the most remarkable instance of this power occurred at a dinner with Queen Victoria. At Windsor the royal hostess informed her guest that he had been called a woman-hater. Rhodes did not hesitate. "How can I hate a sex," he gallantly countered, "to which Your Majesty belongs?" Victoria found this reply satisfactory, but not nearly as pleasing as the one he gave when she inquired, "What are you engaged on at present, Mr. Rhodes?" The preacher's son modestly blinked down on royalty. "I am doing my best to enlarge Your Majesty's dominions."

Rhodes had in mind the land to the north of Kimberley, between the Limpopo and Zambesi Rivers, where gold deposits had recently been discovered. More fanciful explorers thought this territory might be the biblical Land of Ophir, ancient source of precious metal. Ruins of an ancient city had been found there—a place the natives called Zimbabwe, complete with immense circular walls and terraces. That was enough evidence for the old South Africa hand H. Rider Haggard; he made it the center of his romantic novel *King Solomon's Mines*. The Colossus thought in more practical terms: discussing his ambitions in a letter to a London paper he spoke glowingly of a "Providence" that might furnish "a few paying gold reefs." He added, "Please understand that it is no personal avarice which desires this, but . . . gold hastens the development of a country more than anything."

This expression of altruism was Rhodes's latest strategy. In the *Fortnightly Review*, an article by a De Beers engineer boomed the proposed Cape-to-Cairo railroad: "The iron way is the great civilizer. . . . What has been done hitherto towards developing the mineral resources of South Africa may be set down as nothing compared with what must be done in the near future, for almost the whole of that vast zone to the Zambezi . . . may be said to be auriferous."

And who would underwrite this extensive exploration? The article continued: "Perhaps the best way of effecting what we are bound to do would be by granting a charter to some powerful company or corporation."

British officials took the bait. They asked Rhodes for more details. He permitted them to share his vision. Queen Victoria's beloved government, he asserted, was the real power behind De Beers. It could also be the power behind his new Chartered Company, a separate entity from De Beers, but with a greater potential for profit and power. With a nod from Whitehall Rhodes would be free to exploit the northern territory, with its promise of ingots and new jobs and homes for the English-speaking peoples. This land might yet be Victoria's greatest ornament—a more dazzling jewel in the crown than India.

He did not mention that it would put the Colossus in the most exclusive club in the world. The Americas honored the Christian name of the Italian explorer Amerigo Vespucci. In South America, Bolivia echoed the surname of its Great Liberator, Simon Bolivar. Closer to home there were the Victoria Falls and Stanleyville. But a whole African *country* named for one man? One would have to square it with the natives, of course. But after that, what would prevent white citizens from running up the Union Jack and calling the new country Cecilia? or better still, Rhodesia?

7

LYING IN STATE

THE COLOSSUS got everything he wished for. He organized the British South Africa Company, and late in 1889 Whitehall granted it a charter with almost unlimited powers. The Charter Company, as Rhodes preferred to call it, could venture as far as it wished to the north. It could make treaties and enforce pass laws, maintain its own police force, acquire new concessions from native chieftains. It could build roads, railways, and harbors wherever it pleased. The capital of the Company was fixed at one million pounds in one-pound shares. De Beers subscribed for two hundred and ten thousand of those shares.

Immensely pleased with himself, secure in his achievements, extravagant in his ambitions, Prime Minister Cecil Rhodes began to make public addresses in which he dared to state what other eminent South Africans would only whisper. Those speeches were to frame South Africa's racial policies for more than 100 years.

"If I may venture a comparison," he remarked after one formal dinner. "I would compare the natives generally, with regard to European civilization, to fellow tribesmen of the Druids. . . . Just suppose that they were to come to life after two thousand years." To see the blacks as equals would be "to get rid of the two thousand years that lie between us and the natives."

Underlying his speeches was a sexual fear that saw darker peoples as subhuman, forever drinking and fornicating when they should be working. In the past, Rhodes reminded his audiences, native populations were controlled by acts of God. But the iron laws of Malthus had lately been repealed by doctors and administrators: "The old diminution by war and pestilence does not occur. Our good government prevents them from fighting, and the result is an enormous increase in numbers. The natives devote their minds to a remarkable extent to the multiplication of children."

Therefore, "there must be class legislation . . . there must be Pass Laws and Peace Preservation acts . . . we have got to treat natives where they are in a state of barbarism, in a different way to ourselves. We are to be lords over them." This rhetoric was to find concrete expression in the De Beers compounds, and eventually in the government's Europeans Only signs and statutes. Throughout the 1890s many sought to harden racial lines, to deprive blacks of their lands and their votes—none had the financial and political authority of Rhodes. When the question of civil rights arose in the Cape Parliament, the Prime Minister challenged the delegates. "Does this House think it is right that men in a state of pure barbarism should have the franchise and vote?" He was emphatic. "The native is to be treated as a child and denied the franchise."

Rhodes censured those British preachers who supported equal rights for all races. The minister's son knew all about churchmen with soft heads. "I would have liked to have seen the missionaries come down to the House on the important question of liquor; not on this trivial question of the franchise." Besides, the "natives do not want" the privilege of deciding their fate at the polls. They "know nothing about the politics of the country. They have told me time after time that they do not understand these policies. 'Leave us alone but let us try and deal with some of our little questions.' "

Under pressure Rhodes conceded that a black man might be allowed to cast his vote—if he owned a house worth £25 and was a "useful citizen" according to federal standards. However, liberals should keep in mind that "in India there are 150,000,000 people with a civilization far in advance of that of our natives and not one of them has a vote."

Given his attitudes, Rhodes could have surprised no one with his activities in the north—no one, that is, except the blacks who had not seen him before and who had no idea what the Prime Minister had in mind. First among them was Lobengula, chief of the Matabele.

One of Lobengula's ancestors had been a general in the great Shaka's army. By contrast, the present chief was a peaceful figure, content to rule Matabeleland surrounded by opulence, space, and obedience. These had marked his reign since the day of his installation. A missionary witnessed the ceremony: "The soldiers numbered about seven thousand and constituted a semi-circle about twenty deep. . . . Lobengula had a long staff in his right hand, an ample cape of black ostrich feathers and a bandeau of yellow otter skins. . . . To a looker-on from the adjoining hillock, where I stood at the time, the view was a fine one. The motley, moving mass of people presented themselves with black and white, red and white, and other colored shields in their left hands . . . swelling their songs of praise to their illustrious ancestors and former kings, like the chanting of a great cathedral."

Lobengula located his kraal in Bulawayo, his father's "place of slaughter." Although he owned several large huts and a great brick house, the chief preferred to sleep in an old wagon, given to him long ago by a white trader. The huts were used to house the King's treasures, among them a portrait of Queen Victoria, framed in gilt, and two large, rusty biscuit tins. According to tradition they held the royal collection of hard shiny pebbles, tributes purloined from the diamond mines by black laborers. No white man was permitted to see the accumulation of stones; it was estimated to be worth more than £5 million.

Lobengula matched his grand holdings. He stood six feet four inches tall and weighed close to 300 pounds. Wherever he strode, usually in a kilt of blue monkey skins, an official praisemaker walked before him, crying: "Behold, the Great Elephant, he comes! When he walks, the earth trembles! When he opens his mouth, the heavens roar!"

The Great Elephant presided over a contented people, growing crops, breeding cattle, collecting wives—he had over sixty—and seeing to it that the young men honed their military skills without actually going to war. The King could be as volatile as his predecessors: a tribesman who was caught stealing the royal beer was ordered to have his lips cut off because they had tasted the beverage, his nose severed because it had smelled it, and his forehead peeled down to cover his eyes because they had seen it. The thief was then thrown to the crocodiles.

And yet the chief was no absolute monarch. He consulted his wise men before making a political decision, and he saw to it that the strangers from the south were treated with civility and decorum. Not for a moment did he entertain the notion that the Matabele could win a war with European imperialists. That was why he had adroitly kept peace with the white man across what Kipling remembered as "the great, gray-green, greasy" Limpopo River, "all set about with fever trees."

Then had come the discovery of gold in the 1880s and with it the concession-hunters. A few arrived from Portuguese or German colonies, but the main seekers of permission were now the English and the Boers. As it happened, the Charter Company was just beginning its push northward when the South African Republic (formerly the Transvaal) was concluding a treaty with Lobengula under the direction of its President, Stephanus Johannes Paulus Kruger.

Oom Paul ("Uncle Paul" to his countrymen) had taken part in the Great Trek of 1837 at the age of eleven. Three years later he killed his first lion. "As far as I know," he wrote in his memoirs, "I must have shot at least thirty to forty elephants and five hippopotamuses. And I know I have killed five lions by myself." His physical courage was not confined to hunting dangerous beasts. Out on the veld when an infected thumb grew gangrenous, he amputated the infected part himself with a hunting knife.

Elected to the Presidency of the South African Republic in 1883, Oom Paul presented himself as the quintessential Boer—hardy, self-reliant, biased against any native and suspicious of all Britishers, reactionary in everything from social policy to religion. He was a member of the rigid Dopper sect of the Dutch Reform Church. By his own reckoning, the term "was derived from the word *dop*, a damper or extinguisher for putting out candles. The meaning would seem to be that, just as a *dop* extinguishes a candle, so the Doppers extinguished all new thoughts and opposed all progress."

The English thought of him as an unmannered and dangerous clown. A British official described Kruger as "an elderly man, decidedly ugly, with a countenance denoting extreme obstinacy, and also great cruelty. His conduct at the public luncheon on Tuesday was as the Belgian Consul described it 'gigantically horrible.' His dirty wooden pipe was visible, for it stuck out of his breast pocket; his scanty hair was in such a condition of greasiness that it lay in streaks across his head, the drops of rancid coconut oil gathering at the ends of each streak of hair, and thus rendering the use of his pocket comb [necessary] during lunch. The napkin was turned to strange uses during lunch."

Although the shocked dinner guests failed to realize it, much of Kruger's warthog approach was performance art, staged in order to discomfit the *uitlanders*—the foreign strangers he regarded as his natural enemy. He would do his act again and again, snorting, grunting, sweating in his anachronistic morning clothes and top hat. But in matters that counted Oom Paul was not only an incorruptible leader, he could also be a subtle and tragic prophet. "Do not talk to me of gold," he told some burghers who approached him with news of yet another African El Dorado. It is "the element which brings more dissension, misfortunes and unexpected plagues in its trail than benefits." He lowered his head. "Pray to God, as I am doing, that the curse connected with its coming may not overshadow our dear land. . . . Pray and implore Him Who has stood by us that He will continue to do so, for I tell you today that every ounce of gold taken from the bowels of our soil will yet have to be weighed up with rivers of tears."

According to the Lobengula-Kruger treaty, a white consul would be stationed at Lobengula's kraal. He would be granted jurisdiction over the Afrikaaners, mostly farmers and lone prospectors, who lived in Matabeleland. According to Oom Paul, that would be the full extent of Boer authority. Rhodes saw it differently. He believed that Kruger would use the agreement to thwart British expansion, and he mounted a counterattack.

Before the treaty could be ratified, Piet Grobler, the go-between who carried papers from Kruger to Lobengula, was stabbed to death on his way home. Evidence pointed to a neighboring Bantu tribe unfriendly to Lobengula. Kruger bitterly disagreed. "This murder," he declared, "was due to the instigation of Cecil Rhodes and his clique." He offered no proof, and he needed none. The Boers felt that the Colossus was capable of any crime, and they may have been right; Sarah Millin, one of Rhodes's early biographers, implies as much; if "inconvenient emissaries" got in Rhodes's way, she says, they had a "tendency to vanish from his path."

Whatever Rhodes's accountability, he wasted no time once the news of Grobler's death came out. The British High Commissioner was on

Christmas holiday in the Eastern Cape, but that made no difference to the petitioner. He paid a surprise visit to Sir Hercules Robinson (no relation to J. B.) and urged that Matabeleland be declared a British protectorate.

Rhodes appealed in the name of imperialism; he dilated on his Cape-to-Cairo vision; he spoke of the possible encroachments of Britain's European rivals. In the end the Commissioner succumbed. Sir Hercules sent off a dispatch to Lobengula asking him not to enter into treaties with any foreign power or to part with any land without the sanction of Robinson himself. The words were simple and the message behind them clear. Under the right circumstances Britain could be generous, but once roused the all-powerful nation would make a bad enemy. The king withdrew to think about the alternatives and emerged to announce his decision. He would negotiate only with representatives of the Great White Queen from across the sea.

Days later a formal agreement was drawn up. The paper was delivered in style: a contingent of Royal Horse Guards galloped up to the kraal, caparisoned in silver breastplates and plumed helmets, escorting a coach emblazoned with V.R. and drawn by eight silver-bearing mules. Surrounded by witnesses and an aura of good feeling, Lobengula majestically made his mark on a treaty of "peace and unity" between the Great White Queen of England and the Mighty Elephant of Matabeleland. It was his death warrant.

Now that matters were settled with Britain, Rhodes sent three representatives to negotiate further with Lobengula. The trio presented him with one hundred gold sovereigns. This, they said, was to be the first of many gifts. The King had only to agree to Rhodes's proposal. As Lobengula understood it, a few prospectors—no more than ten— would be allowed to explore Matabeleland for a valuable mineral. Should they come upon a deposit of that mineral they would dig no more than one hole. For this favor the king would receive £100 on the first day of every lunar month, plus a thousand Martin-Henry rifles and one hundred thousand cartridges. A steamboat floated down the Zambesi with guns "suitable for defensive purposes" was to be thrown in as a bonus. The king made his mark on their paper as well.

The boat never arrived. However, an expedition did deliver the rifles, despite some objections from Parliament. Rhodes dismissed the complaints out of hand; in his experience the natives always raised the gunsights too high, in the belief that it made the bullets go faster. The resulting misfires would actually make Africa safer than in the days of the short knives. The ink had scarcely dried on the treaty with Rhodes when a group of white traders and missionaries stopped by Lobengula's kraal. He invited them to inspect his newest paper. They told him what the writing really said. The king struggled to understand.

Then, he demanded, "if gold is found anywhere in the country . . . white men can occupy the land and dig for it?"

"Yes, King!"

"If gold is in my garden, can they come and dig it?"

"Yes, King!"

"If gold is in my royal kraal, can they enter and dig?"

"Yes, King!"

The young men of Matabeleland heard the exchange and grew restive. They made noises about going into battle with the deceitful English. Lobengula knew that he could not hold them off for long, and he made a remarkable decision. He was ruler of his state; Victoria was sovereign of hers. As an equal, he would send two ambassadors with a letter properly translated and addressed to the White Queen: "Lobengula desires . . . to ask her to advise and help him, as he is much troubled by white men who come into his country and ask to dig for gold."

Umshete, first among Lobengula's representatives, would express the King's desires in the right words. Babjaan, the second, celebrated for his phenomenal memory, was to remind the Queen of her promises. Early in 1889 the two Matabele sailed aboard something they called "a great kraal which pushed through the water." In London they were met by a special train and taken to Windsor. A royal carriage conveyed them to the palace. Men of the Second Life Guards stood at attention, lining the approaches to St. George's Chapel. They were stuffed—or so Babjaan thought until one of them shifted his eyes. In the Audience Chamber, while the party awaited the Queen, "an awkward contretemps occurred," a report said, "such as often happens to excited children." It was therefore decided to present the Matabele ambassadors in a less intimidating gallery.

Victoria formally received Lobengula's letter and addressed the men. "You have come a long way to see me. I hope it was made a pleasant journey and that you do not suffer from the cold." Rain had been their constant companion, but Umshete knew how to flatter royalty: "How should we feel cold in the presence of the Great White Queen?"

During the luncheon that followed, lemonade was discreetly substituted for champagne in the ambassadors' goblets. Otherwise the Matabele were treated with courtesy and toasted with dignity. South Africa was very much in the news that season, and London regarded its newest visitors with lively interest. Outfitted in western clothing, Babjaan and Umshete were great social successes. They went to rounds of parties, attended the ballet, and visited the London Zoo, where Babjaan tried to attack a lion with his furled umbrella. The Matabele saw their first telephone and concluded that while it was an astonishing invention, it would never learn their language. The White Queen's treasure house, The Bank of England, was especially appealing. Umshete pointed out that when the representative of a foreign government visited Lobengula's royal herds he was honored with a gift of the fattest ox. The hint fell on deaf ears.

At last the Matabele boarded the *Grantually Castle* and sailed home. Exactly what had been accomplished no one could say. One of the white Africans who completed the round trip recalled that the ambassadors, thinking of the reception they might receive at the kraal, "began to be afraid of wearing the English clothes which they loved so well." After their arrival in Cape Town, "first one garment disappeared then another. When we got to the frontier and were going to be doctored with the mystic rites, Umshete appeared with nothing but his monkey tails around his loins." Babjaan was more sentimental. He kept his waistcoat as a souvenir of the country he would never see again.

While all this was going on, Rhodes acted to square Lobengula before any outsiders could interfere with the Charter Company's plans to dig up all the gold in Matabeleland. The Company was represented by Rhodes's old friend and roommate, Dr. Leander Starr Jameson. He was an inspired choice. Lobengula had been suffering from gout that season, and none of his wise men had been able to diminish the pain.

Jameson supplied the King with morphine and made an immediate friend. Over the next few weeks he persuaded Lobengula to allow "some miners" to head northeast in a search for gold. Later, when the Matabele chief hesitated, Jameson pressed him: would a great leader go back on his word? Lobengula fell into the trap. "The King never lies," he answered proudly.

"Some miners" turned out to number more than a thousand. In June 1890, the explorers started on a 450-mile journey into Matabeleland. Their equipment included eighty ox wagons, many Maxim machine guns, and a complete sawmill. They were observed en route, and as they approached their destination the king confronted Jameson. "Has the King killed any white men, that a regiment is collecting on his border?" The doctor mendaciously replied, "These men are a working party, protected by some soldiers and are going along the route already arranged with the King."

A month later the pioneers took possession of the land in the name of Victoria Regina. No sooner had the news reached England, than shares of De Beers shot up on the Stock Exchange. The Colossus could scarcely contain himself. "When at last I found that they were through," he crowed, "I do not think there was a happier man in the country."

Still there was unfinished business with Lobengula. He had let his worries be known: "The Chief is troubled. He is being eaten up by Mr. Rhodes." Yet Lobengula did not act. He knew the consequences of going up against Britain's well-armed, well-supplied intruders. "Rhodes has a very lucky star," wrote one South African. "The bloodless nature of the enterprise has astonished everyone." So it went through the early 1890s, with Lobengula dissatisfied and confused, Rhodes sanguine and expansive. *The Cape Argus* picked up his tone and began to refer to Matabeleland and its neighboring territory, Mashonaland, by the name of Rhodesia. "Has anyone else had a country called after their name?" Rhodes exulted. "Now I don't care a damn what they do with me!"

In May 1893, the fragile peace was finally shattered. Members of the Mashona tribe stole five hundred yards of wire from the English engineers in order to make bracelets and necklaces. A chief named Gomola was held responsible, and police from Rhodes's Chartered

Company showed up at his kraal to demand restitution. The chief paid his fine in cattle. But the cattle were not Gomola's to give away. They belonged to Lobengula.

Furious, the Matabele king sent a force of 300 men into Mashonaland to teach the smaller tribe a lesson. The terrified Mashona fled to the local Company fort for protection. Jameson had been waiting for just such an incident. He cabled Rhodes for permission to march against the "fat naked savage." The Colossus was only too happy to give the nod.

On August 14, 1893, Jameson enlisted, by secret agreement, 672 men to march against the Matabele. Each one was promised 6,000 acres of land and 20 gold claims in Rhodesia. "The loot," said one paragraph, "shall be divided half to [Rhodes's] company and the remainder to officers and men in equal shares."

Without governmental sanction of any kind, the troops assembled and began moving toward Bulawayo. The Foreign Office learned of the march and expressed its official outrage. Attempts were made to forestall the Colossus; but he was nowhere to be found. With considerable amusement Rhodes told a colleague, "I had to hide in the bush and to make it impossible to receive orders by cable from Whitehall prohibiting us from invading Matabeleland. But now that Dr. Jim has disappeared into the blue nobody can deter us any longer from this adventure."

The force of volunteers, bolstered with 1,500 Bechuana warriors, traditional enemies of the Matabele, kept moving relentlessly toward Lobengula's kraal. They crossed the Shangani River on October 24 and camped for the night. Five thousand Matabele attacked the next morning. Rhodes had been right about the Martin-Henry rifles: the natives fired high and ineffectively. The resulting massacre was later summed up in a couplet by Hilaire Belloc:

> Whatever happens we have got
> The Maxim gun, and they have not.

It was the end for Lobengula and he knew it. Everything had gone against him: thousands of his best young men were dead, and now he fell ill with smallpox. Feverish and in great pain, he ordered the royal kraal to be burned to the ground. A small group of loyal soldiers loaded his treasures on the big wagon and took their king to the banks of the Zambesi River. There he called a halt. A cave was found, and the ten young men who escorted him were ordered to store his possessions in the cave and make the entrance inaccessible. They rolled a great rock in front of its small opening.

Afterward, one by one, the men were executed by his old and trusted bodyguard, Bosungwana. On January 24, 1894, Lobengula died, wasted by pox and misery. Bosungwana buried him sitting in his favorite chair, and then obscured the grave with rocks and plantings. The Great Elephant's final resting place and his trove of diamonds and gold passed into legend along with King Solomon's mines. Hundreds of men, black and white, have searched the ground of Rhodesia (now Zimbabwe) for over a hundred years. But the Matabele enjoyed a final vengeance. Lobengula's treasure has never been found.

Many members of Lobengula's family survived him. Rhodes took several of them to work in his estate. For the amusement of his guests and himself, he had one of the grandchildren renamed Rhodes.

Even Rhodes's flattering biographers Lockhart and Woodhouse turn their eyes from this "adventure." They concede drily, "it must be admitted that the treatment of Lobengula does not form a chapter in the history of Africa of which white men should be proud." Contemporary judgments were harsher. A London-based magazine called *Truth* spoke out against "these filibustering and massacring expeditions . . . of Mr. Rhodes and his pernicious company, a wretched, rotten, bankrupt set of marauders and murderers." Parliament censured Rhodes for the massacre on three separate occasions. An anonymous pamphlet circulated in Cambridge, headlined THE MATABELE SCANDAL and signed by "One who remembers the punishment which fell upon Cain for killing his brother, and is jealous of the honour of Great Britain."

Rhodes took the sniping with his customary bad grace, but also with the feeling that he had passed above criticism and beyond the law. His actions grew more reckless. When he decided to exploit another territory, Pondoland, the local native chief demurred. He was taken to a cornfield. At Rhodes's command, machine guns fired at stalks of maize in the distance. They fell away, as if the Colossus had seized control of the wind itself. When the sound died, Rhodes issued a warning: "And that will happen to you and your tribe if you give us further trouble." Pondoland was folded into the Cape-to-Cairo scheme.

Intimidation was not Rhodes's only game. He could be very generous when the occasion required. It came to his attention that Sir Hercules Robinson was nearing retirement. Here was a man who had acted in the best interests of the Colossus; he would be squared. When the Commissioner left the government Rhodes invited him to join the board of De Beers.

Even Queen Victoria was squared. She invited him to the royal presence in 1894 and inquired: "What have you been doing since I last saw you, Mr. Rhodes?" About Matabeleland and Mashonaland he was succinct: "I have added two Provinces to Your Majesty's dominions." The Queen expressed delight in this "tremendous strong man," and suddenly the critics at Whitehall grew quiet.

◆　　◆　　◆

SITTING ON THE *STOEP* of his house in the Transvaal, Oom Paul watched all this and puffed on his pipe, silently planning his next moves. He'd been outmaneuvered by Rhodes in Matabeleland and had said nothing. For the last decade he had watched the English rushing to the gold fields, and he had kept his own counsel. The depraved city of Johannesburg had risen up 50 miles from his home in the good city of Pretoria, and still he was quiet. To him Johannesburg, situated in his own Republic, was too evil for contemplation, and there were many who agreed with him. Olive Schreiner visited the place that whites referred to as Judasburg or Joburg or Jewhannesburg, and blacks called *Igoli*—City of Gold. In a letter to friends she gave her return address as Hell.

The city contained 97 official brothels employing more than a thousand prostitutes; 650 licensed bars, some of which were little more than whorehouses; a racetrack; a boxing ring; and a permanent circus and menagerie. It also had a frantic stock market, eight-story, marble-fronted buildings, bright new electric lights that banished the night. On every street and in every office there was the constant play of fortunes made and lost in gold futures.

In brief, Johannesburg held everything that Kruger despised and feared, including a surplus of *uitlanders*. These, especially the English, he commonly referred to as "thieves and murderers." He compared them unfavorably to the baboons in his back yard, and refused to even think about English voters. "If we give them the franchise tomorrow," he maintained, "we may as well give up the Republic."

Kruger tied the mine owners' hands by taxing them heavily. There was a Water Concession, an Electric Light Concession, a Bread and Jam Concession, a Dynamite Concession. All served to increase the government's income and deepen the *uitlander* resentment of Oom Paul and his people. A group calling themselves Reformers gathered in pubs and private houses to discuss the possibility of a revolt against the state. At the very least they would demand to have English taught in the schools instead of the abominable Afrikaans, plus a reduction in taxes and freedom from military duty. After all, the Boers were outnumbered seven to one in the city. How could Kruger possibly cope if Rhodes decided to march against him, as he did against the black king?

Such *uitlander* grumbling did not worry Kruger. He was an experienced jungle fighter, and for more than fifty years he had made a practice of studying his enemy closely. He knew the English as a formidable people. But he also knew their Prime Minister, Cecil John Rhodes, to be proud and incautious. Oom Paul counseled his burghers to be patient. "Take a tortoise. If you want to kill it, you must wait until it puts out its head, and then you cut it off."

The tortoise lumbered on, and in 1895 obligingly stuck its neck out for the man with the axe.

♦   ♦   ♦

Now THAT THE BUSINESS of diamonds was under his thumb, Rhodes turned his attention to South Africa's other underground treasure. In the 1890s, ten financial houses controlled most of the gold production in South Africa. They and their subsidiaries represented a combined capital of over £50 million, and they employed some 75,000 workers —nine blacks to every "European."

Second only to the great house of Wernher, Beit was the Consolidated Goldfields of Cecil Rhodes. After this came Barney Barnato's Johannesburg Consolidated Investment Co.—"Johnnies" to the trade.

To all appearances Barney had settled into ultimate respectability. The flash of diamonds had been augmented by the solidity of gold, and in 1892 he astonished the world by marrying the woman with whom he had been living for years. Fanny Bees, onetime barmaid and actress, was the daughter of a Cape Town tailor. She claimed to be from an old Huguenot family. Others were not so sure. A contemporary called her "an Afrikander of the St. Helena type," a euphemism for Cape Colored. Fanny's olive complexion and dark tightly curled hair gave some credence to the rumor, and in South Africa miscegenation was not looked upon kindly. It is a measure of Barney's authority (and of his affection) that he insisted on a very public wedding in London. Fanny converted to Judaism before the civil ceremony; then the Barnatos returned to Johannesburg to start a family.

After Johnnies came a group controlled by the indomitable J. B. Robinson. The Buccaneer had left the diamond town without a backward glance and recouped his fortunes in the gold city. Even more surprising were Sammy Marks and Isaac Lewis, the two peddlers squeezed out of the diamond business in Kimberley only a few years before. They had enjoyed phenomenal successes as merchants and put their profits in real estate. Now they held about 300 separate farms covering more than three million acres of the Transvaal.

The place where the gold strikes were heaviest was called the Witwatersrand, "white water ridge" in English. Thus some wag on *The Times* of London dubbed the South African millionaires Randlords. The executives began to think of themselves as a business aristocracy, and with the appropriate use of funds and lobbying, many of them did indeed obtain titles from the court of King Edward VII. In 1895, however, they were anything but noble. The Kruger government was taxing them heavily, and they decided to strike back. The instrument of their reprisal was Dr. Leander Starr Jameson, the man who had so effectively subdued Lobengula.

Dr. Jim, as he was popularly known, once boasted that it would take 500 men with bullwhips to vanquish the Boer militia. He saw it as the Matabele business all over again, this time with simple whites in place of primitive blacks. Late in 1895 he had far more than whips under his command. A miscellaneous band of pioneers, adventurers, and policemen from the country now officially known as Rhodesia awaited orders for the Jameson Raid to begin. This secret military operation had been funded by the Chartered Company along with money from Beit, under the rubric of "New Concessions." Lionel Phillips, the high-ranking Wernher, Beit executive, was entitled to draw on it; so was Rhodes's newest expert on gold mining, the American engineer John Hays Hammond.

From its inception the Jameson Raid was a fantasy concocted by the naïve, carried out by the inept, and built on a total misunderstanding of timing and terrain. "Our general scheme," Hammond later admitted, "was to get some thousands of guns into Johannesburg [smuggled past Boer police in De Beers oil wagons], and then, on some dark night, to take Pretoria, the Boer capital, seize the arsenal, carry Kruger off with us, and to negotiate at leisure for the redress of our grievances." The chief plotters communicated by telegraph in code: the raid was known as "flotation" and the officers as "subscribers."

Unreliability became the order of the day. When Jameson paid a last-minute visit to Johannesburg to organize the "spontaneous" uprising, he dropped in on a co-conspirator. The house was empty. A note from one womanizer to another explained: "Dear Jimjams, sorry I can't see you this afternoon, have an appointment to teach Mrs. X. the bike." Jimjams understood. He kept on with his plans and made ready for his military strike.

In Rhodes's eyes, that strike would complete the dream. The Boer government would fall under his jurisdiction and he would fold it into his Cape-to-Cairo plan. No other magnates need apply; the Colossus informed friends that he was not, for example, "going to change President Kruger for President J. B. Robinson."

The timing of the Raid seemed perfect. In June 1895, England's Liberal government fell, making way for the avid new Colonial Secretary, Joseph "Pushful Joe" Chamberlain. The Secretary was informed of the operation; careful not to put anything in writing, he gave his advice and consent. Others in the government were "unofficially" informed. No objections were entered. The High Commissioner for South Africa was Sir Hercules Robinson, now deeply involved with De Beers and with many of Rhodes's other enterprises.

Having financed the Jameson Raid, Rhodes pulled back and awaited its outcome. There were many Afrikaaners in Cape Town, and it would not do for the Prime Minister of the Cape Colony to have any knowledge of the plot. Dr. Jim understood; he and his troops were content with Rhodes's words of warning and encouragement: "The only justification for revolution is success."

Late in December 1895, Jameson's group of some 400 armed volunteers moved toward Johannesburg. Most of them carried an extra rifle to hand out to sympathizers, known as "Reformers" in the city. At the rear were eight Maxim guns hauled down from Rhodesia. "I shall draw a zone of lead [around] each mile of my column," vowed Dr. Jim, "and no Boer will be able to live in it."

The doctor had forgotten a few details. Raider headquarters were located near the border of the Cape Colony. That was 176 miles east of the outskirts of Johannesburg. Even hardened soldiers would be unable to complete the planned march in two days. Then there were the Maxim guns themselves. They had done very well against the Matabele, who for all military purposes were unarmed. But the Boers held the high ground. They were expert marksmen, and they could hold out for weeks and months until the Maxims were out of ammunition, or, more likely, overheated and jammed. None of this interested Jameson. He dismissed the Afrikaaners as thick-necked and slow-witted, no more than a big target for skilled English gunners.

One of those slow-witted Afrikaaners was aware of almost every move the English doctor was making. Kruger's men had cracked the code long ago. Besides, Raider security was so porous that anyone could read about the plot in the local paper. On December 28, the day Jameson was to set out, a Reuters bulletin, dateline Johannesburg, was published in the South African press. "Persistent rumors are afloat, of secret arming of miners and warlike preparations. Women and children are leaving the Rand." Meanwhile, in Pretoria, "the political situation is the talk of the town."

Jameson took this as an affront: how dare the newspapers know so much? He wired the Company offices on a Friday, "Unless I definitely hear to the contrary shall leave tomorrow evening." Now came the first of the small disasters leading to the great fiasco. Jameson's telegram did not arrive until Saturday, when the offices were closed. The doctor interpreted silence as approval; that evening his troops marched.

According to contemporary accounts, Jameson ordered all the main telegraph lines cut as the raiders advanced. But he made the mistake of paying his operatives in advance. The men got so drunk on their wages that they cut down five miles of fencing wire and left the telegraph wires vibrating over their heads.

By the first rays of morning, Raiders spotted the first Boer commandos. Some were watching their flanks, others were in front. No one bothered to check the rear, where Kruger's men had already cut off any possibility of retreat. On Tuesday morning, January 2nd, Jameson and his troops had gone 169 miles only to end up in a valley surrounded by high stony ridges. Rifle fire broke out. The Raiders found themselves penned in so tightly that the Maxims were useless. They tried to back up; more rifle fire cut down the *uitlanders* at the rear. At 9:15 a.m. it was all over. Hoisted on a wagon whip, a white apron fluttered to signal defeat.

Jameson was given various terms, but they added up to unconditional surrender. "Shaking like a leaf," according to witnesses, he removed his hat, bowed to the Boer officers, and replied, "I accept your terms." An immediate count showed 17 Raiders killed, 55 wounded, 35 missing. The remainder, along with their leader, were marched off to Pretoria as prisoners of war. A new song had recently come over from America, and the men chanted it as they went off to jail. "Many's the heart that is broken," it went, "After the Ball."

♦   ♦   ♦

RHODES's HEART was afflicted in every sense. He had been unwell even before the Raid, subject to minor attacks and seizures of various kinds. Jameson's failure left him even more depressed and isolated. The Colossus resigned as Premier and sulked in his room. When he emerged he inquired anxiously about Rhodesia: "They can't take it away from me, can they? You never heard of a country's name being changed?"

In Pretoria 300 men awaited sentencing. At first, matters were treated lightly. Solly Joel, one of the chief Reformers, puffed away at the expensive cigars his wife had smuggled into prison. Mark Twain, who happened to be touring South Africa, stopped by the jail to visit John Hays Hammond, an acquaintance from the old silver mining days in Virginia City.

"How did you ever find your way into this God-forsaken hole?" Hammond inquired.

"Getting into jail is easy," the humorist said. "I thought difficulties arose when it came to getting out."

A reporter came around to see the literary celebrity. Twain told him that he was "very pleased with the jail; he had found some very charming gentlemen and he thought it was an ideal rest cure for these tired businessmen. He only regretted his stay was so short that he could not take advantage of the peaceful conditions in the jail to rest his own tired nerves. He said he could not imagine a place where one would be less troubled by the importunities of his creditors, and the only feature he did not like about the jail was that there were too many lawyers among the prisoners, and somehow or other he could never hit it off with lawyers."

But as the weeks dragged by the smiles congealed. A rumor shuddered through the jail: a piece of the gallows at Slachter's Nek had been sent to Johannesburg. One of the prisoners grew hysterical, slit his throat and bled to death. In late spring, the Judge confirmed the Raiders' worst fears. Several main conspirators were to hang, among them Lionel Phillips and John Hays Hammond. The ringleader, Jameson, would be sent back to London where Whitehall promised to deal with him harshly. Barnato's nephew Solly Joel got off with a stiff fine, but neither he nor his uncle was grateful. Barnato cursed the bench, vowing to shut down his mines, upsetting the Rand economy and putting thousands out of work, unless every prisoner's sentence was reduced or canceled. Running into Barney on the street, the presiding official exploded, "You are no gentleman." Barney returned, "And you are no judge."

Barney was serious. For the next few days he appeared in mourning clothes, bound his hat with crepe, and stopped his mining operations. Kruger tried to dismiss these maneuvers as so much grandstanding, but privately he was worried, and he granted Barnato an interview. Barney did not stint on the money or the charm. He ordered two marble lions delivered to the President's house in Pretoria, where they remain to this day. During the discussions he alternately smiled and snarled, depending on whether the subject concerned the future of Solly Joel or the name of Cecil Rhodes. A few days later the sentences were dismissed and the fines reduced. Most of the prisoners were released. "No one else could have done what I have done," Barney crowed. But he could—and would—do nothing for Jameson and Rhodes. Dr. Jim and the most important co-conspirators would be sent to London under arrest. The Colossus would follow in short order. And then, with the tidal change that affected every aspect of his life, Rhodes suddenly found events going his way. The Kaiser, who had his own designs on Africa, sent a widely publicized telegram to Kruger: "I express my sincere congratulations that without calling on the aid of friendly Powers you and your people . . . have succeeded in re-establishing peace and defending the independence of the country against attack from without."

The Raiders could not have asked for a more effective antidote. Queen Victoria herself sent a wire admonishing her German grandson, and the Poet Laureate, Alfred Austin, assumed the voice of a Raider to hack out some doggerel for the occasion:

> Wrong! Is it wrong? Well maybe
> But I'm going boys, all the same
> Do they think me a Burgher's Baby
> To be scared by a scolding name?
>
> There are girls in the gold-reef city
> There are mothers and children, too,
> And they cry: 'Hurry up! For pity!'
> So what can a brave man do?
>
> So we forded and galloped forward
> As hard as our beasts could pelt
> First eastward, then trending northward
> Right over the rolling veldt.

Soon all London was repeating the poem; especially the final truculent stanza:

> We were wrong, but we aren't half sorry
> And, as one of the baffled band,
> I would rather have had that foray
> Than the crushings of all the Rand.

Popular opinion rallied to Jameson and company, and they were released on bail with the proviso that "for the sake of the peace of this country [they] keep away from any place where their presence may cause public excitement." Still, when they came up for trial the Lord Chief Justice took no note of popular support; he sentenced Jameson to fifteen months in prison.

While all this went on Rhodes retreated from Johannesburg to Kimberley, scene of his early triumphs. A cheering crowd met him at the station. "In times of political adversity," he told them, "people came to know who their friends were." He held out as long as he could, but early in 1897 he was summoned to London. A Committee of Inquiry wanted to question Rhodes about the Jameson Raid.

The most hostile member of the Committee was Henry Labouchere, editor and member of the House of Commons. Labouchere was out to topple the Colossus. Riding the waves of the three-year-old Dreyfus case, he called Rhodes "a mere vulgar promoter masquerading as a patriot, and the figurehead of a gang of astute Hebrew financiers with whom he divided the profits."

Rhodes was helped by the presence of sympathetic onlookers and friends. Alfred Beit accompanied him to the room, and seated in the crowd was the Prince of Wales, flanked by the Duke of Abercorn, chairman of the Chartered Company, and Lord Selborne from the Colonial Office. Rhodes's testimony went on sporadically for almost six months; a wag accused him of "Lying in State at Westminster," and that is exactly what he did, evading direct answers and claiming a faulty memory. He acknowledged that he had sent letters and cables to Jameson during the period in question. But they had nothing to do with the Raid, Rhodes insisted, and in any case the copies were lost.

The Colonial Secretary supplied more fiction. Joseph Chamberlain had elbowed his way onto the Board of Inquiry, and was thus in the position of investigating himself. Naturally, he found no evidence that he had secretly given permission for the Raid to go on. "Pushful Joe" gave hypocrisy a new voice, calling the Colossus "a man of honor," and inquiring in a schoolboy tone: "What is there in South Africa, I wonder, that makes blackguards of all who get involved in its politics?" Under his direction compromising telegrams were lost, and the name of Chamberlain went unsullied until a son, Prime Minister Neville Chamberlain, sought to appease Adolf Hitler two generations later.

In Rhodes's South African home he had always shown a preference for "teak and whitewash." He received plenty of the latter from his hearers. After a minor scolding he was free to go. The Prince of Wales made a point of shaking his hand. A few weeks later *The Westminster Gazette* summed up the Inquiry with a mock tombstone:

> In Memoriam
> The South African Committee.
> It respected confidences. It discovered the obvious.
> It avoided the obscure. It compromised no man.
> Fortified by unctuous rectitude and an unsuspicious
> disposition, it was unsparing of whitewash.
> Died in the odor of inanity.

Yet if the Randlords were finished with the Raid, the Raid was not quite finished with them. Cecil Rhodes was ill and out of favor. Leander Starr Jameson's appeal was denied: he would serve every day of his prison sentence. Barney Barnato had squandered time, energy, and money at the trial. When South African gold shares declined on the South African exchange the Barnato Bank faltered. Barney folded it into the larger Barnato creation, the Johannesburg Consolidated Investment Company.

Many investors had bought bank shares at the top market price, and they were given "Johnnies" stock at a much lower value. The financial press hinted broadly at sharp practice. Some big losers sent anonymous letters threatening Barney's life. Barnato put up a show of bravado, gesturing with spectacles in hand, telling jokes on others and himself, alternately attacking and laughing at his critics. But he was painfully aware that in Paris the anti-Semites were using him as the latest instance of Jewish swindling. London would not be far behind.

In England a story was already circulating, unsubstantiated but generally believed. A young clerk had shot himself after losing his life savings. The suicide note was supposed to have read, "Regret I have made a mess of it all. Barnato's Bank is the cause of everything."

Driving by one of Barney's London properties, Labouchere pointed out a row of gargoyles on the roof. A companion asked if the statues had any significance. The journalist said they were Barnato's creditors who had petrified while waiting for their money.

Barney started to drink heavily and act irrationally. Fanny had given him a son, Jack, and a daughter, Leah, and in his early forties Barney had settled happily into family life. Now he scarcely glanced at his children. His millions meant nothing; during most of 1896 Barney had expressed the conviction that bankruptcy might be only a week or two away. Any dip in the market drove him to the pub, and he stayed there for hours, getting full of malt liquor and self-pity. As before, fits of mania were followed by troughs of paranoia, aggravated by bad dreams. One evening Fanny found him clawing at cracks in the wall, searching for hidden diamonds. On another occasion he ran out of the house and banged on a neighbor's door. "They're after me!" he pleaded. "Let me in!"

By the spring of 1897 Barney's behavior had become the talk of Johannesburg. Late in May it was decided that he needed a rest cure, and on June 2 the Barnatos sailed for England, ostensibly to attend Queen Victoria's Diamond Jubilee. Solly Joel was persuaded to come along in order to keep an eye on his uncle. At first Barney appeared to be on the mend. He played dominoes with his old skill and engaged his fellow passengers in lively conversation. But all too soon he started to fret about the market and begged not to be left alone.

On the thirteenth of June the ship neared the island of Madeira. Barney ordered champagne at lunch and then asked Solly to accompany him on an exercise walk around the deck. The two men tramped forcefully for nearly an hour. Exhausted, Joel broke away, sat on a deck chair, and caught his breath. Barney kept on. A little girl, Nellie Mackintosh, witnessed the next few moments. Barney suddenly "called out 'They're after me,' rushed to the nearby railings, climbed up and jumped over. As he went, the back of his coat blew up and over him; the suit was a dark brown with stripes in it and I can see it distinctly still." The ship's fourth officer vaulted over the rail and swam to the body floating face down. Engines were stopped and a lifeboat lowered, but it was too late.

"We were told the next day," Nellie recalled, "that Mr. Barnato had died and we must be very quiet. I remember too when we reached England, the sailors carrying the coffin: it was roughly painted very black and had raw rope handles. Mrs. Barnato, Leah and her little brother, both small, walked behind it. We had not seen them to play with from the day after his death as they had all stayed out of sight."

"Death by drowning while insane" read the coroner's verdict. Barney-watchers refused to believe it. Accusations circulated: Solly had pushed his troublesome uncle into the water; a man ruined by Barnato's stock manipulations had killed the financier; the other Randlords had wanted him out of the way. A hundred years later some Kimberley folk could still be found clinging to the notion that Barney was murdered. The evidence does not support them. Barnato had been unstable for a year before his death. A worried friend had provided an obituary well in advance of the suicide: "Some day that marvelous vitality will cease. Either brain or life will go."

After both had gone, London magnates gathered to pay their last respects. Two hundred carriages accompanied the body to the Jewish cemetery in Willesden. The Lord Mayor of London was among the mourners, along with Alfred Beit, who had never liked Barney but believed that a Randlord—any Randlord—deserved a first-class funeral. Rhodes was conspicuous by his absence, and that was the way he wanted it. He had been making a night trip across Bechuanaland when his secretary received the news about Barney's drowning. The young man waited until morning to hand over the telegram. Rhodes snapped at him. "I suppose you thought this would affect me and I should not sleep. Why, do you imagine that I would be in the least affected if you were to fall under the wheels of this train now?" The engine chuffed on. What if a Life Director of De Beers had fallen? No man was irreplaceable.

Even so, the idea of mortality had hit a little too close to home. "It would be very ridiculous to lose one's ideas by death," Rhodes noted, relieved that he had drawn up papers with little Alfred and some of his other associates. The will, however, would have to be revised once more. As soon as the Colossus got back to his desk he informed his financial manager: "It will amuse you. I am almost superstitious. I knew Barnato would not outlive me, so I made no arrangement with him. If Beit had not made [an] arrangement with me, he would have also died first. Now the thought has come that I might go first." The writer's heart grew weaker with each day, but he was wrong. In South Africa, as a native proverb has it, death tiptoes politely with rude surprises in its hands.

8

EXIT RHODES, ENTER HOGGENHEIMER

LESS THAN A YEAR after Barney Barnato's funeral his nephew received a disturbing letter. "Kismet," as the writer signed himself, demanded the sum of £12,000. Otherwise he would seek out the addressee and kill him rather than face "ruin or disgrace." He rambled on. Woolf Joel's death would "not be murder, but your own doing really, though I will willingly admit all the blame for removing you to a better world, this or the other side of the river Styx, where Barnato may be glad to see you again."

Woolf ignored the warning. Other messages arrived, this time threatening Woolf's brother Solly. From what the Joels could gather, Kismet had been injured in some way by Barney's shady financial dealings. The brothers must have decided that there was something to his complaint; they agreed not to call in the police. Solly scurried off to the safety of Cape Town. Woolf stayed in Kimberley to take charge of the matter.

He placed an advertisement asking Kismet to meet him outside the Barnato building in Johannesburg. A tall and imposing figure strode up at the appointed hour, introducing himself as Baron von Veltheim. In a pronounced German accent he related his grievance: after the Jameson fiasco Barney had conscripted volunteers to overthrow the Transvaal government. Kruger would be kidnapped and replaced by an accommodating stooge. The coup was to have been financed with Barnato money, but with Barney's suicide everything had fallen apart. The kidnappers were vulnerable and broke. They needed money to go underground or leave the country.

Baron von Veltheim threatened to make his story public; Woolf, whether he believed him or not, agreed to pay the blackmail. But he refused to meet the stated price. It was lowered to £2,500, and the Baron agreed. This led Woolf to conclude, in the manner of Cecil Rhodes, that the man could be "squared for a fiver."

On March 14, 1898, nine months to the day since Barney took his fatal plunge, von Veltheim entered Woolf Joel's office. Woolf was not alone; his office manager, Harold Strange, stood by with a loaded revolver in his pocket. The Baron hotly demanded his £2,500. Woolf countered with the offer of a £200 loan. The blackmailer darkened. "If that is your final decision, you know too much and neither of you will leave this room alive." He produced a pistol and began firing. By the time Strange drew his own revolver, von Veltheim had shot Woolf three times. More bullets went off wildly in Strange's direction; they missed their target. Alarmed at the noise, Woolf's office staff burst in, captured the Baron, and disarmed him. They were too late to save their employer. The "bright-hearted boy" who had become a millionaire at 20 was dead at 34.

The murder of Woolf Joel was premeditated, and there were letters to prove it. However, these were unusual times. The Jameson Raid was fresh in the minds of the jurymen, many of them Boers. They were unpersuaded by the prosecution's revelations: the "Baron" was really a commoner named Karl Kurtze. The German record showed him to be a deserter from the navy, a bigamist, and a confidence man who had pulled various stunts on four continents.

But Kurtze evidently *had* met Barney Barnato in his wanderings, and that was enough to save his skin. The defendant posed as the tool of cynical *uitlander* capitalists who wanted to overthrow the Boer government. Contrary to what the prosecution claimed, he said, Joel had threatened *him*, and the shots were fired in self-defense. Without much debate the jury found for the defendant. He was free to go. The judge publicly denounced the verdict, and the Baron's lawyer refused to shake his client's hand. Even Kruger was embarrassed by the judicial miscarriage, and after a few weeks he arranged to have Kurtze deported from his territory as a "public nuisance."

Oom Paul's gesture did nothing to calm the growing social malaise. To *uitlanders* the trial showed that the Afrikaaners would not be satisfied with English money; they wanted English blood. As if more proof was needed, Johannesburg's "Zarps"—arrogant young Boer policemen—got involved in a series of brutal encounters. When an unarmed man of English origin was gunned down by a Zarp, a court coldly dismissed the charge of murder. A widow and her child were left penniless. *Uitlanders* demonstrated in Johannesburg market square and handed a petition to the British vice-consul. The nation edged closer to civil war.

Matters worsened with the appointment of Sir Alfred Milner as Britain's South African High Commissioner. Unlike Sir Hercules Robinson, who had allowed himself to be squared by Rhodes, Milner was incorruptible. He had distinguished himself as an administrator in Egypt and began his new assignment by denouncing the Jameson Raid as wrong-headed and irresponsible. Milner assured the press that the friction of Briton and Boer could be peaceably resolved. But his exercise in public relations had no basis in reality. In his own words, Milner was a "British Race Patriot." He thought of Kruger, then 75, as a pious fraud. How dare this frock-coated Neanderthal deny *uitlanders* the franchise? What were Boer rifles and thunder compared with British imperial might? Milner let it be known that Her Majesty's troops and munitions were at his back. Where Rhodes and his friends had faltered, he would prevail. English women and children needed protection in the Boer Republic where Kruger presided.

So they did. But the real basis of conflict was not what happened above the earth's surface. It was what went on below it. The diamonds of Kimberley had made South Africa's millionaires—most of them of English origin—and these men had gone on to found the gold mining industry. Gold stood behind the British pound. In the United States, the "Silver Democrats" from the West challenged the gold standard Republicans from the East. No one could beat William Jennings Bryan for oratory ("You shall not crucify mankind upon a cross of gold"), but no one could beat William McKinley for votes. The new President took office in 1896 with the clear understanding that United States currency would be backed with gold. The metal grew more precious every day. In order to control South Africa's mines, the English had to control its politics.

Meetings between old Kruger and Milner, then in his mid-forties,

only exacerbated matters. The cultural differences, the imperial ambitions, and finally the gulf of three decades made negotiations impossible. Oom Paul's intransigence was met with Sir Alfred's arrogance,
and from June to October 1899, both sides prepared for armed conflict.
It was to be Britain's first military action against whites since the
Crimean battles of 1853–1856.

In order to sell the British public on war, propagandists worked
overtime. At the head of the jingo brigade was the reliable Rudyard
Kipling, urging his readers to stop talking about patriotism and start
paying for it:

> When you've shouted "Rule Britannia"—when you've sung
> "God save the Queen"—
> When you've finished killing Kruger with your mouth—
> Will you kindly drop a shilling in my little tambourine
> For a gentleman in khaki ordered South?

Once the poet started demonizing Oom Paul, Cecil Rhodes felt safe
enough to come out of retirement and take on his old role of Imperial
visionary. He could easily have stayed at his Cape estate, Groote Schuur
(Great Granary). He could have sailed to London, where he had many
friends in high places. Instead, on October 10, 1899, Rhodes returned
"with gray hair and a face like a jubilee bonfire" to his spiritual
sanctuary, the city of diamonds. He was still Kimberley's local hero:
De Beers had subsidized the local school of mines, the sanatorium, the
design of the new town hall.

Nevertheless, some residents wished he had chosen another refuge.
David Harris, who had taken his cousin Barney's place in Parliament,
"trembled to think what might happen . . . to defenseless Kimberley,
500 miles from the nearest port, bounded on one side by the Free State
and on the other by the Transvaal. I feared that the [Boer] forces would
make a dash for Kimberley, where Rhodes housed the bulk of his
fortune, which would have made a rich haul for the invaders." Word
circulated that the Boers intended to capture Rhodes and exhibit him
in a cage throughout the Transvaal. But there was no time for the
Colossus to change his mind, or for Harris to change it for him. The
day after Rhodes settled in, war was declared between the British and

the Boers. Less than a week later telegraph lines leading into Kimberley were cut.

As far-off guns sounded, the Colossus rose to the occasion—on his own terms. Thousands of refugees poured into Kimberley from the surrounding areas, homeless and frightened. Rhodes put them to work. His personal relief agency hired able-bodied men to repair roads, dig trenches, plant gardens, patch up municipal parks. It organized committees to find shelter and provide medical aid for needy families. By the end of the year De Beers had paid out more than £6,000 in relief wages to 185 whites, 730 coloreds, and 1,457 Africans.

A veteran of that time was to remember Rhodes in extravagant terms: "I do not know what we should have done without [him] during the siege. His name will forever mean that of a true friend to everyone who was in Kimberley." The Mayor and the town councillors agreed with her. Others were not so sure. The British army had assigned Lt. Colonel R. G. Kekewich to protect the town, and Rhodes regarded the officer and his troops as toy soldiers. In defiance of army orders he raised and equipped his own Kimberley Light Horse and got one of De Beers's engineers to produce a large cannon, "Long Cecil." It boomed deafeningly and uselessly at Boer installations several miles away. The Boers retaliated with their own big gun, "Long Tom." One of its shells landed in town and caused a lone casualty: the De Beers engineer.

All this drove Kekewich wild, but there was nothing he could do about it. The Colonel knew very well that there would have been no Kimberley without De Beers, and no De Beers without Cecil Rhodes. Kekewich huffed and strutted. Rhodes cursed and fumed. Each went his own way. The Colossus got the best of it. He offered one of his diamond mines as a bomb shelter, and he fed the townspeople. At Christmastime plum puddings were cooked and handed out gratis, courtesy of De Beers. The town's highest ranking officials enjoyed a seven-course dinner complete with roast chicken, even though the next day Kimberley went back to consuming donkey and horse meat.

The Colonel's final humiliation came in February, when the city was rescued by a force under the command of General J.D.P. French. Kekewich rode out to greet the troops, but in the confusion they missed each other. He returned to find a party under way at the sanatorium. French and Rhodes were there, fast friends already, drinking champagne toasts to the Queen. Kekewich complained to superior officers; he had "borne with this man" long enough.

They were not reassuring. "You should remember that Mr. Rhodes, or 'this man' as you call him, owns the place and that he is a power not only in the Empire but in Europe, and you should have tried to work with him."

"I thought *I* was in supreme command," Kekewich protested. He thought wrong, and the authorities made sure he would never make that mistake again. When he took his own life fifteen years later, the Lt. Colonel had risen only one step in rank.

Rhodes did not have long to enjoy his one-upmanship. De Beers's enemies were gathering force in Johannesburg and, worse still, in London. There, a growing number of anti-imperialist Britons wanted to be known as "Little Englanders" or "Pro-Boers." They dismissed the adventure in South Africa as mean and corrupt. It had already given the world the term "concentration camps"—places where captured Boer families suffered from disease and malnutrition. The war was wasting manpower and ordnance, money and moral capital. And for what? According to some respected voices, for the profit of a few plutocrats. Commenting bitterly on "Recessional," the novelist George Moore observed that Kipling "would not have written the most hideous verses ever written in a beautiful language if he had not lived in a specially hideous moment—the moment of the African millionaire."

That was the mildest criticism. In an outspoken pamphlet the *Manchester Guardian* correspondent H. B. Hobson blamed a highly visible white minority. Several years before he had written contemptuously of a type with "superior calculating intellect . . . used unsparingly to enable him to take advantage of every weakness, folly and vice of the society in which he lives." In London he found the press falling "more and more under the control of Jews." In South Africa, Hobson maintained, the same people had their fingers in nearly every financial enterprise. "Johannesburg is essentially a Jewish town." The stock market closed on Yom Kippur, and it was "worthwhile to mention that the directory shows sixty-eight Cohens against twenty-one Joneses and fifty-three Browns." Furthermore, "the Jews take little part in the Outlander agitation; they let others do that sort of work. But since half the land and nine-tenths of the wealth of the Transvaal claimed for the Outlanders are chiefly theirs, they will be the chief gainers."

The radical Henry Labouchere used his weekly, *Truth*, for some private sniggering. One column, run irregularly, was entitled "Letters of Moses Levin of Whitechapel to Isaac Levin of Johannesburg." The Irish Nationalist John Dillon argued in the House of Commons that "Mr Rhodes and his associates—generally of the German Jew extraction—found money in thousands for propaganda. By this league in South Africa and here they have poisoned the wells of public knowledge."

Before the same audience John Burns, leader of the London dockers, claimed that "the British Army, which used to be for all good causes the Sir Galahad of History, has become in Africa the janissary of the Jews. . . . Wherever we examine there is the financial Jew operating, directing, inspiring the agencies that have led to this war."

Edward Carpenter, whose previous pamphlets advocated socialism, spiritualism, and homosexual love, published an influential booklet on New Year's Day, 1900. In it he described Johannesburg as "a hell full of Jews, financiers, greedy speculators, adventurers, prostitutes, bars, banks, gaming saloons, and every invention of the devil." He cursed England's officials, military men, and politicians: "none of these classes have any ideal but a commercial one; and half the time they are being led by the nose by the Jews."

In this climate Hilaire Belloc felt free to write a sarcastic verse about "Jew Power" in South Africa. In a mock dirge, he portrayed the richest Randlords in the most unlikely role he could think of: brave and fallen soldiers.

> We also know the sacred height
> Upon Tugela side,
> Where those three hundred fought with Beit
> And fair young Wernher died.

He went on to describe:

> The little mound where Eckstein stood

And:

The little empty homes forlorn
The ruined synagogues that mourn
In Frankfurt and Berlin . . .

Belloc did not know—and did not want to know—that Randlord
Hermann Eckstein was the son of a Lutheran pastor, or that Beit's
partner Julius Wernher was a German Protestant; or, for that matter,
that Beit's parents had converted to Christianity before Alfred was
born. To the British anti-Semite, as to the German thirty-five years
later, it was enough to have a name that sounded Jewish, or to have
a Jew as a business associate; somehow, the villainy rubbed off. One
hostile biographer, unwilling to accept Rhodes's character flaws as
English, describes him as having "aquiline features, slightly Hebraic
and distinctly predatory."

Others had better reasons to hate Rhodes. The South African novelist
Olive Schreiner, herself of Jewish origin, turned on the Colossus when
he backed a bill granting whites the right to flog their black employees.
Trooper Peter Halket of Mashonaland was a screed disguised as a novel,
but it became to the Little Englanders what *Uncle Tom's Cabin* had
been to American abolitionists.

In an early chapter the hero sees a vision of Jesus Christ. "Why,
you seem to have been everywhere," the soldier exclaims. "Have you
seen Cecil Rhodes?"

"Yes, I have seen him," says the stranger.

"Now, *he's* death on niggers," replies Peter Halket, warming his
hands by the fire, "they say if we had the British Government here
and you were thrashing a nigger and something happened, there'd be
an investigation, and all that sort of thing. But, with Cecil, it's all right,
you can do what you like with the niggers, provided you don't get
him in trouble."

Jesus preaches on, Halket is born again, helps a black prisoner escape,
and in the denouement is martyred for his efforts.

Schreiner worried about her melodrama. Would it be credible to
those outside South Africa? She acquired a military photograph and
persuaded the publisher to add it as a frontispiece. The first edition
of *Trooper* shows several Africans dangling mutilated from a tree. The
lynch mob is clearly visible: its members are supposed to be mercenaries

of the Charter Company, in the pay of Cecil Rhodes. Readers recoiled, and the picture was dropped from subsequent editions. But it had accomplished Schreiner's purpose. Rhodes was increasingly perceived as a racial tyrant and a discredit to Victorian England.

The Little Englanders' contempt for Rhodes was crystallized in G. K. Chesterton's ironic comment—that Cecil Rhodes, instead of promoting Western ideals, "illustrated almost every quality essential to the Sultan, from the love of diamonds to the scorn of woman." There was a further irony. In the end it was not diamonds that finished Rhodes, nor his insidious political maneuvers, nor his racial brutality. The great misogynist was undone by a woman.

Princess Catherine Maria Radziwill tended to natter on about her early life in the *haut monde* of St. Petersburg and Berlin. But she was not a female version of Baron von Veltheim. Her credentials were legitimate. The Princess was the only daughter of an exiled Polish nobleman living in Russia. He had married her off to a German prince at the age of 15. Five children later the couple separated, and Maria Radziwill, her beauty beginning to fade, went off to London to seek the main chance. She thought she saw it in the bachelor Cecil Rhodes, and made advances at a dinner party.

Predictably, Rhodes showed no interest. She contrived to meet him again, this time during an ocean voyage aboard the fateful *Scot*—the same ship from which Barney Barnato had leaped a few years before. Sailing from Southampton to South Africa, the Princess treated Rhodes to a barrage of coquetry and flattery. Out of courtesy he invited her to tour Groote Schuur some time. Catherine Maria misinterpreted this as the opening move in a courtship, and after the first visit she took to dropping in unannounced. Rhodes, who could order whole countries around, was incapable of dealing with a female. Instead of asking her to go away, he kept a horse saddled so that he could retreat whenever a servant announced that the Princess was at the door.

As he galloped off one morning she wandered into his study. Late in the afternoon Rhodes's secretary reported that some important papers were missing—probably the missing telegrams from the days of the Jameson Raid. For a while it seemed that the Princess had disappeared as well. In 1901, as the Boer War raged on, Queen Victoria died; Catherine Maria seemed far away from the tribulations of Cecil Rhodes.

From time to time he heard about the Princess: she had founded a short-lived newspaper; she circulated promissory notes bearing his signature; she claimed that Rhodes had asked for her hand in marriage.

At first he ignored the reports, then realized that he had to take legal action, claiming rightfully that the checks were forgeries. Men were sent around to bargain. If she returned his missing papers, all charges would be dropped. She refused. The Colossus bore down. "It was necessary," Catherine Maria was to recall, "that I should be punished and besides disgrace me [sic], so that anything I should say later on should be disreputed."

In order to discredit her, Rhodes had to appear in a Cape Town court. His doctors advised against it; his heart condition had worsened, and any strain could prove fatal. But the Colossus insisted on having his way. Nothing about his health was allowed to leak out: the stock market might panic. Journalists were squared. The man who headed De Beers, who controlled so much of the world's gold supply, Mr. Cecil Rhodes—said *The Cape Argus* of February 4, 1902—looked to be in "capital health."

Witnesses in the court had a different view. Rhodes, overweight and short of breath, a florid old man of 48, gave his testimony. He had signed no notes for Catherine Maria. Papers she had shown the banks were bogus. After his painful speech Rhodes returned to Groote Schuur, where he lay near an open window, desperate for an alleviating breeze. From that point on, nothing went well for the Colossus or the Princess. He was obviously failing, and she was about to be convicted of forgery and sentenced to two years' imprisonment and permanent obscurity.

Rhodes never learned of her punishment. On the night of March 26, 1902, his heart gave out. "From the cradle to the grave, what is it?" he had once asked, and answered himself: "Three days at the seaside." In those three days he had literally put his name on the map. He amalgamated the diamond fields and built De Beers into a financial superpower. From his headquarters in a sere and difficult country he created more capital than any other civilian in the nineteenth century. Even in death the Colossus continued to exercise enormous power; his last will established the Rhodes Scholarships that would educate thousands at Oxford and exert enormous international influence.

The funeral was of course a grand affair, held in Cape Town Cathedral. The body was then conveyed north by rail, "accompanied," says one awed account, "by all the outward and visible signs of mourning which as a rule are only to be witnessed on the burial days of kings." As the car passed by, farmers doffed their caps, troopers presented arms, local dignitaries stood at attention. The Matabele, high in the Matopo hills, shouted their highest word of tribute— "Bayete!"—to the white chief they had held in awe.

Before the echoes died out, critics began chipping away at the pedestal, then at the whole statue. An obituary in *Le Temps* expressed the Continental view. Cecil Rhodes "was without religion, without love, and without ideals; he lived only for his schemes, and enjoyed life only as a cannon ball enjoys space, travelling to its aim blindly and spreading ruin on its way. He was a great man, no doubt—a man who rendered immense services to his country, but humanity is not much indebted to him." In England his grandiose fantasy was recalled: "The world is nearly all parceled out," Rhodes had said, "and what there is left of it is being divided up, conquered and colonized. To think of these stars that you see overhead at night. . . . I would annex the planets if I could. I often think of that." Many heads nodded in agreement when Olive Schreiner said the Colossus was "too big to get through the gates of Hell."

Rhodes's defenders—and there were many—pointed to the man's lack of personal self-aggrandizement. To the end he had dressed and lived without ostentation: "I want the power," Rhodes liked to say, "let who will wear the peacock's feathers." His friend Rudyard Kipling provided some memorial verses, saluting the

> Dreamer devout, by vision led,
> Beyond our guess or reach
> The travail of his spirit bred
> Cities in place of speech.
>
> . . .
>
> The immense and brooding spirit still
> Shall quicken and control,
> Living he was the land, and dead
> His soul shall be her soul!

As evidence of that vision, Kipling could point to Rhodes's will. The estate was worth over £6,000,000, an enormous fortune at the time. Hardly any of it went to his survivors. Oriel, his old college at Oxford, received a generous bequest for its faculty and for a series of new buildings. Groote Schuur was left in trust as a residence for future Prime Ministers. Rhodes had mistakenly assumed that Rhodesia would keep his memory green for at least 4,000 years. Actually, the provision that saved his name was the establishment of the famous Rhodes Scholarships. This was the final version of his Secret Society, concocted when he and the diamond fields were young together. The grants would ensure, he thought, a steady procession of stalwart Anglo-Saxon males. They would be chosen for their scholastic achievements, their love of sport, their manly and moral characteristics.

In short, for everything that Rhodes had never been.

◆   ◆   ◆

THE BOER WAR wound down in the early months of 1902. To Americans the battles bore an eerie resemblance to their own Civil War. Just before the fighting began South Africa's Chief Justice accurately predicted, "What a legacy of hate for the future!" As in America, the losers had begun with sudden victories and a sense of euphoria. The winners, smarting, announced that they had the bigger forces, the better equipment. It would be a short conflict; the boys would be home for Christmas. Both sides were wrong. Spectacular triumphs on both sides gave way to guerrilla warfare. It ground on for almost four years. More deaths were caused by fever and infections than by bullet wounds. In the end the Boers were undone by casualties and desertions, and by Britain's ruthless scorched-earth policy that ruined farms and towns.

The echoes of Antietam and Gettysburg resounded across the Atlantic. To many American minds, England was still the enemy of the Revolution and the War of 1812. For them, Britain's enemies were automatically friends of the United States. So it was that a New York congressman proposed that the Secretary of State "invite the whole Boer people to settle on the public lands of the United States," and that the governor of Arkansas offered five million acres as a gift to the Boer nation. Colorado made a similar suggestion. The official answer was always the same: "The Boers love Africa too well to think of emigration."

On May 31, 1902, the fighting stopped. A peace treaty was signed, and Lord Kitchener, Chief of Staff, held out his hand to the Boer delegates. "We are all good friends now," he said. Of all the lies told during the conflict, this was the biggest. Neither side expressed remorse or forgiveness. The British had lost 22,000, the Boers 24,000, of whom 20,000 were women and children, dead of starvation and disease in the concentration camps.

Only a few Britons gained any repute from the conflict. Sir Randolph Churchill's son Winston, a war correspondent, became famous with dispatches about his daring escape from a Boer prison. Lt. Col. R.S.S. Baden-Powell did almost as well. He admired uniforms and young men and combined them by going on to found the Boy Scouts. Lord Milner reigned as High Commissioner, determined to maintain British rule over the whole of South Africa. He promised that military administration would be succeeded by civil government "as soon as circumstances permit"—meaning that voting for civilian representatives would take place at his pleasure. "The ultimate end," he wrote, "is a self-governing white Community, supported by well-treated and justly-governed black labor from Cape Town to Zambesi."

Perhaps the greatest triumphs were enjoyed by the Randlords, who retained their mines and their bank accounts and their friendships with the Crown. The gold and diamond mines were reopened, and once more the profits flowed to the companies Cecil Rhodes had founded. From the Boer ranks only one man, a steely officer named Jan Smuts, emerged as a leader with a global reputation. Much would be heard from him in the next decade.

Both sides suffered permanent changes. Paul Kruger went into exile in Switzerland, where his life ended four years later. He never saw his country again. "Born under the British flag," he wrote after the war, "I have no wish to die under it." Queen Victoria and Cecil Rhodes had expired during the conflict, and with them had died the Cape-to-Cairo fantasy. The rallying cry at the start of the fighting—"We are all imperialists now"—gave way to feelings of revulsion and self-doubt. Of all people, Kipling's aunt hung out a black banner from her window, with the device, "We have killed and taken possession." George Bernard Shaw, who could never bring himself to condemn the conflict, wrote that "two hordes of predatory animals" had fought for the possession of a country "where neither of them has, or ever had, any business to be. . . . the moral position of the Boers and the British is precisely identical in every respect; that is, it does not exist. Two dogs [fought] for a bone thrown before them by Mrs. Nature, an old-established butcher with a branch establishment in South Africa."

The bone was mineral wealth, and in the bitter peace the Randlords became everyone's favorite target. Labouchere and Hobson continued to rail about the Hebrew profiteers, and in London a musical entitled *The Girl from Kay's* had as its central character a comic South African millionaire called Hoggenheimer, referred to by the chorines as "Piggy." Nothing more needed to be said: the name and the country of origin indicated that he was a Jewish parvenu, ripe for parody.

At the finale, the leading lady sang of her ambitions:

> When driving through the Park
> Perhaps you may remark
> A silver-mounted perfumed petrol motor trap;
> You'll see me on the box
> In furs of silver fox,
> With just a few big diamonds in my cap.
> I'll marry Hoggenheimer of Park Lane,
> The money he is winning
> I'll set it gaily spinning;
> And ev'ryone that sees me will explain
> That I'm Mrs. Hoggenheimer of Park Lane.

The chorus concluded:

> He may be made a peer
> A baron, a viscount or a belted earl
> He'll be Lord Hoggenheimer of Park Lane,
> And prove he is descended
> From Norman barons splendid!
> And she'll have royal blood in every vein
> When she is Countess Hoggenheimer of Park Lane!

The Girl from Kay's traveled to Johannesburg, where it played for one season. The caricature, however, came to stay. Late in 1902 a political cartoonist co-opted him, and Hoggenheimer entered South African mythology as the big-bellied, hook-nosed Shylock in search of profit and reputation. A young German Jew could not have chosen a worse time to enter South Africa. And if his name was Oppenheimer, he was practically begging to be savaged. But what was Ernest Oppenheimer to do? That was his surname, and he had no intention of hiding his identity. Instead he would have to cloak his ambition.

Ernest was born in Germany in 1880, the fifth son of a bourgeois merchant with modern ideas. Eduard Oppenheimer encouraged his sons to move on, preferably to England because "in England everything is allowed except what is strictly forbidden. In Germany everything is forbidden except what is specifically allowed." And what was forbidden most of all was a future for young Jews.

Bernard and Louis Oppenheimer honored their father and found jobs in the diamond business. Bernard was first in Kimberley, followed by Louis, who then went on to London. Ernest watched their careers enviously and, at the age of 16, left school to follow their example. Louis got him a job with Anton Dunkelsbuhler, a frowning taskmaster who believed in winning by intimidation. His bald head caught the light as he walked around his London establishment, terrifying the young clerks. Once when Ernest was filling the inkwells, he spilled some ink on the boss. "Diamond expert!" The boss exploded. "Diamond expert! Why, you wouldn't even make a good *waiter*."

He kept the young man on anyway. The other Oppenheimers had worked out; and besides, Ernest was beginning to show a unique gift for sorting diamonds. He appeared to know instinctively which rough stones would be jewels of the first water and which would have to be cut up into small, undistinguished baubles. "Dunkels" expected his staff to work long hours, but Ernest worked longer than the other clerks. He not only studied diamonds, he studied South Africa, examining records of mining operations, profits, futures. And he read continually and enviously of the Randlords.

They had gone to Kimberley when it was New Rush, when a man with a shovel and a pail and a mind could make millions. Those days were long gone. Since he could not be a man of wealth, Ernest decided, he would be a man of leisure. He would work hard, save £50,000, invest it wisely, and live on the interest. The rest of his life he would spend as an Edwardian gentleman, reading and filling in the blanks of an abbreviated education.

But first one had to get on at the office. He redoubled his efforts. One of his young colleagues recalled that, watching Ernest, "I sometimes told him 'you'll emulate Cecil Rhodes,' but he did not like my teasing him or my mingling into his business." On November 21, 1901 Ernest became a naturalized British subject. The following May the Boer War ended, and after some industrious office politicking he boarded a boat for South Africa. The old man had decided that his Kimberley office needed a younger man in charge of things.

The current Dunkels representative took the news hard. Leon Soutro was a middle-aged bachelor with an impressive business background. The upstart who had elbowed him aside was 22 years old. Soutro sent what must have been an uncordial wire. Up until then Ernest had been a model of conciliation, unfailingly polite and accommodating to his elders. For the first time he bared his teeth. "Your telegram received," he wrote back. "Meet me at station to look after luggage. Oppenheimer." And Soutro did.

Aside from the luggage, £50 was all Ernest had to his name. To save money he resided with his mother's cousin Fritz Hirschhorn, another diamond connection. Hirschhorn had been on the fields since the early days, and he had become a considerable personage. He held a position at Wernher, Beit and served on the board of De Beers. It was clear that Ernest could expect no favors; the young man had to make his own way. Still, the home was luxurious and full of servants, a far better situation than anything an immigrant could find on his own. And in the evenings some celebrated guests came for drinks or dinner: David Harris, Solly Joel, Alfred Beit, Gardner Williams, De Beers's consulting engineer. All of them, Ernest knew, would be invaluable to his career—if only it got started.

A fellow employee at Dunkels remembered the first time he saw Ernest: "He had just got to the town and I noticed him immediately; [Kimberley] was a little place and you always did look twice at strangers in those days. It was 1902 and a warm sunny day. His sleeves were rolled up and I noticed his arms immediately. I thought I'd never seen such muscular arms on any man. . . . 'Well,' I asked the man in charge of the office, 'who's that fellow with the big arms?' And he said it was a new man, Ernest Oppenheimer, who'd just been sent out from London. He said, 'I don't think very much of him from what I've seen so far. He's terribly shy, and he doesn't seem to be very bright.' "

Judgments like that had a way of getting around, and Ernest felt that he had to do something to establish his credentials in a town of young men on the make. He consulted one of his cousin's guests. "Every day I go there," Oppenheimer complained, "and I work as hard as anybody in the firm, if not harder. I sit down and sort diamonds with them. Yet somehow they don't respect me." "Of course they don't respect you for working hard," said Leander Starr Jameson. "If you want to be someone in the town, leave the task of sorting to others."

Dr. Jim was the greatest living authority on fame, obscurity, and rehabilitation. Only a few years before he had been jailed and disgraced following the Jameson Raid. He had nearly died of a circulatory ailment. But he refused to succumb to bad health or ill fame. Upon his return to South Africa, he had assumed the leadership of Rhodes's Progressive Party. He had unabashedly run for office and got himself elected to the Cape Parliament. These days he made no secret of his ambition to become Prime Minister. In past years he was a dangerous man to know; now it was dangerous *not* to make his acquaintance. Ernest hung on his every word. Here was the beginning of his true education. He heard of the dreams of Jameson's great friend Cecil Rhodes, and how they could still come to pass. He heard about the right people to cultivate, received the proper formula for mixing politics and business, the correct English attitudes toward race and ethnicity.

And yet he nourished the idea of £50,000 and independence until the day he was invited into De Beers's boardroom in Kimberley. It was then, as it is today, austere and hard-edged, looking out to a small courtyard, with matching fireplaces at each end. Portraits of great men looked down at a long table and leather-backed chairs. Rhodes, Barnato, Woolf Joel—only the dead would ever be allowed space on these hallowed walls. And there in a frame was the celebrated check for over £5 million. The life one could lead with that kind of money . . .

Solly Joel was in attendance. By this time he *had* that kind of money, and he let the world know what it meant to be a Joel, shuttling between opulent houses in London and Johannesburg, promenading on the decks of his steam yacht, strutting around his stable of racehorses. During a lull in the meeting he dipped into his pocket and pulled out a glittering piece of rock. It had come from banks of the Vaal River that morning.

"How much do you think it's worth?" he asked Hirschhorn and the others. The stone passed from hand to hand. Estimates rose with each man; this was a prize of prizes. Finally it came to rest in Ernest's hands.

"Well, Oppenheimer?" inquired Solly. "What's its value?"

"Nothing. It's not a diamond."

Joel looked indignant. "What do you mean?" he demanded.

"It's glass."

"You prepared to put £50 on that?"

Ernest took a breath and nodded. A diamond evaluator was brought in. He judged the rock to be nothing more than broken bottle glass, worn smooth from years under water and sand. Joel handed over the £50 and gave the audacious young bettor a rueful look. One day Ernest Oppenheimer would accrue more gold and diamonds than Rhodes and Barnato and Joel combined. But he savored that first victory more than any other. It was, he concluded, "the best £50 I ever earned."

PART TWO
SPERO OPTIMA

The prince being thus obliged to know well how
to act as a beast must imitate the fox and the lion,
for the lion cannot protect himself from traps,
and the fox cannot defend himself from wolves.
One must therefore be a fox to recognize traps,
and a lion to frighten wolves.

NICCOLO MACHIAVELLI

9

THE SPECTRE,
THE SCAM, AND
SATYAGRAHA

LATE IN 1898, the owner of a Johannesburg brickworks took time off to do a little diamond prospecting. On a patch of farmland his eye caught some suggestive gleams. He picked up one of the stones and pressed it against a small piece of plate glass. It made a deep scratch. Thomas Cullinan's heart beat a little faster: this was the most promising discovery he had ever made, and it belonged to someone who probably had no idea what the land was worth. Back in town Cullinan discreetly asked around; the farmer was Joachim Prinsloo, a Boer of deep religious conviction. More than once he had expressed a disdain for those who would seek earthly treasures instead of spiritual riches—diamond hunters, for example.

Aware that he might be recognized for what he was, Cullinan sent an emissary to do the bargaining for him. The man spotted Prinsloo, shouted a greeting in Afrikaans, and froze. A rifle was aimed directly at his heart. Negotiations ended there.

But time and circumstance were on Cullinan's side. The years of war had exhausted the family finances, and when old Prinsloo died his son and daughter agreed to listen. The prospector harangued and charmed them, just the way Rhodes and Robinson had done with pious Boers in the early diamond days. As 1902 drew to a close the Prinsloo children surrendered the farm for £52,000 cash. That was more than Cullinan had in hand; he raised the money by offering shares in something he called the Premier Transvaal Diamond Company.

Several years before, Rhodes had complacently informed his stockholders, "whenever you hear that a new mine has been discovered . . .

if De Beers are not there, they are very near the spot." Now Rhodes was gone, and De Beers was nowhere near the spot. The new Chairman of the Board, Francis Oats, looked over Cullinan's prospectus. Oats had been a mining engineer, and he thought he smelled a hustle. "The whole thing," he insisted, "was a fake." Someone—he named no names—must have salted the mine.

The new Premier mine went on without him, the native laborers and white supervisors working with the most primitive machinery, hauling up the yellow and blue dirt, pulverizing it, and sifting through the soil for precious stones. The process took much longer than Cullinan intended, and long before he could show a profit his money trickled out. New investors were needed—a whole flock of them. Or better still, one or two big capitalists. Bernard Oppenheimer, executive of the Lewis and Marks mining house, was invited to have a look at the diggings. Bernard brought along his brother Ernest, the man from Dunkels. They liked what they saw. Over a chorus of protests, both men persuaded their employers to invest in the new mine.

As Cullinan's diggers came upon more and more diamonds, Oats conceded that perhaps he had been a *little* hasty in his accusations of fakery. Nevertheless, he maintained, at De Beers "we are not alarmed or disturbed by these new discoveries, for judging by the work done up to the present our five mines are high grade in comparison with any of these new propositions."

Alfred Beit begged to differ. He had become a key member of the De Beers Board of Directors, and on a tour of the new Premier he realized at once that the company had let a fortune slip through its hands. Physically he had never been strong; the shock seemed to weaken him a little more. Little Alfred suffered a paralytic stroke and retreated to his country house in England. Cullinan went on to establish his own selling operation in London; the De Beers monopoly was broken. Within three years, production of the Premier Transvaal Diamond Company rose from 750,000 carats to 1,890,000. The Oppenheimers had been vindicated.

In 1905 a delighted Dunkels gave Ernest six months' paid leave. Not a moment of it was wasted. The young man visited his parents in Germany, then came to London to court Mary Lina "May" Pollack, a plump and comely young woman with a great deal in her favor. For one thing, she was a known quantity. She was Louis's sister-in-law: Louis Oppenheimer had married Charlotte Pollack in 1902. May was also uncommonly intelligent: she had just been accepted at Girton College, Cambridge. And, perhaps more significantly, she was the daughter of a past president of the London Stock Exchange. Once again, family ties were crucial in the rise of the Oppenheimers. Like his brother before him, Ernest would be marrying up into wealth and social position.

On June 19, 1906, newspapers reported that Ernest Oppenheimer, a bachelor of 26, diamond merchant by profession, son of Eduard Oppenheimer, gentleman, wed according to the rites and ceremonies of the Jewish religion Mary Lina Pollack, 19, daughter of Joseph Pollack, stockbroker, at his mansion in Kensington Palace Gardens. For May it was an especially large step: Ernest had decided that his future lay in Kimberley rather than London. That meant leaving her beloved father, forfeiting all plans for higher education, and settling in an unknown country. Ernest must have given her glowing accounts of South Africa. The young couple would live in the City of Diamonds, and it was not impossible to imagine themselves in a great house attended by a large staff. With luck and industry Ernest might become a latter-day Randlord, and May would be his lady. Maybe he could run for public office like Barney Barnato and Cecil Rhodes. One day he might even receive a title from the Crown. Stranger things had happened to white men in South Africa: Wernher had just been made a baronet; it was *Sir* Julius nowadays. One thing was certain: there would be no more talk of retiring on £50,000 a year.

◆   ◆   ◆

THE PROBLEMS OF ALFRED BEIT acted as counterweights to the general euphoria. First there was the business of his cousin, William Lippert, head of a Cape Town wool-buying firm. In order to save a troubled bank, Lippert had forged Alfred's name on a bill. Beit said nothing and, when the bill came due, he paid up. Emboldened, Lippert forged his cousin's name to another bill. It, too, was paid in silence. Only upon receipt of a third bill did Beit speak out, denouncing the forgery. The bank failed, and scores of depositors lost their savings. Lippert, formerly a leading citizen of Cape Town, fled to the United States where he changed his name and eked out a living as a bookseller. After five years he sheepishly returned to South Africa, throwing himself on the mercy of the court. It was in no mood for indulgence. In the witness chair Alfred struggled uncomfortably with the question: Why had he let the deceptions go unreported? Beit looked smaller than ever as he squirmed uneasily and answered, "I thought of only one thing—to save the family." It was not saved. Cousin William received seven years' hard labor, and Alfred was portrayed as an accessory to the crime.

The Raid was next. "Mr. Beit," the investigating committee had found, "contributed large sums of money to the revolutionary movement, and he must share full responsibility for the consequences." Those consequences amounted to little more than sneers from Labouchere and the other hostile commentators. Besides, in Alfred's mind he had really been guilty of nothing more than loyalty to his financial associate, Cecil Rhodes. He thought the criticism unfair, and he took it hard. Then had come the death of Rhodes, the war, the appearance of the new Premier mine, the stroke, and the terror that stalked him to the grave. An editor of *The Cape Argus* was to recall that Dr. Jameson "first let me into the secret that Rhodes's devoted friend and fellow millionaire, Alfred Beit . . . was firmly persuaded that artificial diamonds could be manufactured cheaply and that Kimberley and the diamond industry were faced with ruin. There appears to be little doubt that this 'spectre of the night' aggravated Beit's failing health and hastened his end."

The hideous disclosure had come from Paris. At the turn of the century a Nobel Laureate in physics announced that he could make tiny artificial diamonds in his laboratory. Henri Moissan regarded his experiment as little more than a chemistry lesson. The cost of creating tiny and imperfect stones had been prohibitive, and he saw no way to produce large, high-quality jewels at any price. One of his assistant engineers thought otherwise, and in 1905 Henri Lemoine let it be known that he had invented a process for creating ring-sized gemstones.

Beit's partner, Sir Julius Wernher, decided to see for himself. In the basement of a Paris warehouse, Lemoine gave a performance worthy of the medieval alchemists. He entered the room nude, in order to show the witness that there was nothing in his hands, nothing up his sleeves. Before Wernher's astonished eyes the Frenchman heated up a large electric furnace, placed his mysterious concoction on a long-handled spade, and thrust it into the crucible. After a sufficient delay he brought out some shapeless, ash-covered material. This was plunged hissing into cold water and then put on a table, where Lemoine picked through the mess for diamonds. He found twenty-five. Wernher took one stone in his fingers, held it to the light, and squinted through his loupe. There was no escaping facts: it was indeed a diamond, every bit as hard and flawless as the kind they were pulling from the ground back home.

Wernher arranged for a second demonstration with his partner in attendance. More diamonds came out of the furnace. Alfred Beit went pale. Something had to be done to keep this process out of unscrupulous hands; it could be more ruinous than I.D.B. Wernher took over. He agreed to underwrite further experiments if they were kept from the public. He added another demand: Lemoine would not be expected to reveal his formula, but he had to secrete it in a London bank. The sealed envelope could only be opened with the joint consent of Wernher and Lemoine, or in the event of Lemoine's death. The Frenchman agreed.

A laboratory was set up in the town of Argele in the Pyrenees. Gradually the costs mounted up until the final reckoning stood at £64,000. Wernher and Beit felt they had no choice. At least this way they could limit the production of artificial diamonds, and if necessary stop the process altogether.

Then came the first inkling of swindle. Wernher learned that the inventor was spending his days selling electricity from his generators to the neighboring towns. When a telegram suggested that the manufacture of diamonds was more important than the peddling of amperes, and that men would be soon coming up to see his magic furnace in operation, Lemoine replied that he had better things to do than entertain a bunch of prying executives.

Alarmed, Wernher sent word of the situation to South Africa. Francis Oats sailed for Europe at once. One of the chairman's first calling points was London, where he scrutinized a Lemoine diamond. He thought it bore a peculiar resemblance to the stones found at one of the Kimberley mines. He crossed the Channel and appeared at Lemoine's laboratory. Together, he and Wernher persuaded the physicist to grant one more encore.

Again the Frenchman entered in the nude, palavering about his miraculous discovery. But this was a different audience. If Oats had hurt De Beers's chances during the Cullinan business, he more than redeemed himself now. In the chairman's opinion, Lemoine smacked more of the music hall than of the laboratory. Oats saw ample opportunities for skullduggery even with a naked ringmaster. As the diamond maker chattered away, Oats did his own sleight of hand, palming a small South African diamond and flipping it into the furnace just before the electricity went on. According to Lemoine, the heat would be so intense that any ordinary diamond—as opposed to the created kind—would be reduced to ashes. But when the speaker's back was turned, Oats fished out his jewel and found it unchanged. Outside, he and Wernher talked over what had just occurred and concluded that the entire adventure, from the days in London to the mountain factory, had been an elaborate scam.

Wernher loathed the idea of summoning the police: the press would have a field day mocking De Beers and caricaturing the Randlord as goat. But pride had to be set aside; the diamond industry could never afford to let criminals go unpunished. Lemoine was arrested and brought to court with all the expected publicity swirling around him. Journals reported every legal nuance as prosecutors and defense attorneys wrestled with the fine points of the case. Lemoine offered to perform his experiment openly and let the people be the judge. Wernher wanted no more theatrics. He demanded to have a look at the formula. During the lengthy crossfire Lemoine was released on bail and fled to Constantinople, well beyond reach of the authorities.

With the confidence man out of the way, Wernher persuaded bank officers to open the sealed envelope. His worst suspicions were confirmed. Lemoine's great secret was expressed in a few sentences: one took carbon, such as coal, and heated it to a temperature somewhere between 1,700 and 1,800 degrees Centigrade. At this point, said the paper, it would obediently crystallize into gemstone. Any first-year chemistry student knew how preposterous this was, and soon all of Paris was chortling at *l'affaire*. Louis Cohen expressed great delight; it was always a pleasure for him to see a Randlord's top hat knocked off. Mrs. Lionel Phillips wrote a friend that "They roar with laughter at Wernher's name."

One of the laughing Parisians was an aspiring writer named Marcel Proust. The affair of the diamonds, he remarked, was "just like something in Balzac"—except that the novelist would have made something serious out of it. Proust could see nothing but comedy in the tale of Audacious Thief versus Humiliated Millionaire. He began "Pastiches and Mélanges," using the diamond scandal as a premise for parodies of Balzac, Flaubert, the Goncourt brothers, Saint-Simon, and many others.

In one passage Proust commented on his own misadventures in the market, where he held shares in De Beers. The mock diary of the Goncourts notes that "an eccentric friend . . . named Marcel Proust," ruined by the slump in diamonds, has killed himself. Edmund Goncourt plans to write a popular tragedy about the suicide. The next morning he is desolated by more bad news. The rumor is false; Proust is in excellent shape.

That was more than could be said for Lemoine. In the relaxed, not to say giddy atmosphere of *l'affaire*, the swindler thought he could safely return to France. But he had not reckoned on the persistence of De Beers. One night as he sat dining with his family, gendarmes appeared at the door. Without turning a hair he let them in and gestured to the table. "We are having our dessert, Messieurs. Would you like to have something to eat yourselves, or would you prefer a glass of Bordeaux?" He tried to maintain a similar nonchalance throughout his trial, but Sir Julius was not impressed. Nor was the judge, who discovered why Lemoine's "manufactured" diamonds looked so much like stones from Kimberley. They were from Kimberley. Lemoine had bought them from a dealer and hidden them in various crannies for use during his experiments. The defendant was sentenced to six years' hard labor for the crime of fraud.

♦   ♦   ♦

THE END OF THE AFFAIR came too late for Beit; he died at his palatial summer home in England on July 16, 1906, convinced to the end that artificial diamonds were about to destroy all that he had built. Little Alfred was the last survivor of that fateful night in Kimberley when

De Beers was created. Barney Barnato had jumped off a ship and drowned at the age of 43; Rhodes had perished in political disgrace at 48; Woolf Joel had been murdered at 34. Beit outlived them all, but photographs taken just before his death show him to have been a wispy and careworn old man at 53.

Beit's Christian funeral was heavily attended not only by British dignitaries but by every prominent South African in the country. His beloved mother came all the way from Germany, sitting on a hard wooden chair at the gravesite. When her view was blocked she spoke gently, and one could hear the source of Alfred's quiet manners: "Good friends, stand aside, if you please, I would see the last of my dear son."

Among his colleagues Alfred's Christian upbringing had always been a source of confusion. *The Cape Times* offered a posthumous salute to the Randlord. Recalling Beit's loyalty to Rhodes during the Jameson debacle, the *Times* concluded that the British learned "to be patriots from a Jew." The journalist W. T. Stead had a different view: he believed "there was something Christ-like about Alfred Beit." Beit's posthumous biography lists him as Sir Alfred, although he had never been knighted. The feeling was that King Edward *meant* to confer the title; like many others he had simply overlooked little Alfred in the crowd.

Exaggerations aside, Beit does appear to have been a higher type than the other diamond and gold men. Even his mistakes were born out of misguided loyalty to relatives and friends. He was the most cultured of the Randlords, a box holder at Covent Garden, owner of a fine library of German classical writers and English novelists (George Eliot was his favorite), and a collector of paintings by Rembrandt, Hals, and Reynolds.

No other South African magnate ever showed so much concern for his employees. Beit's correspondence is preoccupied with personnel matters: "We must treat X generously in this matter." "Have we been fair to Y?" "I think in this case Z deserves a bonus." His philanthropy was not as widely publicized as Rhodes's, but it benefited more people (Beit left a fortune of nearly £8,000,000; Rhodes's estate added up to some £6,000,000). The man who had never attended college endowed a chair at Oxford for the study of colonial history. His legacy financed railways, bridges, schools, and public buildings in Rhodesia; it provided real estate and money for the foundation of a university in Johannesburg. Some time before Beit had been asked how he wanted to be remembered. "Mark me as one who loved his fellow man," he had stated. Alone of all the Randlords, he got his final wish.

One way or another, all the rest suffered disappointment, humiliation, or exile. In his reminiscences, a veteran hand of the diamond and gold fields appraised the great men he had known: those "who dug for gold and diamonds and were lucky enough to find what they sought appeared to be unlucky in everything else." In the judgment of one P. Tennyson Cole, "they were the unhappiest men on earth. A camarilla of spite, envy and hatred engulfed them fiercely on all sides immediately they grew rich." That summarized the old crowd. Young Oppenheimer was part of the new one. Traditional German folk wisdom held that money couldn't buy happiness. Ernest had been studying the behavior of British gentlemen for ten years, and he knew better.

◆　◆　◆

THE NEWLYWEDS stepped into a different country from the one Ernest had left only six months before. The friends who greeted them had much to report, and very little of it was good. South Africa's economy was limping from its war wounds, and the politics of race and ethnicity stained every aspect of national life. Alfred Milner, now Lord Milner, High Commissioner in South Africa and Governor of the conquered Boers, set the ground rules. Primarily he wanted an "Anglicization" of the region. He intended to change the ratio of Boer to British by encouraging English families to immigrate. Meantime, he would "denationalize" the Afrikaaners by suppressing their language and culture. To help him accomplish these goals, Lord Alfred hired a group of young Oxford men—"Milner's kindergarten" they were called, though not to their unlined faces. Before they could deal with the Boers, they had to learn the official attitude toward natives. According to Milner, "A political equality of white and black is impossible." The white man, he elaborated, "must rule, because he is elevated by many, many steps above the black man, steps which it will take the latter centuries to climb, and which it is quite possible that the vast bulk of the black population may never be able to climb at all." For that reason, as Lord Alfred saw it, the natives would remain witnesses to, rather than participants in, national life, barred from voting and from having a say about where they lived or how they were educated. Blacks did retain one right. They could choose not to work in the mines. And they took full advantage of that freedom.

In the faltering postwar period, De Beers and other large companies had felt the need to cut costs. They began by reducing the salaries of their unskilled and semi-skilled workers. Singly, and then in groups, the blacks walked away. The number of African mineworkers dwindled to about 45,000, half as many as before the war. The owners felt pleased with that figure as long as conditions stayed on a downward course. But when the economy improved, the short-sighted Randlords suddenly realized their labor-intensive industries would be short of men—as many as 196,000 in the next five years. The Chamber of Mines actively recruited a group of Italian miners willing to work for low wages; or so they said. A boat bobbed in the Bay of Naples, waiting to take them across the ocean. The men never showed up. A correspondent came up with another idea. What if American blacks were sent back to their country of origin? Surely the United States would be glad to get rid of the people who had caused the Civil War, and "notwithstanding the inherent laziness of the race" they might be just what the mines needed. The kindergartners dismissed this suggestion as attractive but frivolous.

With the counsel of some mining executives, Milner finally hit on a practical answer. He would import Chinese workers. The low-priced coolies would be locked into three-year pacts, instead of the familiar three-month contracts. As bizarre as this sounded, the Imperial Government in Peking announced its enthusiastic approval. White laborers were aghast. Furious demonstrations against the "yellow peril" took place on the streets and squares until Sir George Farrar, president of the Chamber, issued a reassuring statement. Asians would "only be brought in under government control, and only as unskilled laborers, prohibited to trade, prohibited to hold land or compete with any white man." Yet an iron tone underlay his words. Sir George made it abundantly clear that nothing could dissuade him from bringing coolies to South Africa. Without them the mining industry would be crippled. It might even fold, along with thousands of positions for whites.

This was an argument the protestors could follow, and the objections ebbed away. Within three years some 60,000 Chinese made the long journey to a nation whose populace feared and despised them. For the Randlords, the arrangement could not have been happier. White miners would be earning an average monthly wage of more than £26; blacks, 52 shillings, threepence; and Chinese, 41 shillings, sixpence. No one bothered to ask the Asians what they thought about the situation, but their feelings may easily be guessed. From the moment they stepped on foreign soil, coolies could feel the resentment seething from both black and white onlookers. Other than shouted orders, no communication took place between the races, and the Chinese withdrew into their own sullen and insular society. They passed the time in the crowded compounds smoking opium, gambling, and fighting. Sometimes arguments erupted into violence and murder; sometimes the violence took place away from the compound, when coolies broke out and attempted to rob a local farmer. To the ruling powers, crime was a small price to pay for a revived mining industry. Milner's plan went down in their diaries and bankbooks as a success.

So it was until the repercussions began. A year into the arrangement, anti-Chinese demonstrators reappeared with a new message. No wonder the immigrants behaved like criminals: obviously China had emptied its prisons and dumped the occupants in South Africa. To quiet the crowds, Britain rescinded a postwar law: once again Boers would be allowed to own guns for "self protection." This only stirred up the British public. London journals ran stories of floggings, shootings, and physical intimidation. Parsons sermonized about the vice that might flourish when foreigners were locked up together for three years. Posters showed Chinese workers manacled to each other, marching dejectedly to "forced labor" in the mines. Old-style American abolitionists wrote letters to their newspapers. British Liberals and radicals made much of the horror stories, and Lord Milner found it necessary to declare that despite what they read or heard, corporal punishment was absolutely forbidden in the compounds. His enemies countered with evidence proving that managers regularly beat the Chinese offenders rather than bring them to court. The South African establishment stood exposed as liars and exploiters, and in the British election of January 1906, Liberals handed the Tories a resounding defeat, largely on the coolie issue.

Two months later a motion of disapproval was heard in the House of Commons. Winston Churchill, under-secretary for the Colonies, read an amendment designed to protect Lord Alfred: "This House, while recording its condemnation of the flogging of Chinese coolies in the breach of the law, desires in the interest of peace and conciliation in South Africa to refrain from passing censure on individuals."

Churchill's maneuver failed to mask the obvious. The British had lost their taste for imperial brutality. Milner was out, and so were the Chinese, who found themselves herded onto ships, headed back to their homeland. Only a few would avoid the net, to settle in this hot and hostile land that they now preferred to the Far East. Ambitious men saw a lesson in all this. Every issue in South Africa was a political issue. And politics now reached past the shores of Cape Town, to invade the corridors of Whitehall and Washington, D.C. To prosper in this land of diamonds and gold, one had to enter the government's arena.

That was a truth Leander Starr Jameson had learned from his friend Cecil Rhodes, and which he strenuously applied to his own career. From the disgrace of the Raid he had returned to South Africa and slowly climbed back to prominence, getting elected to Parliament and assuming leadership of the Progressive Party. Finally he felt strong enough to ask the voters a central question: who better than Jameson to assume Rhodes's old job? In 1904 they answered by making him Prime Minister of the Cape Colony. He had staged the most extraordinary comeback in South African history.

From the sidelines, Jameson's young protégé took notes and formulated his own political plans. Four years later Ernest Oppenheimer enjoyed a triumph of his own, getting himself elected to the Kimberley town council. It was a critical time for the diamond industry. Recession had begun in the United States and worked its way to Europe. Luxury items like diamonds and gold were the first to go. The residents of Kimberley witnessed something they had never seen before: soup lines and armies of the unemployed. To increase the distress, diamond discoveries had just occurred across the border in German South West Africa. Again, Oats dismissed the finds as "superficial deposits." De Beers turned up large stones, the only kind the rich were buying nowadays. From what he had heard, the German diamonds were small. Any large production in the South West, claimed the chairman, "will affect our competitors therefore in a far greater degree than they will affect the De Beers Company."

All the signs pointed to another Oats miscalculation, and Ernest knew it. But there was nothing he could do except muse and speculate. If only he were sitting on the board of De Beers . . . This was a form of idling, however, and the Oppenheimers were not known as wasters of time—their own or their employers'. The young executive turned back to his job at Dunkels, his City Council work, and his burgeoning family. The Oppenheimers' first son, Harry Frederick, arrived on October 22, 1908; the second, Frank Leslie, on October 17, 1910.

Everything was looking up. In the year of Frank's birth, the Afrikaaner colonies were granted responsible self-government. They united to form the Union of South Africa. The country would be part of the British Commonwealth, but it was to be autonomous. Elections followed; the South African National Party won an easy victory, under the leadership of two Boer generals. Louis Botha became the Union's Prime Minister. Jan Christian Smuts was named Minister of Defense, Mines, and the Interior. Although Smuts had to maintain a pose of absolute objectivity, he knew that the progress of South Africa depended on its mines. In an indiscreet moment he had admitted as much to Julius Wernher. The Party and the Randlords, the general said, had a number of "identical interests." Ernest knew about that conversation; he would find ways to get close to Smuts in the very near future.

Unlike most of the area's rising businessmen, Ernest preferred his home to the Kimberley Club. He and May attended some of the club dances, but the all-night gambling sessions were not for him. The diamond business had enough risks without the artificial stimulus of card playing. When Ernest was not at the office or at home, he was negotiating at the horseshoe-shaped table at City Hall. His newest enthusiasm was the amalgamation of Kimberley and the adjacent territory of Dutoitspan, now known by the grand name of Beaconsfield. This seemed an arcane issue, but a great deal turned on it. The other councillors were persuaded by his arguments, and in 1912 the merger was written into law. Each ward voted in its new representatives, and they in turn voted for the new mayor. Their choice was unanimous: Ernest Oppenheimer.

The senior partners and grand old diamond men took note of this anomaly, a politician who won the enthusiastic approval of other politicians. Clearly, the 32-year-old Mayor was one of the coming personalities. Still, he was a comparative youth, and they waited for his first speech. It could not have been more reassuring. "Efficiency," he announced, "rather than new ventures must be the watchword." So young and already a fiscal conservative; Ernest was in. Jagersfontein, an important diamond company, elected him to their Board. He put on a bit of weight, not as a matter of indulgence, but to give himself some physical authority. A contemporary oil painting shows him in his fur-trimmed mayoral robes, a gold ceremonial chain draped around his neck. Ernest might be one of the prosperous Jews who had fascinated Rembrandt.

He assumed office at exactly the right time. Western economies had begun to right themselves, and conspicuous consumption had returned to the drawing rooms and parlors of the Western world. The City of Diamonds was vigorous once more. Crowds queued up impatiently at the new motion picture palaces with magical names: the Trocadero, the Vaudette, the Olympia. Indian and colored storekeepers returned to the market square, presiding over mounds of brightly colored vegetables and fruits. Long-silent auctioneers boomed the virtues of secondhand furniture and clothing. Evenings no longer depended on the stars and moonlight; under the humming electric street lamps Kimberley had an American dazzle, heightened by polished plate-glass windows on most of the storefronts.

In 1913, women—white women—received the franchise. Ernest ran for reelection and won in a walk. To almost everyone he represented affluence, responsibility, optimism. Under the Oppenheimer administration, De Beers agreed to supply the trams with electricity from its mineside generators. Finally, in the summer of 1914, the company took over the entire tram concession. Critics opened their mouths to protest this collusion with the diamond powers, and promptly shut them as fares dropped and efficiency increased.

Another vital decision took place that summer, although it was given light coverage in the local press. For many months Jan Smuts had been negotiating with an Indian lawyer, Mohandas Gandhi. The barrister had come to South Africa to appear for Indian clients, most of whom had come as laborers or as shopkeepers. The country's racial laws had defined them as "colored," and they were therefore disenfranchised. Then an additional insult was tacked on: they were to pay a special £3 tax. For his efforts and protests, Gandhi had been arrested many times. But prison had not broken his spirit, and he had never relaxed his demand: the tariff on his countrymen must be rescinded. After several strikes and some pressure from London, Smuts agreed to a face-saving "Indian Relief Bill." It scrapped the tax forever. In July, Gandhi triumphantly returned to India, to the relief of white South Africans. They believed they had seen the last of the irritating policy Gandhi had called *satyagraha*—passive resistance. Ernest had no reason to believe it would ever touch his life or the life of his industry. That July he was riding too high to look down.

But the very next month came the guns of August, and with them the end of Oppenheimer's mayoralty and, nearly, the end of Oppenheimer himself. The first weeks of the Great War almost destroyed Kimberley. With Europe in turmoil, diamond sales abruptly ceased. Once again thousands of miners were thrown out of work. Talk of black protests and white riots rippled through the town. Ernest assigned extra police to the compounds and organized public works; he knew all about hard times. The mayor's air of calm soothed the townfolk, and he was asked to serve an additional term.

Oppenheimer was reluctant to devote three more years to municipal affairs. But now he had something to prove: city councillor Fred Hicks had called for the mayor's resignation. A man with a Frankfurt accent, he said, should not be in a position of leadership at this time: "it would be graceful on his part if he retired at the present juncture." At one meeting Hicks filibustered until Oppenheimer banged the gavel and called for adjournment. Hicks objected: "It is a German ruling, not a British." In the ensuing weeks Ernest responded by trying to out-Kipling Kipling. He raised a battalion for the Kimberley Regiment, vigorously canvassed for the Red Cross, and saw to it that every man on active service received a signed Christmas card from the mayor himself. "We know you will be a credit to Kimberley," Ernest told one troop of foot soldiers, "and to the Empire of which Kimberley is a part."

To his enemies, showy patriotic gestures proved nothing. They circulated a handbill headed "A Lesson in Manners for Mr. Oppenheimer" on the streets, noting that the German-born mayor of Coventry had resigned. In May 1915 they got their wish. That month the *Lusitania* was torpedoed and sunk by a German U-boat off the coast of Ireland. Some 1,300 men, women, and children drowned in the disaster, and when the news hit South Africa, it ignited a series of anti-German demonstrations. Johannesburg was first to feel the wrath of the mob; several days later the torches of angry men lit the streets of Kimberley.

Oppenheimer got the message and unhappily gave up his office, too late to slow the momentum of protests. A knot of angry men passed by a barbershop whose proprietor had a Teutonic name, Pfeffer, and burned his establishment to the ground. From there they went on to smash windows and break down doors, to destroy bars and stores. The uniformed Defense Force stood by, partly in sympathy, partly in fear; the police were vastly outnumbered. Demonstrators rampaged through the town's Diamond Market, a group of one-story buildings where they broke more windows and tore down the brass plates of F. Hirschhorn and E. Oppenheimer. Someone shouted an address, and the others followed him to No. 7 Lodge Road. By the time the mob arrived, Ernest had taken his wife and small children to a less conspicuous home. From there the Oppenheimers could only wait until the violence spent itself.

The following day May and the boys were spirited off to the peace of Cape Town. Ernest stayed behind to take care of business, but he never got to the office. A group of agitators, still seething from the night before, spotted his automobile en route. They picked up rocks and hurled them at the windshield. One of them scored a direct hit. Ernest cleared away the shards, blinked through a stream of blood, and jumped from the car. He ran down the street toward the Kimberley Club. Footsteps clattered behind him. He plunged into the nearest building. The thugs hesitated at the doorway. Had their quarry entered almost any other structure he would have been followed, beaten, and possibly murdered. But this was a convent belonging to nuns of the Holy Family, and not one man dared to violate it. The sisters bathed Oppenheimer's severe cut, summoned the police, and asked them to escort him home.

But what was home? Not the City of Diamonds; not any more. "I had been a hero to the people of Kimberley," he was to recall. "Now my very name was hated." Not Johannesburg, where riots still went on. Cape Town remained quiet, but no one there knew about diamonds, and diamonds were all that Ernest knew. Well then, where? He joined his family at the Cape and pondered the situation from their hotel. Stories in *The Diamond Field Advertiser* only increased his misery. Hypocrisy was the order of the day. Now that Oppenheimer had left town, the agitators denounced the very violence they had provoked. Fred Hicks was shocked to find that the mayor "had been threatened, as two attempts had been made to burn down his house. His office had also been damaged. This [Hicks] considered to be totally un-British." The rest of the council replied with a hearty "Hear, hear."

That settled it. Since Ernest's city could no longer be trusted, the Oppenheimers would migrate to May's city. The plan was risky: enemy submarines plied the Atlantic, and even if the passengers arrived safely, who could say what awaited them? Liverpool, the *Lusitania*'s home port, had already been the scene of some vicious demonstrations against the German-born. Still, the voyage to London was a necessary risk. At least Ernest and his family would be removed from an ungrateful Kimberley. Forever, he hoped.

10

MONKEYING ABOUT WITH THE CAPITAL

WHILE ERNEST TRIED TO FORGET about Kimberley, his associates could not stop laughing about it. Their merriment had nothing to do with the Oppenheimer misfortunes. Two old diamond field veterans had recently engaged in courtroom battle; they were the ones who provided England with comic relief from the Great War.

By now, many of the Randlords had moved to London, where they had bought mansions and showed off their possessions. Sometimes respectable papers reported their comings and goings; other times their backgrounds were recalled in *The Winning Post*, a London scandal sheet. In 1910 readers were intrigued by an anonymous writer. "I could a tale or two unfold if I liked," he boasted, "but there is a blue pencil suspended over my head, like the sword of Damocles, fear of which stays my hand, to the great relief of certain South African financiers."

Like most people who live under a sword, he eventually became numb to the danger. All sorts of indiscreet and unflattering anecdotes began to flourish in his column. They concerned Barney Barnato, who was safely dead, and Joseph Benjamin Robinson, who was 74, infirm but very much alive. J.B.R. was remembered as "sour-visaged . . . yellow as a bad apple," and his character as craven. During the Boer War the colonel of the Diamond Field Horse had deliberately avoided combat, claimed the writer. *Au fond* Robinson had been "a soldier who disdains to fight, a politician with no politics, an orator without speech, a financier *sans* spirit or tact, a music-lover bereft of hearing, a philanthropist lacking charity, a man without friends and a patriot without country." For lagniappe, J.B.R. was accused of cheating customers from his earliest days as a trader. One Boer had bought a sack of coffee from him only to find it weighed down with pebbles.

Whatever the validity of the other charges, it was not true that Robinson lacked spirit and tact. Some years before he had vigorously spread his wealth around in the right places, and in 1908 King Edward VII had made him a baronet. Perhaps that was why Sir Joseph made such an inviting target. Certainly that was why he made no reply: aristocrats never swatted gnats; they affected not to feel their stings. However, when the cascades were published in book form in 1911, entitled *Reminiscences of Kimberley* and signed with the name of Louis Cohen, J.B.R. reverted to type.

Then again, so did Cohen. As Barney Barnato's first partner, he had been in on the ground floor at Kimberley. But he had had no luck and no instinct for diamonds, or for money in general. Men he regarded as his inferiors accumulated huge fortunes; all Cohen possessed was his pen. He had dipped it in vitriol and composed his memoirs, assuming that his would be the final word on the old diamond days. He had reckoned without Robinson.

The retired financier left nothing to chance. He hired Edward Carson, the brilliant prosecutor of Oscar Wilde, and at considerable expense sent for a number of prominent witnesses from South Africa to testify on his behalf. Weary of war news, the press closed in, much to the distress of the principals, who paced nervously on the sidewalks, consulting with friends, puffing cigars, and pretending to ignore the photographers. Inside, both opponents seemed to wither in the artificial light. J.B.R., bent and moving slowly, was heavier than he had ever been and almost stone deaf. Cohen, aged 60 and still handsome in a music-hall way, put on a show of bravado that fooled no one. A harrumphing Boer general appeared for the prosecution, and a notorious jailbird for the plaintiff. Robinson shouted at reporters in order to hear his own voice. "The whole thing," he grumbled, "is a farce."

So it seemed when Cohen's defense called its first character witness, Emile Berger. The prosecution quickly exposed him not only as a confidence man, but as a person who scarcely knew Cohen. Step by step Berger was induced to confess that he had never been to the diamond mines, never been to South Africa, never in fact been to Africa at all. From there on it was all downhill. After several weeks the judge found Cohen "steeped in malice" and awarded Robinson £1,000 in damages. *Reminiscences of Kimberley* was ordered to be withdrawn from the bookstores. Deprived of his income, the defendant declared bankruptcy.

For Cohen there was much worse to come. J.B.R., dissatisfied with merely ruining his accuser, brought him to court once more. This time it was to face charges of conspiracy to commit perjury with Berger. Again Cohen lost. The judge lectured him for "wickedly suborning" his witness "to tell deliberate lies, which he knew were lies . . . I should pass a more severe sentence. . . . But you are an old man, and I think I can meet the justice of the case by passing on you the same sentence as was passed on Berger . . . three years' penal servitude." Robinson retreated to his great house in Park Lane, and Cohen to the confines of his prison cell. Londoners assumed that they had seen the last of both men.

◆   ◆   ◆

As soon as the Great War commenced, Otto Oppenheimer enlisted in the artillery and went off to France, hoping to redeem the German family in English eyes. His brothers Gustav, Louis, and Ernest continued to work in the British diamond industry, vigorously contributing to wartime charities. Bernard outdid them all. Before the conflict he had risen to full partner at Lewis and Marks, then gone on to form his own South African Diamond Corporation. Bernard had depended on the master cutters of Antwerp. But when the Kaiser's troops marched into Belgium, he made the dramatic gesture of abandoning jewels for bullets, importing "the latest and most wonderful machinery" from America and setting up a huge munitions factory in Hertfordshire. Three thousand men, most of them Belgian refugees, worked overtime. By the beginning of 1915 they were producing 10,000 shells a day. Salutes came from General Kitchener himself. "If we only had a half-dozen [like] Bernard," declared the Secretary for War, "there would never be a shell shortage on the Western Front."

If Bernard Oppenheimer had an ulterior motive, no one was unmannerly enough to mention it. Nevertheless, everyone at Whitehall knew that the German colony of South West Africa had recently posted a *Sperrgebiet*, a Forbidden Zone, along its beach. There, under close guard, natives were crawling with shovels in their hands and gags around their mouths to prevent them from swallowing the diamonds they were prying from the sand. The Prime Minister himself had called the German diamonds "a hideous calamity for us all," a calamity that might be eliminated by this convenient and well-timed war. As if to underline those words, Bernard got a message to General Smuts, back in Africa at the head of an expeditionary force. It was known that the general and his troops were headed for German territory in Africa; Bernard Oppenheimer would give £100 each to the first four soldiers to win the Victoria Cross. The first four to become members of the Distinguished Service Order would get £50. This information was received with the appropriate gratitude and huzzahs.

Now that his brother was held in such esteem by the government and the soldiers, Ernest began to have second thoughts about South Africa. Perhaps in this new climate it would be possible to return after all. Still, Kimberley had been vicious and London was safe. . . . Then one morning a letter arrived from De Beers's management, thanking the ex-mayor for services rendered. The company wanted to reward him somehow; would Ernest make an appropriate suggestion? He would. "I want," he informed them, "to be a director of De Beers." The disdainful reply was not long in coming: "Some time ago, it was tacitly agreed not to fill any vacancies in the directorate during the war and further, when the time arrives to do so, the prior claim of others will have to be first considered."

Instead of discouraging Ernest, this seemed to prod him. He would go back after all. Not immediately, and not to the thankless precincts of Kimberley; only a masochist would attempt that. But to some locale where a man was judged by the power of his brain instead of the thickness of his accent. There he might rise again and give the lie to those who had driven him out. The notion of revenge was not unpleasant; with it one could get through many a bad night.

In London Ernest went to work on a master plan. Through his brother Louis he got to know William Lincoln Honnold, an American mining engineer. Honnold held a number of executive positions with various gold companies. Yet desk work had never truly satisfied him; he was a man of action, and at the age of 49 gave up his profitable business concerns to direct the Committee for the Relief of Belgium.

Public-spirited as he was, Honnold refused to allow good works to occupy all of his time. Before he returned to his home in the United States he explored the city and its clubs, conversing in their spacious rooms.

In Ernest Oppenheimer Honnold found his ideal listener. The young man absorbed every lecture about precious metal. Prevailing wisdom held that finding gold was just like digging diamonds; the discoveries, however large, would be isolated in discrete spots around the land. Honnold disagreed. He believed that in South Africa the deposits were connected in what amounted to a vast underground sea of gold-bearing earth, stretching from Johannesburg to the Far East Rand. The area covered more than 100 square miles.

If he was right, then almost any mine had a fabulous potential. Ernest examined Honnold's theory from every angle. It could be the musings of a crackpot American. Or it just might be the story of Barney and the blue ground, rewritten for the new century. In ordinary times an owner could test things out, order his diggers to keep shoveling until they saw the glint of ore. But these were not ordinary times.

The troubles of Consolidated Mines Selection Ltd. showed why. Ernest's employer, Dunkels, owned a sizeable portion of CMS—and so did stockholders in Germany. The wartime British press were baying for blood and gold, demanding that the government take over such "enemy" holdings. Would the company be seized as the booty of war? Or would Britain hesitate to act? Should the directors sell out now? Or should they take their chances, hold on, and wait for the shooting to stop?

Someone had to go to South Africa and assess the situation. Minutes of the CMS board note that in April 1916, "On consideration of the various schemes now in progress requiring attention on the spot, Mr. E. Oppenheimer expressed his willingness to proceed to South Africa in the company's interest and the board accepted this offer with thanks."

And so at the age of 36, less than a year after he swore never again to set foot on the ungrateful land, Ernest boarded a ship of Indian registry and set off for South Africa. The Atlantic was infested with submarines and the vessel followed a winding route across the Mediterranean, through the Suez Canal, and down the east coast of Africa to the port of Lourenço Marques in Mozambique. From that point Ernest traveled the route used by Winston Churchill in his great escape from a Boer prison camp, rolling down to Pretoria and then on to Johannesburg.

After last year's humiliations and this winter's wet London weather, Ernest felt a reassuring warmth. No one in Johannesburg questioned his political loyalties or the fact that he was a diamond man among gold men. The company he represented was too powerful to ignore, and he was ushered into every significant office. What the executives told him was not so welcoming.

Lionel Phillips, now Sir Lionel and very much the grand seigneur with stud farm and English mansion, happened to be in Johannesburg looking after the interests of Wernher, Beit. He received Ernest Oppenheimer. So the chaps at CMS were thinking about selling off the company's gold mines, were they? The old man reminded his visitor that these were not the free-wheeling old days when investors pushed their pledges through windows and under doors. Today money men depended on researchers and technical advisors. Why, just the other day Sir Lionel's councillors had told him that time was running out for the gold fields of South Africa. In 20 years they would be depleted. If there was any precious metal in the East Rand it must lie at very deep levels, and the recovery of gold was not at all like digging up precious stones. The human cost of elevating ore to the surface—blasting, hauling, extracting—would be prohibitive. And there was this rapacious war that ate up capital while you watched. Well, he would not buy the CMS mines. And neither would anyone else in his right mind.

Ernest faced an excruciating and lonely decision. Honnold could not help him now. The American had gone back to the United States, and all he could offer was an occasional letter of advice and encouragement. Honnold agreed that the CMS properties could go one of three ways. They could be sold at a loss—in the unlikely event of a willing buyer. They could be held—but then the British government might take them over. Or—and this was the longest shot of all—Ernest, backed by CMS, could exploit the mines himself, searching for the gold that just might be within reach. According to the most conservative calculations that would require an investment of close to two million pounds. There would be land to acquire, equipment to purchase, men to hire.

Ernest took some deep breaths and sent word to CMS in London: he was ready to act independently, in the spirit of Cecil Rhodes converting a liability into a resource. The directors scratched their heads; obviously they had made a mistake sending this opportunist to South Africa. The chairman was most emphatic. He and his colleagues were "not prepared to monkey about with the capital of the company."

Having been ejected from Kimberley and refused in Johannesburg, Ernest had every reason to give up, go home to May and the children, and settle into the comfortable life of a middle manager. No doubt that was what the diamond men expected when he returned to London, waiting for an appointment with the CMS directors: poor Oppenheimer, this was just not his year.

They would have been astonished at the conversation behind closed doors in the boardroom. While the whisperers went on about Ernest and his failures, the Oppenheimer brothers had worked out a secret proposal. If CMS would provide the backing, Ernest would match the company's contributions pound for pound. His price was 50 percent of any new business CMS initiated in the East Rand over the next seven years. The executives reasoned that if Ernest could attract £1 million on his own, he would be a sound risk. They decided to go along. The agreement would need a few months of analysis and probing. If everything was in order, a contract would be drawn up dating from June 8, 1917.

Very well then, CMS was set; now all Ernest needed was money —pounds and pounds of it. Useless to look for investors in London; the European conflict was bleeding the banks dry. No group in South Africa could come up with adequate funding. Only one major nation still had investors with venture capital, because it was not yet at war. Ernest began to express himself in the grand terms of Cecil Rhodes: amalgamation was the key to power. He communicated with his main contact in the United States: with vision and sufficient funds, the Eastern Rand companies could be brought into the fold. He wrote Honnold, "It does not seem too optimistic to think that we shall be able, within a reasonable time, to bring about a willing combination of the . . . companies, which would straightaway make us the most important gold group in Johannesburg." Could Honnold put him in touch with some American capitalists?

He could. In a return message, Honnold advised Ernest to meet an American mining engineer now on his way to England. This person was more than the usual technocrat, Honnold went on. Herbert Hoover was an influential figure with broad contacts in the financial and political communities—someone definitely worth cultivating. Although Hoover's schedule was crammed with humanitarian and business meetings, he made time for Ernest. Three men shook hands in the lobby of the Savoy Hotel—Ernest had been advised to bring along a new acquaintance, the former Finance Minister of the Transvaal, Henry C. Hull. "If American capital wishes to obtain a footing in South Africa," Ernest began, "the easiest course will be to acquire an interest in our company." Hull provided assurances at every turn. It says much for their teamwork that, before the presentation ended, Hoover had already given the signal of approval. What would Mr. Oppenheimer think of bringing in J. P. Morgan as an investor?

Ernest attempted to suppress his excitement, but he could barely sit still. As soon as the men parted company he wired Honnold to proceed with the roundup of capital. Once the name of Morgan was dangled before them, other bankers fell in line. A pleasant difficulty arose: the investors wanted to know the name of this new company, and nobody had come up with one yet. The title, Ernest wrote to Honnold, ought to be one "which will make the American connection apparent, but the 'Africa' must also appear."

Back came a wire: "How about Union of South African Mines or United South African Companies? Either of which in market parlance would probably be abbreviated USA and thereby serve the purpose aimed at." Although the first name seemed "acceptable and excellent," Hull felt that the South African government would not be pleased with those initials. What about "African American Corporation Limited"? Honnold brought up the omnipresent topic of race: *"African American would suggest on this side our darkskinned fellow countrymen and possibly result in ridicule."* After some additional go-rounds, Ernest found a name that pleased everyone: "Consider it very necessary American identity should form part of company's title. Suggest the Anglo-American Corporation of South Africa, Limited."

Next Ernest tried to get approval from the upright war hero Jan Smuts. The general's prestige would lend Anglo-American some badly needed credibility and respect. Smuts was in Britain serving on the Imperial War Cabinet. He could hardly refuse an audience to the brother of Bernard Oppenheimer, benefactor of the expeditionary forces. One day later another auspicious message went out to Honnold. "I had a private talk with General Smuts some days ago on our new company. . . . The only doubt in his mind was whether it was not a case of taking an interest in a promising business, snatching a profit, and clearing out quickly. I satisfied him that this was not the case."

There were those who wondered whether Smuts was truly satisfied. They warned Ernest that the general was first and foremost a politician, anxious to please all sides while committing to none. Besides, in a Johannesburg brimming with potential labor problems, taxes, legal technicalities, what good was the unwritten word of a statesman? They were talking to the wrong man. Ernest felt that at times like these you had to go on instinct, or you didn't belong in the game. Over all objections he saw to it that the Anglo-American Corporation of South Africa, Ltd. was officially registered on September 25, 1917.

Before the creation, writers and editors expressed some doubts. Afterward, the press amounted to a cheering section. *The Rand Daily Mail* blared the news in a headline: AMERICAN MILLIONS FOR THE RAND. *The Times* of London took a long and approving view: "The link means the beginning of a new epoch, for it is the first occasion on which a definite arrangement has been made for the employment of American capital on the Rand."

Planning for the new epoch absorbed most of the next year, and it was not until the early fall of 1918 that Ernest was ready to nail things down in Johannesburg. He boarded the *Galway Castle* on September 25, two months before the armistice. Almost every day the papers carried reports of U-boats plying the Atlantic, but not many passengers took the threat seriously. Since America's entry into the war, it was obvious that the German navy was doomed.

Two days out, at 7:40 a.m., a violent explosion nearly tore the ship in half. An enemy torpedo had destroyed the boilers and cracked the keel. Steam rumbled and hissed through the corridors. The lights and wireless abruptly went off. Over 700 confused and terrified passengers thronged the entryways. Some of them were wounded soldiers returning from battle, lame and in several instances blind. They surged onto the crowded decks and vied for room in the damaged lifeboats. Ernest had been in his bath when the explosion occurred; all he could do was throw on shirt and trousers, clamber up the stairs, and urge the others to remain calm. When he looked out it was impossible to tell the difference between the gunmetal sky and the sea. One of the officers pushed him into a boat with seven other men and a woman, and lowered it into a chaos of water and wind.

They could count themselves lucky. Bodies floated by them, face down. Some lifeboats hit the water and broke apart. Others were swamped and disappeared. Their little craft bobbed and shuddered in high seas. Ernest's massive forearms were never more useful; he and the other rowers strained at their oars, attempting to get clear of the *Galway Castle* before she capsized and pulled them under.

By the time the wind abated they had lost sight of the ship and of the other lifeboats. Gray morning turned into sullen afternoon. Evening came on swiftly. Someone thought he saw a ship materializing on the horizon. For a moment it seemed to be an illusion, then an enemy boat cutting through the waves. As it approached they could make out the lineaments of a British destroyer. Frantically they fashioned a white flag from a handkerchief and waved it from an oar. The destroyer spotted them, pulled alongside, dropped a ladder, and plucked them from the water.

Hand over hand they ascended a rope ladder, to be received by waiting crewmen. Ernest was one of the last to come on board. An officer had been told to look for a short man with a moustache and an authoritative air.

"Mr. Ernest Oppenheimer?" he inquired.

"Yes, I am he."

"General Smuts wanted to know if you were lost or saved."

Any doubts about Ernest's importance vanished with that message. Ernest went below to sip a hot drink and put on some dry clothing. The head of Anglo-American regarded himself in the mirror with considerable satisfaction. The reflection showed a very fortunate 37-year-old, outfitted with the secondhand jacket of a chief petty officer. It fit rather well. But Ernest knew now that if there were a uniform commensurate with his civilian status, he would have to be dressed as an admiral.

◆　　◆　　◆

DURING THE WAR YEARS only a few men seemed as concerned about South African capitalism as Ernest Oppenheimer. One of them lived in Zurich, an isle of neutrality in the midst of conflict, and in 1916 he completed his pamphlet, *Imperialism*. "I naturally suffered somewhat," V. I. Lenin was to remember, "from a shortage of French and English literature and from a serious dearth of Russian literature. However, I made use of the principal English work on imperialism, the book by J. A. Hobson, with all the care that, in my opinion, that work deserves."

John Atkinson Hobson, South African correspondent for *The Manchester Guardian*, had recently found his "opinions and feelings were beginning to move in the direction of Socialism." His book, also titled *Imperialism*, was angry, accessible, and full of big villains—just the sort of tract that Lenin would find congenial. Hobson never advocated the abolition of private enterprise, but in the Russian's view that was because he was an Englishman and therefore hobbled by tradition. No matter; the revolutionaries would enlarge upon his opinions, particularly the ones about the Boer War. Hobson regarded that conflict as the connivance of "a small confederacy of international financiers working through a kept press" in the hands of "Hebrew mining speculators."

Hobson was one of the first twentieth-century writers to promote the conspiracy theory of history. His work righteously disavowed any hint of *Judenhetze*—Jew hatred—and then pointed to "men of a single and peculiar race" who make up "the central ganglion of international capitalism." Those of the Hebrew persuasion are "united by the strongest bonds of organization, always in closest and quickest touch with one another, situated in the very heart of the business capital of every State, so far as Europe is concerned." Johannesburg was particularly objectionable. Hobson was shocked to find that "the newspapers of September 13th contained the announcement 'There will be no performance of the Empire [music hall] today by reason of the Jewish

Day of Atonement.' The Stock Exchange was also closed that day."
He lashed out at those who "have behind them many centuries of
financial expertise." They were in a "unique position to manipulate
the policy of nations. No quick direction of capital is possible save by
their consent and through their agency." In his summing up Hobson
paused to offer a solution: an "international political organization" that
might someday oversee "a repression of the spread of degenerate or
unprogressive races."

Lenin was very impressed with all this; he particularly liked the
notion of South Africa as a capitalistic "shell which may remain in a
state of decay for a fairly long period . . . but which will inevitably be
removed." The Russian saw to it that *Imperialism* was widely read by
the young Bolsheviks. They would soon write their own words about
Johannesburg, much of it secondhand and most of it ignorant. Hardly
any whites, radical or reactionary, bothered to read a volume far more
revealing than *Imperialism*. Its author was an eloquent young Bantu
who produced *Native Life in South Africa* at almost the same moment
that Lenin was working on his own book. Sol Plaatje plaintively attempted to reach a white audience. "Some readers may think perhaps
that I have taken the Colonial Parliament rather severely to task," he
explained. "But . . . if you see your countrymen and country-women
driven from home, their homes broken up, with no hopes of redress,
on the mandate of a Government to which they had loyally paid
taxation without representation—driven from their homes, because
they do not want to become servants . . . you would, I think, likewise
find it very difficult to maintain a level head or wield a temperate
pen."

Plaatje was referring to the results of the Natives Land Act, which
delivered the coup de grâce to English notions of democracy. The act
forbade all blacks from buying or leasing any land outside designated
territories known as the Reserves. Africans were henceforth forbidden
to settle in areas marked for whites; they could stay there only as
laborers, even though more than a million of them had been working
as productive tenant farmers and sharecroppers.

The natives—two thirds of the population—would be relocated onto
22 million acres. To outsiders this seemed an enormous land grant;
what it actually meant was that 65 percent of South African humanity

was being forced onto 7 percent of the country. Allegedly, the act was meant to create "parallel institutions" for blacks and whites (more familiarly known as the principle of separate but equal facilities). In General Smuts's words, the races should be kept apart "in our institutions, land ownership, in forms of government, and in many other ways. As far as possible the forms of political government will be such that each will be satisfied and developed according to his own proper lines." The principle of separate but equal facilities was a canard from the start. The truth was that the mines were drastically short of manpower. After the law was passed the natives, taken from productive farms, would be left without any means of support. The government and the Randlords were counting on that; sooner or later blacks would have to turn to the mining fields, digging up gold and diamonds.

Originally Plaatje had trusted the liberal English speakers. Now he spoke out indignantly: "If anyone had told us at the beginning that a majority of members of the Union parliament was capable of passing a law . . . whose object is to prevent natives from ever rising above the position of servants to whites, we would have regarded that person as a fit subject for the lunatic asylum."

The act had swift and tragic consequences. Hardly any funds were provided for the adjustment period, and the native farm system totally collapsed. Poverty, with all its concomitants, took over. Infant mortality rose: every fifth child died in its first year. Crime became rampant. Blacks could neither go backward nor forward; their immemorial customs and common laws were shattered, yet their education was left to the ill-equipped missionary societies. Untrained, geographically limited, hampered by selective pass laws and taxes, the natives crowded back into the compounds.

♦   ♦   ♦

VETERAN DIGGERS never forgot the powerful culture shock they had experienced at New Rush: the strange, upside-down weather when it snowed in July and seethed in December; the primitive sanitation and the terrible spread of disease; the fortune-tellers and spider fights; the women auctioning themselves off to the highest bidder; the thefts and beatings in a place without laws or regulations. But all that was gentle buffeting compared with the new world of Johannesburg. The Kimberley of the past had been little more than a frontier town with quirky regulations and haphazard social arrangements. Mining took place in the open, the governmental hand was shaky, and native policy a matter of improvisation. The gold city presented a very different scene. A visiting Australian journalist attempted to describe it: "Ancient Nineveh and Babylon have been revived. Johannesburg is their twentieth-century prototype. It is a city of unbridled squander and unfathomable squalor."

Native life represented the squalor. For black men to take a freight train from their villages to Johannesburg was like entering some dreadful time machine. They stepped aboard in the tenth century, with its intense village life and age-old rites. They exited into the twentieth-century city of technology and segregation. At night the gold miners lived in all-male compounds; during the day they tunnelled deep into the earth, a dark, hazardous place of explosions and cave-ins. No matter what their ages, they were addressed as "boys," and mine owners made sure that they never matured into adult citizens. There would be no more bargaining for higher wages or better conditions. Natives were forbidden to go on strike, to hold office, to become managers of any kind. Schools, poor in every sense, served as little more than holding stations. In early adolescence children were expected to leave the classroom in order to refill the reservoir of cheap labor. Every native knew that he could be replaced overnight; hundreds of unemployed black men clamored for his job. The oversupply of native labor affected every aspect of Johannesburg life. No matter how underpaid, how menial the position, candidates were pathetically eager to take it.

Blacks were not the only ones to be appalled by their situation. Olive Schreiner wrote that "if, blinded by the gain of the moment, we see nothing in our dark man but a vast engine of labor; if to us he is not a man, but only a tool, [if] we reduce this vast mass to the condition of a vast, seething, ignorant proletariat—then I would rather draw a veil over the future of this land."

Because she was a white woman, Schreiner could only perceive the tragedy from the outside. Plaatje was at the heart of it. During a bicycle trip to the Orange Free State he saw a blizzard strike. "Native mothers," he remembered, "evicted from their homes shivered with their babies by their sides. When we saw on that night the teeth of the little children chattering through the cold . . . we wondered what these little mites had done that a home should suddenly become to them a thing of the past."

The plight of a rural black was even sadder. Kgobadi had been making £100 a year working for a white farmer. As soon as the law was passed the farmer reduced his salary by 75 percent. The native refused to work for starvation wages, and the farmer handed him a note. It ordered Kgobadi to "betake himself from the farm of the undersigned by sunset of the same day." Refusal to comply meant that "his stock would be seized and impounded, and himself handed over to the authorities for trespassing on the farm." No appeal was possible. Just then Kgobadi's baby fell ill. The family moved from their house to a drafty ox wagon, and two days later the infant died. It had to be buried illegally in the dark "lest the proprietor of the spot, or any of his servants, should surprise them in the act." Plaatje reminded his readers that "even criminals, dropping straight from the gallows, have an undisputed claim to six feet of ground in which to rest their criminal remains. But under the cruel operation of the Natives Land Act, little children, whose only crime is that God did not make them white, are sometimes denied that right in their ancestral home."

The writer, along with a group of like-minded black leaders, called a conference at Bloemfontein, near Kimberley, to determine the fate of their people. This "gathering of tribes," as one black observer put it, "had never before met except on the battlefields." On a feverishly hot day in January 1912, the keynote speaker set the tone of collective rage. "Chiefs of royal blood and gentlemen of our race," he began, "the white people of this country have formed what is known as the Union of South Africa—a union in which we have no voice." His message had been stated before, in periodicals as well as speeches: "The demon of racialism must be buried and forgotten." The natives of South Africa would have to band together for the good of all. Intertribal conflicts must go, for they had "shed among us sufficient blood. We are one people."

The man who held the floor was a firebrand called Pixley Ka Isaka Seme, related by marriage to the Zulu royal family. The audience knew all about him. Missionaries had arranged for his education at Columbia University in New York and at Jesus College, Oxford. Both places honed his sense of injustice, and the sight of blacks forcibly ejected from their homes had driven him to a number of notorious acts. Once he had actually settled into a Whites Only railway carriage. When his fellow passengers objected, he drew a pistol and was promptly disarmed and arrested. After a brief detention, he explained haughtily, "Like all solicitors, I, of course, travel first class."

In deliberate contrast, the Reverend John Dube called for "a hopeful reliance on the sense of common justice and love of freedom so innate in the British character." Surely "perseverance, patience, reasonableness, the gentlemanly tendencies of Africans, and the justice of their demands" would "even force our enemies to be our admirers and our friends."

Elections were held, and the moderate Dube won the presidency. In a rare compromise Seme accepted the title of treasurer, and Plaatje became secretary-general. Not one white newspaper reported the occasion. On the coalition went, warring with itself, arguing with the white leadership, challenging laws and customs, confident that one day history would make room for the African National Congress.

11

A SIDE ENTRANCE
TO DE BEERS

ONCE THE CONFLICT in Europe was over, most of the Randlords prepared to resume business as usual. Not Ernest. Even as Anglo-American explored the gold of the East Rand, he turned his attention to his first love, diamonds. The Diamond Syndicate was still in power. It was composed of Kimberley's four great diamond producers. De Beers dominated the group, accounting for 51 percent of the stones, followed by South West Africa (21 percent), Premier Mines (18 percent), and Jagersfontein (10 percent). In theory the syndicate was carrying out the ideal of Cecil Rhodes, engineering the price of stones by controlling the supply. In practice, things did not work out so neatly. When demand ebbed during World War I, for example, the syndicate acted exactly like any other group with merchandise on its hands; it simply lowered the price of its goods. To Ernest this policy seemed weak and self-destructive. A true cartel had to exert its authority under all circumstances, controlling the supply, creating shortages when necessary, hanging tough through catastrophes, depressions, and wars. Otherwise what was the point of having a syndicate at all? In his view the fault was not so much with the system, but with its practitioners. What the diamond industry needed was fresh thinking and new faces. Naturally, he wanted one of those faces to be his.

At the time he was still an executive at Dunkels, whose participation in the syndicate amounted to 12½ percent of the diamonds to be sold. None of that portion was Ernest's—not yet, anyway—and none of it gave him the power to move the syndicate in the direction he wanted. But he had a very clear idea of how to proceed. He would join the board of directors at De Beers. "Step by step," he told a colleague, he would work his way to "a leading position in the diamond world."

Ernest made no secret of his intentions, and the top executives at De Beers felt threatened by this ambitious climber. They resolved to keep him outside with his nose pressed against the windowpane. Frustrated, Ernest began to search for a side entrance, and in 1919 he found one. Some diamond mines in the German colony of South West Africa had been seized by the British victors. When the war ended, German owners sounded out the Bureau of Mines. Would it make sense for a recent enemy of the Crown to resume operations? Would it be better to sell the holdings and clear out? Friends in government told Henry C. Hull about these conversations, and he passed the information on to Ernest.

A few days later, Fritz Hirschhorn, De Beers's man in Johannesburg, called on Prime Minister Botha to inquire about the purchase of the same German properties. He was shocked to find that his own cousin Ernest had already come and gone without saying a word to him. Wounded and anxious, Hirschhorn fired off a cable to the London-based directors of De Beers: "From the conversations with General Botha there is no doubt that [our competitors] are endeavoring to obtain interests in South West Africa. . . . It is very important therefore that we should be first in the field . . . and, if possible, acquire rights from German holders subject to ratification by the Union Government."

After De Beers made further inquiries, it sent a cool reply: "German holders under belief they will remain in possession of their property and from our inquiries in Germany these holders are not disposed to sell at present."

While De Beers was busy cutting itself out of riches, Ernest and his associates were busy putting on long faces and persuading the German owners that they faced an uncertain and difficult future in Africa. Having talked down the diamond properties, they negotiated a price of £3,500,000 and pounced. Much of the money would come from J. P. Morgan's bank, and from Louis Oppenheimer's connections at Dunkels. On November 3, 1919, De Beers's Kimberley office sent some distressing news to headquarters. "The whole of the diamond interests in German South West Africa," said the cable, "have been acquired by Hull on behalf of Anglo-American."

A new corporation, Consolidated Diamond Mines of South West Africa, was established, with Ernest as both Chairman and Managing Director. The syndicate agreed to accept Consolidated's output of precious stones. In its first year the company would produce 20 percent of the syndicate's diamonds. Pushed, Ernest would have to admit that it was a pity about Hirschhorn; the man had been a generous host, and he had been so indulgent to May when the young couple appeared in Johannesburg—can it have been only four years ago? With enough diamonds in your hands, though, you no longer really needed indulgences. And with enough brothers in position, you no longer really needed cousins.

◆　　◆　　◆

IN 1869, QUEEN VICTORIA underlined her feelings in a letter: "To make a *Jew a peer* is a step she *could not* consent to. It would be ill taken and would do the government great harm." Not until 1885 would she consent to name any Hebrew a Baron of the United Kingdom, and then it was the irresistible Nathan Rothschild, whose father had loaned the British government four million pounds sterling for its great Suez adventure.

So much had altered since that time; Victoria had been succeeded by Edward VII, a collector of Jewish friends and their dialect jokes. And he had been followed by George V, a ruler with no objections to knights with names like Solomon and Abrahms and Oppenheimer. The London *Gazette* carried the announcement in 1921: Ernest Oppenheimer had been created a Knight Bachelor for taking "a leading part in recruiting of both combatants and laborers for various fronts during the war." The same list elevated Bernard a step higher than his younger brother. He had not only recruited war workers and manufactured ammunition; in peacetime he had established a diamond polishing industry for disabled veterans. For all these benefactions he was to be made a baronet.

These proclamations were greeted with a volley of cheers and a few lofty grumbles. It might have been thought that Winston Churchill would welcome a South African peer. His father, Randolph, had gone out of his way to cultivate the first diamond men; Winston established himself as a journalist in the Boer War, and he counted some mining men as his friends. But the Secretary of the Admiralty was displeased with the King's list. In a letter to Bonar Law, Britain's next Prime Minister, Churchill complained about the "disposition of peers" in the lists of honors. He specifically mentioned Bernard Oppenheimer as a type who buys his way into the House of Lords. The brothers got their awards nonetheless, and Ernest immediately selected a coat of arms and motto. He allowed himself a small and subtle reprisal against the town that had wounded him. On Kimberley's official stationery was the phrase *Spero Meliora*: I hope for better. For his motto Ernest chose *Spero optima*: I hope for the best.

He had every reason to hope. In America, William Honnold and J. P. Morgan promised to supply more capital for his business ventures. In South Africa, Jan Smuts, the politician Ernest had so assiduously cultivated, had just been made Prime Minister. Prosperity seemed to beckon from every corner, and in a burst of optimism the Oppenheimers bought a magnificent new home in Brenthurst, a prosperous suburb of Johannesburg. There Harry, now eleven, and Frank, nine, commuted to the Parktown School in scarlet blazers and red caps, little English gentlemen in the making.

And then the first crack in the facade appeared. Six months after he had knelt before the crown, Bernard suffered a fatal heart attack. He was fourteen years older than Ernest, more of father figure than a sibling, and he was irreplaceable. For a time, Ernest took the unaccustomed role of bystander and watched while history caught up with his country.

A vigorous new radicalism was rippling across the postwar world, challenging the old assumptions of authority. South Africa was no stranger to strikes, but in the prewar period, these had been wildcat, disorganized, and brief. In 1913, several white mine workers had been fired in a dispute over working hours. Hundreds and then thousands of their fellow laborers had gone out in a show of solidarity. Speaking for Wernher, Beit, Lionel Phillips had commented, "A general strike would of course be a serious matter from a dividend-paying standpoint. I do not think, however, that it could last very long and, if it does happen, we must make up our minds once and for all to break the unions here." The Randlords, working with government troops, had ended the strike at a cost of more than 100 lives.

Then, seven years later, labor unrest shook the black compounds. On Monday, February 16, 1920, two African gold miners, Mobu and Vilikati, were arrested for trying to organize a strike on the East Rand. The following day, 2,500 native workers refused to go to work unless the men were released. Mobu and Vilikati stayed under lock and key, and the strikers escalated their demands. They would settle for nothing less than improved working conditions and a cost-of-living increase of three shillings a day. After two weeks 771,000 workers—more than half the black working force—were out.

The government sensed that something extremely ominous was under way. Johannesburg was put on notice that "this is not, as all previous native troubles have been, a riot; it is a regular strike organized on the European model." The entire future of labor relations was at stake here; the disruption would have to be put down abruptly and absolutely. Federal troops were brought in to aid the private police. They surrounded the compounds, identified the ringleaders, and marched them off to jail. The next day black miners were forced back to their posts at bayonet point. Some went with an air of resignation, others protested vigorously. Confrontations were met with gunshots and beatings; before the strike was put down, 11 miners had been killed and 120 injured.

Ernest knew that these were only the first indications of a dangerous and possibly lethal new attitude. All over the world, workers were beginning to speak out in a different, defiant tone. They had effected severe changes in America, and they had taken over Russia entirely. Was South Africa next? Its labor troubles were in every sense just below the surface, waiting to erupt. Ernest sensed that the next few years might be the most dangerous in his life; he would have to act very cannily to control the mines and the miners. Otherwise they would control him.

◆　　◆　　◆

IN 1921 LOUIS COHEN, sprung from jail and feeling alternate twinges of rheumatism and nostalgia, paid a visit to the gold city he had known a generation before. The old mixture of buccaneering and bonhomie was gone. Everything was regulated in the British style; the Union Jack flew over the town hall. Cohen always had an eye for pretty ladies, and he found the streets crowded with them. Still, there was no doubt that this was a provincial place: they wore dresses that had long gone out of style in London. Prices were astronomical and inconsistent. One proprietor would charge 25 percent more than his neighbor for the same article, and customers were met with calculated indifference.

The visitor stopped by the old stock exchange. There may have been a touch of autobiography in his description of the building, now abandoned: "disreputable and frayed, like a broken-down rake who had rooked his friends, lost his name and was avoided by everybody." Malice colored his picture of the new stock exchange as an "immense structure, forlorn and despairing, like a giant without vitality, stately as a museum, hungry as a workhouse—a hopeless center, busy doing nothing."

Cohen was right to see the skull beneath the skin. Johannesburg's prosperity was largely bluff and promises. The war had taken 5,000 men from the mines. Five hundred of them had been killed in action, more had been wounded, and still more chose not to return to their old positions. Since the war, gold had fallen from 130 to 90 shillings an ounce, while the cost per ton of mining it had risen from 21 to 25 shillings. All this might have been peacefully surmounted if labor and management had worked out a modus vivendi. But the owners were determined to drive costs down, and they had slowly allowed Africans into semi-skilled positions. A mining engineer calculated that a full 50 percent of the white workers could be let go, and a rumor circulated that the Randlords would soon replace all white laborers with Africans.

The Chamber of Mines neither denied nor affirmed the scuttlebutt. It refused to say anything at all until January 28, 1922, when it decided on a formal increase in the ratio of black to white workers. There had been 8.2 blacks to every white; now it would be 10.5 to one. The information acted like kerosene on a brushfire. By March, when the workers met at Trades Hall, all hopes of labor peace had vanished. The handful of moderate leaders were thunderously drowned out. Two men broadcast a new message from the balcony. Messrs. Fisher and Spendiff were Leninists imbued with the spirit of Bolshevik Russia, and they convinced the crowd that the hour of revolution had struck. One man produced a Red flag; another announced a general strike.

The crowd erupted into the streets, ready to express its anger against people and property. In the following days post offices were stormed, trains and trams boarded and halted. Electric light and power was cut off, and trucks hauling food were stopped in their tracks. *The Johannesburg Star* saw the strike as part of a "revolutionary movement aiming at establishing Bolshevism" in the country. If it was Bolshevism, it was the kind that disappeared from the official record. Soviet historians were particularly anxious to expunge the time when radicals marched through the streets of Johannesburg under the banner: WORKERS OF THE WORLD FIGHT AND UNITE FOR A WHITE SOUTH AFRICA.

Led by a group called the Council of Action, these workers grew increasingly violent. They barged into shops, forcing customers and salespeople to leave. A bomb was thrown into a miner's house after he criticized the Council's tactics. A cabdriver who refused to go along with the crowd came home to find his residence dynamited. Bands of strikers raided the suburbs, stoning cars and firing at police. Rumor had it that the natives were on the verge of an organized uprising; before it could be denied, several Africans were murdered in vicious racial attacks.

Prime Minister Smuts was advised to declare martial law. He hesitated. The mining industry was not merely integral to South Africa, it *was* South Africa. And yet to break the strike would be to repudiate the rights of white workers. While he debated with himself, almost all of Johannesburg fell under control of the radical leaders. A magistrate concluded that "the character of the revolt was fast approaching that of the French Revolutionaries," and it was "practically certain that all Government officials in this town and a number of others" would suffer "death at the hands of the revolutionaries."

Smuts decided to see for himself. He boarded a special train from Cape Town and headed north. Strike leaders were sure that he had set his face against them, and they had the railway line blown up. But Smuts was no longer on the train. He had decided to stop 80 miles outside Johannesburg and drive the rest of the way in an anonymous-looking automobile. Even then his life was in danger: someone spotted him in the back seat, and the car was peppered with rifle bullets. The driver made some evasive maneuvers and brought his passenger safely into the city.

As soon as he was barricaded behind closed and guarded doors, Prime Minister Smuts reverted to General Smuts. He declared martial law and called out 20,000 troops, backed by tanks, field artillery, and airplanes. It was as if World War I had returned from the grave. The strikers were better organized than the government had been led to believe, and for the next four days neither side could gain a foothold as fighting raged from the inner city to the outlying districts. The air stank of cordite and gunpowder, and the ground shook from the incessant pounding of artillery. Several police stations were overrun and the constables summarily executed. Some natives unlucky or unwise enough to be on city streets were lynched. Stray bullets cut down a number of uninvolved civilians caught in the crossfire.

Then official South Africa went on the attack, rolling and booming its cannons through the streets, strafing the rebels from biplanes circling overhead. Smuts personally took charge, visiting field positions, counseling his officers, positioning his artillery, offering instructions to pilots. The rebel leaders stopped, retreated, and slowly made their way back to their headquarters in suburban Forsburg. On March 14 the Prime Minister confidently prepared his troops for the final assault. Civilians were told to abandon their houses and leave the area. Most of them obeyed; others defied Smuts's edict, peeping out from their windows or gathering at a nearby ridge to watch the battleground below. From there they witnessed the kind of event that would receive far greater coverage when it occurred in Spain a dozen years later: a government bombing and shooting its own citizens. By now the odds had tilted heavily in favor of the army and police, and the rebel leaders knew that it would be suicidal to go on. They continued, regardless. Deafening barrages went on for several hours; planes unloaded bomb after bomb and continued to circle noisily over the rebel stronghold. Just before nightfall a white flag appeared, and men began to pick their way through the rubble and come out into the daylight with their hands raised. In the background two shots suddenly rang out from deep within a building. The radical leaders Fisher and Spendiff had both chosen death over surrender. One day later the strike came to an end, and the men returned to their jobs.

In the bloody aftermath it was difficult to decide who had won. Certainly not Smuts: even his ardent supporters believed that the Prime

Minister had been too slow to react, and too harsh when he did. His government, the South African Party, stood accused of fatally exaggerating the "Red Threat." As the press pointed out *ad nauseam*, most of the strikers were politically unsophisticated. Hardly any of them wanted to shake up the existing social order. They had simply reacted to Randlord insensitivity and agitators' promises.

As the detritus got cleared away and the grave diggers did their work, the acts of the government looked more and more irresponsible. The final death toll came to 214, of which only 76 were strikers; 78 troopers and 62 bystanders had been killed by shells or bombs, and 30 Africans had been lynched. Over the course of eight weeks, more than 4,700 men had been arrested, 40 of them charged with murder. Prosecutors could only obtain 18 convictions; of those, four were hanged. The doomed men saw themselves as the latest in a long procession of South African martyrs. They chanted "The Red Flag," a new Communist hymn, on the way to the gallows.

If the Prime Minister and his party had been damaged; if the mining companies had suffered huge financial losses; if the white laborers had to return to work and the Africans were no better off than before, who had won the strike? At first it seemed a battle with no victors and no spoils. Then, gradually, the truth emerged. The decline of one politician invariably meant the rise of another; South Africa's new political star appeared to be James Barry Hertzog. He too had been a Boer general, a war hero, and a politician. But he was far to the right of Smuts. Hertzog regarded the Prime Minister as the "valet of Britain," too hard on his fellow Afrikaaners and too tolerant of the natives. Hammering away at the South African Party, Hertzog headed the opposition National Party under the rubric "White South Africa First."

The Randlords were not wholly uncomfortable with the outcome. They balanced their deficits with the consoling knowledge that, given the choice between men and commodities, the government had come down in favor of gold and diamonds. Social agitators remained out of sight. Stability returned to South Africa, and once again cheap labor was back where it belonged, in the mines.

Yet at least one mining executive was unhappy with the results.

Ernest Oppenheimer had deliberately kept himself out of the crossfire, but at election time he had felt compelled to defend Smuts and his party. In one speech he reminded an audience, "If you had a good watch dog and you discovered the dog had fleas you would not drown the dog. But you are asked to kill the South African Party because of a few unpopular measures, which our great leader has already promised to put right." Yet even as he had campaigned for Smuts, Ernest was aware that he had backed the wrong dog. Wary of social disturbance, J. P. Morgan's company announced that it would dispose of its holdings in Anglo-American. Other United States investors followed, precipitating a stampede for the exit. South Africa, a haven for investors only a few months before, now looked to be a risky proposition.

Just then J. B. Robinson emerged from retirement to fight yet another courtroom battle in London. The old belligerent had not lost his touch: his timing was, as always, catastrophic.

♦ ♦ ♦

ROBINSON'S TALENT for making money was exceeded only by his genius for creating enemies. Some years before, he had decided to get rid of his South African holdings and withdraw from mining altogether. He offered his companies to Solly Joel, Barney Barnato's nephew, for £4,500,000. The prospective buyer had become a Randlord in his own right, and he was no fool; Solly knew Robinson for a hard-bitten Scrooge who would never willingly part with a farthing. But the glittering properties looked too good to pass up, and J.B.R. got his price. Only after the ink was dry and the money paid did Solly realize that his pocket had been picked clean by an expert.

First, Robinson had neglected his companies for years. Although the gold mines looked healthy enough on the surface, vast sums would have to be invested before the deteriorated shafts could turn a profit. Second, and far more important, J.B.R. had not been content to cheat Solly Joel. He had also shortchanged his stockholders.

Secretly, Robinson had been purchasing the mineral rights to land —and then selling them to his own companies through third parties. In one typical scheme he bought a half-share of the Watervaal farm for £60,000 and several weeks later peddled it to one of his firms for

£275,000. Less expenses and commissions, Robinson cleared a fast £210,000. As this and other incriminating revelations came to light, Solly Joel sued for damages.

For half his lifetime Robinson had warmed himself at the fire of prosecution and defense; he regarded the courtroom as a second home. But this was different. The newspapers tried him before the testimony began. They called it The Secret Profits Case, and noted that for once the old man had a foeman worthy of his steel. Solly was a millionaire with his own set of high-priced barristers, and he gave them a case full of evidence.

Not that Robinson gave up easily. He acted the part of an ancient innocent badgered by the predatory young. His celebrated deafness became a secret weapon: whenever Joel's lawyers tried to prod his memory, J.B.R. seemed to have trouble understanding the question. When his own counsel made a gentle inquiry, he was no longer hard of hearing. Onlookers enjoyed the theatrics, but neither the public, the press, nor the court was deceived. Robinson was ordered to pay Joel £462,000 plus costs. Undeterred, the old man fought on in the appeals courts. Here, too, he was denied. Counting penalties and legal fees, he came out poorer by £750,000.

That was not the end of his losses. In 1922 Lloyd George, Britain's Liberal Prime Minister succumbed to aggressive lobbying—and incalculable bribes—and recommended Robinson for a peerage. The House of Lords expressed collective shock. In 1907 Robinson had been made a baronet; to address him as Sir Joseph was bad enough. Coming so soon after the Secret Profits Case, the notion of *Lord* Robinson was intolerable. On June 22, 1922, Lord Harris, Chairman of Rhodes's old Gold Fields Company, led the attack on Robinson. He was followed by speaker after speaker who rose to protest.

These stings were too great even for J.B.R.'s elephant hide, and the following week Lloyd George received a letter. "It is now some 60 years since I commenced as a pioneer the task of building up the industries of South Africa," it began. "I am now an old man, to whom honors and dignities are no longer of much concern. I should be sorry if any honor conferred on me were the occasion of such ill-feeling as was manifested in the House of Lords. . . . I would wish, if I may without discourtesy to yourself and without impropriety, his Most Gracious Majesty's permission to decline the proposal."

The letter was pure fiction. Rejection had stunned and humiliated the old man. As Lord Robinson he would have built himself a great country house in England and strutted through the streets of London as he had in Kimberley. Now he closed his mansion in Park Lane, turned his back on everything British, slammed on his pith helmet, and sailed off to South Africa. Perhaps he consoled himself with the fact that at least one Robinson had a title beyond the reach of the House of Lords. His daughter had married an Italian aristocrat, and she was currently Countess Labia.

♦   ♦   ♦

ACCORDING TO LONDON WAGS the Secret Profits Case was good for *a* Jew but not *the* Jew. Even though they had no use for Robinson, the British newspapers could see little difference between the cheater and the cheated. In victory Solly Joel was characterized as yet another Randlord reaching out for more money than he could ever spend, and during the trial "Hoggenheimer" leapt from the cramped square of the editorial cartoon and into the public imagination.

The Communists, who had lost the battle of the unions, spoke of Hoggenheimer as a beaky predator who had bought his title and rented his opinions from the Tories. The Afrikaaner right saw him as a Johannesburg Fagin, stealing and spoiling whatever and whomever he touched. Either way the Jews lost, and the uneasy coincidence of Hoggenheimer–Oppenheimer made life and business difficult for Ernest. More than the other rich South Africans, he would have to watch the way he acted and lived.

Precautions had already been taken. Although his sons had been circumsized, neither Harry nor Frank was to have a bar mitzvah. Parktown was a Christian school, and except for their surname the boys had no Jewish identity. The Oppenheimers moved from their pleasant home to a 50-acre county seat called Marion Court. It was no accident that Ernest chose this property. The accompanying mansion, a unique amalgam of ostentation and understatement, had been designed by Herbert Baker, official architect for Cecil Rhodes.

These splendid surroundings would not be enough to ward off the critics. Something more was required. To that end, Ernest reneged on the promise he had made to stay out of public life. In the summer of 1924 he ran for Parliament, representing, of all places, Kimberley. And he won. It was as if there had been no stone-throwing, no riot, no acrimonious flight to England less than ten years before. His victory speech barely alluded to the past, and then only to refer to Kimberley as the "place which gave me my start in business, and which has now given me my start in political life."

But Oppenheimer's enemies had not forgotten the old days. They waited with long knives when Ernest—Sir Ernest, as he preferred to be called, annoying them even more—made his maiden speech. He began modestly enough, discussing the technical aspects of finance. Then, as he warmed to the subject, Sir Ernest was unwise enough to reveal his ambition: "I have the honor of being a vice president of the Chamber of Mines and I hope in the years to come that body will do me the honor of electing me its president. I am also largely interested in the diamond trade, both as a producer and a merchant." Yet he emphasized that money and power were not his true goals. In lofty tones he stated, "My presence here shows that I put country before business and that I have only one desire, that is to be able to render useful service to South Africa."

The unwritten law of Parliament called for debuts to be received with polite applause. However, one Labor M.P. had a low tolerance for self-promotion and he broke with tradition. "I have not risen to reply to the mining questions mentioned by the previous speaker," he informed the assembly, "but I would like to say that it takes a great deal more courage for a man to go down a mine than it does for a man to sit in comfort on the surface and invest money in mining enterprises."

Parliament's newest member refused to return fire. He knew his enemies were waiting for him to act in the Hoggenheimer manner, all greed and wind. Instead, Ernest took the high road. Rather than apologizing for his Randlord role he embraced it, presenting himself as a twentieth-century Rhodes. Let other politicians stress the separation of the races; he spoke as the Colossus did, of "equal rights for all civilized men," an attractive phrase to the Liberals whose votes he might need some day. (No mention was made of Anglo-American's dependence on black labor at bargain prices.) Let other politicians demand press coverage of their every move. Ernest talked with a quiet, deferential voice, scrupulously polite to reporters.

The journalists happily jumped through his hoop: they had never seen anyone like him. One reporter, assigned to interview Sir Ernest recalled "the biggest name in diamonds . . . confronting someone who, in the newspaper industry, ranked less than the dust. Yet he acted considerately, kindly. It takes a big man to do that, when things aren't going too well for him personally. . . . He doesn't shout. He talks, and because he talks common sense in a kindly, understanding way, he gets things done."

Among the things he got done in the mid-twenties was the expansion of Anglo-American and the invasion of De Beers. At this point Anglo was not yet a major financial house; its mines were responsible for only about 5 percent of South Africa's gold supply. Still, every business Ernest controlled was growing rapidly, and he had big plans for acquiring more of the gold and controlling all of the diamond supply. He also had formidable allies. The closest was his brother Louis, now a senior partner at Dunkels in London. The two Oppenheimers discussed the situation in South Africa. It was time, they decided, for the assault on De Beers. To that end they had to go beyond the family, to the most influential diamond man they could find.

They located him at Barnato Bros., one of the few solid legacies that Barney had left behind. The concern was led by his nephew, Solly Joel. Even before the showoff victory over Robinson, Solly had been a flamboyant type, very much in Barney's tradition. He owned racehorses, had an exuberant wardrobe, and made no secret of his desire for money and power. In short, he exactly fit the profile of the Jewish Randlord—just the image that Ernest was trying to avoid. On the other hand, in the complicated ways of Kimberley, Solly had absorbed smaller companies like Jagersfontein; and, more significantly, he was not only on the board of De Beers, he was its largest individual stockholder.

Solly had not bought his way to the top of the diamond industry. He had climbed there with a combination of good timing and predator's instinct. At the beginning of the decade, for example, the Bolsheviks had begun to sell off the jewelry they had confiscated from the White Russian aristocracy. The market, suddenly flooded with diamonds, drove down the price of precious stones. In South Africa's shaky postwar economy the Russian move could have triggered a depression. Many other magnates held their heads in their hands; Solly reached for his checkbook. He bought £390,000 worth of stones, staved off a panic, and pocketed a variety of bargains that he would unload when the prices went back up.

Ernest considered all this and worked out a strategy. Solly would be convinced to act on the Oppenheimers' behalf. There was no law that said only one syndicate could rule the diamond industry. In 1925 Ernest threatened to create a new one. Members of the existing syndicate were livid; battle lines were drawn. Solly, an accomplished fence sitter, tried to reconcile the warring factions. But Ernest rebuffed all attempts at peace talks.

His intransigence was no bluff. Oppenheimer had a lock on the diamond production of the Congo and Angola, the two biggest producers outside South Africa. Early in the year he had lined up two great banking concerns, J. P. Morgan in New York and Morgan Grenfell in London. Finally, in July, Solly did something that went against his deepest convictions. He chose sides, joining hands with Ernest. With so much firepower arrayed against it, the old syndicate shuddered and collapsed. Ernest then made good on his threat: he created an entirely new diamond syndicate with himself as chairman. After considerable haggling and backstairs maneuvers, it was agreed that De Beers would account for 51 percent of the diamond production. The remaining 49 percent was to be divided between companies controlled outright by Ernest Oppenheimer and Solly Joel.

Forced into a new and uncomfortable situation, the directors of De Beers took the only revenge open to them. They knew how anxious Ernest was to join the board, and they blocked the entrance. Again and again Solly tried to effect a reconciliation: what would be wrong with having Ernest inside shooting out, he wanted to know, instead of outside shooting in? But he was outvoted by men who had resented Ernest since the days before the Great War when Oppenheimer–Hoggenheimer had audaciously demanded a seat on the board.

Ernest made no more appeals. He had anticipated the hostility and, with typical sangfroid, simply acquired shares of De Beers whenever they came up for sale. By the spring of 1926 he owned almost as much of the company's stock as Solly. The directors had nothing left in their arsenal. Solly worked on them one by one, and in July 1926, Louis Oppenheimer received a cable from his brother. Ernest had been waiting for ten years to send it: "For your private information only De Beers board of directors unanimously agreed appoint me board."

As head of the new syndicate, as well as De Beers's newest director, Ernest enjoyed an unaccustomed prominence. One newspaperman was speaking to General Smuts when he saw a member of Parliament come into the room.

Someone remarked contemptuously, "Enter Ernest Oppenheimer's jackal."

Smuts rose in defense. "But what a splendid man to be jackal to!"

Other newsmen came around and pressed the General for more information. What was the big fuss about Oppenheimer, anyway? There were other financiers in the country, men with greater personal style and charisma. To say nothing of the leaders in Europe and America.

The General sat back and made one of his confident prophecies. "Yes, yes," he agreed. "They make headlines, but Oppenheimer makes history. Wait and see."

12

THE DEATH OF HOPE

No MATTER HOW HIGH HE ASCENDED, Ernest knew that he could never become a British gentleman. That role would have to be played by the next generation of Oppenheimers. And so in early youth Harry and Frank Oppenheimer were sent away from South Africa to the English county of Surrey. There, at a top public school, Charterhouse, they would pursue their studies and acquire the requisite education, manners, and polish.

The brothers bore little resemblance to each other. The elder, Harry, was short and dark; Frank was fair and tall. Harry was introverted and inclined to intellectual pursuits. Frank was sunny and gregarious. Harry's excellence in French won him a scholarship to Christ Church College, Oxford. Frank went up to Trinity College at Cambridge. Throughout his academic career, Harry was always the more studious. But his academic career remained generally undistinguished, and his twenty-first birthday party might have been staged by one of the half-mad young fauns celebrated by his Oxford contemporary, Evelyn Waugh.

The event took place in October 1929, at The Spreadeagle, a raffish hotel whose publican, in Waugh's view, was "Oxford's only civilizing influence." Ernest and May were in England at the time and attended, along with a disoriented General Smuts, who wondered why he was being dragged "into the bush." The atmosphere was heady, and in one of his memorable and quixotic gestures Ernest tipped the servants 25 percent of the bill—and why not? He had just become the chairman of De Beers. In the afterglow they would have followed him to Cape Town in a canoe. Everyone was having such a good time that one of the guests wished it might go on for a month. And in a sense it did.

Not until November was Wall Street to experience the seismic shocks that led to a global depression. In very quick order diamonds became the last item on anyone's shopping list. Even so, South Africa was a long way from the centers of bad news, and mining processes went on with metronomic regularity, the stones brought up to the surface, sorted, and stored as if buyers were waiting in line. A few months into 1930 there were no buyers at all. Diamonds began to pile up in Kimberley until the safes and drawers overflowed. Matters grew so dire that De Beers used butter churns to store the jewels. Sorters went through the motions of separating and grading the stones every day, then mixed them up at night in order to give themselves something to do the next morning.

It seemed obvious that the situation could not continue, but it only seemed obvious to Ernest. The government wanted no part of his announced intention to close down the mines under his control. The new Minister of Mines, Adrian Fourie, suspected that the Oppenheimer plan was a typical Hoggenheimer move: making an artificial shortage of diamonds, and in the process throwing thousands out of work in order to protect his company's position in the stock market. Ernest did not help matters when he insisted, "I am not going to be pointed out as the chairman of De Beers company who saw it brought to bankruptcy." To keep white men employed, without giving them anything to do, was "to ruin the shareholders."

Except for this outburst, Ernest avoided direct confrontation with the government. He sought to win allies by waging a campaign of public relations. De Beers had been running the town tramways as a subsidized service; he handed them back to the city, gratis. And he presented De Beers's (unprofitable) Belgrave Hotel to the nuns of the Holy Family, the convent that had saved him from a mob in 1915.

During this struggle his sons inconveniently came of age. The price of sending Frank to England was that the young man preferred that country to the land of his birth. If Ernest was disappointed he showed no sign of it: Frank was suitably installed in Anglo's London office.

Harry played the dutiful son; he decided to come home and learn the diamond business from the ground up. He would begin as his father did, sorting stones in Kimberley.

Another family member came aboard soon afterward: Bernard's son Michael, a barrister who had fallen on hard times in England. Now in his late thirties, he had married a famous English beauty, Caroline "Ina" Harvey, daughter of an English baronet. In spite of these family connections, Michael had made some unwise investments and had been forced to declare bankruptcy. Relocating to South Africa seemed an act of desperation. But Michael, Ina, and their small son, also named Michael, immediately took to the climate and the work; they enjoyed great social success. For all its ornaments of power, Johannesburg remained a provincial town, and Ina's listeners doted on her girlhood recollections of Queen Mary, a forbidding figure who always insisted on examining the terrified child's needlework.

After training at Kimberley, Harry moved to Johannesburg. There he rubbed shoulders with yet another relative, May's brother Leslie Pollack, who had become a managing director of Anglo-American. Theoretically Harry reported to his uncle, and the two of them did make some out-of-town trips together. But much of Harry's time was spent writing speeches for Ernest. The son was used to communicating with brisk efficiency; he told friends he had some difficulty adapting to his father's "rather diffuse" style.

Harry may have written the address Ernest gave to Parliament in the winter of 1932. "The diamond industry has been struggling against collapse for years," he reminded the members. "The producers have spent vast sums to prevent unemployment. From the Minister, instead of gratitude and help, they have received insults and accusations of bad faith. . . . The only conclusion they can come to is that he does not understand the position." All this was to say that Ernest had determined to close his mines regardless of the immediate human cost.

Fourie resentfully countered, "We have the spectacle in South Africa that there is one man who is chairman of all the producing companies in South Africa. . . . He alone is the center of the whole diamond industry and, moreover, he advocates his own case in this House. . . . It is necessary for the government to take this great industry under its protection."

This was pure bluster, and it would prove deeply embarrassing to the Ministry of Mines. Fourie talked tough, and he created a commission to dig into the workings of the new syndicate. But he had no legal weaponry to back him up. Ernest and his executives defiantly refused to testify, and the investigation folded as rapidly as it had been set up.

With the diamond industry safe from governmental interference, Ernest turned his attention to another precious commodity. Thus far the depression had not seriously damaged gold prices. Miners worked on, and Anglo continued to pay dividends. But there were troubling signs. For more than fifty years the United States and most of Europe had been on the gold standard: their currencies were backed with gold bullion, payable on demand. The price of gold per ounce was fixed by international agreement—but this agreement had come to an end after World War I. Britain, and other countries that enjoyed a favorable balance of trade, received gold in trade for exports. Initially that meant falling interest rates and vigorous economic activity; this, in turn, led to inflation and higher prices for their goods. Exports fell, the export trade diminished, and more imported goods came in. The price for those goods was gold. The economy diminished, and unemployment rose. And so the cycle began again. Governments gradually recognized that the gold standard had outlived its time. In 1931 Britain announced that it was simultaneously abandoning the standard and devaluing the pound. Members of the Commonwealth could follow suit or stay dependent on gold. The choice was theirs.

Ever since Hertzog deposed him, Smuts had been seeking a way to restore his political career. Gold provided him with just the issue he was looking for. As leader of the opposition South African Party, he demanded that his country follow Britain's example. By continuing to back its currency with gold, he pointed out, South Africa had devalued its pound; the note bought next to nothing overseas, and the country found itself paying far too much for imported items. Meantime inflation was eating into the economy, and South Africans were paying too much for items like foodstuffs and repairs. The Hertzog government refused to listen: damned if it would copy England. Soon a gold debate erupted in Parliament and echoed in the streets.

Throughout the controversy Ernest had stayed loyal to his old friend.

Now Smuts asked him to present the case for the opposition in Parliament. Listeners, paying close attention to Oppenheimer's diction and phrasing, thought they could detect the work of young Harry. "There is no such thing as financial independence," the Member for Kimberley pointed out with a new clarity, "and there is no such thing as a 'natural' currency system. At the present time we have to choose between two systems. . . . One of them, the 'international' gold standard, is leading [to] the ruin of the primary producer. England has broken away from this system. To follow [her] we must increase the price which we get for our products in the markets of the world. Are we to throw away this advantage . . . simply because we cannot or will not understand that the gold standard, as it existed before the war, has gone never to return?"

The government saw Oppenheimer's advocacy as one more Hoggenheimer move, and refused to capitulate. The fight might well have gone against Ernest, had it not been for Tielman Roos. The former Minister of Justice thought he saw a way to promote himself to the top job. He announced his return to politics by calling for a coalition government—his own and Smuts's—to replace the current one. Roos, not a man for fresh language, saw himself at the helm, steering his country through the shoals of the depression. He declared that his first move would be to abandon the gold standard.

When the country and the newspapers gave Roos a favorable reception, Hertzog was trapped. To avoid being toppled by a vote of no confidence he had to give in, and on December 28, 1932, South Africa stopped backing its currency with gold. Now Ernest was the vulnerable one; he had been the advocate, and he would be blamed if the move failed to spur the economy. The public and the politicians hung back, waiting to call for cheers or blood.

The results were surprisingly quick. Almost as soon as the currency deflated, the tide of foreign investment flowed back into the country. At the end of 1933 the price of gold rose from about £4 to £6 an ounce. Almost overnight, consumer confidence returned, the Johannesburg stock exchange grew lively, the mines hired more workers, subsidiary industries and stores started to move their goods, and massive unemployment—white unemployment—became a thing of the past. Ernest had shown that he was not only a magnate, he was a prophet.

The good news continued. Smuts, wary of Roos and his unbridled ambition, sought a private rapprochement with Hertzog. The two formed their own coalition government, and several administrators were replaced, among them Adrian Fourie. The new Minister of Mines, Patrick Duncan, pledged to be more conciliatory with Anglo and De Beers. That promise capped Sir Ernest Oppenheimer's most brilliant year. The man who had never liked to gamble, even at a game of bridge, became known for an astonishing gesture. Several years before, a geologist named Hans Merensky had made many important discoveries of diamonds and platinum, but by the time he came to see Ernest he was nearly broke. All he had left were some shares in an independent diamond mine. No one knew just how much they were worth. Nevertheless Merensky insisted on an astronomical price. He and Ernest negotiated behind closed doors, and Merensky departed smiling. Afterward Oppenheimer reflected, "It is not often that a man comes in without sixpence in his pocket, and leaves with a million pounds." Nevertheless, Ernest had not acted out of charity. The property he so generously bought was to quintuple in value.

It was that kind of period for Sir Ernest Oppenheimer, chairman of De Beers, creator and director of Anglo-American, Knight, Member of Parliament. Syndicate panjandrum, King of Diamonds were no longer fit descriptions of the man; he was also one of the most important producers of gold. And now he was reaching out to invest in Rhodesian copper, coal, platinum, explosives, agriculture. At the age of 52, surrounded by relatives, supported by friends in and out of office, he had become one of the wealthiest and most influential businessmen on the continent of Africa. Not even the great Cecil Rhodes had come so far.

◆　　◆　　◆

THE REVERSAL OF FORTUNE began on a quiet September morning in 1933. A small group gathered at an airport just outside Johannesburg to see their friends off on a trip to Rhodesia. The plane was a de Havilland Dragon, a twin-engine six-seater with only two men aboard: the pilot, Major Cochrane-Patrick, a much-decorated flying ace of World War I, and Ernest's nephew Michael.

The Dragon lifted off, soared into the brilliant sky, and then banked at a height of some 250 feet in order to let the major and his passenger signal farewell to the knot of friends enthusiastically waving from the ground. Without warning the plane slipped into a dive, whether from wind shear or mechanical failure no one could tell. Seconds later it crashed nose-first into the earth. The ground engineer rushed to the burning wreckage and dragged the pilot away. He was too late. On impact Michael had been thrown through the fuselage and over the port engine. He, too, had perished instantly.

Ernest was prostrated by the tragedy. It had been a special comfort to have his brother's son so near, to see a new generation of Oppenheimers newly rooted in South Africa. Michael's young widow, Ina, put up a brave front but she was devastated. For a time she spoke about returning to England with little Michael, but Ernest persuaded her to stay: he needed someone close to look after his wife.

May's health had been deteriorating rapidly. Although ten years younger than Ernest, she was afflicted with a series of ailments. Ina helped to nurse her back to health, and in February 1934, May finally felt well enough to accompany her husband to the opening of Parliament in Cape Town. When he returned to Johannesburg she stayed on, recuperating in the sea air. The day she planned to return to Brenthurst, May suffered a slight heart attack. Ernest was notified; he dropped everything and made plans to leave Johannesburg. At 10:00 that night she had another attack, and this time it was not minor. May Lina Oppenheimer died before Ernest could reach her bedside.

The two losses seemed almost too much for him to bear. May had been at his side for almost thirty years. Unlike the wives of other Randlords, she had always been absorbed with the ins and outs of finance, and she remained that way to the end. The daughter of a past president of the London Stock Exchange had much to say about daily decisions, and her advice was unusually sound. Moreover, May had been born to wealth, and her ability to preside at parties and formal functions brought Ernest the social position he had craved since the early days at Dunkelsbuhler's. The widower tried to right himself. A letter to Honnold mentioned an unshakeable melancholia: "I feel very tired and weary and am toying with the idea of retiring. I should not like you to think that I am ill, but I find it very difficult after my bereavement to concentrate on work."

He was still in mourning when May's brother collapsed at a dinner party. No one at Anglo knew that Leslie Pollack had been suffering from walking pneumonia; he had hidden it from the staff, and by the time he was taken to a hospital there was nothing the doctors could do. The 46-year-old had been worn down by overwork, and he died the next morning.

Anglo-American was unexpectedly left without an experienced manager. Ernest had planned to give Harry a few more years of seasoning before moving him into a corner office. Pollack's death gave him no choice; from here on Harry would move to the center of all company decisions. Still, matters were not quite as dire as they appeared. Ernest tried to comfort himself by noting that, with Harry in charge, his other son Frank could coast for a little longer.

The trouble was that, unlike Harry, Frank had never quite settled down. There were too many distractions in the London of the 1930s for a light-hearted young man. The 24-year-old was known to enjoy fast cars and good meals—too many good meals, it seemed. In April 1935 he and some similarly overindulged friends decided to take a holiday in Madeira where they would swim, sun, and diet. After a few days of Spartan living they agreed to have one Lucullan feast, then work it off by taking a vigorous dip in the municipal swimming pool. Frank was the last to emerge from the water. He tried to get out, then fell face down in the shallow end. The companions attempted to revive him, but no amount of artificial respiration could bring Frank around; the Portuguese doctor attributed the cause of death to bathing too soon after eating.

Ernest received the news on shipboard. He had been en route to Madeira at the time and was barely able to grasp what had happened. There had been too much anguish in too short a time. He seemed bewildered and numb during the interment of Frank Leslie Oppenheimer at Madeira's British cemetery. The next day Ernest made a decision which was to cause more intense speculation and resentment than any other act in his lifetime. He would be baptised and received into the Christian faith.

Did he imagine himself the victim of some horrific Jewish curse? Or was this a grieving attempt, once and for all, to rid Oppenheimer of Hoggenheimer? The family would always refer to the conversion in identical words: it was the result of "a spiritual crisis." Given the sad circumstances, that has always seemed a plausible explanation. Still, that crisis must have made itself felt long before the Madeira tragedy. Like her husband, May Pollak had been raised in the Jewish faith. The Oppenheimers had been married and their children had started their lives as Jews. Yet the year before, May's memorial service did not take place in a synagogue; indeed, the ceremony was held at St. George's Church in Parktown.

For months after Frank's funeral, Ernest journeyed aimlessly through Europe and back to South Africa. It was the death of hope. Everything had lost its savor. He had never been religious; now he kept a Bible by his bedside, trying to wring some solace from the Book of Job. The poem on the inaccessibility of wisdom must have had a special pertinence, speaking as it did of "a place where gold is refined." There,

> Man puts an end to darkness,
> Every recess he searches.
> Through dark and gloomy rock
> He sinks a shaft far from habitation.
>
> . . .
>
> He puts his hand to the flint,
> Overturns mountains at the base.
> In the rocks he hews out channels,
> His eye sees every precious thing.
> The sources of the rivers he probes,
> Brings hidden things to light.
> But wisdom, where can it be found?
>
> Where is the place of understanding?
> Man knows not the path to it,
> It is not found in the land of the living.
>
> . . .
>
> Wisdom's value surpasses rubies.
> The topaz of Ethiopia cannot equal it,
> It cannot be bought with pure gold.

Ernest brooded on the futility of human endeavor. He had built a structure, a fortune, a reputation. And for what? For whom? In less than a year his immediate family had been cut in half. He had material wealth but no wife to share it with, gardens but no grandchildren to play in them. His old colleagues, and even his enemies, were gone. Solly Joel was dead; David Harris, who had enticed Barney Barnato to South Africa, had retired from the board of De Beers. So had Ernest's disappointed cousin Fritz Hirschhorn. Lionel Phillips had retired to his Cape estate. Nearby was J. B. Robinson, embittered, deaf, brooding over his disappointments.

During the long period of mourning Ernest toured his estate at Brenthurst, frequently alone, sometimes in the company of Ina, who was still grieving for Michael Oppenheimer. On one of his trips to London, Ernest brought her along, and in the spring of 1935 he surprised much of the world by proposing marriage. On the first of June his niece became his wife, and thus young Michael came to be both his grandnephew and stepson. Ina's mother, Lady Harvey, was one of the official witnesses; Harry was another.

One month after the marriage, Ernest created a new company to safeguard the family—new members and old—against his own death or disability. The institution was given an unassuming title. The other companies kept their names—De Beers, Anglo-American, and the subsidiaries that dealt with coal, copper, agriculture, real estate, and so on. But they might just as well have assumed the new one. From here on, E. Oppenheimer and Son would be the symbolic umbrella that covered them all.

♦   ♦   ♦

IN THE DEPRESSION YEARS a new word entered the vocabularies of South Africans: apartheid—an Afrikaaner word meaning a literal "apartness" of the races. Even though the term would not work its way into lawbooks for more than a decade, it had already found a home in the conversations of a worried white populace. To the poor among them, and there were many, blacks represented an economic threat and a moral quandary. Natives would settle for lower wages than whites, and they would accept working conditions that whites found intolerable. They were poised to take the Europeans' jobs away. The only way around this situation was to force the natives to compete for the same wages and conditions as white workers. Yet to do that would be to grant them a kind of equality. That no Afrikaaner, and precious few other whites of any ethnicity, could accept.

During the Smuts administration the government had sought to placate its white constituency by following the recommendations of a Transvaal Commission. Headed by the hard-line segregationist Frederick Stallard, it stated a "recognized principle": natives, "men, women and children—should only be permitted within municipal areas in so far and for as long as their presence is demanded by the wants of the white population . . . [because] the masterless native in urban areas is a source of danger and a cause of degradation of both black and white." Convinced by Stallard's conclusions, the Smuts government pushed through the Natives (Urban Areas) Act, a law that made segregation an official policy. From now on, blacks would be forbidden to live in or visit white towns. They could only work there, and when their day was finished, they had to return to their own segregated areas.

What Smuts started, Hertzog intensified. It would no longer suffice to have Whites Only facilities and railroad carriages. His Native Administration Act gave the white government extraordinary powers over all black people. The appointment of chiefs and headmen was up to white administrators, not natives; groups were moved from area to area at their pleasure. They could determine dress codes and censor any speech or action made "with the intent to promote any feelings of hostility between natives and Europeans."

What they could not do was reverse the mounting tide of African sentiment. It had started with the African National Congress; then had come the Industrial and Commercial Workers' Union. The ICU originated in 1919 on the Cape Town docks and then fanned out from the city to the rural farmland. En route it redefined its political character, changing from straight trade unionism to militant black nationalism. Its founder Clements Kadalie, a clerk from Rhodesia, spoke no African language; he made his appeals in English, and he dared to tell his audiences the most subversive statement some of them had ever heard: "What is good enough for the white man is good enough for you."

Others had already awakened to the new black consciousness. They had read the tracts of Marcus Garvey, a West Indian who had moved to the United States during the Great War. From his headquarters in

New York City, Garvey argued that the blacks could never find justice in countries where they were a minority race. His "back to Africa" movement argued for an autonomous black state where African-Americans could find their destinies.

As these revolutionary thinkers shouted out their programs, the Communist Party of South Africa added its peculiar voice. Before the abortive civil war, Bolshevik organizers had urged workers to unite for a white South Africa. In the late 1920s, party policy was overturned; now it recruited among the native population, denouncing the Pass Laws, rejecting all discriminatory legislation, and advocating a "democratic, independent native republic" to throw off the yoke of capitalist oppression.

Each group pursued its own course, and each met with failure. The ICU switched its militant tactics, attempting to cooperate with white landowners. The gesture was interpreted as a sign of weakness; white farmers took the blacks to court, evicted them from their homes, intimidated organizers, and got local magistrates to ban union meetings. The Garveyites lost momentum when their leader was arrested for mail fraud and exiled to Jamaica. Although he lived until 1940, his influence waned and sputtered through the 1930s. The Communists took their policies to the polls. White voters rejected those policies out of hand, and the membership of the CPSA spent the rest of the decade in internecine arguments, fighting over ideology and calling each other traitors to the cause. The ANC leaders also quarreled among themselves. A conservative faction expelled those it considered radical and sent out the word: "Having noticed the spread of bolshevik tendencies among the non-Europeans . . . [the] Congress is of the opinion that leaders and propagandists with communist doctrines should not be allowed to address meetings organized by Congress." Those on the left tried to organize their own counter-Congress, and the resultant split weakened the movement for a generation.

At this point the blacks outnumbered the whites by about six to one, and the Afrikaaners represented about 60 percent of that white minority. As the Boer right saw it, social chaos lay just around the corner: left unattended, the Kaffirs and the white liberals would overcome their many differences, band together, and drive the Afrikaaners into the sea. That scenario was nothing new; to prevent it a Broederbond—Band of Brothers—had been created back in 1917 by a group of Afrikaaner zealots who opposed their country's participation in the Great War. The Bond had gone underground when South Africa joined with the dreaded British, and many South Africans thought—incorrectly—they had heard the last of it.

The Bond organized itself in a manner virtually indistinguishable from that of the dreaded Communist Party. Membership was secret —even wives were not supposed to know their husbands had joined. The group was divided into cells, and each Brother checked the others for loyalty. "He who betrays the Bond will be destroyed by the Bond," warned the oath of initiation. "The Bond never forgets. Its vengeance is swift and sure."

In 1938 the Bond surfaced in a ritual of white supremacy and Afrikaaner identity. One hundred years before, the Great Trek had occurred. On August 8, the centennial of "the sacred happening" was restaged. After much advance publicity and fanfare, two stinkwood ox-wagons were named after heroes of the Boer War, the martyr Pieter Retief and Andries Pretorius, victor at Blood River. The wagons pulled out of Cape Town and wheeled north. At every turn they were cheered by large, defiant crowds. For the occasion, the men had grown Voortrekker beards and put on waistcoats and knotted scarves. The women had decked themselves out in the voluminous homespun dresses fashionable in their great-grandmothers' day. The primitive vehicles rolled to Pretoria, where a team of torchbearers caught up with the trekkers. Speeches and sermons followed. At the foot of the Voortrekker monument a great bonfire was lit, providing a cue for three thousand torchbearers on the surrounding hilltops. They ignited other fires, in a circle of "white civilization." One of the three thousand recorded her emotions: "The hill is on fire; on fire with Afrikaaner fire, on fire with the enthusiasm of Young South Africa! You are nothing—your People is all. One light in the dusk is puny and small. But three thousand flames. Three thousand! And more! There's hope for your future, South Africa!"

In the style of Adolf Hitler at the Nuremberg rallies, Dr. Daniel François Malan exhorted the crowd to think with its blood. Malan was used to public speaking: for many years he had been a Dutch Reform clergyman. But he had abandoned the pulpit for politics, and now he led an organization called the Purified National Party. Illuminated by the fires, possessed by the past, he reminded Afrikaaners of their glorious victory over the Zulus a century ago. Then, "the muzzleload [had] clashed with the assegai." Today the battle raged on; there were just as many savage enemies, and they were of the same color and ferocity. It was the duty of modern Afrikaaners to continue the fight, for once and for all "to make South Africa a white man's land."

◆　　◆　　◆

UNCOMFORTABLE WITH BLACK NATIONALISM, wary of the Afrikaaner right, Ernest wondered whether he should continue in elective politics. It was the one aspect of his life that had failed to mend. The mourning period was over. He had happily remarried; his remaining son, Harry, was at his side. Anglo-American prospered: zinc and lead mines had been added to the Oppenheimer holdings. Events were going De Beers's way: jewels were back in demand. More significantly, a use had been found for *bort*, tiny diamond crystals formerly consigned to the slag pile. Until the 1930s, steel blades had been employed to cut the precision tools for industry. These were constantly getting blunted, and a new tungsten alloy was developed. But what was hard enough to cut that metal? At the end of the decade, a method was found to bind diamond dust with resin. The mixture was then molded in the shape of cutting and grinding wheels. The rearming nations of Europe lined up to order these new tools: "industrial diamonds" became the heart of the automotive and defense industries, and De Beers could scarcely keep up with demand.

Meanwhile, Anglo-American had outgrown its headquarters. Rather than occupy another old edifice, Ernest ordered an elegant new five-story building to be constructed, framed in steel and concrete and faced in stone. It was the focus of Anglo's and De Beers's—and by extension Johannesburg's—financial network, just as his Brenthurst estate was the center of the city's social life. With Ina in charge, the Oppenheimers' bridge parties and dinners were pronounced the equal of any in London. Black tie was the usual dress; meals were served on gold plate. The family car was a chauffeur-driven black Rolls, and many of the guests arrived in automobiles of the same manufacture. Money and power radiated from every corner of the Oppenheimer empire.

Every corner but one. Ernest fancied a cabinet post, yet with all his power and influence, he was kept from the government's inner circle. Hertzog and Smuts were walking a fine line in South Africa; given the thunder on the right and the agitations of the large black majority, they had to appear independent of any influence—particularly the pressures of diamond and gold capitalists. Ernest knew better than to rail against circumstance. He kept his distance and announced in 1938 that he would not seek reelection. For once his actions were not magnified and analyzed by the press. It had more urgent matters to discuss. Nazi Germany was rolling over Europe, and South African leadership was of two minds about it. Smuts regarded the rise of Hitler as horrific; Hertzog saw it as the result of the injustice done to Germany in the postwar era. The Purified Nationalists naturally found much to admire in the Third Reich. One of their leaders, the Rev. Koot Vorster, was chosen to articulate his group's policy: "Hitler's *Mein Kampf* shows the way to greatness—the path of South Africa. Hitler gave the Germans a calling. He gave them a fanaticism which causes them to stand back for no one. We must follow this example because only by such holy fanaticism can the Afrikaaner nation achieve its calling."

In 1939 the battle lines were drawn in every sense. All through the year Smuts argued against the tactics of appeasement, and after Hitler seized Czechoslovakia Smuts urged South Africa to join the allies. On the other side of the aisle, Hertzog advocated a strict neutrality—what business did South Africa have in the affairs of Eastern Europe? By the time Parliament convened the two leaders were barely speaking to each other, and their fusion government headed for collapse. All debate came down to one question: should South Africa enter the war or stay out of it? On September 4, the matter was put to a vote. By a margin of 13, Parliament agreed to a declaration of war on Germany. Two days later Hertzog resigned to join forces with Malan, whose Purified National Party spent much of its time decrying the latest "British-Jewish conspiracy." A number of crypto-fascist organizations sprang up: the Grayshirts, the Blackshirts, *Ossewabrandwag*—"Ox-wagon sentinel"—all of them armed, all of them backers of the Nazi cause. The Rev. Wilhelm Luckoff, pastor of the German Lutheran Church at Bloemfontein, refused to pray for the Führer ("To ask God's blessing on Hitler's person would be a mockery of prayer"). A shocked congregation forced him to resign.

The pressure groups gained strength until the Germans overran Holland, the Afrikaaners' mother country. Smuts seized the day to promote the Allied cause, asking for able-bodied volunteers to end South Africa's isolation from the Western world. "Don't be left out of the greatest adventure of all time," said one of the government's recruiting posters. Another asked, "Was there ever a girl who didn't prefer a man in uniform?"

The African National Congress knew that if South African racial policies were oppressive, the Third Reich's would be even worse, and the organization quickly fell in line. It endorsed Smuts's call for war, and its members volunteered for frontline duty. For their efforts, they were informed that black men were welcome in the defense force so long as they were used in noncombatant roles—ambulance drivers, trench diggers, cooks, medical orderlies.

There were to be no exceptions. During an early battle in North Africa some African stretcher bearers were killed and given a common burial with white soldiers. South African Army Headquarters learned of the incident and ordered the bodies to be disinterred and buried in segregated graves. Africans from Bechuanaland and Basutoland were supposed to be issued firearms, but when they reached the North African front the supply sergeants gave out assegais; sharp knives were all right, but to allow natives to hold rifles, it was thought, would be to give them subversive ideas.

With more and more colleagues, employees, and servants joining up, Harry felt the obligation to put on a uniform. In January 1940, the 31-year-old volunteered for duty, took his training, and received a commission in Army Intelligence. His qualifications were impeccable—except to the National Party member who sat on a military review board. He commented obliquely on the lieutenant's shocking lack of Afrikaans: "Unilingual," said his report. "Knows French and German."

Late in the year the 4th South African Armored Car Regiment dug in at El Amiriya. From his listening post near the Libyan border Harry tapped into German messages, translated them, and sent relevant information back to headquarters. In mid-September he reported that General Rommel was planning an immediate offensive. The next day three German columns charged through the open desert at the phenomenal speed of 30 miles an hour, and the South Africans were forced to retreat. Not all of them made it. A truck carrying personnel records and ciphers was surrounded and captured. From the German propaganda station at Zeesen, word went out that the men of the 4th had been either captured or killed. Prominent among the names was Lieutenant Harry Frederick Oppenheimer of Johannesburg.

13

CLEAVING A DIAMOND WITH A BUTTER KNIFE

SEVERAL DAYS LATER, military intelligence determined what had actually happened: the Germans had seized paperwork, not soldiers. The South African soldiers reported as wounded or killed were just names from captured files. In the next few days the "casualties" straggled back to their base camp, were debriefed, and went on with their assignments as before. Harry continued to tap enemy wires and interrogate prisoners, wryly amused by the notion that he had been listed as missing and presumed dead.

After some delay the mail caught up with him. Ernest was Harry's principal correspondent, and his letters from Brenthurst brimmed with information. The elder Oppenheimers had loaned their home to the army. It was now a medical center, and in a further gesture of patriotism the Oppenheimers volunteered to pay all the bills. Wounded men from the Mediterranean theater—Britons, Free French, Poles, Greeks, Australians, even Italian POWs could be found chatting in the polyglot wards. "To show you how much Brenthurst is . . . a hospital," the father informed his son, "I walked in yesterday and was stopped by nurses who told me visitors were not admitted after 4:30. I assured them that I once owned the place."

In the half-superstitious hope that Harry would soon return, his house, Little Brenthurst, was being redesigned. From a suite at the Carlton Hotel, Ernest sent out assurances that the changes were "those which you discussed with Ina and me on many occasions. . . . The old dining-room has become the entrance-hall; the gables are pushed out, now have better bedroom and servants' accommodation, even for the

Natives. The new dining-room (where the old *stoep* was) is big enough to seat 35 people."

Every guest was appraised. "On Sunday," Ernest proudly noted, "the Crown Princess of Greece is lunching with us. She is a charming woman. You see your old man is getting famous." Another visitor was not so impressive: "She belongs to the oldest profession in the world."

Beneath the business and social intelligence from home Harry could read a subtext of melancholy. Anniversaries seemed especially hard. "On the 30th July," read one letter, "was your Mother's birthday. I thought of it all day long." Another tersely commented, "My thoughts are today especially with Frank and your Mother, in the firm belief they are happy and we shall meet again." Harry's expressions of concern got a mixed reply: "I am fit," Ernest told him, "but there is just no question that one is not so energetic when one is over sixty than one was in one's younger days. I do look forward to the time when you return and take active charge and I can play the role of an Elder Statesman."

No longer middle-aged, not quite old, Ernest in his early sixties began to show signs of deterioration. Where once he was tolerant, for example, he now grew impatient. Native ingratitude became the subject of an unusually irritated letter. With government aid, De Beers had gone out of its way to create a clean, handsomely outfitted camp for black mine workers. No, not a camp, "nor even a mining town, but a mining Utopia. The layout of the town, the houses, the amenities, the free services to our employees do not exist anywhere else. The whole thing is a dream town, something which—if mining is carried on in Paradise—one imagines it to be like."

And what was the native response? Ingratitude. "Anyone might have imagined that our workmen who had all these favors *forced* upon them would be loyal. Not a bit of it." The improved living conditions "made them an easy prey to Bolshevik propaganda. Why should we not supply more homes, more benefits, when our managers lived in palaces, when we kept a beautiful guest house for the benefit of directors, who pay an occasional visit?"

No doubt Harry would have viewed native affairs with better grace. However, neither he nor the army was ready for his demobilization. Authorities did pull Capt. Oppenheimer back from the front in 1942, posting him to an island in Table Bay off Cape Town, safe from the enemy and far from the family holdings. Or so it was assumed until a Japanese submarine got close enough to send four crewmen ashore. Captured, the quartet revealed its destination and plan: demolition of the African Explosives and Chemical Industries dynamite factory. The AECI was not unfamiliar to Harry; his father was chairman of the board.

During Capt. Oppenheimer's off-duty hours he struck up conversations with other officers. One of them was an attractive young lieutenant in the Women's Auxiliary. Years before, Bridget McCall's parents had been acquainted with Ernest and May in Johannesburg, and the young couple found no shortage of subjects to talk about. A few months later the discussions grew serious, when Ernest and Ina visited the Cape, Lt. McCall sailed ashore to meet them.

The Oppenheimers approved of their son's choice, and in the spring of 1943 Harry and Bridget exchanged vows at a military wedding. In keeping with family tradition, Harry's best man was a relative: his cousin (and stepbrother) Michael. A few months later Harry applied for a leave to attend to the family businesses. He never returned to active duty. Before Bridget gave birth to their first child, Mary, in December 1943, her husband was back in civilian life as the managing director of Anglo-American, sharing quarters with his father, the commanding officer of De Beers, at 44 Main Street in Johannesburg. Although Harry had been on the board before the war, this appointment served as notice that no matter how big the Oppenheimer empire, it was still a family concern.

He found his desk overflowing with papers and complications. They were as nothing compared with the trouble at De Beers. In Harry's absence industrial diamonds had assumed a vital importance. Gyroscopes, bombsights, guidance systems, airplane and automotive parts depended on precise cutting tools made with diamonds, and the Allies were attempting to govern the industry, stockpiling any stones they could get. But that industry was already ruled—by Ernest—and he had no intention of relinquishing his hold.

The first test of authority came with President Franklin D. Roosevelt's order for 6.5 million carats of industrial diamonds. Ernest balked at the amount: he thought there was an "artificially created fear of a shortage," that the size of the American demand was "farcical." What if the war ended quickly, leaving America with a surplus of stones? Obviously the demand would slow, prices would crash through the floor. De Beers might never recover. Ernest refused to fill the United States order.

F.D.R. searched for a diplomatic solution. His State Department asked for help from Winston Churchill's War Cabinet, only to find that Ernest's men had already been there, pleading De Beers's case. Without exactly turning down the President's request, the British failed to go along with it. American investigators did not have to search far for the reason: His Majesty's government had been staffed with De Beers executives, mobilized for the war. In a secret memorandum, the United States War Production Board fumed, "the diamond section of the government and the Syndicate seem to be the same."

There was only one thing left to do. Another confidential memo, dated April 16, 1942, was brief but eloquent: "It was said unofficially that we would not give planes to England if the Syndicate would not sell us the diamonds with which to make them." Without those attack planes London would be virtually helpless against the Luftwaffe's bombing raids. A few communiqués later, De Beers yielded. Even then, the surrender was arranged on its own terms.

The company agreed to sell the United States one million carats, a mere fraction of the original request. Irritated, the Roosevelt administration escalated its demands. Each time pressure was applied, De Beers offered another reason for noncompliance. It did not have enough diamonds on hand. Its London vaults "had been bombed shut" in an air raid. It needed more time to prepare an inventory. As 1943 came to a close, the administration ran out of patience and enlisted the aid of the Justice Department. An investigation of the diamond industry got under way. It amounted to a war within the war, complete with maneuvers, casualties, and atrocities.

The investigators took full advantage of their wartime powers to operate outside the law, opening the mail of Oppenheimer associates in the United States, secretly rummaging through records, leaking stories to journalists. De Beers responded with its own public relations campaign. *Time* magazine reported that the diamond cartel was meeting all charges "with a dignified silence. If De Beers was disturbed by the charges of price fixing, control of production, quotas for diamond merchants, etc, it was comforted by the belief that [Attorney General Francis] Biddle had no more chance of denting the cartel than of cleaving a diamond with a butter knife."

Perhaps; and yet Ernest could not have been happy with revelations unearthed by the Office of Strategic Services. Intercepted mail showed that De Beers was stifling its competitors all over the world—including those in America. Nelson Rockefeller and some associates had investigated the possibilities of diamond mining in Venezuela. De Beers's advisors learned about the project and warned Ernest to be "ruthless in stamping it out." According to another letter, a De Beers mine in the Belgian Congo called Forminière was being overworked and depleted years before its time—for the mine threatened South Africa's position as the world's principal source of diamonds, and Ernest wanted "complete control over the market."

The company's reach extended to British Guiana, where De Beers had bought areas rich in precious stones; and, astonishingly, to Arkansas, the only state where diamonds had been found in quantity. Ernest's colleagues had acquired control of an on-site United States company. They selected a De Beers engineer to build a plant for separating and sorting stones. The machinery was flawed, perhaps deliberately. In any case it failed to produce a sufficient quantity of diamonds, and the company was shut down. "An inference could be drawn," said a Justice Department memo, "that the property was sabotaged and then closed at the insistence of Sir Ernest Oppenheimer."

More incidents came to light when the OSS began a crucial inquiry: how was it that the Third Reich was still able to buy all the industrial diamonds it wanted for the manufacture of, among other things, V-2 rockets? Company defenders sent a confidential report to the Justice Department stating that De Beers's hands were clean: "Almost the entire [diamond] production of Africa is policed through the operation of elaborate controls extending through every mining area of the continent." The diamonds were then sent "in a closely guarded stream" to London.

But the OSS had evidence that the stream was being freely fished by poachers. Working backwards from black-market diamond dealers in Cairo and Tangier, a United States agent traced the stones to Forminière. A chain of Belgian Congolese smugglers had been suborned by the Nazis. Corruption reached up to the Police Chief of Leopoldville. To confirm his findings, the agent gave a Belgian citizen some money to purchase illegal diamonds. It was an unfortunate tactic. The citizen was arrested, and to save his skin he identified the agent as his source of cash. The American was promptly expelled, ending the investigation.

The OSS tried to work its way around the Congolese authorities by going public, proposing a wartime "advisory commission" on diamond smuggling. The British had a better idea. They would employ a security expert and an engineer to oversee the situation, the men to be selected by the most reliable diamond authority in the world: Sir Ernest Oppenheimer. "Thus," an OSS memo acidly commented, "the responsibility for security" would be "turned over entirely to the industry."

To quiet their ally, British Intelligence stepped in and imposed a new plan for halting the flow of diamonds to Germany. The OSS remained exasperated and suspicious. Its officers thought the new British operation would be "unable to cope with the Syndicate's control of the industry and its dealing with the enemy." Yet the Americans were unwilling to go further. A secret memorandum sent to the Assistant Attorney General conceded, "we could not make any allegation that [De Beers] themselves have prevented effective control of leakage of industrial diamonds to Germany. . . . Any theory of this nature would seem to depend upon supporting action by some units of the British Government." Those units never appeared, and the Justice Department reluctantly withdrew. It would not "be involved in a controversy of this nature." De Beers had won another small victory.

Yet it was an uncomfortable one, because the diamond smuggling went on unimpeded. That could only aid—deliberately or inadvertently—Germany's war efforts. A vicious new rumor arose. The real reason Sir Ernest had converted to Christianity, it was whispered, was in order to do business with the Third Reich. Germany, after all, had been paying 30 times the diamonds' official price; profits would have been enormous. The rumor was patently untrue: why would Hitler, whose Final Solution condemned those with one tainted grandparent, whose Minister of Culture said "I decide who is a Jew," deal with so recent a convert? Calumny dies hard, however, and 50 years later the slur could still be heard in Johannesburg.

♦   ♦   ♦

THE COUNTRY had a lot to celebrate on VE Day, 1945. Smuts's enthusiasm for the Allied cause had been vindicated, and even his enemies took to calling him *die Oubaas*, the old master. Notions of universal freedom were promoted in newspapers throughout the Western world. Blacks had every right to expect postwar dividends. In mid-May they were encouraged to see the Afrikaaner right remain silent as 20,000 Africans marched in a euphoric "People's Day of Victory" in Johannesburg, organized by the Council of Non-European Trade Unions, the ANC, and a revived Communist Party.

Reality began to seep in when the government published its list of veterans' benefits. Whites were to receive £5 in cash and a £25 clothing allowance. "Colored men" would get £3 and £15 respectively, and Africans £2 and a khaki suit worth £2. During the war only 750 housing units had been built for natives, and now the outskirts of Johannesburg were filled with thousands of shacks put up by squatters who had no place else to live. The administration expressed regret for the overcrowding, but only regret. No money could be found for new dwellings. On the diamond and gold fields, War Measure 1425 remained in force: since left-wing agitators might manipulate the workers at will, it was forbidden for more than twenty men to congregate on mine property.

Conditions for Africans continued to deteriorate even as the officers and shareholders of De Beers and Anglo enjoyed new prosperity and power. Demand for industrial diamonds dipped briefly as factories retooled, then went up again. A drill burrowed deep into the earth of the Orange Free State and came up with a load of pure gold—the richest deposit in the world. Investors fell over themselves in a rush to put money in Oppenheimer companies. *The Economist* reported that "All the achievements of Aladdin's Lamp pale beside the £20 million boom in the . . . mining exploration shares which the speculating public has built up in a fortnight."

Aware that De Beers and Anglo would need every mine worker they could find, Ernest told his executives what needed to be done.

The Oppenheimer companies must "pay special attention to the welfare of our employees. . . . It is our aim to have the best possible housing conditions for our European population, and to improve their amenities of life to the greatest possible extent."

The African situation, he allowed, was a special and enduring "problem." He could not see past the traditional ways of segregating blacks in the same old labor reservoir. Somehow they had to be kept energetic enough to work hard, yet docile enough to stay away from organizers and agitators. "The compound system must be continued for some time to come," Ernest thought, "but I feel sure our ultimate aim should be to create, within a reasonable time, modern native villages from which the mines would ultimately draw a large proportion of their native labor requirements."

D. F. Malan denounced this mild suggestion as a prescription for social catastrophe. His Purified National Party predicted that liberal policies would lead to "black spots"—small native enclaves—breaking out in European areas. Next would come racial clashes and revolution. Disillusioned and bitter, the 4-year-old African Mine Workers Union made frantic efforts to propagandize and recruit new members. In the summer of 1946 the leaders got hold of a governmental report admitting to the landlessness, poverty, and malnutrition endemic in the black homelands. Using it as a weapon, the AMWU demanded a minimum 10-shilling raise for every worker, and the repeal of War Measure 1425. The Chamber of Mines ignored the union, and on Monday morning, August 12, some sixty thousand gold miners put down their picks and shovels and walked off their jobs.

Union leaders expected Smuts to play the statesman in this confrontation. They were fatally mistaken. To the Prime Minister this labor dispute was the result of outside agitation, and he assured the mine owners that the government would take whatever "appropriate action" was necessary. The action took the form of summary arrests and violent police raids. On August 13 the compounds were sealed so that no one could get in or out. At one mine, as the noise level rose and laborers jostled with guards and policemen, an order came to fire on the crowd. Six men fell dead. A panic followed, and another six were trampled to death.

Forced back to work the next morning, the miners tried a nonviolent approach. Their sit-down protest only served to raise the stakes. Police formed outside the mine entrances and fingered their nightsticks, ready to attack. On a given signal they plunged down to the bottom shafts. Excavation by excavation, level by level, they beat and drove the blacks upward until they reached the outside. Laborers were then pushed and marched back into their compounds. By Saturday the 17th it was all over. The miners had been wholly defeated. No deal was necessary, no raises, no compromises. As an added twist of the knife, it was revealed that during the strike a group of conservative blacks calling themselves the Natives Representative Council had met to discuss the situation. Normally they were allowed a room at Pretoria City Hall. This time they had been herded into narrow quarters in the Labor Department, where all the lavatory doors were clearly marked Whites Only. To go to the toilet they had to leave the building and seek relief in a Blacks Only building. They had better get used to segregation, said City Hall; this was not only the natives' past, it was to be their future.

After his victory something seemed to wither and die in the Old Master. Twelve men had died, and more than a thousand miners had been injured. These statistics made South Africa appear to be a barbaric country, constantly at war with itself. Smuts tried to refurbish his reputation and the United Party's image, spending more and more time at United Nations headquarters in Paris. It was in that city that he drafted the historic Declaration of Human Rights—rights denied to most people in his own country. The irony was not lost on the black populace. As native protests grew more strident and whites nervously sought help from the politicians, *die Oubaas* returned, brandishing a new idea: the United Party would play its English card.

In 150 years of imperial history, no British king or queen had set foot in South Africa. To Smuts, this seemed the ideal time for a royal visit. Throughout World War II, no matter how badly the battles had gone, the royal family had given the impression of solidity and historical power. Its members were now regarded as icons of victory, and the Prime Minister hoped to gain strength from the regal association. With much fanfare he sent forth an invitation to King George VI, his Queen, and their daughters, and early in 1948 the family arrived for its unprecedented visit.

Threatened anti-British demonstrations failed to materialize, but the leading Afrikaaner newspaper continued to regard the Windsors as non-persons: not a single story mentioned them. Townspeople in Stellenbosch did the journalists one better; they met the king in total silence. Smuts was pleased to see Kimberley reverse the trend. Sir Ernest was there, an impeccably tailored figure slightly taller than the princesses Elizabeth and Margaret. Ina came along; so did Harry and Bridget and the 3-and-a-half-year-old Mary. The newest member of their family, Nicholas Frank, was considered too young for state occasions, and he stayed back at Little Brenthurst.

Dutifully, the regal guests made their way to the historic and long-abandoned Big Hole at Kimberley, where they approached the guard rail and gazed blankly down at the green, stagnant water. Lunch was served at the nearby Kimberley Club, then as now a Victorian place of polished mahogany, diamond power, and inedible food. At the appropriate interval both princesses received sizeable jewels from the De Beers collection, after which Smuts dramatically announced that British rule would continue to be a "guarantee of universal peace." Several days later Elizabeth responded with an address to the Commonwealth, broadcast from Government House in Johannesburg. It was her 21st birthday, and listeners throughout Africa, India, and Canada heard the young princess make history when she told them, "Through the inventions of science I can now do what was impossible for bygone heirs to the Throne. I can make my solemn act of dedication with a whole Empire listening."

Her speech recalled the great days of Victoria and Cecil Rhodes, and banking on the royal afterglow Smuts called a general election for the fall of 1948. It became the most fateful decision in South African history. The Prime Minister and his United Party saw social progress as a ramp rather than a staircase: gradualism was the answer to all racial problems. Smuts believed that labor migration to the cities had become "irreversible" and that territorial separation of white and black was "utterly impractical." This did not mean that he endorsed radical or even liberal legislation. To him, social progress was a matter of tiny increments. Blacks would be "uplifted" with the progress of time.

Whites would be strengthened by the increase of European immigrants to the land of diamonds and gold.

To the hard-liners of the National Party, Smuts's philosophy of reconciliation was nothing less than surrender parading as statesmanship. They called for a vote of no confidence in the government, building a new campaign around *swart gevaar*: the black peril. Academics contributed theses about tribalism; Dutch Reform ministers reminded their congregations of Deuteronomy 32:8: "When the Most High gave the nations their inheritance, when He divided the sons of man, he fixed their bounds according to the numbers of the sons of God." According to their interpretation, "divided sons of man" meant whites in one part of the country, blacks in another. And who were humble South Africans to defy the prescriptions of the Lord?

No one could accuse the National Party of ambiguity. Its program openly proclaimed that the choice facing the country was "either that of integration, which would in the long run amount to national suicide on the part of the Whites; or that of apartheid, which professes to safeguard the future of every race." The Party platform went on to condemn "Churches and missions which frustrate the policy of apartheid." And it demanded that blacks in urban areas "should be regarded as migratory citizens not entitled to political or social rights equal to those of the Whites."

Politicians in Europe and America spoke out against the insolent builders of apartheid. Seething newspaper editorials made it difficult for readers to look away from South Africa; and then a 45-year-old white teacher made it impossible. Alan Paton's novel, *Cry, the Beloved Country*, belongs on that small shelf of books that, without any advance publicity or critical acclaim, make their way onto the international bestseller lists. In narrating the tragedy of a Zulu family it distilled the essence of a people in extremis. The father is a minister—an *umfundisi*—who attempts to guide his son by Christian principles. When the boy reaches maturity he is tempted by the lure of mining money and big-city life, and abandons his rural home for the teeming slums of Johannesburg. Crime and violence become his lot, and in the end he is condemned to death for the unintended murder of a white man.

The book, published in 1947, had its shortcomings: repetitiveness, an unstable mix of the poetic and the editorial. But Paton had been the principal of a boys' reformatory outside Johannesburg, and his work was crammed with intimate detail. No one could question the authenticity of his reportage or dialogue. Indeed, many readers made their first acquaintance with a real magnate when his name was invoked in Chapter 23. Sir Ernest Oppenheimer is mentioned as "one of the great men of the mines," one of the few decent Randlords, willing "to try out the experiment of settled mine labor, in villages, not compounds, where a man can live with his wife and children. They want to hear your voice again, Sir Ernest Oppenheimer," says the narrator. "Some of them applaud you, and some of them say thank God for you, in their hearts, even at their bedsides."

The *umfundisi*'s story entered hundreds of thousands of homes in the United States and Europe, and eventually became a film and a Broadway musical. This, outsiders were persuaded, was what it meant to be black in South Africa, where drought no longer signified a shortage of water but a lack of compassion: less than 20 percent of the population imposed legal restrictions on the other 80 percent. Voices were raised against the Nationalists in Europe and the northern United States, and political analysts gave the party little chance of victory. Its platform smacked of the worst kind of extremism, even of jackboot Nazism. Moreover, Smuts had not only led his nation through World War II, he had become internationally famous as an architect of the U.N. Surely this prosperous and decently conservative country would not want an abrupt change of leadership. As the polls closed, United Party candidates confidently prepared their acceptance speeches.

Harry Oppenheimer was among them, hoping to represent Kimberley in Parliament as his father had before him. Harry's candidacy had presented some technical difficulties: his home was not in Kimberley, it was in Johannesburg. Horses provided the solution. Harry, who had shown little previous interest in racing, would breed champions at Mauritzfontein, a stud farm about seven miles from the diamond mines. Never mind that the farm had no suitable house; Harry would have one built, and he would live there long enough to establish residence.

The United Party's feeling of euphoria evaporated 24 hours after the polls closed. As expected, the UP pulled in large majorities in most of the towns and cities; Harry led his opponent by more than two thousand ballots and kept the right to represent Kimberley. But the Nationalist candidates swept almost every rural district, and in a special humiliation Smuts lost his supposedly safe seat in the town of Standerton outside Johannesburg. "My old comrades have turned against me," he was heard to complain. That was not quite true. As someone cruelly reminded him, "How could they? Your old comrades are all dead." The final count showed that the white supremacists had won an unpredicted and shocking victory.

At the next convening of Parliament, Daniel Malan replaced Smuts as Prime Minister. Malan provided a sharp contrast to his predecessor. Smuts was spare and white-bearded, his manner high-toned and evasive. Malan was fat and clean-shaven, crumpled in appearance and confrontational in style. He exhorted his followers to remember the ancient Boer victories over the Zulu nation: "your Blood River lies in the cities. . . . In that new Blood River, black and white meet together in much closer contact and much more binding struggle." Settled in office he and other Nationalists began their politics of revenge, assuming supreme command of all South Africa from the upper reaches of Parliament to the lowest levels of the mines. The imposition of apartheid was to grant a final victory to the Boers, almost 50 years after their loss to the British.

In a perverse way, the Nationalist triumph strengthened Oppenheimer's hand. Had the United Party won, Harry would have been identified as the man from De Beers and Anglo, a parliamentarian only slightly more progressive than his father. Now, as the Nationalists began to implement their harsh racial laws, he appeared to be the essence of moderation and decency. Recognized as the Opposition's most articulate representative, he spoke out freely on two topics, money and race. There were those who thought his attacks on apartheid had less to do with morality than with the foreign investors' image of a neolithic South Africa and with the maintenance of a plentiful and docile labor force. Others thought that liberalism had found a fresh voice.

Harry took a pragmatic approach: whatever the moral background, racial divisiveness was driving investors away. That was bad for business, bad for South Africa, bad for whites as well as blacks. Few dared to challenge him in the arena. "Arguing with the honorable member for Kimberley City in a financial debate is rather like arguing with the Bank of England," said a columnist in *The Rand Daily Mail*. "Other members may wonder where the capital influx has gone since the Nationalists came and why it hesitates to come back. Harry Frederick Oppenheimer, though he looks disconcertingly young, does not wonder. He knows."

The trouble with the man from Kimberley, Nationalists complained, was his unpredictability. Better to have an out-and-out enemy than a man who seemed conciliatory one moment and confrontational the next. In a typical speech Harry pleased the Nationalists by acknowledging that "It is all very well to be separated from the Natives and walk in separate corridors at Johannesburg station." Then he turned around and unnerved them by adding: "while we still have the Native working in our houses and looking after our children . . . apartheid is getting us nowhere." Then he switched tones again, insisting that the United Party aimed for prosperity, not revolution. Its members were never in the business of making the native an equal, he said; they simply wanted to give black laborers a chance to improve themselves, to be better educated, to keep their families intact. These efforts would produce internal stability and a greater South Africa.

The new leaders never trusted the two faces of Harry Oppenheimer. They felt that he was overarticulate, too wealthy and too clever by half. Left alone he might become a political star and a very formidable rival to Malan. If that were to happen, God alone knew what rights and privileges might be ceded to the Kaffirs.

So when Harry raised money to resuscitate the United Party, the Nationalists countered with a barrage of speeches, editorials, accusations, and ad hominem cartoons. Their tactics were so blatant that *The Economist* commented: "South African Nationalists play a complicated game of politics with only three well-thumbed cards. These are the black bogey, the British connection and 'Hoggenheimer'. . . . 'Hoggenheimer' represent[s] 'money power,' which in South Africa has traditionally meant the gold and diamond mines. It is no accident that 'Hoggenheimer' rhymes with Oppenheimer."

Addressing the Harry Problem, Malan proclaimed: "What we have against us is money power, principally under the leadership of Oppenheimer. He has become a power in the land. Oppenheimer—the one who sits in parliament—has control of millions of pounds, and he puts this at the service of our opponents in this struggle. Oppenheimer with his millions exercises a greater influence than, I think, any man in South Africa has ever had." Nationalist spokesmen continued the fight in Parliament. According to one of them, the United Party had been invented by Jews and reinforced by Englishmen. Now "that Party sits in Opposition. General Smuts is no longer there. There is a Leader on that side who . . . has a 'snowball's hope' in South Africa to get that party returned to power."

Harry returned the fire. The government was using its majority to push South Africa backward. But the vindictiveness and racism of the Nationalists would not endure. "What is happening is that people are waking up . . . in reaction to what the government is doing. I don't expect hon. members opposite to like that. I can assure them they will like it a great deal less when the [next] general election comes along."

At the time of Jan Smuts's death in 1950, the battle was joined. In the looking-glass politics of South Africa, a conservative Christian multimillionaire, born in Johannesburg, was portrayed as a conniving English Jew. And his party, which for half a century had kept black labor available, cheap, and docile, was maligned as a group of irresponsible radicals.

♦　　♦　　♦

BETWEEN THE SALE of industrial diamonds during the war, and jewelry immediately afterward, De Beers found itself with a surplus of £25,000,000. There was some talk about portioning the money out to the shareholders; Ernest quickly put a stop to that. As in the past, he followed the lead of the Colossus: extend your reach, put the capital to good use.

As the financial world looked on in wonderment, a De Beers diamond selling and buying subsidiary, Diamond Corporation, reproduced itself by splitting in two equal parts like an amoeba. One half kept its original name and function. The other became known as the De Beers Investment Trust. Its purpose was to put the surplus to work in whatever way the trustees (i.e., Sir Ernest Oppenheimer) wished it to work. Some shareholders raised hell; the rest went along with a man who had made few, if any, fiscal errors. *The Economist* reported the contretemps: "it is claimed shareholders might have been allowed to decide themselves whether to invest money in speculative ventures . . . but Sir Ernest will have none of it. He claims he is 'reviving the tradition of Cecil John Rhodes.' So shareholders of this group follow Sir Ernest pioneering with the mantle of Rhodes around his shoulders whether they like it or not. So far they have come to no harm."

Nor would they. Nearing 70, the old autocrat outdid himself. Diamonds and gold, copper and coal would have to step aside. He was pleased to announce that a fresh and exciting source of wealth had been found on company properties. Since August of 1945, the world had been repeatedly informed that it had entered the Atomic Age. It was no secret that the metallic element uranium, central to the making of fissionable material, was frequently found on the site of gold mines: South Africa was known to have a handful of minor uranium fields, markedly inferior to those found in Canada, Europe, and the Congo. Recently, however, an American physicist had examined some gold ore from the Witwatersrand. His report was so encouraging that geologists had come with Geiger counters, wandering the fields and judging for themselves. According to their calibrations, the Reef was one of the biggest uranium fields in the world. Almost depleted of their gold, the Anglo mines would be reappraised as prime sources of atomic energy. For hardly any capital investment—the mounds of discarded earth and the deep excavations were already in place—millions more pounds were going to come to South Africa.

The government tactfully reappraised its relationship with the Oppenheimers. By the early 1950s uranium was the most anxiously hunted element in the world. It was neither an ornament, like diamonds, nor a method of exchange, like gold; if it fell into any category, uranium would have to be considered a weapon. Properly, it belonged in the hands of the administration. Yet Malan could hardly countenance the nationalizing of an industry; that was the sort of thing the Communists did, not the "purified" right. After many months a modus vivendi was hammered out. The sale of uranium to foreign governments would be overseen by an official Atomic Energy Board, the profits to go to the producers. They would then pay the government back through a process of land leases and income taxes.

The Big Hole at Kimberley in the 1870s, when diamond digging began in earnest

McGregor Museum

McGregor Museum

The two men who triggered the diamond rush: Schalk van Niekerk (left) found the first stone; Jack O'Reilly sold it

De Beers Centenary AG

"Never has any eye seen such a marvelous show of mining as was given in this grand amphitheater": like strings of an enormous harp, the metal ropes reach down to hundreds of separate claims, twanging in various keys as they haul rawhide buckets of diamondiferous soil up to the surface

Leander Starr Jameson, physician, politician, speculator, and self-designated soldier, who led the notorious Jameson Raid

Barney Barnato (né Barnett Isaacs), the cockney "Jew d'esprit" who left London to go diamond hunting and became a multimillionaire

Cecil John Rhodes, the "Colossus," who saw no conflict of interest between his jobs as chairman of De Beers and prime minister of his country

Joseph Benjamin Robinson, one of the earliest and most aggressive Randlords —a man whose favorite weapons were the horsewhip and the lawsuit

Alfred Beit, Rhodes's indispensable advisor and South Africa's first financial genius

Stephanus Johannes Paulus Kruger, "Uncle Paul" to the Boers who elected him their leader; he predicted quite accurately that "every ounce of gold taken from the bowels of our soil will have yet to be weighed up with rivers of tears"

McGregor Museum

Miners' families were expected to pitch in: women and children spent long days on the diamond fields, washing and sorting the stones

McGregor Museum

Dressed in antelope, leopard, and jackal skins, black tribesmen arrived at the diamond fields ready to work for low wages in order to buy guns and brides

By the 1880s, "horse whims" took the place of human labor

Until women arrived at the fields, unisex Saturday night dances were all the rage

When the workday was done, African laborers climbed the great human anthill of the Big Hole to go home

Sorting could be a career in itself, requiring a meticulous eye and scrupulous honesty. Most employees had the eye; the honesty often had to be reinforced by an overseer with even keener vision

Dealers' Row in Kimberley, where immense fortunes were made and lost in corrugated iron shacks

As the mines grew deeper, new ways had to be found for conveying laborers from the surface to the claims below; three "boys" make their way down on a rudimentary cable car, pulled by horses

Groote Schuur, the "Great Granary" that became Cecil Rhodes's country estate and his favorite retreat

As the racial lines hardened, blacks were given an unambiguous message: if it was luxurious, it was for Europeans only

Natives were separated from their families and segregated in compounds. There they could be supervised and physically inspected. In case the security force overlooked a stone, netting was placed overhead so that the thieves could not throw jewels to confederates

Later, inspection grew far more refined—and infinitely more humiliating as black overseers examined every possible orifice for illicit diamonds, while other miners watched and the camera looked on

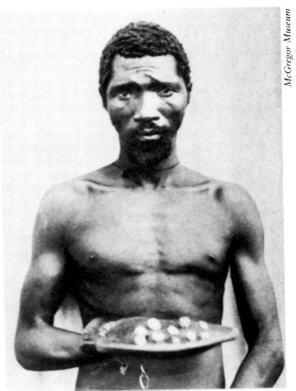

Occasionally, a laborer would swallow a diamond or two. This one gulped down ten and, like most other thieves, was forced to give them back

"The largest check yet written," for 5,338,650 pounds sterling, sealed the amalgamation of the De Beers and Kimberley mines, and literally provided the rocks on which the last empire would be built

PARTNERS!

South Africa's classic anti-Semitic caricature, "Hoggenheimer," portrayed the Jew as a fat, grasping profiteer, whose greed endangered the very life of South Africa. This Frank Holland cartoon appeared in *The Johannesburg Star*

As the Rothschilds had proved, brothers were the key to financial success. Ernest Oppenheimer had four. Top row: Gustav, Bernard, Ernest; bottom row: Louis, Michael (Bernard's son), and Otto

Ernest was elected the Mayor of Kimberley in 1912 and remained in office until the start of World War I, when a German accent was considered a liability

De Beers Centenary AG

Ernest and his second wife, Ina, visited
Johannesburg's Shantytown to see conditions
firsthand. Shocked, Ernest provided funds for
a new township; it was originally to be
named after him, but was later called Soweto

De Beers Centenary AG

Harry, Ernest's son, wearing
the uniform of the South
African army, took Bridget
McCall as his bride in 1943

UPI/Bettmann

Mary, Harry's daughter, with her
first husband, Gordon Waddell,
whose relationship with De Beers
outlasted the marriage by many
years

Nicky, Harry's son and heir to the Oppenheimer empire, married Orcillia "Strilli" Lasch in 1968

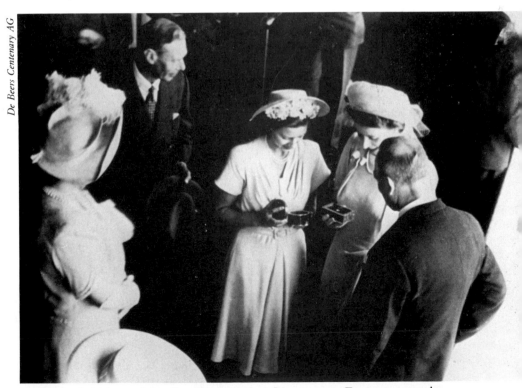

When the British royal family visited South Africa in 1947, Ernest presented the princesses with diamonds

Harry socializing with a few of his thousands of employees at a club in
Zambia's copper mining district

Harry confers with Charles
Engelhard, the precious metals
magnate who was the model for
Ian Fleming's *Goldfinger*

Petrus Ramaboa, a digger,
flashes his find, the Lesotho
Brown, one of the largest
diamonds on record

In the Siberian tundra, diamonds were actively mined—and silently sold
through De Beers, even though the Soviet Union was loud in its denunciation
of South Africa

Directors of Anglo American: Nicholas Oppenheimer, far right, flanked by Julian Ogilvie Thompson. At far left, Gavin Relly

Kimberley's Big Hole today, a tourist attraction and a repository for rainwater

The arrangement was Solomonic. Each party got exactly what it needed: for Anglo, large revenues; for Malan's government, international power. An Anglo executive put it neatly. "As things stand today," he told a study conference, "our position in the field of uranium is of paramount importance to the future. Even though we may not be the largest individual producer, our position as a source of uranium is assured until at least the end of the century." So much for money. As for the "very important factor" of politics, one might be critical of the Nationalists, but one had to be pragmatic. After all, "the world will want our uranium and for that reason," no matter who runs the government, "South Africa will be regarded as a very important bastion of Western civilization."

14

GETTING AWAY
WITH IT

A HUNDRED YEARS EARLIER, John T. Williamson would have been one
of Africa's eminent Victorians. The diamond hunter displayed all the
characteristics: high intelligence, retarded sexuality, unstable temper,
and most important, an attachment to subtropical lands far from home.

Home in his case was Canada. As an undergraduate at McGill
University in Montreal, the lumberman's son became fascinated, not
to say obsessed, with geology. He received his Ph.D. in 1933 and took
a job copper mining in Rhodesia. Coworkers thought that the young
man had been born with sand under his skin. Hardly a day passed
without some sort of argument, and after a couple of years Williamson
was only too happy to part company and go it alone. During his time
in Rhodesia he had heard prospectors speaking of isolated diamond
strikes in Tanganyika (now Tanzania). The geologist journeyed to the
area, made soil tests, and convinced himself that a lake of precious
stones lay beneath the parched earth, if only one knew where to look.

For the next three years he explored vast stretches of land. Several
times he fell gravely ill with blackwater fever and malaria; twice he
nearly went bankrupt. Undiscouraged, he pushed on. In 1940 he stumbled on a lone diamond in an isolated region called Mwadui, south of
Lake Victoria. The requisite leases and licenses were obtained, and a
team of hired hands began to pick over the soil. After a few false starts,
they unearthed the classic blue ground. It continued for five miles.
Williamson had found his lake.

Over the next few years Mwadui grew into a millionaire's private
city-state. It had paved streets, shops, a school, a club, an airstrip,

sporting facilities, and a reservoir big enough to hold Williamson's new yacht. Tanganyika's British administrators hinted that the Union Jack should be hoisted up the town flagpole, and the master of Mwadui agreed. But only if it fluttered beneath the company pennant, a white diamond on a red background carrying the inscription W D Ltd.

With all of this wealth, the owner remained an isolate. He had only one or two friends, the men who had staked him when he was an indigent prospector. Through World War II, the story of Mwadui became a favorite of feature writers; images of the lanky and moustachioed figure enlivened newspapers in Britain and on the Continent, and sheaves of marriage offers came in. Williamson ignored them all. He had no use for women. "They only want me for my diamonds," he protested.

Yet he treated those stones with a disregard that amounted to contempt. Jam jars full of diamonds sat untended on his mantel, and security at the mine was so lax that workers brazenly sneaked the stones out in their hair and navels, in plaster casts and chunks of butter. It was some time before British authorities could convince him to hire Detective Inspector Percy Burgess, newly retired from Scotland Yard—and then it was because the stolen diamonds were being used to finance groups of radical blacks, agitating for independence. Here, at least, Williamson and the British saw eye to eye.

Inspector Burgess was to note many exotic sights in his tenure, and the strangest of them was Williamson himself. For all his humorless demeanor, the magnate delighted in practical jokes. He scattered fake diamonds on his property, waited for guests and staffers to make the inevitable cries of discovery, then laughed in their faces. He carried a pair of scissors in his pocket, so that when he felt the urge he could snip off a visitor's tie. (Several days later a new cravat would be sent as compensation.) One night he sneaked into his own club, stole all the furniture, and secreted it in his own house.

When he was not creating mischief, Williamson amused himself with a series of collections: antique furniture, rare Persian carpets, first editions, and mongrel dogs, which he allowed to bark, scratch, and shed all over the house. He prided himself on his knitting; he had twice won the Aylsebury Women's Institute Silver Distaff Award for Needlework.

These were the lighter signs of eccentricity. Williamson drank heavily, usually a noxious combination of whiskey and lime juice, and he alternated between long, brooding silences and bursts of manic glee or fury. Burgess recalled the day when "a quarrel suddenly flared up between him and the woman who was his secretary at the time. She had just raised some query, I think, nothing very important.

"I hesitated to go because I thought he might be on the verge of having one of his recurrent attacks of fever and knew from experience how unreasonable he could be at such times. He got more excited and continued to shout and finally flung all the diamonds around the room, rushed into his bedroom and locked the door behind him." Burgess and the secretary spent hours on their hands and knees tracking down the stones and placing them back in their containers. It was, he told friends, just another day at Mwadui.

For those who knew all the parties, it would be hard to imagine a greater contrast than the one between Williamson and the Oppenheimers. The former prospector regarded De Beers as a pack of jackals out for his fortune, and for some years he totally refused to deal with the diamond syndicate. Instead, the jewels of W D Ltd were sold on the open market through banks in London. In 1948 Williamson finally reached an agreement with the Oppenheimer interests, only to break it off in 1950, when he concluded that the syndicate was not rewarding him with the profits he deserved. He withdrew from competition and began to stockpile stones. Ernest and Harry realized that this situation could not be allowed to continue: at any time W D Ltd might unload its stock, flood the market, and precipitate a crash.

In the spring of 1952 Harry flew to Mwadui to see if a rapprochement could be arranged. Burgess remembered the day: Oppenheimer, he noticed, was "short, slight and remarkably ordinary-looking. Ordinarily dressed, too; it was difficult to think of him as being in command of a vast financial empire. This first impression, however, was dispelled as soon as one began to talk to him. I was interested to see how he at once put Williamson at his ease."

The ease vanished after the first day. Williamson did everything he could to throw his guest off guard. Meetings were scheduled at odd hours—sometimes as late as 11 p.m., sometimes in the early morning. As the negotiations heated up, he made a point of Delphic silences.

One morning Harry made up his mind not to respond; he would sit in his chair and refuse to say the first word. Twenty agonizing minutes ticked by. . . . Williamson finally won the war of nerves when his guest could stand no more and shattered the atmosphere by making a few tentative remarks. Other gambits followed. On certain occasions the host demanded to be left alone in order to ponder De Beers's latest offer. Harry and his assistant would take strolls in the sun, along the gravel paths of the mine compound. Wherever they walked they were flanked by trained maribou storks. The birds seemed to be eavesdropping on every confidence; when the men reached the end of a path and went back, the storks also turned around and retraced their steps.

Once Williamson had made Harry sufficiently uncomfortable he got around to stating his case. What he wanted was the annual right to produce up to 10 percent, by value, of the world's diamonds. Otherwise he would stay out of the syndicate. The decision was excruciating for Harry. He could not afford to allow a major source to operate outside of his empire. It would break the cartel. Yet to allow Williamson to produce so many stones would be to cede millions of dollars to a known maverick; there was no telling what the man might do. In the end there was no choice. Harry was trapped and he knew it. He capitulated quietly and left town. Exultant, the mad king of Mwadui returned to his throne. The friends of labor waited for the worst to happen.

He surprised them by becoming shockingly and perversely liberal. His black employees were allowed to bring their families into the compounds, a policy De Beers had still not adopted. Mwadui miners were carefully searched, but they were not given purges, South African style, and they could quit whenever they wished. Although Burgess tightened up security, there were always some holes in his fences, and from time to time the detective inspector had to report another incident of diamonds missing. Williamson never seemed to mind. "What I never have I'll never miss," was his philosophical reply.

The Oppenheimers could not afford to be so sanguine. Unlike Williamson, they were responsible to stockholders and directors. And from time to time I.D.B. still made the headlines; embarrassing stories circulated about smuggling in Angola, the Congo, Rhodesia, Mozambique. The cartel had to act. Legally or otherwise, it had to plug the holes. Harry took his cue from Mwadui. Williamson had engaged an ex-Scotland Yard man; why shouldn't De Beers do the same? Sir Percy Sillitoe, the famous chief of MI-5, Britain's counter-intelligence organization, had recently retired. What if Sir Percy could be persuaded to work for the Oppenheimers? Ernest dispatched another knight, Sir Reginald Leeper, head of the Diamond Corporation in London, to locate Sillitoe.

Leeper found his man ringing up sales at a sweetshop in Sussex. The counterspy who had tracked down Soviet agents was now meekly handing out peppermints to suburban matrons. It was no undercover operation; Sir Percy had bought the place for his son and stayed on to help. He claimed to be quite content with his new life, but the fact was that he missed the old drills. Sir Reginald knew what bait to dangle, and the MI-5 man agreed to an all-expense-paid tour of South Africa.

To the Oppenheimers' displeasure, journalists learned of the visit, and there was a flurry of speculative reports and editorial cartoons. *Sir Percy, They Presume*, said a drawing in *The Rand Daily Mail*. "They" were the press, flourishing magnifying glasses and bloodhounds. A caricatured Sir Percy sat with his back to a sea wall. He was heavily disguised in an inky beard and moustache, affecting not to see the newspapermen. Denials did no good; the cover was blown, and everyone guessed why the Oppenheimers' guest had come. De Beers could not afford to be coy, and as soon as Sir Percy agreed to sign on, the official word went out. An International Diamond Security Organization was being created to wipe out illicit diamond buying. It would center in Johannesburg, with branches throughout the world reporting to the former head of British counter-intelligence.

Sir Percy's six-week tour of the diamond mines revealed all sorts of leakages and opportunities for smuggling. "How far up do you want me to go?" he asked his employers. Given carte blanche, he and a group of handpicked assistants began their unpleasant work. One operative noted that "when we started on the job we were amazed to find how few white men had to go through security. I suppose it was considered undignified to do much about the whites." Within the year IDSO men brought their own kind of equality to the mines: everyone was suspected, regardless of color.

The company installed X-ray machines; in addition, inspectors painted diamonds with a radioactive substance that could be picked up by Geiger counters. "Mark you," said a security man, "these sort of gimmicks are most useful against the colored workers. Sort of White Man's Magic. But they all help. Just like an occasional flight by helicopter over big mining areas, and setting up television cameras, real ones and dummies, at various points in the plant. These things frighten the small man, but they don't frighten the big ones. The big ones have their own planes for landing in the bush—probably even frogmen for swimming up rivers."

One of the big ones turned out to be a De Beers field inspector, an Englishman in his late twenties with an impeccable record. In a diamond-rich inlet called Chamaais Bay along the Atlantic coast, he and an assistant were responsible for counting and sorting stones turned up by African diggers. Proximity to so much wealth turned his head, and when the assistant was otherwise engaged the inspector began to help himself to the odd jewel. New methods of examination made it impossible for him to smuggle the diamonds out; he had to secrete them somewhere and come back for the treasure at a later time.

Inland seemed too risky; air surveillance would spot the tracks in the desert and give him away. He decided to use the ocean, secreting all of his stolen goods in a canister buried along the beach. Then he went back, empty-handed and cheery, and resigned. Five months later the former employee and a pilot force-landed their Auster Autocrat on Chamaais Bay. But in the intervening time security had been tightened. An investigator spotted the pair and had them arrested. After a few nights in jail, along with some unpleasant interrogation, the thief cracked. He led the IDSO to the canister. It contained over $100,000 in diamonds. Considering the potential haul, the judge's sentence seemed relatively mild; then again, these were men of good backrounds with no previous arrest records. More significantly, they were white. The thief received nine months' hard labor; his pilot-accomplice, three months on the same rock pile.

Still, these were isolated instances of dishonesty. To the west practically everyone was on the take. In Sierra Leone unlicensed diggers turned up stones and smuggled them across the border to Liberia, where government officials steered them onto the black market. A

British Commission of Inquiry found that "dishonesty has been accepted as a normal way of life to such an extent that no one has been concerned to fight it or even complain about it." Pursuing new arenas for his hero James Bond, novelist Ian Fleming visited South Africa in the mid 1950s and persuaded one of Sir Percy's assistants to talk under an assumed name. "John Blaize" spoke of some interesting IDSO choices. Having infiltrated big smuggling operations in the two African nations, he concluded that "short of exterminating the illegal diggers, the only solution was to legalize them."

Pressure was applied to the right officials until, early in 1956, Sierra Leone granted 1,500 mining licenses to former smugglers. The number soon rose to nearly 5,000. Deep in the interior, trading posts were set up overnight, manned with De Beers's Junior Valuers. Each was a young university-trained Englishman, equipped with a safe full of cash and, it was fervently hoped, an instinct for the Real Thing.

Nighttime in the bush is never restful for the stranger; one typical newcomer had just managed to shut his eyes when he was awakened by insistent shouts. The caller was an intimidating native with a large diamond wrapped in his linen handkerchief. The valuer looked at the stone and at the man and back at the stone again. It might be worth his life to refuse the offer; it might be worth his career to give cash for glass. He examined the diamond from several angles, made some rudimentary tests, took a deep breath, and offered £10,000. The native nodded and waited while the notes were counted out on a wooden table. Then he grabbed them and vanished back into the night. It took several days for the De Beers man to learn that the jewel was actually worth far more than he had paid.

To support the Junior Valuers, Sir Percy recruited Fred Kamil, a tough Lebanese dealer who had once been on the wrong side of the law. Kamil had been caught and turned informer. Sir Percy had dealt with such men for decades; he thought Kamil might be useful as the head of a private army, patrolling the jungle of Sierra Leone. In turn Kamil recruited 15 mercenaries every bit as vicious as their chief. They made a profession of ambushing diamond smugglers on the way to Liberia and seizing their loot. Those miscreants who were not shot were chased onto minefields. Very few got out alive.

IDSO's combination of intelligence and ruthlessness made it too successful to live. Supremely pleased with Sir Percy's work, Harry dissolved the organization and the Oppenheimer empire set up its own corporate security system. "There was nothing more for us to do that couldn't be done by the mine security staffs and by the local police forces," recalled a supervisor. "After the excitement of the previous two years and the tension there was nothing but anticlimax as our men gradually drifted off to other jobs. Some have gone back to intelligence or security work and others to appointments with De Beers and Anglo-American."

Sir Percy himself wanted no further part of the diamond business. "I'm sick of crooks and sick of spying on them. All I want is a nice quiet job as a country lawyer or administrator in a university, or some other job where I can clear all this muck out of my mind."

In the mid-1950s a senior IDSO operative was allowed to go public with his memoirs, and the editors of *Punch* had such a good time reading them that they offered a piece of doggerel about the whole affair. It recalled the espionage novels of E. Phillips Oppenheim, fashionable in the 1920s:

> Fiction's frequently sublime
> But fact is far sublimer,
> For fiction may be Oppenheim,
> But fact is Oppenheimer.

♦   ♦   ♦

FACT GREW SUBLIMER STILL on the evening of December 5, 1955. Harry Oppenheimer was on safari in the Belgian Congo, and his son Nicholas was away at preparatory school. Bridget and their daughter Mary were at Little Brenthurst, along with the customary staff of servants and guards. A dinner invitation arrived; Mrs. Oppenheimer decided to go alone. She chose a few pieces of jewelry from the bedroom safe and returned the key to its resting place, a dilapidated bluish-green satin box that held bric-a-brac, cigarette holders, and badges from various horse shows.

In those days Johannesburg dinners began early and ended early; she was back home by 10 p.m. Bridget noticed nothing peculiar about the bedroom except for one detail: a pillowcase was missing. Nothing to worry her personal maid about; she would say something in the morning. Upon arising Bridget decided to put back the jewels she had worn the night before. Strange, she thought: the satin box was not in its familiar resting place.

She went to her handbag, fished out a duplicate key, and opened the safe. Someone had picked it clean. Sixty-three pieces were gone, including a pure white emerald-cut diamond ring weighing more than 23 carats, an emerald-cut pink diamond ring with emerald and sapphire shoulders, a blue marquise diamond ring, a white marquise diamond ring, and a ring of white gold and platinum with a blue-white brilliant of more than eleven carats. Some brooches had vanished as well, along with a string of pearls and two Buddhas set in platinum and diamonds.

Here was no incident of a native sticking a stone in his hair, or even a high-born company man siphoning off some private treasure. The Prince and Princess of Diamonds had been robbed in their own castle. Because Harry was in the jungle, beyond the reach of a telephone, his assistants were notified at their offices. Hurriedly, a phalanx of gray-suited executives, company security men, and local police moved in. Trailing them were the reporters, and behind them De Beers's public relations staff. A spokesman set the Oppenheimer tone. He declined to give the press a list of stolen jewels because, "After all, we don't want to flaunt our wealth in front of the public." His statement was not materially aided by Bridget's remark, "I'm now left with about as much jewelry as the average city typist." Or by her husband's casual wire, sent when he finally got the bad news: "Don't worry. Love. Harry."

The PR men might have spent their time more creatively; the Oppenheimer wealth had been a subject of speculation for years, and withholding information only served to sharpen public interest. In pubs and clubs and restaurants, new theories were advanced. De Beers had "lowered the diamond curtain" because of embarrassing revelations. "Fancy old Harry being caught like that," said a barroom critic. "Should've known better than to keep all that ice lying in the fridge." Taxi drivers laid fingers alongside noses and spoke of hanky-panky at Brenthurst. One speculator decided that little Mary Oppenheimer had lifted the jewels in her sleep and hidden them somewhere on the grounds. "Call in a hypnotist," came the advice. "He'll soon make the kid remember." Others thought that African witch doctors and psychics should "throw the bones" and locate the treasure.

Every notion, no matter how bizarre, seemed as plausible as the next. There were no clues, no footprints or fingerprints, no revealing fibers. No disturbance had aroused the night watchmen. The dogs did nothing in the nighttime, a signal for all Sherlock Holmes readers to conclude that the Brenthurst robbery was an inside job. Yet inquiries showed that every one of the staff had an impermeable alibi. Very well then, it was an outside job, meticulously planned. But Interpol investigators reported that none of the major jewel thieves had been spotted in South Africa, and such a theft could not have been accomplished by amateurs or small-time crooks.

The first major development in the case came on December 9, when the insurers offered a reward of $56,000 for information leading to the whereabouts of the stolen treasure. Scores of self-appointed sleuths materialized at Brenthurst, complete with magnifying glasses and cameras, ready to comb the grounds. They were all turned away by a 24-hour police guard ringing the house. The one investigator who was allowed through came with impeccable credentials. Representing the insurers, Dudley Strevens had flown in from London. The retired army captain played down his role: he dressed in a deliberately nondescript manner and told reporters that he was merely a claim adjuster who had found, through the years, that sooner or later a "squealer" would turn up and provide a way to crack the case. Had any candidates contacted the police? he inquired. There had been, replied one of his colleagues, but they were "mainly cranks." He did not know what to make of "one persistent chap with an Australian accent who so far refuses to speak to anyone but you." Strevens thought he might look up that particular chap right away.

The police had other ideas. Colonel Ulf Boberg, chief of the Witwatersrand Counter Intelligence Division (CID), was a small, Napoleonic officer with a bristling moustache and cold blue eyes, much given to assertions of authority. He issued a severe warning. The Londoner was to do no private detecting. If anyone attempted to reach him with information, he was to report it to the police immediately. Violation of this order would be prosecuted to the full extent of the law. Strevens agreed—and then went off to his rendezvous anyway.

In a well-appointed hotel suite, the mysterious Australian identified himself as William Linsay Pearson, 33. He was a rather dashing combat veteran of World War II, with strong survival instincts. A beating dispensed by a gangster in Sydney, Pearson said, "was the greatest lesson of my life. Now I do the other bastard before he can do me whether it's business or brawling." His business was gambling in hotel rooms and hanging around Johannesburg bars, looking for the main chance.

It came one evening at a hotel bar, where a drunken stranger mumbled something about a big job about to be pulled off. That had been some weeks before. When Pearson read the headlines he was certain that the job in question was the Oppenheimer robbery. He checked the city bars until he located the stranger and confirmed his suspicions.

The Australian confidently offered Strevens some choices. He, Pearson, would buy the jewels from the thieves, then claim the reward. If the insurance company balked, Pearson would go to Europe on his own, disposing of the treasure piece by piece. There *was* an alternative: Pearson could hand the jewels directly to Strevens. In that case, the finder's fee would be $112,000.

Strevens went away to ponder these proposals. He was still considering them when a call came in from Boberg. The colonel got straight to the point. He suspected that, despite official warnings, Strevens had been in touch with the underworld. If the captain had information, and if he failed to share it with the police, he would be charged with conspiracy. Cornered, Strevens told him about Pearson's impudent offers. The policeman hardly knew which way to turn. He was furious with the insurance man for acting alone, yet he needed him to trap the thieves. In the end he forced Strevens to call Pearson with an ultimatum. Either he came downtown to the insurance offices, or any deal was off.

Rather than being frightened away, Pearson was only too delighted to show up. Upon his arrival Col. Boberg stepped forward to demand: "I want to know something about you. Who you are, where you are from, and what you are doing here." A few days before, Pearson had watched Alfred Hitchcock's *To Catch a Thief*, and he responded with a Cary Grant insouciance. "I'm a crook." He smiled wickedly. "I live by my wits. I do no work and I never have worked. Satisfied?"

"You are very frank, Mr. Pearson; you call a spade a spade. So do I. Now you'd better tell me damned quick everything you know."

It was bluff and Pearson knew it. He showed no signs of intimidation and stayed with his story. He claimed to be nothing more than an entrepreneur, shady perhaps, but operating within the law. If he was so innocent, Boberg demanded, then why had he consorted with thieves? Because, said the Australian, they were so easy to con. He had bragged of his intimate relationship with an old Mafia chieftain: "I told my contact that Lucky Luciano wants the jewels."

The policeman realized that he was dealing with an uncommon criminal. Boberg muted his hostility and offered a fresh idea. What if the insurance company were to supply a trunk full of money? The thieves would be invited to Pearson's hotel, where they would bring the jewels and examine the cash. A plainclothes detective would be in attendance, posing as Luciano's man in Johannesburg. While the crooks were palavering, the police would surround the place and spring their trap. Pearson would get his reward; the authorities would capture the malefactors; the Oppenheimers would regain their treasure. What could be more equitable? The Australian shrugged. "There is no honor among thieves," he told Boberg, and asked for his instructions.

On the warm evening of December 15, 1955, Boberg saw to it that the Carlton Hotel was surrounded with unmarked squad cars. Shortly before 9:30 p.m., two visitors arrived separately and rode the elevators to Pearson's floor. One man had nothing with him; the second carried a suitcase. Pearson extended a warm greeting and introduced them to "Luciano's rep." As planned, the Mafia man was one of Boberg's plainclothes detectives; four others waited in the hall, just out of sight. Someone lifted the lid from the suitcase. There, among some silken material, lay almost all the Oppenheimer jewels, minus a few brooches and rings. Satisfied, the plainclothesman went to the door, ostensibly to get some air, and signaled four waiting colleagues. The quartet barged into the room shouting, service revolvers drawn.

Neither visitor offered any resistance. The first was a tall, fair man; his companion was slightly shorter, with slicked-back dark hair. Both protested their innocence all the way to the police station. There a few more facts emerged. The dark-haired man was Percival William Radley, 42, who claimed to be credit manager of Tropic Airways, a small charter company operating between Johannesburg and Amsterdam. The fair-haired one was Donald Ernest Miles, 34. He identified himself as a private detective, but he had been without visible means of support for more than a year.

Their story was simple, unshakeable, and just this side of plausible. Radley said that he and Pearson had just met, and that the Australian had invited him up to his hotel suite for a drink. There had been no talk of diamonds or thievery or anything illegal whatsoever. As for Miles, he maintained that he had been drinking in a bar earlier that evening, when a slight acquaintance whose name he did not know— "a Jewish chap"—came in. He and Miles got to talking, as drinkers will. The chap was on his way out of Johannesburg and asked Miles to do him a small favor: deliver a parcel to a friend at the Carlton. Out of the goodness of his heart Miles agreed. Upstairs he went, and there were Radley and Pearson. He had never seen either of them before and, like them, was astonished at the police invasion. The disgruntled Boberg had all three men thrown in jail, where detectives tried to break down their collective plea of innocence.

Through Christmas and New Year's they refused to budge from their accounts. Radley had the best alibi: he had been spotted going into a cinema the evening of the robbery. But there was no hard evidence incriminating the other two either. Then, on January third, the first fissures appeared. Pearson asked to see Boberg and informed the Colonel that he might give evidence in return for his unconditional freedom. That seemed agreeable to Boberg. He went back to Miles and Radley with the news: the Australian was about to rat on his friends. Miles remained firm; Radley began to weaken. In England he had accumulated a long police record, and he knew it would go against him in South Africa. Several more days went by, and then he cracked for a price: the police could have his evidence, but in exchange he would have to be made immune from prosecution. Boberg nodded, took him to a private room, sat him down in a luxurious leather armchair, plied him with cigarettes and tea, and invited Radley to talk. A stenographer wrote down the confession in shorthand. It took six hours.

The adventure had begun on a rooftop, according to the confessor. A year before the robbery, Miles had been employed by a roofing firm.

One day he found himself working on Little Brenthurst, fireproofing Harry and Bridget's home. The Oppenheimers happened to be overseas during the construction, and when the roofer spotted her safe and the key in the dish, he saw his way to a life of ease. Unhappily for him, the safe was nearly empty. But that was just as well, Miles decided. Better to wait until the roof was finished and the jewels returned to their resting place. Johannesburg was not London. No one hurried in this part of the world.

Underworld connections put him in touch with Radley, and they took to each other instantly. During the time the partners were working out their scheme, Pearson arrived from Australia. He and Radley had indeed met by chance in a hotel bar and, after some mutual inquiries and background checks, agreed to work together. Miles and Radley would pull off the job. Pearson had contacts with major fences; he would arrange to peddle the stolen goods overseas.

Detectives went over the testimony and investigated his story. They even flew to Italy in order to interview Lucky Luciano. Graying and overweight, the old godfather lived under relaxed house arrest in Naples. He insisted that his modest income came from the sales of surgical instruments, and wished that people would stop bothering an honest businessman. Putting on his best Damon Runyon intonation, Luciano denied any knowledge of Pearson. "Never hoid of da bum," he insisted. He was also ignorant of "Johannesbug," as he called the city. "Da only Jonannesbug I ever hoid of was a horse I once backed. And dat nag lost, too." No evidence contradicted him; this time, apparently, he was telling the truth. According to police theorists Radley was a small-time crook incapable of a major heist, and Pearson a braggart but not a mastermind. Prosecutors decided to concentrate on Miles.

The *Sunday Express* took a dim view of these tactics. An editorial writer was reminded of the rhyme about ten little Indians. "It could be varied," he said, "in the following manner:

> Three adult European males
> Charged with a jewel coup;
> Radley turned queen's evidence
> Then there are two.

Two adult European males
Sent for a trial run;
Pearson's told he is released
Then there is one.

One adult European male . . .

"But perhaps it would be unwise, and indiscreet, to attempt to complete the third verse. We shall defer doing so until events themselves are unfurled on the canvas of history."

♦   ♦   ♦

THE UNFURLING took place early in January. Brought before a judge and jury, Miles offered his own version of history: he and Radley had met a year ago for the first time. In the course of their conversation, Radley claimed to be one of Sir Percy Sillitoe's aides, working for the Oppenheimer group. At the mention of Oppenheimer, Miles brightened. He had once done some roofing at Little Brenthurst and noticed how vulnerable it might be to prowlers. Since Radley was so well placed, could he get Miles a job guarding the estate? Radley was warm and encouraging. He asked a lot of questions about Harry and Bridget's place, and suggested that perhaps there might be something he could do to help his new friend.

Nothing came of this offer, and several months passed before Miles paid a call on Radley, hoping to prod his memory. This time Radley was receptive. He thought something might be available after all, and promised to come to Miles's apartment that very evening at 7 p.m. He appeared at the scheduled time clutching a package wrapped in Christmas paper. Radley said it contained uncut diamonds bought by an Australian businessman. There was a scheduling conflict, and someone else would have to deliver the goods to a Mr. Pearson at the Carlton. Would Miles do it? There's a good fellow. Nine o'clock. Room 641.

Miles and Pearson met for the first time that night. When Pearson examined the box in his presence, Miles saw that there were scarves inside. What they concealed, it was impossible to say. He never got a second look because a few moments later the police invaded the place. From start to finish, he claimed, Miles never realized that he had been the courier for the Oppenheimer jewels until a policeman informed him en route to the station.

Such was the account of Donald Ernest Miles. His lawyers served up soft, exculpating questions. Had he talked about the key or the safe to Radley? No. Had he given Radley the layout of the Brenthurst? Never. He had only mentioned, in general terms, the Oppenheimers' "beautiful home" and the lack of guards. What did Miles know about diamonds? Nothing except that ladies wore them in rings. Well, then, who did he think actually pulled off the theft? Here the witness gripped the rail so tightly that his knuckles showed white. He disliked impeaching anyone, but the others were free, and a long jail sentence hung over him. "Radley obviously stole the jewels," said Miles.

The defense expanded upon this conclusion. What if Radley had used Miles as his cat's paw? He had the motive and, more important, he had the skills and the brains that Miles so evidently lacked. The jury listened impassively, and when the twelve men went out to deliberate, some Indian gamblers offered five to one against the witness. They were still quoting odds when the jury filed back in. Deliberations had taken less than an hour.

The tumult of Indian dialects, English, Afrikaans, and Zulu quieted as the judge waited for the foreman. He hesitated, then spoke the answer: "Not guilty." The silence lasted for another beat, and then the spectators erupted into applause, stamping and whistling. Part of this was the expectation of getting five rands to every one they had wagered; the rest was from the agreeable surprise of seeing the government blow an open-and-shut case.

For official South Africa, things grew even more embarrassing. The matter of the trial was raised in Parliament, where the Minister of Justice blamed everything on the jury system. Immune from prosecution, Pearson and Radley blithely peddled their memoirs to newspapers and magazines, and then Pearson added the crowning outrage: he claimed the insurance company's reward. After all, he had found the Oppenheimer jewels, and they were now back at Brenthurst. Try as they might, the insurance executives could not wriggle out of the situation, and they had to hand over a check for $56,000. Ever afterward, Col. Boberg would regard this case as his greatest success and his most notorious failure: he had almost immediately recovered the stolen goods, made three arrests—and not a single person had been locked up for the crime.

The trio of suspects were deported; all ended up in England. Pearson and Miles changed their names and vanished into private life. Radley wanted no such anonymity. As he stepped from the *Athlone Castle* at Southampton, he saw a familiar face. It was Robert Fabian, a former Scotland Yard inspector. Since his retirement, the policeman had become a journalist specializing in crime stories. Would Radley consent to an interview? Radley would do better than that. Now that he was beyond the law, he would submit a confession.

He said that he had indeed been at the movies on the night of the burglary. But he had slipped out unseen, driven to Brenthurst, opened the safe, grabbed the Oppenheimer diamonds, and returned to his seat, all within 45 minutes. Radley reminded Fabian that even after the police raid a few pieces were missing; those jewels turned up later in Johannesburg pawn shops because Radley had left them there "for a measly $2,800." The inspector believed him; "I had," he wrote later, "a feeling in my bones" that Radley had done the job.

The South African authorities were not so certain. It was all too neat, too much like a B movie. Radley seemed to have adopted too much style and lingo from the cinema. He wore a camel's-hair overcoat, black-and-white checked suits, and blue suede shoes, and when the name Pearson came up Radley spoke out of the side of his mouth. In America, he said, the mob knew to take care of such men: "they sew you up in a cement bag and drop you over Brooklyn Bridge—and they call it an accident. [Pearson] thinks he has got away, but we are watching every move that he is making." (The "we" was unidentified.) Instead of regarding such remarks as ominous, the police thought they were pure swank and refused to reopen the case.

It has never been solved. Nearly fifty years later the opinion of *The Sunday Times* has lost none of its salinity: "So nobody stole the Oppenheimer diamonds after all, and they arrived in a room at the Carlton Hotel of their own accord. This is surely the most remarkable ghost story in South African criminal history."

15

CROWNING THE NEW KING

THE BRENTHURST ROBBERS purloined more than the Oppenheimers' diamonds; they took away their privacy. For many decades, public relations officers had worked to keep the family out of the papers, except for notices of benefactions and political accomplishments. On those occasions father and son were invariably shown as enlightened business leaders guiding their companies and their nation serenely into the second half of the twentieth century. Ernest's chosen motto, *Spero optima*, I hope for the best, characterized their work. Stability and philanthropy radiated outward from their offices. Much was made of the Honorary Doctorate of Civil Law conferred by Oxford in 1952. Sir Ernest's "high reputation" and "humane spirit" were praised at the university. Later they were celebrated in South Africa, along with his endowments for the study of surgery, engineering, and history at local colleges.

The robbery changed all that. Ernest and Harry's extreme wealth became topic A, not only at home, but in many parts of Europe and America. Once more the name Hoggenheimer was heard in South Africa, and hostilities reopened on the left and right. Radicals pictured Ernest and Harry as major hypocrites. Underneath the facade of social concern, they warned, were two ruthless plutocrats who would stop at nothing to extend their diamond cartel and their golden touch. A Freedom Charter, endorsed by the ANC and other organizations of African workers, called for "the nationalization of the mines, banks and industrial monopolies, for trade and industry to be controlled for the benefit of the people, and for all people to have equal economic and job rights."

At the same time, the Nationalists were busy implementing their strategy of "Grand Apartheid." After the reign of D. F. Malan had come the administration of Johannes Gerhardus Strijdom. The new Prime Minister intensified his party principles in 1955: "I am being as blunt as I can. I am making no excuses. Either the white man dominates or the black takes over. I say that the non-European will not accept leadership—if he has a choice. The only way the Europeans can maintain supremacy is by domination." In the early 1950s domination meant vigorous enforcement of the Immorality Act, banning sexual contact between Africans and whites. This was augmented by the Population Registration Act, dividing the population into various racial groups. Physical criteria were used, along with such categories as social "repute." Once it was decided who was "colored," "native," "Indian," "Malay," and so on, people were subject to the Group Areas Act. Here was the main pillar of apartheid. It condemned mixed areas as "deathbeds of the European race," and restricted each group to its own residential and trading sections of cities and towns.

Further regulations forbade the entry of blacks into universities and set up "alternative education" for natives, teaching them their "proper place." Bantu, the code word for members of the Negro race, was substituted for "native" and "African." For those words, said the Nationalists, could just as well apply to whites. The newly appointed Minister of Native Affairs, a former psychology professor named Hendrik Verwoerd, encapsulated the new situation when he inquired: "What is the use of teaching a Bantu child mathematics when it cannot use it in practice?"

The Oppenheimers tried every way they knew to mollify both sides: the dangerously restive black activists and the iron-handed lawmakers of apartheid. Harry made conciliatory political speeches; Ernest adroitly described Anglo's and De Beers's personnel policies: "amenities now being provided for African employees include electric light in their houses and individual water-borne sanitation facilities, which even today are not available to about half of the population of Europe. Never in the world's history has more rapid progress been made by any section of its people." Then in the next sentence he bowed to the government:

"This extraordinary progress has been made possible solely by the leadership and control of the European with his discipline and his knowledge. It can continue, or even be maintained, only under his leadership and control." He concluded in a patronizing tone: "The African has learnt a very great deal in the short space of thirty years. It is much to his credit that he has done so, but a whole gulf remains between his capacity and his aspiration."

As usual when speakers try to accommodate both sides, they pleased neither. On the left, the ANC and its affiliates knew that the mines, more than any other factor, had destroyed traditional African life. No doubt the workers enjoyed well-balanced meals and outstanding medical care; that was simply because physical fitness was in the interest of the employer. Social health was something else entirely. At the time of Sir Ernest's speech the average monthly wage for a black laborer at the gold mines was about £5 a month, and if he were married that wage would have to support two homes—in South Africa wives and children were forbidden to live with their husbands on mine property. The white workers earned more than 15 times as much, without being burdened with the problem of dual residence.

On the right, the government regarded Harry with great suspicion. He was a member of the opposition United Party, and his opinions were slippery. One moment he would concede that "we must maintain the standard of living of the European people, and it certainly would not help the Natives to lower that standard. I think people would also agree that it is very desirable to have residential segregation. I think everyone in this House is agreed that it is most undesirable to put political power into the hands of uncivilized, uneducated people." The next moment Harry would attack the Strijdom government's policies of racial discrimination: "I am quite sure that the attempt by systems and theories to determine the history of this country for a hundred years to come is nothing but folly and nothing but arrogance."

At last Verwoerd could stand no more, and he attacked the Member from Kimberley. Hoggenheimer capitalists like Harry, he informed Parliament, "have well-tried methods by which they usually attempt to serve the interests of their undertakings and of capitalism. This method is to pretend that they are acting in the public interest, in the interest of the community as a whole."

In the mid-1950s Ernest and Harry proposed to build new African towns where Anglo's black workers could live with their families. They had already done so in the copper belt of Rhodesia; why not in the gold fields of South Africa? Verwoerd set his mind against the plan. "Every mine can then establish its own native town with married quarters," he complained. "That will mean a series of native towns in the vicinity of the big cities." And what about the inevitable day when the vein of gold ran out? "A large number of towns will remain. . . . They may amount to 20 or 30 or 40 within that area." Verwoerd shuddered at the vision of blacks in hideous proximity to whites. The plan was condemned out of hand.

Harry continued to protest, and every now and then, when his criticism hit home, a Nationalist minister would burst out, "Perhaps we ought to raise taxations on the mines. How would you like that?" Neither Oppenheimer responded to the taunts. In private Ernest scoffed, "They talk. They talk, but they don't carry out half what they threaten against us." Both sides glowered and withdrew to make new battle plans. And the fuse burned on.

♦   ♦   ♦

NOTHING MANAGED to shake the composure—some said arrogance—of Sir Ernest Oppenheimer until a slight and modest Anglican priest published *Naught for Your Comfort*. Unlike *Cry, the Beloved Country*, this South African book purported to be factual. It was not destined for the stage and cinema. There was an absence of rhetorical flourish. It contained no fine writing or great characters. Father Huddleston's work was in every sense a little book. Still, he had been a friend of the Christian Oppenheimers for some years; on several occasions Ina had even helped him raise money for some charitable projects, and when a copy came to Brenthurst Ernest decided to give it a look.

The author began with an encounter with six Africans, victims of the latest government move to force blacks out of the cities and into the Group Areas. The men had awaited him at the steps of his mission in a black township outside of Johannesburg. "In the morning," wrote the reverend, "they had gone to work as usual, leaving their wives and children still asleep under the blankets. They had returned in the dark evening to find the roofs stripped from their shacks: their families squatting in the open round a brazier: their children crying with cold and the desire for sleep."

Father Huddleston went with them to see for himself. "I found a woman in labor amongst those round the brazier and her baby was born under the winter stars that night." The Biblical parallel was obvious: "In that dejected little group . . . the picture of Bethlehem and the rejection there, came to life."

From this incident, the narrative moved on to anecdotal evidence of black misery all over South Africa. "There was an instance not so long ago when an African, standing at a bus stop (second class) dared to put on a pair of white gloves. This was so offensive to a group of European lads waiting for their bus (first class) nearby, that they set on him: had him down in the gutter, and kicked him so that he died."

Father Huddleston recalled the day one African knifed another. The murderer turned out to have "six previous convictions, several of them of a serious nature, although he was only nineteen. The charge was reduced to culpable homicide. He was sentenced to one year in jail. So far as I know he is still walking the streets of Sophiatown. After all, it was only another stabbing in a native area. . . . Neither the boy who murdered, nor the man who was murdered, had any real value as a person. Both were natives: a different category, another species living in a world apart."

This polemic set the country on edge. At least two books were published in angry and wounded reply. *You Are Wrong Father Huddleston* took 113 pages to dismiss *Naught for Your Comfort*: "What a sad figure, this influential Priest blinded by love for a slum into a common cause with agitators." Subsequently a more detailed attack, entitled *Without Fear or Favor*, came from a conservative politician. "I would say that it is men like . . . Huddleston who cause mischief and mistrust among countries. Should trouble indeed arise they would have contributed greatly to it through their unjust criticism."

The familiar arguments surfaced again: the blacks were naïve, immature, and incapable. "How can you give a child a knife and expect it not to cut itself? Many of the 'Liberals' know only the educated Africans in the towns, but do they know the majority? The primitive African who lives in the country? By trying to drag these problems into the political arena the White people of South Africa are making of the primitive Zulu, this fine upstanding people, a nation of thieves and prostitutes.

"These are strong words, I admit, but unfortunately true . . . thanks to the blundering of the White Man with his mistaken idea of human rights."

Ernest and Ina tried a more open-minded approach to their friend's book, but they too had difficulty with its tone and approach. Surely Father Huddleston must have been exaggerating for literary effect when he compared the Strijdom–Verwoerd policies to Adolf Hitler's. Surely Africans lived more decently than this appalling depiction of a black hell. Ernest had never ventured into Shantytown, on the outskirts of Johannesburg. He had been warned that a white man, particularly a wealthy white man, might be taking his life into his hands if he went there alone. Never mind, he replied; there were some things one had to see firsthand. No guards, thank you; no priest, no company officials. Just himself and Ina serving as their own witnesses to Bantu life.

The Oppenheimers were not attacked, or reviled, or remarked upon very much. They saw what all visitors saw if they bothered to look: a breeding place for aimlessness and despair, occasionally relieved by religious celebrations and the distractions of family life. The situation had been born of Verwoerd's iron policies. The law demanded that blacks be removed from their "illegal" quarters in white areas and sent to "serviced" areas in specific African locations. These areas were supposed to be the equal of white dwelling places. In fact they were vacant acres equipped with water taps. Those who went there were supposed to assemble their own shacks until the mythical day when the government came to their relief.

Ernest concluded that Father Huddleston had been accurate in his reportage and justified in his rage. For the past three years Johannesburg's City Council had turned back all new housing plans for Africans because of Nationalist objections. Over that time squatters had come and set up a maze of shanties and shacks built of whatever material they could scrounge: packing crates, cardboard, plastic, even corrugated iron, the material that had been used a hundred years before by Rhodes and Barnato and other diamond hunters. There were at least 10,000

Africans living in conditions of extreme squalor, and thanks to official indifference, no public aid was in sight.

At the age of 74, after years of mild concern, Ernest abruptly became an activist, speaking in the tones of a social worker. "Anyone who has visited the Native areas on the outskirts of this city, as I have done," he told newspaper reporters, "would be impressed by the urgency of the need for action in clearing away the slums that have grown almost as rapidly as the industrial development of Johannesburg." He took the occasion to remind his white listeners that "these Native people are, in general, the employees of European citizens."

Morality was almost beside the point. Rhodes had looked upon public works as "philanthropy plus five per cent," and Ernest's overview was not very different. He used the imperialists' old term "enlightened self-interest" to justify his actions: improved living conditions for the natives "should make for healthy, efficient, law-abiding and contented service." By badgering his fellow mining executives, Ernest raised £3 million and arranged for the building of some 15,000 houses over the next three years.

The Shantytown construction was the last truly vigorous activity for the King of Diamonds. Celebrations of his 75th birthday took place in London, where he opened new company quarters. Ernest told employees that he had "always dreamed of seeing the London office of the diamond group and the Anglo-American Corporation under one roof." And now here it was, in High Holborn. Nevertheless the occasion proved to be exhausting for the speaker; Ernest was rarely comfortable at public events, particularly away from home, and he had to steel himself before getting up to speak. Once on his feet, though, he made no mistakes, fielded questions in a relaxed manner, quoted statistics fluently. Then when the reporters were putting away their pencils, he fainted.

"It was the smoke," Lady Oppenheimer theorized, after the couple was safely back in Johannesburg. "What else he could have expected after behaving as he did I don't know. All that excitement and the bad air. He's not used to the tension of London in any case, and there he stood in a crowded, smoke-filled room for more than half an hour, and he was talking the whole time. . . . After all, he's an old man, but he's very strong."

Strong enough to return to his office, and to increase his good works. In the next months Ernest donated £100,000 for the establishment of Queen Elizabeth House, a center for colonial studies at Oxford. Other funds went to the Faculty of Engineering at the University of Stellenbach and to the Institute of Medical Research in South Africa.

He also found time to sit for yet another portrait, add to his already huge collection of books on Africa, and accumulate a few more oil paintings. But he was slowing down; Harry was unobtrusively assuming the burden of his father's duties. The elder Oppenheimer gave up his flat in London. His collection of paintings, including rare oils by Renoir and Goya, were shipped to Brenthurst. Possessions seemed to be losing their appeal. When a big diamond was discovered at the Premier mine, a rumor circulated that Ernest would buy it for his wife. Only recently he had stated his sentiments about precious stones. "Diamonds," he recalled, "were my first love. I never lost the feeling. Diamonds speak to me."

Now, pondering the dimensions of this new stone, he pronounced it lovely. "Why don't you buy it, then?" he was asked.

The old man shook his head. "It would cost a lot of money."

Ernest reduced his office schedule. After a noontime whiskey and soda with associates, he went home for lunch and usually did not return. In July 1957 there were more intimations of mortality. At the opening of a gold mine, Wes Deep, Ernest told a small crowd that he expected to see the first yield, but doubted whether he would live to see the mine in full production five years down the road. Several weeks later he collapsed during a country amble. The mild heart attack was followed by a series of more serious relapses.

Ernest regarded his latest illness as a personal affront, and he fought back. After six weeks, signs of the old vigor returned. The patient began making jokes and showing renewed interest in Anglo and De Beers. Ina had been at his bedside almost every hour, and she was visibly worn. Ernest encouraged her to take a holiday in London, visit her sister, take a holiday from nursing an old nuisance. Ina protested at first, but she knew she had been depleted by the ordeal, and Ernest prevailed.

Being on his own did not mean being alone. A nurse was in attendance; his personal physician frequently dropped by; Harry and

Bridget visited almost every day. The weekend after Ina's departure, Ernest felt hale enough to attend a dinner party, and early Monday morning, November 27, 1957, he and Harry went over some business matters. The doctor made an examination and agreed that Ernest could spend a little time in the office. When he left, Ernest chatted with his nurse, Sister Pam Walton. A servant announced that breakfast was ready and the old man looked up to see Sister Walton watching him from the banister at the top of the stairs.

"We're just like Romeo and Juliet," he called up, and sat down to eat. The attack came before he could lower his fork to his egg; Ernest clutched his chest, cried out, and crumpled over the table, still conscious but in very obvious pain. The servants rushed to his side and called for the nurse. "What's going on?" He gasped for breath. "You don't feel very well," Sister Walton explained in a soothing voice. She and the servants carried him to the living room and gently lowered him to a couch. "What's happening?" he repeated suddenly, breathed heavily, and lost consciousness. By the time Dr. Kaplan arrived, Sir Ernest Oppenheimer was dead.

Later that morning Anglo issued the official announcement, and South Africa went into mourning. A tribute from Father Huddleston might have astonished the deceased: "Above all it was his simplicity which was always so endearing. He retained a quality of childishness which one could hardly have believed possible in one with such vast material concerns." Other encomia were less effusive. International business leaders paid their respects; Queen Elizabeth II sent a message, and now that a Hoggenheimer was safely dead, condolences came from Prime Minister Strijdom. Another salute issued from the opposite corner, the black South West Township where new housing had begun to replace the battered shanties. The occupants wanted to name the new place after their benefactor, Sir Ernest Oppenheimer, but the Johannesburg city fathers thought this might fan some smoldering animosities, and they chose a less controversial name: Soweto, the abbreviation of South West Township.

Ernest's will was published a few days after his cremation. One sentence summarized the contents: "I give and bequeath the whole of my estate and property whatsoever situate and of every description to my son Harry Frederick Oppenheimer absolutely." The amount of money mentioned was absurdly small: £3,500,000. The fortune had been channeled into a maze of trust funds and investments, and no one outside the family would ever be able to find the way through it. Ernest had been the richest man in South Africa; now Harry was.

♦   ♦   ♦

THE NEW KING sat at 44 Main Street, head of Anglo and De Beers, controlling at least 40 percent of South African gold and more than 80 percent of the world's diamonds. No doubt Harry would have preferred a period of tranquil adjustment. Tranquillity, however, had vanished from South African life.

The wild prospector John Williamson died seven weeks after Ernest. Williamson's brother Percy inherited his mine and put it up for sale. He wanted more than £5 million. The price was extravagant, but De Beers could not afford to let him sell it to anyone outside the cartel. Harry flew to Tanganyika to provide the personal touch, sans lawyers or advisors. The two men sat up all night, conceding here, demanding there, until they agreed on a deal. When Harry returned he showed the paper to Anglo's legal department. "A little unorthodox," was their judgment. CEOs were not supposed to negotiate personally with the opposition. That was left to the attorneys; it was like sending a general into the trenches without a rifle. Nevertheless, they conceded, "it seems to hold water."

A larger obstacle remained. The Williamson Mine was in Tanganyika. The country had been a British mandate since World War I, but that relationship was about to end. Black power advocates had found their voices and Whitehall, uncomfortable with its colonial past, was about to give in. Harry reacted quickly; better to make terms with the native leaders before they took over, he realized, than to risk the future nationalization of the mine. He spoke with the incoming native Tanganyikan administrators: how about a fifty-fifty proposition, with De Beers providing whatever loans were needed for expansion of the mine? As soon as he got an acceptance, Harry went in search of investors. He found them in an unaccustomed place: West Germany. Not since the days of Kaiser Wilhelm had Deutschmarks been sunk in an African venture.

The ink had scarcely dried on the Williamson papers when some other unsettling news came in. Diamond fields had been discovered in the Siberian tundra. Since the late 1940s Soviet geologists had been exploring the banks of the Vilyu River, where an explorer had accidentally come across some miniscule diamonds. Early in 1955 a Soviet geologist, Yuri Khabarin, stumbled onto a foxhole. Digging itself a burrow, the animal had turned up a lot of blue earth. Khabarin did considerable digging of his own before sending back a code message: "I am smoking the pipe of peace." By 1958 engineers had determined that it was more than a pipe; it was a whole field of diamonds, seventeen acres long and a half-mile wide.

The discovery of precious stones always signaled prosperity in South Africa. In the Soviet Union it meant misery. Siberia resisted every form of diamond mining. In the winter, temperatures dipped to minus 80 degrees, freezing oil in blocks and shattering rubber tires and steel tools. In the summer, ice and earth became a sea of mud. In order to recover the diamonds, the U.S.S.R. had to create Aikhal, a city on stilts, cocooned in translucent plastic to shield it from the weather, heated and dehumidified from within. Using jet engines and dynamite, the Soviet diamond hunters blasted big holes to loosen the diamond-bearing earth. The floors of Aikhal could not bear the weight of the soil, so it was hauled to a separation plant 20 miles away.

A complicated process but, as far as the Soviet government was concerned, worth every ruble. For once the world learned of the Siberian explorations De Beers shares dropped from 114 shillings, sixpence to 82 shillings. The U.S.S.R. now had the upper hand. At any time, it could flood the market with stones and bring down the entire diamond industry. A hundred years of history might vanish in a week. Harry had to act decisively and fast. His cousin Philip, Otto Oppenheimer's son, flew to Moscow with a question and an offer. Why sell the stones independently? It would only impoverish every retailer and wholesaler—including those in Russia. Suppose De Beers were to buy the Soviet Union's entire production this year and every year thereafter. Suppose that production was always to be purchased at prices higher than the market rate. "A single channel," as Harry pointed out on numerous occasions, "is in the interest of all diamond producers whatever the political difference between them may be."

The Soviets, who spent their days and nights maligning capitalism, found the deal irresistible. All it required was carbon and hypocrisy. Russia would sell 100 percent of its uncut gemstones to the syndicate, provided the route from mine to retailer was heavily camouflaged. De Beers created a path impenetrable to outsiders: diamonds would travel from Siberia to a series of small corporations huddled under the umbrellas of various holding companies. Those companies would in turn be held by other companies, and so on up to De Beers. This arrangement would give the Soviet delegate license to pound his fist on the tables of the United Nations, denouncing monopoly, condemning the racist capitalists of South Africa, and urging a boycott of the country's exports—even as his country was wholesaling its stones to the enemy.

With the emerging nations De Beers used the same methods. Tanzania, Ghana, and Sierra Leone would naturally refuse to trade with an apartheid state. Yet who could criticize them for selling their unpolished jewels to the Diamond Development Corporation and Mining and Technical Services Ltd., unaffiliated companies licensed outside Africa, in Switzerland, Luxembourg, and England? It was not the African countries' fault that the diamonds were subsequently sold to De Beers. And so it continued from the 1950s onward, and if everyone's hands were not exactly immaculate, they were at least well laundered.

The United States presented Harry with more complexities. Seventy-five percent of the diamonds sold for rings and jewelry were sold to Americans. And yet not a single office could bear the De Beers sign: anti-trust laws barred any cartel from operating within the national borders. As important as Americans were as customers, they worried Harry: the stones being bought in the United States were low-priced and small. Not much profit there; not much chance for growth. Once a man gave his fiancée an engagement ring, chances were he would never buy another diamond. It was "the result," said a De Beers analysis, "of the economy, changes in social attitudes and the promotion of competitive luxuries."

Altering the economy was beyond the resources even of De Beers; attitudes and promotion were not. Harry had first come to New York in the fall of 1938 to meet Gerald M. Lauck, president of N. W. Ayer. The advertising agency had been recommended to Oppenheimer by the Morgan Bank, Sir Ernest's old friend. Ayer was an inspired choice. It became the company's American arm, shrewdly carrying out

Harry's injunction to keep diamonds before the public as the preem-
inent symbol of romance and durability. Perhaps more importantly, it
orchestrated corporate public relations in the United States.

From the 1930s through the war years, Ayer had one aim in mind.
As a De Beers memo put it, Americans must be convinced that "the
Diamond Industry, though an admitted monopoly, operates fairly and
in a manner that accords with American interests. This must be done
in a way that will stand up under direct attack even from a government
source."

The agency knew that consumers were made, not born, and that
image was everything. It homed in on America's dream factory, convincing Hollywood producers to change the title of a film from *Diamonds are Dangerous* to *Adventures in Diamonds*, and arranging for stars
like Merle Oberon and Claudette Colbert to flaunt their jewels on
screen. Later, newspapers were spoon-fed upbeat stories with such
headlines as "War Gives Impetus to Diamond Cutting" and "How
Diamonds Spark the Wings of War and Peace."

After VJ Day, with an increased budget and higher goals, Ayer
submitted a new strategy to strengthen the century-old tradition of the
diamond engagement ring, making it "a psychological necessity capable
of competing successfully at the retail level with utility goods and
services." To begin with, the principals of selected high schools were
persuaded to allow visiting speakers to address student assemblies.
Their subject: the unique and fascinating history of diamonds. "All of
these lectures," said a confidential memo to De Beers, "revolve around
the diamond engagement ring, and are reaching thousands of girls in
their assemblies, classes and informal meetings in our leading educational institutions."

Indoctrination continued outside the classroom. Another strategy
paper reported, "We spread the word of diamonds worn by stars of
screen and stage, by wives and daughters of political leaders, by any
woman who can make the grocer's wife and the mechanic's sweetheart
say 'I wish I had what she has.' " To increase sales of bigger and more
expensive jewels, men were encouraged to buy "the biggest diamond
they could afford."

In 1948 the slogan "A Diamond Is Forever" was concocted by an
Ayer copywriter; it became a much-parodied, fervently imitated hall-

mark of American advertising, a classic headline to be put alongside "Pepsi Cola Hits the Spot" and "There's a Ford in Your Future." A diamond, of course, is no more "forever" than an amethyst or a garnet. The stones are all about the same age, and like any other jewel the diamond can be accidentally shattered, chipped, or burned. No matter; the phrase took hold in the American mind, and De Beers's product came to crystallize hope for marital success and material accomplishment. In the heady postwar period, who dared to call hope a luxury?

At the beginning of the 1950s half of America's engaged women were presented with a diamond ring by their fiancés. Under Harry's prodding, Ayer stepped up its efforts, with admirable results: as the 1960s approached, the figure had risen to nearly 80 percent. In the 1953 film *Gentlemen Prefer Blondes*, Marilyn Monroe and Jane Russell sang "Diamonds Are a Girl's Best Friend," and everyone got the message at no expense to De Beers ("square cut or pear shape, these rocks don't lose their shape"). An expansive mood pervaded the company. The gross national incomes of Japan, Germany, and Brazil were increasing dramatically. There would be a lot of discretionary income; no reason why diamond sales shouldn't consume a good portion of it. True, there was no tradition of diamond buying in those countries, especially Japan, but that was what ad agencies were for. As one diamond executive saw it, "The Japanese can be advertised anything."

Meantime, another problem for Harry surfaced far from the mines and the jewelry stores of America and Japan. All through the 1950s, chemists at a Swedish company, Almanna Svenska Elektriska Aktiebolaget, had attempted to manufacture synthetic diamonds. In 1953, using a process that involved pure carbon, intense heat (about 5,000 degrees Fahrenheit), and pressures equal to about 90,000 times that of the Earth's atmosphere, ASEA produced some 40 tiny crystals with all the characteristics of natural diamonds. Scientists at General Electric had been working along the same lines, and two years later, using pressures up to 100,000 times the Earth's atmosphere, GE turned out its own artificial diamonds. Economists published their grave doubts about the future of the diamond industry. De Beers had undergone depressions, disease, political strife; and it had always emerged stronger than before. But it had never done battle with science.

Bearing in mind the many fraudulent attempts to produce jewels in furnaces, Ernest clung to his belief that only God could make a diamond. His faith now appeared to be a false creed. All the same, Harry refused to panic. The tactic of encircling the enemy had always worked before, and it would be invoked again. First, De Beers issued warm congratulations to General Electric for its interesting technical experiment, all the while reminding the world that these synthetic crystals were not gemstones. They were really only a form of grit. Perhaps they could be used as abrasive powder, *if* they could be made cheaply. That was hardly the case at present: the thimbleful of Swedish stones had cost more than $300,000 to produce.

Privately, De Beers managers acknowledged that the industry could be facing its most profound crisis. They moved to stage two. There was only one way to beat science, and that was to co-opt it. A diamond research laboratory already existed at Crown Mines; Harry now issued fresh marching orders. A division called Adamant—from the ancient Greek word for diamond—was to find a new process so that De Beers could make its own synthetic diamonds. With the finest experts money could buy, plus virtually unlimited funds, Adamant came out with its own artificial product in 1958. The first crystals were extremely small, useless for anything except grinding operations. They were also costly: nearly twice the price of industrial diamonds dug out of the earth. But that was beside the point. De Beers could now negotiate with ASEA and GE on level ground.

That brought the company to stage three. After protracted negotiations, a settlement was announced. For $8 million plus royalties, General Electric would allow De Beers to use its patented process to make diamonds. Harry turned his attention to ASEA and, for an undisclosed sum, purchased the Swedish factory, its technology and patents. Within two years De Beers would create its own artificial diamond division, Ultra High Pressure Units Inc., with 75 hydraulic presses in South Africa, plus the ones in Sweden and a new factory in Shannon, Ireland. "I wasn't sure when Harry took over," one of the Nationalists grudgingly admitted. "Pampered Oxford boy I thought. Then I heard about the business with Russians and the blacks. And I saw him myself going from a position on the sidelines, to major player in the field of artificial diamonds. He's his father's son all right. Someone who could cause a lot of trouble."

◆　　◆　　◆

FOR MOST OF THE NATIONALISTS, Harry was irritating enough in the private sector. The thought of a famous anti-apartheid businessman in the political arena was intolerable. Party officials were pondering their next anti-Oppenheimer move when Harry took the matter out of their hands. Just before the election of 1958, Hendrik Verwoerd, Nationalist candidate for Prime Minister, read an official statement from the Chairman of De Beers: "My father's death has brought me heavy business responsibilities which cannot be discharged properly if I remain actively engaged in political controversy.

"I have, therefore, informed the leader of the United Party . . . that I will not be available to stand for Parliament in the next election."

The Nationalists campaigned across South Africa with a fresh confidence. They had beaten Hoggenheimer without firing a shot. Standing on a platform of white supremacy, the party had won a tremendous victory over "British-Jewish liberalism." The new Prime Minister, Hendrik Verwoerd, not noted for his religious zealotry until now, proclaimed his belief: "It was the will of God that was revealed in the ballot."

Harry made no secret of his disappointment. Even so, he professed to be bullish on South Africa. Visiting London he said as much to the members of the Royal African Society: "South Africans often fail to grasp the extent to which they are united about the things that matter most. . . . It is surprising to how small an extent the economic development of the country has been affected by political controversy."

He would willingly have bought back those words in 1959, when the United Party split open on the issue of the black vote. The conservatives felt that there should be no more talk of extending the franchise to non-whites. The liberals, Harry among them, wanted to 'leave the door open.' The debate grew rancorous, and some members, among them a liberal named Helen Suzman of Johannesburg, were ready to bolt then and there. Harry made no move, hoping for some kind of rapprochement. When it failed to occur, he wrote a letter that shook the party, and, in time, South Africa itself. "While I have completely retired from public life and have no intention whatever of returning to it," he wrote the UP leaders, "I have naturally followed with close interests the recent developments of the United Party. . . . In the circumstances, I think it would be improper for me to remain a member . . . and I have accordingly tendered my resignation." Several months later the Progressive Party was founded. For many years Harry was to provide its principal financial support, and Suzman its sole Parliamentarian. Their enemies on the far right, near right, and center yawned. Even with all of Harry's wealth, these two did not seem much of an opposition. "We have a lot to learn," Harry acknowledged early on. So did his enemies.

In the early winter of 1960 Verwoerd became greatly distressed by a speech of Britain's Prime Minister Harold Macmillan. The Englishman had the temerity to speak of "the winds of change" blowing over the Congo, Kenya, and the rest of Africa. Verwoerd knew what that meant: it heralded the social mixing of Bantus and Europeans, desegregated universities, political chaos, and the death of white ideals. He stepped up his apartheid program, and in response the African leaders called for massive demonstrations of civil disobedience.

An active new movement, the Pan African Congress, broke away from the ANC and declared March 21, 1960 as "Anti-Pass day." Its followers were to protest the law by deliberately leaving their passes at home. Other such protests had begun well, but they had ended with brutalities on both sides. The year before, four white and five black policemen had been clubbed to death in an incident outside Durban. The PAC was determined not to let such things happen in the orderly and pleasant town of Sharpeville, 50 miles south of Johannesburg. Citing the words and spirit of Gandhi they planned to offer no resistance to the arresting officers. The jails would swell with thousands of PAC followers, thereby embarrassing the administration and forcing changes in the law. It was a grave miscalculation. On its side the government had no give at all; on the Africans' side, the demonstrators were untrained and poorly organized.

So were the police. At 10 a.m. a group of some 5,000 blacks assembled outside the Sharpeville police station. The officers had no idea what to do. They were intimidated by the crowd, and yet the jails were too small to hold so many people. The standoff lasted for more than three hours. In that time the government sent Sabre jets to fly low, hoping to disperse the demonstrators. The tactic had worked for some civil disturbances in the past; here it only served to roil the crowd. At about 1:45 p.m. someone shoved a policeman, and a scuffle broke out. A group surged forward to see what had happened. Police later claimed that rock throwing began at this point. The constables had no orders to shoot, but some of the younger ones were rattled. They drew their pistols and opened fire. The demonstrators turned back and started a frenzied flight. It was too late. A schoolteacher named Michael Zondo heard chattering noises and fell from his bicycle. "I just saw brains," he reported. "Skulls were bursting open in front of me."

He tried to walk away when he spotted some of his students. "They started shouting *'Tichara othunswe! Tichara othunswe!'* which is Sosotho for 'Our teacher has been shot!'

"I was shocked. I thought, am I dead? I remembered magazine stories I had read as a child, of King Arthur's soldiers in battle, who kept on running after they had been beheaded, and I wondered if that had happened to me."

The children indicated his leg. He looked down, saw that his calf muscle had been shot away, and collapsed.

The Sharpeville Massacre, as the papers called it, was the watershed of modern South Africa. Overnight the brutality of apartheid was graphically displayed in a flood of photographs and international reportage. No other incident, dating back to the worst excesses of the Boer War, did more damage to the country's reputation. Pretoria was condemned in the United Nations, castigated in Europe and the United States. Verwoerd's government angrily responded: The disturbance, it claimed, came from "a planned demonstration . . . the demonstrators shot first and the police were forced to fire in self-defense."

When the official story failed to persuade the world, the Prime Minister had an epochal tantrum. On April 8 his government passed the Unlawful Organizations Act, banning the ANC, PAC, and lesser groups. A young black leader named Nelson Mandela ominously recalled that "We . . . had always stood for a non-racial democracy, and we shrank from a policy which might drive the races further apart than they already were. But the hard facts were that fifty years of nonviolence had brought the African people nothing but more and more repressive legislation, and fewer and fewer rights."

South Africa edged closer to social dissolution. Two weeks after Sharpeville, a disturbed white farmer pumped two bullets into the Prime Minister. He told police that he was seized with "a violent urge to shoot apartheid—the striking monster of apartheid that was gripping the throat of South Africa and preventing South Africa from achieving his [*sic*] rightful place among the nations."

Verwoerd not only survived, he prevailed. Thoroughly persuaded that he had been saved by divine intervention, the leader demanded harsher racial statutes. Strikes were broken; thousands were arrested and held without charge. Stung by the criticism from England, he pulled out of the British Commonwealth, ending a 150-year association. And he continued to fulminate against one particular enemy of the state: a white man who insisted that apartheid was worse than dangerous, it was impractical.

"The Oppenheimer group," Verwoerd complained, "is an octopus" with "branches in all spheres of the economic life of South Africa." Its head, Mr. Harry Oppenheimer, "makes political statements; he discusses political policy, he tries to exercise political influence. . . . He can secretly cause a good many things to happen. In other words, he can pull strings. With all that monetary power and with this powerful machine which is spread over the whole of the country he can, if he so chooses, exercise an enormous influence against the Government and against the State."

A member of parliament agreed: on the fingers of one hand he could count South Africa's "most pressing problems—the United Nations, the English Press, the Liberal Party, the United Party and Harry Oppenheimer." Harry held his tongue. If they wanted to believe in Hoggenheimer's vaunted influence, let them. The stock market had other ideas: investors were panicking and moving toward the exits. From January 1960 to June 1961 foreign reserves dropped 50 percent. The Oppenheimer empire was forced to borrow, and borrow heavily, from American banks. So much for Hoggenheimer power.

Harry had always looked to history for consolation and enlightenment; but it was of no help here. The 1960s were unprecedented times;

the politics were changing, the country altering almost beyond rec-
ognition. Rhodes, Barnato, Beit, Robinson, and all the other Randlords
were now merely names on statues, their stories as irrelevant as Black-
beard and Captain Kidd. Dead less than five years, Sir Ernest himself
seemed to have flourished in a nineteenth-century romance. Musing
about his father one day, Harry presented him in a cold light. He
recalled that Ernest "was often written of as an 'international financier,'
but this was quite wrong. There was nothing international in his look
or outlook, and he saw his financial success as a by-product in building
up South Africa. The South Africa he thought of, however, did not
stand alone but was a member of the Commonwealth, as the Commonwealth used to be but can never be again.

"I have often wondered how he would have felt about the Commonwealth and Africa today. I do not think," Harry concluded, "that
he would easily have adapted himself to the changes that have come
about, and it may be that he was fortunate in his death as in his life."
It was a strange thing for a devoted son to say, and some executives
at De Beers and Anglo were shocked by the appraisal. Yet no one
could refute a word. Ernest Oppenheimer had indeed been fortunate
in his death as well as his life. These days, King of Diamonds was a
far more difficult role to play. Perhaps it was impossible.

PART THREE

CONNOISSEUR
OF CHAOS

I

A. A violent order is disorder; and
B. A great disorder is an order. These
Two things are one. (Pages of illustrations.)

II

If all the green of spring was blue, and it is;
If all the flowers of South Africa were bright
On the tables of Connecticut, and they are

. . .

WALLACE STEVENS,
"Connoisseur of Chaos"

16

A NASTY SORT
OF SURVIVAL

"IN SOUTH AFRICA, politics have the habit of going one way, life another." Harry Oppenheimer could always produce an aphorism for foreign investors to take home—until the early 1960s. Then, for the first time, the members of his audience began to smile politely and turn away. They were in no mood for empty reassurances.

This was the third decade of Nationalist rule, and Pretoria's racial formulas seemed set in stone. Mandela led the ANC from various hiding places, embarrassing and infuriating the government. Admirers called him the Black Pimpernel; they taunted South African police every time he surfaced in Britain or Eastern Europe, staying just long enough to raise funds before he vanished. At last Mandela grew careless, and with the help of informers the police caught up with him in Natal. Convicted of sabotage and of seeking to overthrow the government, he was sentenced to life imprisonment on Robben Island. The romantic place where Harry and Bridget had met during the war had been turned into South Africa's Alcatraz.

In the United Nations, vote after vote condemned South Africa, with scarcely a dissenting voice. Foreign capital drained away and economic growth plummeted to zero. Hunkered down, the government was forced to impose controls on imports and foreign exchange. Liberal politicians in Europe and America outdid each other in outrage. They openly compared Verwoerd's country to Hitler's Reich and argued for disinvestment and sanctions, measures which would undermine and perhaps destroy De Beers and Anglo.

In South Africa Harry had lost his famous powers of persuasion.

On the right, the government stepped up its Oppenheimer–Hoggenheimer approach, portraying the King of Diamonds as a rich radical, living well and safely while he urged the natives to revolt. On the left, black critics sarcastically commented that Oppenheimer's benign policies were not really multiracial at all; they were multi*facial*, one profile for the Afrikaaner rulers, another for the African majority.

Some of these opinions were played back to Lyndon Johnson when he greeted Harry at a White House visit in 1964. The President's advisors instructed him to begin by praising Mr. Oppenheimer's "humane policies toward his African workers." LBJ was to assure his guest that the U.N., in the President's opinion, should not "interfere" in South Africa's internal politics. After these bland remarks, however, the President was to remind Harry forcefully that failure to reform was "making it increasingly difficult for [South Africa's] friends."

Harry needed no further goads. That year, in an address at the University of Cape Town, he attempted to bring both factions to his side. He had come to protest the lack of academic freedom at South African universities, forbidden by law to enroll non-white students. The speech began as a history lesson. Except for Egypt, he pointed out, the African continent had never really produced what the West could call a civilized society. Imagining Africa before the days of imperialism, Harry invoked Thomas Hobbes: There were "no arts; no letters; no society; and which is worst of all, continual fear and danger of violent death; and the life of man solitary, poor, nasty, brutish and short."

The colonialists, he reminded the audience, did not invent slavery. Black Africans carried on a traffic in human beings long before the first white men landed. At their best, the Europeans had brought capital and provided markets for African material, aiding and sometimes founding the economies of various now-independent African states. They had erected a solid framework of administration and civil service, calmed tribal conflicts, and provided courts of law.

This part of the speech was to make black Africans nervous. Here they were, warmed by the winds of change, well past the halfway mark of the twentieth century. And here was the nation's most liberal industrialist talking in the self-congratulatory tones of Cecil Rhodes.

In contrast, the Afrikaaner whites found the Oppenheimer history very much to their taste.

They were brought up short. The burden of Harry's argument was that A: whatever their intentions, the colonialists had in fact profited handsomely from slavery until the political climate made it inconvenient for them to continue. And that B: capitalist institutions had risen on the backs of underpaid black labor. How had this happened? Why had the Africans allowed the Europeans to exploit them? No doubt it was because the native tribes had been awakened and prodded by European imperialists after "ages of stagnation." As a result, Harry maintained, "there were those who argued from this general backwardness to some basic inferiority of the Africans"—"those" included every imperialist from Queen Victoria's adventurers, who thought of Africans as children, to the current apartheid government, which treated them like beasts.

"But surely," the speaker continued, "the facts of the case really point in quite a different direction. . . . What is astonishing about Africa is the unexampled speed of advance" by the blacks. Inescapably, this speed would provoke the conflict between, "on the one hand, the new men seeking wider opportunity and eager for change [i.e., Oppenheimer and his followers], and on the other hand, the traditionalists," defenders of the Afrikaaner way of life based on white rule and black disenfranchisement. Harry foresaw that "in this conflict the traditionalists must go under, and much that is good, wise, and beautiful must go with them. That is the price that must be paid to open the way to new opportunities, wider horizons and higher values."

Nothing could have been more threatening to the Nationalists, the Afrikaaners, the Broederbond, and every other group resistant to black participation in the government. It was all very well for Harry F. Oppenheimer to talk of tradition going under; he had made his pile, and a mountainous pile it was. His white critics had no time or room for such palaver; segregation and apartheid had given them their economic and social position, and they had no intention of relinquishing it.

Harry's next move alienated the other side. He served on a Progressive Party commission inquiring into the voting rights of all South

Africans. It concluded that the concept of "one man, one vote" was inappropriate. "Its inspiration," said the report, is "non-White nationalism which, like all nationalisms, is ultimately totalitarian in its logical outcome."

The only answer, as Harry saw it, was the Oppenheimer Thesis. Briefly, it held that the answer to racial oppression lay in financial prosperity. In a growth economy, new, high-paying jobs would be open to blacks. By the hundreds, then the thousands and then the hundreds of thousands, they would enter the middle class. Apartheid would be a hindrance to prosperity, and a sensible government would allow it to wither and die.

Harry pointed to the English example. Britain was originally controlled by a minority of wealthy autocrats. Many in the ruling class had owned slaves. But over the course of time the nation had been forced to develop some form of social justice. Altruism had nothing to do with it. Great changes in the moral landscape occurred, and always would occur, during the years of industrial expansion, "when the supply of unskilled labor ceases to appear inexhaustible and the ruling minority starts to find that it actually needs the rest of the population."

The reasoning seemed plausible to business leaders; here was capitalism with a heart, something they could live with. The Chase Bank agreed to lend $10 million for the promotion of South African business, and a consortium of bankers led by David Rockefeller advanced another $150 million. Anti-apartheid critics raised a squall of objections, but this was to be expected. The Chase prepared a rationale: "We believe it would endanger the free world if every large American bank deprived developing countries of the opportunity for economic growth. If one hopes for changes in the Republic of South Africa or elsewhere, it would do little good to withdraw economic support."

If the bankers were cold and defensive, Charles Engelhard seemed to shed heat wherever he walked. The American was the son of a German immigrant whose company, The Engelhard Metals and Minerals Corporation, had prospered in the New World. Charles used this small fortune to make a larger one. He had first visited South Africa in the 1940s, shopping for gold to sell overseas. At the time a law specifically prohibited anyone from taking ingots out of the country.

The only way precious metal could cross South African borders was in the form of jewelry or *objets d'art*. Where others saw only a net, Engelhard focused on the loophole. He became a jewelry manufacturer: his Precious Metals Development Co. made baubles that lasted just long enough to be exported to Hong Kong. There they were melted down and formed into gold bars to be sold overseas.

Some Americans read of this process in their financial journals; the rest were to learn about it in a bestselling novel. Ian Fleming, vastly amused by the antics of his friend, studied the scam. In his sixth adventure of James Bond he made Engelhard a villain and called him Goldfinger ("Mr. Bond, all my life I have been in love. I have been in love with gold. I love its color, its brilliance, its divine heaviness. . . . But above all, Mr. Bond, I love the power that gold alone gives to its owner—the magic of controlling energy, exacting labor, fulfilling one's every wish and whim."

Later Engelhard and Fleming tried another venture in Africa, developing timber estates on the banks of the Zambesi River. It failed, and they turned their attention to farming vegetables in the same area. This, too, was unsuccessful: hippopotami ate the entire crop.

These events, and the fact that Engelhard's marriage had produced daughters but no male heir, were almost the only disappointments of Goldfinger's career. By cornering another precious-metal market he got himself labeled the Platinum King, and more millions came his way. In America he wrote checks for innumerable Democratic Party campaigns; Presidents and senators sought his advice and consent. The small, rotund figure stood at attention at the independence ceremonies of Algeria, Gabon, and Zambia, formally representing the United States; at the 1963 coronation of Pope John XXIII, he was the official American presence. The ebullience of Johannesburg seemed a reflection of his personality, and he acquired an estate in the city. From there he carried on in the swaggering manner of a Randlord, gambling huge sums on horse races, flying about the continent in his private plane, *The Platinum Plover*, with two butlers aboard. His big dinners were famous for their opulence and their gaffes—when the black singer Miriam Makeba performed for his white guests, they ate in the dining room. She was given supper in the kitchen.

To those who knew both men, Engelhard's life style seemed the diametrical opposite of Harry's subdued and self-effacing methods. But the American's influence and power were simply too great to ignore. Oppenheimer's official biographer put it out that the two men "got along like a house afire from the first time they met," and perhaps they did. By this point Harry had become a genuine enthusiast of Thoroughbred racing and breeding. Engelhard controlled an outstanding stable; at one time he owned 250 steeds, including Nijinsky, winner of the English Triple Crown, and he offered to breed a prize stallion with one of Harry's mares. No one was surprised when the American joined Anglo's board as an executive director.

Engelhard swiftly got richer, and Oppenheimer acquired a lobbyist of the highest influence, an industrialist who urged American corporations, the International Monetary Fund, and the World Bank to join him in his adopted country. Expanded capital would solve all social problems. "If you find somebody who doesn't like living in South Africa," Engelhard proclaimed, "he hasn't been paid enough."

The message took hold, and South Africa's national economy began to right itself. In the early 1960s the national growth rate averaged almost 6 percent, second only to Japan's. Exports, even excluding gold, rose some 135 percent. Foreign investment returned. When Britain's Labour government decided it would no longer supply arms to Pretoria, France rushed in to fill the vacuum with weaponry and Mirage fighter planes. West Germany brought in machinery and tools for atomic research. BMW opened its only foreign plant in South Africa, alongside the giant United States firms of Ford, Chrysler, and General Motors. Financiers were getting a minimum return of 15 percent on their capital investments, a figure that multinational corporations began to find irresistible. With some justification, critics described this as South Africa's "apartheid boom." In the early 1960s shouts from the trading floor all but drowned out the cries from the townships.

In August 1966, the government confidently predicted a long period of tranquillity. The period lasted exactly one month. On September 6, Hendrik Verwoerd cleared his throat and arranged his papers, preparing to give an ebullient speech to the legislature. He had just been seated when a parliamentary messenger approached him, reached out, and suddenly stabbed the Prime Minister four times in the chest and neck. Several members of Parliament saw what was happening;

they closed in, captured the attacker, and pulled him out of the chamber as he screamed, "I'll get that bastard!"—as if his mission had failed. Verwoerd, shirt and suit soaked with blood, was taken off to the hospital at top speed. Before the ambulance pulled up to the hospital doors, he was dead.

Dimitri Tsafendas was the assassin's name, and the merchant ship-man ushered in a new harvest of irony. State guards, who had always searched crowds for a fanatical black face, did not think to look for a simple-minded white one. Tsafendas, the illegitimate son of a Greek father and a Mozambiquan woman, was apolitical. His grievance against the Prime Minister was sexual. Men aboard his ship everlast-ingly complained about South Africa's immorality laws, for they were white and the local prostitutes were colored. Intercourse between the races was strictly forbidden. At the height of their frustration, the men used to grumble that Verwoerd should be killed. A few months later the suggestible Tsafendas found a job carrying messages to the members of Parliament. Pleasing his old shipmates had been a simple matter of timing and a knife.

After the public eulogies and hopes for a more enlightened future, South Africa went on as harshly as before. Verwoerd's successor was his own Minister of Justice, Balthazar Johannes Vorster, a man with firm ideas about "Kaffirs." In 1962 Vorster gave the police the power to hold suspects—almost always black—without charge for 12 days; in 1963 the period was increased to 90 days; in 1965 to 180 days. Eventually Vorster arranged to have suspects held for an indefinite period.

The Prime Minister knew a thing or two about jail time; he had experienced 20 months of it during World War II, when he was held in detention for expressing Nazi sympathies. Not only did Vorster profess no bitterness about the past, he used it to rationalize his current policies. "I had come out in opposition to the government of the day," he remembered. "That government identified me as a threat to estab-lished order and so neutralized me. It did what it felt was necessary at the time. I adopted the same approach."

In the next several years that approach would broaden the definition of apartheid. The Nationalists were uncomfortable with the presence of so many Africans in the shantytowns surrounding major cities, on white-owned farms, in established townships. A generation before, the Third Reich had found a solution to the problem of surplus population. Now Vorster, the one-time admirer of Nazi Germany, imitated some of Hitler's methods. First, black leaders were jailed or put under house arrest; then "superfluous" natives were loaded onto trucks and forcibly removed to "Bantustans"—segregated territories in various parts of South Africa. Vorster's General Circular of 1967 stated that "No stone is to be left unturned to achieve the settlement in the homelands of non-productive Bantu at present residing in the European areas." Non-productive, in the Nationalists' terms, meant:

(i) The aged, the unfit, widows, women with dependent children and families who do not qualify for accommodation in European urban areas;

(ii) Bantu on European farms who become superfluous as a result of age [or] disability . . . or Bantu squatters from mission stations and black spots which are being cleared up;

(iii) Doctors, attorneys, agents, traders, industrialists, etc. [who] are not regarded as essential for the European labor market.

Just as the trainloads of Jews were taken out of Germany in sealed cars, the trucks full of black deportees deliberately avoided the white cities, and the Minister of Bantu Administration carefully disseminated his propaganda across the country and the world. Far from from being discomfited, he claimed, "The Bantu people like being moved. . . . They like the places where they are being resettled."

Visitors came back from the homelands with a different story. A Father Cosmas Desmond reported, "We found the first arrivals [from the cities] sitting in the bare veld surrounded by their belongings looking bewildered and utterly lost. A little distance away was a water tank and a pile of folded tents, which the people did not know how to erect—nothing else." They were joined by other confused Africans, pushed, driven, and sometimes bulldozed out of their homes and farmlands. The number of displaced blacks has never been precisely determined; in the first decade of Vorster's resettlement laws at least 1,820,000 of them were, as the government euphemism had it, "endorsed out" of their dwelling places and livelihoods.

The idea of a future where blacks would outbreed whites spurred on the Nationalists. They were forever reciting history and terrifying their audience with numbers: in the fading glow of Edwardian England, Europeans had comprised one third of South Africa's population. By the early 1950s, they had been reduced to one fifth. At this rate, by the end of the 1960s whites would be a sixth and, early in the twenty-first century, a mere tenth of the nation.

There were other considerations as well. International Communism had found hospitable soil in Africa. In 1963 the old colonial possession, the French Congo, declared itself the People's Republic of the Congo. Who knew what country was next, or what subversive elements—white as well as black—might be at work in South Africa? A Suppression of Communism Act, long in place, was used to redefine Marxism as any activity seeking to force "any political, industrial, social or economic change within the Union by the promotion of disturbance and disorder."

The emerging nations of Africa added another ingredient to the brew. In Kenya the Mau Mau murdered white farmers; in Malawi, the leader Hastings Banda substituted witchcraft for statecraft; in Burundi assassins took the lives of two state ministers. President Omar Bongo of Gabon forbade the word "pygmy," possibly because he himself was less than five feet tall. He took care, however, to surround himself with a bodyguard of tall German veterans who liked to sing the *Horst Wessel* song. The President of Benin murdered a Foreign Minister, found in bed with the First Lady. On Congolese television the corpse of a government official was shown in prime time, his mouth stuffed with dollar bills. In Equatorial Guinea a Foreign Minister was clubbed to death by the head of state.

Every month some fresh atrocity was reported from the north, and the Nationalists used three pretexts—Communism, overpopulation, and violence in the emerging black nations—to stretch the limits of apartheid. International protest rose a few more decibels. Moral outrage echoed down the corridors of Moscow, Whitehall, and Washington. Meanwhile, the U.S.S.R. silently sold its diamonds through the complicated channels of De Beers. And after denouncing Pretoria in various press conferences, Britain's Labour Government quietly advised traveling entrepreneurs not to rock any boats. A pamphlet entitled *Hints to Businessmen* told them, "When engaged in business dealings visitors would be well advised not to become involved in controversy on political and social matters that arouse deep feeling in South Africa."

Aware that they would receive little help from Europe, South African black leaders turned to the United States. They received mixed signals. Presidents Kennedy and Johnson had professed to find apartheid morally repugnant, but did no more than scold the South African government. During the Nixon years, National Security Advisor Henry Kissinger gave an official overview of South Africa: "The whites are here to stay, and the only way that constructive change can come about is through them. There is no hope for the blacks to gain the political rights they seek through violence, which will only lead to chaos and increased opportunity for the Communists."

His message seemed to energize South Africa's business leaders. Confronted by a reporter, the most prominent man in the private sector, Harry Oppenheimer himself, allowed that he was "not very happy about the way things are being handled here, but, as they say in the mining industry, it takes an incredibly bad manager to spoil a good mine."

A good mine: an inspired metaphor. Viewed that way, South Africa could take on a different moral tone. It could be seen as a property rather than a political entity, a place where new machines and new management might yet pull out enough diamonds for everyone and every race. Harry backed up his claim with commitment. Neither he nor any member of his family would make the "chicken run"—saying good-bye to friends, selling the house, and emigrating to Europe or America or Australia. Despite a hostile government, despite the threats of social dissolution, he stated, "unless I'm chased out, I'm going to stay here . . . when things were going badly a lot of people hived off—well, I think that's silly. I think it's not very brave and I think it's bad judgement, too. It's worse than a crime . . . it's a mistake."

Harry had made very few mistakes in his life, and his declaration caused a great many whites to abandon plans to exit South Africa. "The man has a hell of a lot more to lose than I do," said a doctor who had been planning to sell his practice. "I can get more patients overseas. Where's he going to find more gold and diamond mines?

He must know something the rest of us don't. He usually does. I think I'll stick around for Act Three."

♦　　♦　　♦

As foreign investors tentatively moved into South Africa, Harry passed them going the other way. Under Ernest, the Oppenheimer empire had retained its national character and outlook. But a new reality prevailed in the late 1960s and early 1970s: like all great corporate entities of the period, De Beers and Anglo-American had two choices: grow or die. Even a healthy South African economy, nourished by outside investment, would not be large enough to sustain the empire. Its chief officer prepared to extend his grasp to North America.

In Canada Harry arranged for Anglo to buy a 14.5 percent share of the Hudson Bay Mining and Smelting Company of Manitoba, which specialized in lead, zinc, and copper. The stake cost more than $20 million, a sum that Goldfinger had to raise because of South African restrictions on the flow of currency out of the country. Harry had his eye on other foreign investments, and he knew there were only so many times he could go to Charles Engelhard. The Oppenheimer empire had to set up its own financial house beyond the laws of Pretoria.

Charter Consolidated started modestly. From all outward appearances it looked to be independent and British, a world away from the country of apartheid. Actually, the house's every move was made in the interests of De Beers and Anglo, and within three years its assets doubled in value to £324 million.

Harry vigorously pushed on to Australia. On a visit he assured authorities that their country was "a first class place to look for minerals, and if we find anything we will invest on a very large scale." Public relations had something to do with his ebullience, but Harry was speaking from the heart as well as the vault. He liked the place and its possibilities, as far as he could see. The trouble was that he failed to see far enough. Anglo and Charter invested in companies searching for tin and copper in Western Australia, and gold in Victoria. But the idea of diamonds seemed an unlikely proposition Down Under, and no great effort was made to find any. In a dozen years that would prove to be a costly oversight.

Meantime the financial house concentrated on other minerals, buying its way into tin producing companies on both sides of the globe: in Malaysia and in Portugal. In Africa, Charter pushed north to the newly independent black nations, seeking out diamonds, gold, and copper. Zambia, at first delighted with Oppenheimer's development money, later complained that too much of the profit was being siphoned out of the country. President Kenneth Kaunda demanded—and received—51 percent of Zambia Anglo-American (Zamanglo). Shortly afterward Zamanglo transferred its base to the tax haven of Bermuda. From there its long arms reached into the United States.

The other half of the empire, De Beers, carried on its own backstairs operations. The nation of Tanganyika was about to merge with the nation of Zanzibar under the new name of Tanzania. The new country would still produce first-quality stones at the Williamson mine. Harry was aware that an emerging black nation could not afford to be seen holding hands with a South African company. Yet Tanzania was hardly in a position to nationalize the mine; all the technology and expertise belonged to De Beers. Harry made a suggestion. What if the country were to *buy* half of Williamson? The leaders hesitated; there was not enough money in the treasury. No matter, Harry assured them, he would arrange for a loan. *The Nationalist*, Tanzania's leading news-paper, wanted none of this. How could the country advocate a boycott of South Africa "if we are in partnership with the South African corporation openly supporting apartheid?"

Oppenheimer's answer was not to raise his voice but to disguise his operation. The loan went through, and De Beers's half-interest in the Williamson mine was renamed Willcroft Co., with an address in the Bahamas. Officially the African republic of Tanzania had nothing to do with the country of apartheid; its diamonds were dealt to a Ca-ribbean company. Tanzania was now able to enjoy a double freedom, just like the United Soviet Socialist Republic; it could condemn South Africa at the U.N. General Assembly—and it could profitably convey its jewels to the same old stand.

De Beers expected threats of nationalization from the black repub-lics; it was an unpleasant shock to find them waiting at home. During the election year of 1970 Harry's mild but continued opposition to apartheid ran up against something called the *Herstige Nasionale*

Party—the "Reborn National Party"—which regarded the Vorster government as dangerously liberal. To them the Oppenheimer companies comprised "the greatest threat to White South Africa." An HNP representative spoke out in Parliament: "I don't know how, but we will have to break Harry Oppenheimer's power if we want to survive as a White nation." His solution was a governmental grab of Anglo and De Beers.

Harry happened to be in Australia during this attack. A reporter at *The Melbourne Herald* closed in before the interviewee had time to put up his guard. He responded bitterly, "I realize I am living in a country which politically is a failure. But somehow we are surviving. It is a nasty sort of survival and I often wonder what will happen in ten years' time. South Africa could be wiped out; its rulers are so damn bloodyminded."

By the time Harry stepped off the plane in Johannesburg, he found the government in a state of undeclared war against the Oppenheimer empire. It was led by the Minister of Mining and Planning, Carel de Wet. Harry responded cooly. He reminded the ministers in general, and de Wet in particular, that South Africa was emerging from recession because of foreign investment. Did Pretoria want to turn the calendar to the wall? "If business men outside South Africa get it into their heads that people in South Africa not only have to obey the law and conventions that govern our industry, but also have to be active supporters of government policies to get a fair deal, it is a very serious thing for this country."

Whatever his public stance, Vorster had no wish to lock horns with the man whose companies controlled some 50 percent of the Johannesburg stock market. To deal with Harry nowadays was in effect to deal with a head of state. When HFO had an official statement, the press came running; when he made deals, the stock markets on four continents reverberated. British dukes worked for De Beers; friends in Washington and Whitehall, Berlin and Tokyo stood ready to serve.

The last thing South Africa needed was another public relations disaster—especially since the tide appeared to be turning in the West. Here, for example, was that old Christian iconoclast Malcolm Muggeridge writing about Pretoria in *Esquire* magazine, not precisely complimenting the government, but refusing to follow the standard U.N.

line. "In a world full of oppressive régimes and terrorist practices, [why should] the venom and fury of the liberal mind . . . pick on the white South Africans with particular spleen when their oligarchic rule only differs from that of a dozen others—Tito's, Franco's, Ulbricht's, Castro's etc., etc.—in that they happen to be anxious to be on good terms with the English. What but a death wish could bring on so complete a reversal of all the normal worldly considerations of good sense, self-interest and a desire to survive?"

With an eye on Harry, Vorster took the Planning portfolio away from de Wet. A little later on, the Prime Minister went further. He reshuffled his cabinet and removed de Wet from South Africa altogether: he was sent off to London as Ambassador to the Court of St. James. Suddenly Harry could not lose for winning, on the track, in the government, in private life. Only one South African was more famous in the 1960s—Dr. Christiaan Barnard, who performed the world's first heart transplant. And it was the new Chancellor of the University of Cape Town, Harry Oppenheimer, who presented Barnard with his first honorary degree.

At Brenthurst the Oppenheimers lived in a style unseen since the days of the Edwardians. Harry and Bridget dressed formally for dinner even when they dined alone. Taking afternoon tea with Bridget amounted to a ceremony. Gibson, one of a dozen indoor staff members—that number did not include maids—was outfitted in white uniform with scarlet shoulder sash. He laid the table in silver and lace; afterward two other servants, dressed in similar uniforms, cleared away the plates, cups, and saucers.

Imperial style was backed with material accomplishments. Under the Oppenheimer banner, gold and uranium prices continued to rise. From a modest start Anglo had built up its chemical and explosives division until it became South Africa's largest industrial company. Anglo's own merchant bank had grown into the seventh biggest bank in South Africa. A subsidiary company had made itself the country's biggest producer of synthetic fibers. Yet another division was South Africa's fourth largest manufacturer of steel. As lagniappe, the Argus Group, which Anglo acquired incidentally in a takeover, was shortly to take control of 17 out of 20 English-speaking newspapers.

From Harry's point of view, the best part of all this was that De

Beers was the biggest beneficiary of Anglo's success. It held some 35 percent of the company's shares. Those who still doubted the power of diamonds could be referred to international jewelry districts, where the precious stones were appreciating at about 25 percent a year, compounded annually. Better still, they could read the instructive tale of the No Name diamond.

In the mid-1960s Harry Winston, America's leading diamond merchant, acquired a 100 carat diamond from the syndicate. He had it cut down and shaped into an astonishing 69.42 carat pear-shaped bauble. In 1967 its 58 facets caught the daylight and the flashbulbs as it was sold to Harriet Annenberg Ames, daughter of the millionaire publisher Moses Annenberg, for $500,000. But the jewel failed to make Mrs. Ames happy—insurance premiums alone cost her $30,000 a year—and in 1969 she offered to sell it back to Winston.

He claimed that she would do a lot better on the open market; why not put it up for auction at Parke Bernet? Informed that the owner did not want her family's name connected with the sale, the gallery dubbed the stone the No Name Diamond, implying that anyone who bought it would have the right to give the jewel his or her own surname. This was too great a temptation for Cartier—and for two actors. The store bought the No Name for $1,050,000. For four days it was known as the Cartier Diamond. Then Elizabeth Taylor and her then-husband Richard Burton purchased what was to become the Taylor Diamond for $1,100,000. The attendant publicity brought Cartier a fresh prominence, and just when the public thought that no more ink could be given to the on-again-off-again couple, the jewel furnished a new headline and some fresh arithmetic. In 24 months a De Beers diamond had doubled in value. Everyone was ecstatic, Cartier, the Burtons, and Harry. Especially Harry. His happiness was more durable than such shaky institutions as New York retail stores and Hollywood marriages.

17

FUNIGALO
AND FLASH FRED

Mr. Oppenheimer to those beyond his inner circle, HFO to his thousands of employees, Mr. Harry to his servants, had started rich, consolidated the family fortune, and in the 1960s aggressively crashed the exclusive club of world-class billionaires. He enjoyed global attention. Yet on the rare occasions when journalists observed him at work, the Chief Executive Officer was completely disarming, without a hint of pretense or flourish. He tried not to evade questions, kept his voice habitually muted, and issued commands in a tone of suggestion rather than insistence: Would it be wise to challenge the government monopoly in South African steel? Shouldn't we move into forestry and lumber? And what of the natives? Mustn't they be allowed their own portion of the good life?

Accumulation was Harry's specialty, at home as well as at headquarters. Oxford days had given him a special enthusiasm for the works and wit of Lord Byron; the Oppenheimer collection of first editions and letters mounted up. The walls of Brenthurst displayed the Reynolds, the Goyas and Romneys acquired patiently by Sir Ernest; Harry added a number of oils done by the better French Impressionists. He also bought rare china and silverware, providing his wife with an answer to the eternal question: What do you give to the man who has everything? You give him a birthday present of antique sterling. The connoisseur explained his idiosyncratic collections: "I am not one of those . . . who want an example of each type of a particular subject. I am for instance not a stamp collector. In fact I would hate collecting stamps. I think they are only meant to go on letters. I prefer to collect things which look good about the house."

In addition to objects for display, Harry acquired rare items of Africana whenever they came up for auction, adding still more items to his father's old collection of maps, books, and illustrations. In addition to all this there were horses, scores of them racing or foaling or being put out to stud. The family's personal scrapbooks had begun with clippings about business, political, and social occasions; as Harry and Bridget grew more involved in breeding and racing, the pages were filled with as many references to prize-winning fillies and colts, handicaps and derbies. Bridget had a fancy for pink, and the family stud farm at Mauritzfontein was painted that color, down to the pigstys.

Besides the horse place there was a ranch to the north and a flat in London, as well as a fully staffed vacation home in Durban. Milkwood, named for Dylan Thomas's radio play, was an elegant two-story structure with white shutters and sea-green tiles. As many as 30 guests could be accommodated in five suites with ten bedrooms and fifteen bathrooms. A separate dormitory wing housed the visitors' children.

No other Anglo or De Beers executive, no matter how high he rose—there were no women directors and, of course, no blacks—could possibly afford such opulent surroundings. Still, Harry saw to it that the men around him lived well. Oxonians predominated ("We did have occasionally the odd itinerant Cambridge man," observed an Anglo director. "They didn't stay for very long.") Harry's men dressed in conservative and well-tailored dark suits and spoke, as their leader did, in careful modulated tones. Yet below the quiet remark the alert listener could detect a surety that bordered on arrogance: these men worked for a powerful duchy within South Africa, just as Cecil Rhodes's men had flourished in a self-sealed world within the Empire. De Beers executives and "Anglo boys" operated their own private security force, air fleet, and diplomatic corps to smooth the way around and out of Africa.

Long workdays were counterbalanced with munificent salaries and perquisites. Company jets flew the directors to various meetings; cheerful African chauffeurs sat in purring limousines, ready to take them wherever they wanted to go. Left out of the main action, the Anglo wives, like army spouses, took their cues from the general's lady. Bridget Oppenheimer operated behind the scenes, pleading for racial amity, raising money for black charities like the African Children's Feeding Scheme, and providing a moral example. Her chauffeur's cottage was turned into a classroom where black children could be taught to read and to master handicrafts. "We have all lived in various ghettos for so long," she told a reporter. "I think people want to get together."

The idea appealed to selected whites and Africans; more radical blacks had other ideas, one of which was that they were being patronized by rich people with bad consciences. As one of the leaders pointed out, the Anglo boys made sure they knew every aspect of gold mining—except the part about human beings. In the 1960s laborers were still recruited from the independent but land-locked countries of Lesotho and Botswana (formerly Basutoland and Bechuanaland), from Zambia and Angola. Why from so far away? a mine official was asked. He replied with unaccustomed candor, "We prefer to hire these country chaps. Otherwise we would have to compete with local industry in wages, and the urban African gets more money than we're willing to pay." He seemed uncomfortable with this statement and added hastily, "We are doing these men a favor by letting them work in the mines. That way they can supplement the income they get from their farms in their tribal lands at home." The favor was a binding agreement to labor underground for months and often years, six days a week.

Scenes at the Johannesburg labor depot might have been lifted wholesale from the early diamond days in Kimberley. The yard swarmed with local Zulus and Xhosas, as well as with Zambians freshly unloaded from a company plane, still trembling from their first, terrifying flight. They rubbed shoulders with Shangaans from Mozambique, Kwanyamas and Ovambas from South West Africa. Some were Christians, some Muslims; many were animists. Their tongues and accents differed widely. Very few could read; to them the contracts in their hands were nothing more than the white *baas's* ornaments. Supervisors communicated with their various crews by barking in *funigalo*, a pidgin African dialect.

Once the men had made their marks on the contracts, they lined up to be stripped and medically examined, fingerprinted, and issued an identification bracelet, tunic, and trousers. The cost of the uniform would be deducted from their wages. Afterward the various crews were boarded onto trains and sent to gold mines in the Rand or in the Orange Free State.

In the late 1960s Ernest Cole, a black photojournalist, asked the Chamber of Mines if he could interview some miner who had done well for himself. Out of nearly 400,000 "boys," as the supervisors called them, the Chamber chose Joseph Wenene, who had worked his way up to "boss boy" of other black men. On his pay—about one sixth of what a beginning white miner would earn—he supported a wife and five children in one of the "Bantustans," black areas set aside by the government. The Wenenes were not permitted to come to his workplace, and he had not yet earned enough money to go home. He had not seen any of them for four years. "I am happy on the mine," he said gravely, "but my longing for my family is always there." A white official turned to Cole: "You see, he has nothing to complain about."

When the journalist ventured inside the mine he became invisible. "To the white guards, as to the mine official," he recalled, "I was just another Kaffir and they paid no attention to me. As a result, I had considerable freedom to see whatever I wanted to see." What he saw was a hidden and pervasive misery, "worse even than in the worst slums of Johannesburg." Down in the shafts, supervisory tasks were taken by white men; black workers handled the heavy pick and shovel work and operated the loud drilling machines. After hours the miners were quartered, 20 to a room, in long brick-walled structures with corrugated iron roofs. They had no privacy, inadequate plumbing, and nutrition "like pig's food." Breakfast: sour porridge and coffee. Lunch: *nyula*, a stew of cabbage, carrots, and other vegetables supplemented, on occasion, by meat. Supper: maize porridge and beans.

Sunday, the one day of rest, was attended by heavy melancholy and ennui. Separated from their wives and children, deprived of recreational facilities, the miners wandered around in circles, slept, or chatted aimlessly. They were free to go into town, but few ventured out of the mining area: company lectures, stressing the dangers of crime and prostitution in the depraved city, had made a deep impression.

Life in the mines often took on the aspects of a prison sentence, complete with homosexual liaisons—*matamyola*, in minetalk—a big

subject for intramural jokes. Some of the more talented men volunteered for programs of "mine dances," staged for white visitors touring
the gold mines. Signs on the walls informed onlookers that the tribal
entertainment was free; they were not to toss so much as a coin in the
dancers' direction.

Miners who worked for nine consecutive months were offered two
options. They could leave or sign on again for a six-month period.
Those who wanted out had to make their way to the train station,
pockets loaded with cash from the final payday. They might have been
wearing the label, VICTIM. Hawkers and peddlers easily picked them
out of the crowd and shouted, "C'mon brother. C'mon," dangling
gimcrack souvenirs, cowboy hats, and flashy articles of clothing. It was
the first and last time these innocents would ever be called brother by
a white man.

Within six months the vast majority of these laborers were back on
the job. Rural economies could no longer sustain more than a handful
of farmers and hunters. For most, the only way to leave the mines
permanently was as a corpse or a medical patient. The lucky ones
received a grievous injury instead of being crushed to death by a cave-
in. They would then receive free hospital treatment and workman's
compensation. The principle of benefits for the injured was widely
publicized by the mine owners; exact amounts, however, were rarely
disclosed. The case of one miner may be taken as standard: in the mid-
1960s, for losing both legs above the knee, he received $1,036. It was
to be paid out at the rate of $8.40 per month for the rest of his life.

The public rarely learned of such matters, but the miners knew all
about them. It made no difference. As Cole reported, "However they
leave—sick, injured, worn out, or hale and hearty with the savings of
20 years' work at $38 a month—they are rarely missed. For as they
go out the gate, there are always new men coming in."

◆   ◆   ◆

IN HIS TIME every form of flattery had been offered to Harry, from
honorary doctorates to a study in *Fortune*, recognizing him as a financial
powerhouse. Subsequently a newspaper article listed HFO as one of
the "immortals" of South Africa. Still, even the deathless do not get

younger, and as Harry reached his sixties people began to speculate about the next generation of Oppenheimers.

Mary, the eldest child, attended the Sorbonne and played the debutante in London before returning to Johannesburg to enter the family business. Employees watched her with considerable trepidation. Was this unconventionally attractive young woman to be the Princess of Diamonds? The accounting department was her first stop. The debut was somewhat less than triumphant: she and numbers failed to agree. Yet what were Anglo and De Beers but columns, mounds, pyramids of numbers? Perhaps business was not Mary's metier. Harry had another of his inspirations: he installed his daughter as permanent secretary of Anglo's principal charities, the Ernest Oppenheimer Memorial Trust, and the Anglo Chairman's Fund. These duties were not intolerably severe, and most afternoons Mary could be found at her favorite avocation, riding.

Like all unwed daughters of the wealthy she was everlastingly tracked by journalists. They peered at her through field glasses, hung about the family residence, followed closely as she made the rounds of Johannesburg parties. Every man who led her across the dance floor was considered a potential husband. She reacted testily: "It's not easy to be an Oppenheimer. People always watch you, even spy. You must always be careful not to say or do the wrong thing. But even this way you can be hurt."

The jeweled cage would not hold Mary for long. Pressed about her plans she told an interviewer, "I hope one day to marry a South African, but I've no preconceived ideas . . . he can be any shape or size. He needn't have any cash. A bank clerk with the right background can end up the right one."

The first of the right ones was neither a pauper nor a plutocrat. Gordon Waddell, son of a Glasgow stockbroker, was touring South Africa as captain of a British rugby team when he and Mary met at a party. The casual acquaintance ripened into a romance. After his graduation from Cambridge, the massive young Scotsman carried carbon to Kimberley, presenting his fiancée with a three-diamond antique ring. They were married in 1964.

Apart from Queen Elizabeth's televised coronation, no one in Johannesburg had seen anything like the Oppenheimer–Waddell nuptials. They included a procession by vergers, a choir, robed priests, and the bishop of Johannesburg, resplendent in scarlet and gold. Thousands of onlookers lined the streets, craning their necks for a glimpse of Mary. Some of the bolder women attempted to touch her bridal gown for luck, in much the same way commoners used to seek a touch of the royal hand in Tudor England. She pulled at her 20-foot train; police tried to maintain order; guard dogs were brought in to intimidate the crowd. But it was no use. A riot began, and before it was quelled scores of people were injured. An elderly woman suffered a broken arm, and many an onlooker limped away with bruises and abrasions. By the end, abandoned hats, handbags, and shoes lay scattered near the cathedral grounds.

Following the exchange of vows, 1,000 guests attended a party at Brenthurst. Security guards, posted at all the entrances, turned back a host of gate crashers; it took an hour and a half for all the socialites and business leaders to file in. Oppenheimer friends and acquaintances who failed to receive an invitation made certain to be on holiday for the weekend. That way they could explain their absence from the party: they would surely have attended the wedding of the century, if only they hadn't been out of town.

Save for the servants and a couple of journalists, all but one of the faces at the wedding were white. The sole exception: Mary's friend Violet Padayachi, a social worker of Indian origin. The bride had also intended to ask some of her colleagues on the executive Committee of Union Artists, a group that sponsored native theater. Her father put a stop to that. According to *The Johannesburg Star*, Harry had no wish to provoke "controversy" on such an auspicious day. All he wanted was sunshine and celebration. Good weather was denied him; it rained all morning. But the festive mood continued until dark. It reached an apogee when Gordon Waddell received his wedding present. The new Maserati was the first of its kind in Africa.

At the appropriate moment the couple drove off to the airport. To foil the international paparazzi the Oppenheimers gave out the story that they were to honeymoon in Pretoria—and then booked themselves on a flight to Rome under the names Mr. and Mrs. Grant. From Italy they continued on to the garden spot of the Middle East, Beirut. From there they returned to Johannesburg, where Harry had found his son-in-law a job at E. Oppenheimer and Son.

Those employees who expected Waddell to be a kind of Prince Consort, taking up a corner office between lunch engagements and golf dates, were in for a rude surprise. Supervisors handed the apprentice manager various opportunities to fail; he made a success of all of them. In time he was granted a directorship of Anglo-American Prospecting, a small but important subsidiary. Along the way he proved to be a devoted father; Mary gave birth to Harry and Bridget's first grandchildren, Victoria Jane in 1968, and Rebecca two years later.

Gordon's one flaw was as a husband, in Mary's view. To her he seemed far more devoted to Harry's business than to Harry's daughter. The paths of husband and wife diverged. Mary spent her days at the stable, getting to know her horses and her riding instructor, Bill Johnson. The emerging scandal did not escape the notice of the gossip columnists or of the elder Oppenheimers. They made no secret of their disapproval and prevailed on the Waddells to attempt a reconciliation. One did not say no to Harry, and the couple flew to Rome for one last try. The results were negative. Gordon filed for divorce and, after complicated negotiations, received custody of the children.

The watchers at De Beers and Anglo assumed that the ex-son-in-law would bow out and start over in Britain. He astonished everyone by staying on—evidently Mary had been right when she testified that her ex-husband was "much more of an Oppenheimer than I'll ever be." Harry added an additional shock by promoting Waddell to an executive directorship of Anglo-American Prospecting. At the same time, Mary became the recipient of disapproving stares. They issued not only from her parents but from her grandmother Ina, Sir Ernest's widow. The old lady had been living in comfortable and obscure retirement near Brenthurst. But she possessed sharp faculties and censorious views, and she had disapproved of Bill Johnson from the day she laid eyes on him; he was not the Oppenheimer sort.

There is no telling how profound her influence might have been. On November 25, 1970, twelve years to the day since Ernest's final heart attack, Ina set out on a fateful visit to Kruger National Park. About 40 miles from home her chauffeur lost control of the van. It veered off the road, plunged into a deep ditch, and overturned. The driver was thrown clear; Ina suffered head injuries and went into a coma. Two months later she died in a Johannesburg hospital.

Shortly after the mourning period, Bill Johnson spoke up. He had received his own divorce, the disparaging grandmother had gone, and now it was time for a little injection of reality. "We would have married long ago," the horseman asserted, "but for two things—opposition from her family and my wanting her to fight for custody of her little daughters." He conceded that "although Mary has never been exactly hung on babies her daughters are now at an interesting stage of development and they've begun to mean a lot to her."

Mary's second marriage took place quietly in Swaziland, out of the reach of reporters. Once the Johnsons were resettled in Johannesburg, the new groom granted another interview. He allowed that Harry and Bridget were slowly becoming reconciled to Mary's new life, "although I don't think they're exactly thrilled about it. I think Mary's mother is the one who likes it least." Since his in-laws were not free with their praise, Johnson added his own self-congratulations: Mary had "always been a dutiful daughter, never doing anything to displease them. She has always cared too much about not putting a foot out of line. But I think I've taught her to be a little more reckless and not to mind what the rest of the world thinks. I've never given a damn about what people think and Mary is coming around to my way."

In rather stark contrast to his sister, Nicholas Oppenheimer reminded people of the young Harry. He attended Harrow, went on to his father's Oxford college, Christ Church, and then did nine months' South African military service with the Imperial Light Horse near Kimberley. Informal was the one adjective everyone applied to the young man, who insisted upon being called "Nicky." His plans were as guileless as his smile. "I will start at the bottom, sorting diamonds at Kimberley, and work my way up to the top. Eventually I hope to step into my father's shoes."

Although he was one of the world's most eligible bachelors, as one disappointed young woman remarked, "Nicky was only on the open market for about an hour." He had first met Orcillia "Strilli" Lasch on the golf course at the Johannesburg Country Club. She was the daughter of Helli Lasch, a dashing Johannesburg businessman and glider pilot. Nicky was the heir apparent to South Africa's greatest fortune. An ideal pairing—except that he was 13 and she was 17. As they reached their twenties, the difference no longer seemed so formidable, and in 1968 they were married. No grandiose ceremony for them; Nicky and Strilli exchanged vows at a small Anglican church in the suburbs, attended by relatives and close family friends. Their honeymoon, undisturbed by the press, took place in Australia. In November of the following year Harry's first grandson, Jonathan Ernest, was born. The Oppenheimer dynasty would continue.

♦   ♦   ♦

OUT OF HIS INTERVIEWS and probes into I.D.B. Ian Fleming produced two books, *The Diamond Smugglers* and *Diamonds Are Forever* (The jewel was "so pure that it held a kind of truth. . . . In these few minutes James Bond understood the myth of diamonds."). Both works seemed preposterously romantic and full of cinematic intrigue; it took the Kamil affair to show the mildness of Fleming's imagination.

As a mercenary for Sir Percy Sillitoe's International Diamond Security Organization, Fred Kamil had prospered. The Lebanese and his underlings had ambushed any number of diamond smugglers in the West African bush. For every illegal transaction they exposed or stopped, they got to keep one third of the value. When Sir Percy retired in the late 1960s so did Kamil, grumbling that he had not been paid in full.

But sitting still and grumbling was not Kamil's style. He preferred action, legal or otherwise. After several years of silence, the mercenary appeared in London with information for sale. He claimed that two De Beers executives were smuggling diamonds out of Africa and into the Argentine. No proof accompanied the accusation, and the company dismissed the matter out of hand. Without any further communication, Kamil left England with his South African wife and baby. They settled in Beirut, where in 1972 he wrote to Harry asking for money to extend his investigations. There was no reply. He sent another letter. In this one he dropped all pretense of counter-intelligence, and threatened to blow up De Beers headquarters in Johannesburg if his demands for money went unanswered.

Despite what De Beers security men may have felt at the time, Kamil was quite serious. He knew very well that it would be impossible to get to Harry directly; the thing was to make his life as miserable as possible. Explosion was one way to get his attention. Another, he concluded, was to kidnap Harry's ex-son-in-law, Gordon Waddell. Posing as a photographer, Kamil journeyed to South Africa with a Lebanese policeman, Ajij Yaghi, who took a leave of absence in order to come along. En route they found that Waddell, currently on a business trip to London, was scheduled to fly back to Johannesburg on a certain Wednesday at 10 a.m. The plane would touch down first in Salisbury, Rhodesia, and that was where they intended to hijack it. The scheme had all the ingredients of a paperback thriller: shiny-eyed Mideastern conspirators; Kamil's attractive blonde contact, who supplied sticks of explosive and then vanished; and the ultimate destination of Khartoum, where General Gordon had died at the hands of the Madhi and where Kamil intended to bring Harry to his knees.

Everything went off according to schedule. The two men seated themselves comfortably aboard the 727, Kamil on the aisle, Yaghi staring out the window. At the appropriate moment the explosives were revealed, first to a flight attendant, then to a steward, and finally to the pilot himself. When Kamil presented his flight plan, Captain Blake Flemington shook his head. There was not enough fuel to go to Khartoum. They could barely make it back to Salisbury. Kamil thought about it, and while he was thinking he demanded to see the passports of all 70 passengers. A steward went through the aisles collecting them, assuring everyone aboard that there was a small technical difficulty. They would circle back to Rhodesia for some minor repairs. Meantime would everyone please move to the rear of the aircraft?

The steward closed the cockpit door behind him and handed over the passports. Kamil and Yaghi riffled through them, casually at first, then with rising concern. The key name was not among them. A searching look at the passengers confirmed the hijackers' worst fears. Waddell was not on board. (Much later they discovered that their informer had slipped up; quite by chance the target had taken an earlier 747 to Johannesburg. He was already home when the operation began.)

Kamil reconsidered his position. Perhaps a recoup was possible. He and Yaghi still retained the whip hand. The 727 was theirs, and so were the people on board. With these hostages he could go to Khartoum or anywhere else he chose. From there he could hurl his demands at Harry, who would be forced to obey. As the plane moved on, the hijackers began to regain their confidence. During the descent to Salisbury, Kamil ordered Flemington to refer to him as Captain Z and to obey his orders. After refueling they would go on to Egypt. Very well, Captain Z, the pilot responded, but wouldn't it be more efficient to travel light, to rid themselves of at least some passengers and crew? Hostages needed food and water; they were heavy; they could be a nuisance over the long haul. Kamil thought it over. He decided to keep five passengers plus the chief flight steward and Flemington himself.

After taxiing to a stop the plane allowed its doors to swing open. A group of relieved passengers and crew members stepped onto the tarmac. As they moved to freedom, Kamil made Flemington slam the doors and take off without refueling. In the waning sunlight the hijacker barked out a new order: from now on he would only negotiate with the King of Diamonds himself. Flemington relayed this message to the tower. Minutes later an answer crackled over the intercom: Harry was on his farm, out of reach of telephone or radio. The hijackers huddled. They had no way of knowing whether Oppenheimer was bluffing or not, but they were aware that the fuel gauge was pushing empty. They had to land somewhere. What about Mauritius or Madagascar? Capt. Fleming suggested Malawi, home of the Williamson mine. At least that country had formal relations with Pretoria. If they flew north they would be using the hostile air spaces of black Africa, newly independent countries that had every reason to pursue and perhaps shoot down a South African carrier.

The Lebanese agreed. The plane would land in Malawi. From there he would broadcast his ultimatum: Harry was responsible for the fate of all these passengers. If he failed to speak voice to voice with Kamil, De Beers headquarters would be blown to the sky. And Mary Oppenheimer would be kidnapped. Capt. Fleming opened his microphone and relayed the hijacker's wild message to the Johannesburg tower. South African police closed ranks around the Oppenheimers, and all De Beers offices went on 24-hour alert. Round the clock surveillance began on the Johnsons' house. Wherever Mary went, a bodyguard followed in a beach buggy. Waddell and his children were similarly protected.

When Flemington reached Malawi he received permission to land on a runway far from the main buildings. Once the plane touched down, Kamil and Yaghi reiterated their threats. As they did, a ground crew crept under the fuselage and quietly deflated the plane's tires, rendering it incapable of takeoff. They were acting on orders from the President of Malawi, Kamuzu Banda. The chief executive had been about to leave for a holiday in London, and he had no wish to be delayed by these "fools of the air." He wanted them brought to justice within minutes.

Capt. Flemington feared the price might be his life and the lives of everyone else on board. For Yaghi had begun to unravel, shouting incoherently as he prepared the explosives for detonation. Even Kamil seemed leery of him. There was a lot of backing and forthing at the airport; finally a South African security man approached the plane. He had come to hear the hijackers' terms. Warily they allowed him to clamber aboard. Yaghi elicited a guarantee of money and safe passage before allowing the man to go out the way he had come in.

Presently the South African reappeared holding two metal valises. He opened them briefly to show their cargo of high-denomination dollar bills. Kamil lowered the aft ladder and pulled up the trunks. Shouting triumphantly, he and Yaghi fell on the treasure. As they did Flemington signaled to the five passengers, who unfastened windows and threw out ropes. In one hysterical burst Flemington and the hostages made their escape. As the last one looked back he saw the hijackers, oblivious to what had just happened, alternately pawing the money and gleefully throwing it over their shoulders.

An uncomfortable silence followed. By now President Banda had placed his chief Secretary of State in the control tower, and ordered sharpshooters to keep the plane covered. The President made one final offer: the hijackers could blow themselves up, 727 and all, or they could peaceably surrender.

No answer. South African Airways engineers gingerly approached the plane and disconnected the power from a switch on the underside of the fuselage. Without air conditioning the cabin temperature rose into the 90s. After a long, jittery wait Kamil shouted his request: he wanted a priest. It was all but certain that he and his collaborator would blow up the plane and themselves with it. A priest was produced and, from a distance, heard their confessions.

Night fell without any movement one way or the other. Troops slowly came to within 100 feet of the plane. Their commandant again demanded a surrender. Silence. He ordered his soldiers to advance and keep firing until they boarded the craft. A cascade of shells followed, and a few seconds later the hijackers emerged with their hands up. Kamil was unharmed; Yaghi had been shot in the foot. Within a few hours the airport was back to normal and President Banda, content with a job well done, flew off to London.

Pretoria applied for extradition, a move the Nationalists considered a mere formality. But Banda resisted all appeals from the apartheid nation, and in the end his prisoners were tried in a Malawi courtroom. Yaghi insisted that he had never laid eyes on the Lebanese before boarding the plane. Hijacking, he claimed, had been the last thing on his mind. He had simply been unable to communicate his thoughts in English. It had all been a tragic misunderstanding. Kamil offered no statement of any kind. The judge impatiently heard the evidence and then issued his sentence: eleven years' hard labor for each criminal. Defense lawyers called the punishment unduly harsh, but both men could hardly be blamed for nourishing secret grins. In South Africa hijackers received the death penalty. They had got themselves a bargain.

Yet the misadventure was not quite over. After 21 months in a Malawi jail, Fred Kamil and Ajij Yaghi were quietly freed. During his brief sentence Kamil had become the subject of numerous articles in the Johannesburg papers. They referred to him as "Flash Fred" and portrayed the hijacker as a mixture of thief, liar, and psychopath. The recollections of a De Beers security officer were published, portraying Kamil as a double agent who would betray his closest associates without a backward glance. Another newspaper article described the Lebanese as "obsessed . . . determined to harm Mr. Oppenheimer in some way or another." A third piece suggested that while in the employ of De Beers, Flash Fred had been "privately making illegal diamond deals or blackmailing the persons with whom he was dealing."

Ridiculed and held up to public shame, convinced that Harry Oppenheimer had orchestrated the stories, Kamil brooded about the chairman he had never met. "I would paint feverishly," he was to recall, "the shrouded, looming figure of the powerful man, backed by rows and rows of faceless robots. They click and whirr hither and thither, performing tasks like ants. The nest must be defended at all costs against those who do not conform to its laws, laws which are directed to procreation, expansion, the acquisition of even greater power. Transgressors are expelled from the nest."

To carry out his revenge, Kamil now fell upon a new scheme. Evidently he recruited three English criminals to send wreaths to the homes of several Oppenheimer family members. These were followed by hired hearses to "collect the bodies." The trio were amateurs, and police swiftly rounded them up. From a safe base in Spain the Lebanese denied any responsibility: "they were acting on their own without any instructions from me." Nevertheless he declined to go to London to argue his case. Instead he sat down to write a no-holds-barred autobiography. This, he said, would rip the cover off De Beers and reveal the cruel mechanisms beneath.

When it came out between cloth covers, *The Diamond Underworld* turned out to be little more than an exercise in self-justification. In it Kamil presented himself as a scrupulous hunter of thieves, betrayed by his diamond-hearted employer. De Beers had shortchanged him to begin with, then characterized him as a maniac and put detectives on his trail.

Yet through the meandering narrative Kamil did manage to reveal one damaging fact. As derisive as De Beers had been about the mental instability of their agent, they had used him continually and praised him as "an outstanding diamond detective" whose cases "were perfectly planned." Indeed, shortly after Kamil got out of jail the company arranged to send him a bank draft for £50,103 for services rendered. But that was his last payment. *The Diamond Underworld* went ignored by reviewers, and its author fell into a well-furnished obscurity.

Start to finish, the entire episode had been uncomfortable for Harry and his cadre. In the words of one diamond merchant, "De Beers the powerful, De Beers the aristocratic, had consorted with a common thief, and a loose cannon." He still shook his head over it a decade later. Clearly, Kamil had been, as he put it, "useful in his day. And, after all, weird things can happen in the best of families. The important thing was that everything came out all right in the end." The nest had been defended; the transgressor had been expelled.

18

UNDER ANGLO EVERY ONE

It used to be said that a Randlord knew he had arrived when the people hanged him in effigy. Such an event seemed unlikely in 1970s South Africa, where HFO was beloved by some and respected or feared by the rest. So the spring of 1973 brought with it a vivid shock. The image of Harry Oppenheimer was desecrated not on the mines or in Pretoria, but at that most unlikely place, the University of Cape Town. The Nationalists had just banned some "student revolutionaries" for writing and demonstrating against apartheid. In protest, Chancellor Oppenheimer reacted angrily. "We are justified," he told an undergraduate audience, "in believing that the Government has abused its powers. It has trampled out civil liberties underfoot and brought South Africa a long way nearer to being a police state."

In reply, a group of students condemned UCT as a "reactionary campus"—and Harry's liberalism as pure myth. To them, the discrepancy between word and deed originated "from the top." As chairman of Anglo-American and De Beers and as a director of some 70 companies, the students asserted, "our Chancellor assumes a less progressive facade." Oppenheimer's industries, "South Africa's politico-economic base," rested on an "iniquitous migrant labor system, a system of barrack-like compounds, strict reinforcements of a disintegrated tribalism, destruction of family life and payment of starvation wages." In their hands the students held all the incriminating evidence they needed: pictures of the compounds; charts of comparative salaries. Anglo paid its black miners an average of $37.50 a month, plus food, shelter and services valued at another $37.50. Harry's spokesmen pointed out that Anglo was not the only mining concern in South Africa, and that the other gold mines paid their workers much less. The statement made no impact. The students replied that just to break even a family of six needed $120 a month. By contrast, the average white miner earned $600 a month. (Diamond mining had its own racial disparities: De Beers paid black workers about $97.50 for the wage and services package; whites averaged $480.)

Rage overflowed from the campus and onto the streets of Cape Town, where students carried an effigy of Harry along with placards addressed to him: "Hunger Breeds Hatred." "Give Rights and Money, Don't Give to Charity—Pay a Decent Living Wage." Attempting to put the conflict in perspective, Harry asked the demonstrators to bear in mind that "mining is South Africa's oldest industry, and the idea of what is a white man's job is fossilized in ways it is not in newer industries." This was meant to explain, not to excuse, and several days after the demonstrations, Anglo and De Beers announced changes in their policies. The wages of all mine workers, black and white, would be increased, some by as much as 60 percent.

Instead of ameliorating conditions, the announcement made them worse. Harry had set irreversible forces in motion, and on September 4, 1973, they shook the Oppenheimer empire to its foundations. Almost three hundred drill operators, men who made the holes for explosives, refused to go down into the shafts at a gold mine called Western Deep. These were the elite black workers, and they had received some 46 percent in pay raises, whereas men with lesser skills—truck drivers, for example—had been awarded the full 60 percent. Unfair, the drillers said, and demanded more money. Management talked it over and on September 12 informed the dissidents that enough was enough; there would be no additional raises.

Disappointment gave way to fury. A large group of drillers went to the Number 2 Shaft, where the night shift was just coming on. Some of the men they met were willing to go along with the protest; others wanted to keep on working. Fighting broke out; stones and bricks were used as missiles. Mine managers sent an alarm to police headquarters. Twelve officers responded, setting up positions and then firing tear gas to disperse the crowd.

Amid the choking and coughing, looting began. As the darkness closed in, police reinforcements arrived. They raised their nightsticks and charged into the crowd, now armed with knives, crowbars, and bricks. Someone heaved a brick; it caught a policeman full in the face. He went down with a fractured nose and broken teeth. At the sight of blood his partners opened fire.

Still the riot went on. Some 200 strikers advanced on the administration building, intent on burning it to the ground. The police surrounded the building and kept them at bay, but order was not restored until reinforcements arrived two hours later. Next morning Anglo added up the costs. Eleven miners had been shot dead by the police, and one had been hacked to pieces by the mob. Twenty-six others had been seriously wounded.

The toll in lives and property was far less than the Sharpeville massacre, in which defenseless people had been shot in the back. But the feeling of international revulsion was identical. In his autobiography, published at about this time, Malcolm Muggeridge recalled Johannesburg: "a wild feverish city, awash with new red wine and raw brandy; a place of violence, with more to come—smelling already of the blood that must flow. A city of gold and blood; yellow and red." Gold shares plummeted on the New York and London markets. More than 100 students from Witwatersrand University ringed Anglo headquarters and demanded that Oppenheimer pay higher wages. A much larger demonstration took place outside South Africa House in London. Asked about the strike and about the wide disparity between Anglo's black workers and white ones, Harry spoke fluently but he seemed to be a man in shock. "This is wrong," he kept insisting, "We must put it right." He did not say how.

◆   ◆   ◆

> Where have all the houses gone?
> Long time passing
> . . .
> Under Anglo every one.

In its parody of a famous folk song, *The South African Financial Mail* was having a little respectful fun at Harry's expense. Actually, it would have been more accurate to say "under Oppenheimer every one." In the 1970s the very word conglomerate seemed inadequate to describe Anglo-American, De Beers, and all that they had overtaken and absorbed.

Traditionally, major corporations worked in a series of layers, the lowest executives reporting to a smaller group, which reported to a yet smaller group, and so on up to the top officer. Under Harry, the plane geometry of the triangle grew into the solid geometry of the pyramid. A cross-section of that structure was not available to outsiders. They would have found it worth a second look, and a third and fourth. Anglo's investments were varied and sizeable. In terms of market capitalization, however, De Beers was two-and-a-half times as big as the gold mining house. Then there was Harry's invention, Charter Consolidated, the huge overseas investment group with holdings in the United States, Canada, Europe, Australia, and Malaysia. Each of these three companies had its own chairman, its own board of directors, and more significantly, its own group of shareholders. And still the picture was not complete. Every classic pyramid has four sides; Oppenheimer's fourth was Rand Selection. Funded with De Beers money, Rand's main assignment was to finance certain of Anglo's domestic and foreign operations. "While it will not itself seek to initiate new business," Harry stated, "it will be admirably placed, both because of its financial strength and its connections, to participate in business initiated by others."

The empire was designed so that Harry could state just about anything and make it seem plausible. For example, he could turn up his nose at takeovers, hostile or otherwise: "We don't like to make acquisitions. Making acquisitions isn't really very amusing. I like to be in things where you have a possibility of investment, because it's much more difficult to find good business than it is to find money." At the same time, upon the death of Charles Engelhard, he could secure Goldfinger's mineral business under a corporation called HD Development. Through a series of other cross-holdings, the empire could unobtrusively buy, spawn, or control, among other properties, steel and vanadium manufacturing, coal mines, construction, lumber, real estate, agriculture, vehicle construction, computer services.

The Johannesburg Star contributed its own parodic comment about Harry, changing the words of *Alice in Wonderland*:

The time has come, the Chairman said,
    To talk of many things:
Of cashew nuts and curried prawns,
    Of beer and piston rings.

By 1973, Oppenheimer industries accounted for 10 percent of South Africa's gross national product and 30 percent of its exports. Good enough for any other multinational, but not the Oppenheimer empire. Growth—canny, quick, unlimited growth—was its salvation. "Once you get to be pretty big and pretty prominent," Harry informed his staff, "your best protection is . . . to become bigger still, particularly if your views are not those of the government." That, of course, depended on which government. Size and counterpunches would work in the South African ring. The United States opponent would not be so easy to intimidate.

In 1973, just as Harry was settling in comfortably at the pyramid's summit, the United States Justice Department was preparing its case against De Beers. Since 1890, when the Sherman Anti-Trust Act was passed, monopolies had officially been declared un-American. Teddy Roosevelt initiated a "Trust-Busting" campaign against giant corporations that threatened to stifle competition; the succeeding president, William Howard Taft, went after Standard Oil and the American Tobacco Company. The Sherman Act was bolstered by other legal measures, and in the days of the New Deal, Franklin Delano Roosevelt's Justice Department protected small merchants by prosecuting some oversize chain stores. De Beers, with its unbreakable grip on diamond mining and manufacturing, seemed an ideal candidate for such prosecution. Indeed, it had been scrutinized by the Justice Department for years, yet the antitrust division had never been able to present a substantial case. Until now. A grand jury had just been convened, and many prominent diamond dealers had been subpoenaed. The antitrust division wanted to know if what they heard was true: the De Beers cartel was illegally doing business in the States.

Rumors of that business had first been heard in 1967, when informants said that Harry Oppenheimer had tried to purchase controlling interest in an industrial diamond concern in Verona, New Jersey. Supposedly the owner had turned him down. Then came word that some Oppenheimer executives had surfaced in America, seeking jobs in important diamond firms. Finally, in 1970, in the best B-movie style, lawyers in the antitrust division received an anonymous phone call, made from an untraceable pay phone and delivered in a muffled tone.

Rattling off a series of names and places and bank accounts, the unidentified voice accused De Beers of planning a secret takeover of America's industrial diamond business. The informant would only go so far—he steadfastly refused to meet anyone in the Justice Department—but he obviously had an intimate knowledge of his subject. He may have been a disgruntled merchant, or a dealer with a longtime grievance against De Beers. Whatever the motivation, his tips led investigators to damning material and to other informants.

Making the case against De Beers was extremely difficult. Most industrial diamond users refused to incriminate their suppliers, and even those who were willing to talk gave very few specifics. Harry's maze had been ingeniously constructed, and financial facts were buried in the records of some 300 interlocking corporations. Many of them were registered in Luxembourg, Liechtenstein, Switzerland, and other nations friendly to Oppenheimer interests.

After several months of intensive research, the Justice Department closed in on Christensen Diamond Products. Papers were unearthed, witnesses brought before the grand jury to testify under oath. The department learned that De Beers had acquired 50 percent of the company's stock in 1960, and not for investment purposes. Christensen made diamond drill bits for oil rigs. So did several other companies, but they were not supplied with De Beers's best products. By the mid-1970s Christensen and its silent partner had their grip on more than half of the oil drilling business in the United States. Government lawyers concluded that De Beers had engaged in a "conspiracy . . . to suppress competition . . . to require and increase consumption of De Beers processed diamond drill stones." The conspiracy had been hidden in the usual thicket of Dutch and Luxembourg registrations, "so as to be secret and misleading, and much was done with full knowledge that there was grave risk of violating U.S. antitrust laws."

The government's case seemed airtight: De Beers had been caught with ink stains on its fingers. But Harry stayed calm; there was a time to acquire and a time to cut your losses. A signal went out from

Johannesburg. To the distress of the more predatory Justice Department prosecutors, De Beers abruptly sold back all its stock to Christensen Diamond Products. It no longer had any connection with the American company, and thus was not presently in violation of the antitrust laws. All along the Justice Department had one aim in mind: getting De Beers to divest itself of its American surrogate, and so the case was dropped. Diamond people knew that behind the scenes De Beers would still go on supplying and maneuvering Christensen, but the paper trail was gone and, with it, grounds for prosecution. Not until 1975 did the Justice Department actually score a blow against De Beers, and that triumph was so small it went virtually unreported. Anco and DAC, two American companies whose industrial diamond distributorships had been granted by De Beers, were indicted for price fixing. On April 8, both companies pleaded *nolo contendere*. DAC paid a fine of $30,000; Anco settled for $10,000. The sale of one medium-sized jewel would have been enough to cover all of the defendants' expenses, with enough left over for a celebratory lunch.

◆   ◆   ◆

IN THE SPRING of 1974 Europe's last dictator, Marcel Caetano, tumbled from his perch in Portugal. The coup occurred five thousand miles from Brenthurst. It might have been next door. For well over a century, white South Africans had been protected from black Africa by a ring of buffer states. Among those territories were Rhodesia, still holding out against native agitation, and two Portuguese colonies, Angola to the west and Mozambique to the east. Both were about to fall to the black liberation movement. The Portuguese had lost the taste for empire. Their economy was tottering; defense of foreign possessions could cause outright bankruptcy. The new rulers in Lisbon ordered the soldiers to pack up and head for home.

The timing could not have been worse for South Africa. A British arms embargo had left the country feeling vulnerable. Then there had been an erratic and downward movement in the price of gold. The violent mining strikes had taken their economic toll. And as if all this were not enough, OPEC had pushed through yet another increase in the price of imported petroleum.

With an eye to Mozambique's rich oil fields, the usually truculent

Vorster tried a fresh approach. Only a few months before, the Prime Minister had labeled that country's black leaders "evil Marxists" and "murdering terrorists." Now he confidently informed his constituents that "black government in Mozambique holds no fears for us whatever. . . . I wish them well." Mozambique's new leader, Samora Machel, responded positively: he would not allow his country to be used as a base for Marxist guerrillas. Having considered the millions in profits that came from trading with the country of apartheid, he decided that his countrymen "do not pretend to be saviours or reformers of South Africa. That belongs to the people of South Africa." Trade continued, and migrant labor flowed unabated to the gold and diamond mines.

The same conditions did not apply in Angola. As the Marxists began to take over, South Africa grew jittery, and France, also squeezed by OPEC, tried to interest South Africa in a military incursion. Vorster was less than enthusiastic; Mozambique had succumbed to the leftists, yet a rapprochement had been worked out. Given time, perhaps Angola could be brought around.

France raised the stakes. Shortly after Valéry Giscard d'Estaing's election in June 1974, the French government offered to sell Daphne submarines to South Africa. The United States, anxious to add its own influence to the region, guaranteed to supply helicopters and spotter aircraft. Some black nations of Africa joined with the Arab states to protest what they saw as a rebirth of Western colonialism. But before they could act, France outbid its American competition by offering Mirage F1 fighter planes. The United States would not be topped. The administration of Gerald Ford announced a plan to supply South Africa with enriched uranium for its proposed nuclear power stations; whereupon France announced that a consortium of French businessmen was seeking to construct those very nuclear plants.

Pretoria, the international wallflower, was dazzled by all this attention. In the fall of 1975 South African troops were ordered to invade Angola. Under the code name "Zulu" they moved in, driving toward the capital, Luanda. A series of easy victories followed. Then came the counteroffensive, manned by Cuban troops and backed by Soviet artillery with its "Stalin Organ," a rocket launcher of formidable power. South African commanders appealed to Pretoria for reinforcements. The government hesitated; was the risk worth the commitment of more troops against a well-equipped enemy? In a military crunch, could South Africa count on its European allies? Could it depend on the United States? The answers were all negative. France, convinced that South Africa had fallen under American influence, petulantly withdrew its offer to sell armaments. The United States offer never did have firm congressional backing, and in December, when the battles went against South Africa, the Senate voted to stop further aid.

In January 1976 South Africa grimly commenced a retreat. At the end of spring, its troops and equipment were completely out of Angola. By then permanent damage had been done. The outraged governments of Malawi, Botswana, and Lesotho halted the flow of workers to the gold mines. Angola turned to Cuba and the U.S.S.R. for aid. Harry looked to the future and shuddered. The Soviet influence had come within a few hundred miles of home. It was not hard to imagine an African country run from Moscow, with all the Marxist concomitants: state-run industries, the seizure of private property, the overturning of history and tradition. "After the events in Angola," he remarked, "it is not even plausible to suppose that the defeat of South Africa in a war of race would result in rule over the whites by a black majority who were themselves free."

A year of mining strikes, followed by the Angolan misadventure, angered and demoralized the whole of South Africa. Stephen Biko, a medical student at Natal's non-white university, exhorted his fellow students in the new Black Consciousness movement. It sought "to channel the pent-up forces of the angry black masses to meaningful and directional opposition"—in other words, to demand majority rule. The louder the black leaders shouted, the tighter the Nationalists clung to their *laager* mentality. Since the 1950s a law had required blacks to learn Afrikaans as well as English. Because there was a shortage of textbooks and of bilingual teachers, the statute had been ignored for twenty years. Now, at the worst possible time, the government decided to enforce it. Modest objections could be heard—a teacher resigning here, a class boycotted there. Nothing to worry about, said the Minister of Education: "I'm not aware of any real problem." On June 16 he stopped sleepwalking.

Marchers assembled in Soweto at 6 a.m., ready to carry their message through the township and on to a mass rally at the local football stadium. Marshalls handed out pieces of cardboard inscribed with the slogans "Down with Afrikaans" and "Afrikaans Is a Tribal Language." An hour later the demonstrators began moving toward the stadium and ran directly into the police. The drama unfolded as in a slow-motion sequence, the marchers progressing, waving their cardboards and singing a Bantu anthem, *Morena Boloka Sechaba sa heso* (*God Save Our Nation*), the police slowly backing up, half-fearing, half-hoping to see a break in the collective resolve.

As in so many past riots, this one started when the police set off a canister of tear gas. Panic began, and the blacks surged forward. A policeman's shot rang out, followed by a hail of stones, more shots, and more stones. News of the violence spread through the township. Protestors put up barricades across the dusty streets and set fire to government buildings. The plate-glass windows of offices and stores gave back reflections of Africans with red eyes and wet faces, still coughing from the gas. Some were hurt, others dying, still others running for cover or aiming for revenge. A beer hall was looted and thousands of bottles seized; but instead of pausing to drink, the raiders spilled the liquid on the ground, chanting "Less liquor, better education." On a school wall, Bantu education was summarized in a six-word jeer: "Enter to learn, leave to serve."

As expected, the government fought back on all fronts, closing the schools, reinforcing the police, putting the army on alert. Violence continued anyway, and it was not confined to Soweto. Within two weeks of the first incident, at least 80 black communities experienced some form of angry demonstration. Before order was restored, several hundred blacks had perished and 139 buildings had been destroyed. The Nationalists refused to yield to African pressure. "The government will not be intimidated," Vorster boomed in parliament. "Orders have been given to maintain order at all costs." The Justice Minister fixed the blame on outside agitators: "The question one has to ask oneself is why the young people walked with their fists in the air? Why do they walk with upraised fists? Surely this is the sign of the Communist Party?"

In a previous time his tactic might have worked. Not in the era of television. Unlike the Sharpeville Massacre, which was reported days and, in some cases, weeks later, the Soweto uprising went on the air almost as it happened. The world saw jittery black figures put down by uniformed and heavily armed forces. The incidents took place a mere twenty minutes' drive from the green lawns and whitewashed villas of Johannesburg. Investors voted with their shares; in the stock markets and bourses of the world gold prices plunged, and De Beers stock fell precipitously. It was the worst of times.

Whatever the opposition parties and liberal businessmen had done to alleviate black misery, their efforts were not enough. Harry, of all people, knew that; and he thought he knew what to do about it. He had said it over and over again; the only thing that could stand between the white rulers and the angry black majority was a black middle class. But stating it, advocating it, promoting it through the Progressive Party was not enough. A new way had to be found, and it had to be found quickly.

Harry got in touch with Anton Rupert, chairman of the Rembrandt Group, a vast tobacco conglomerate. They and a group of prominent South African magnates created the Urban Foundation, launched in November 1976 at Anglo's Carlton Hotel in Johannesburg. The wife of one of Anglo's division heads recalled the aim of the foundation: It was not to be dominated by Anglo-American "but co-hosted by a kind of business power-house in South Africa and moved away from the strict housing thing into a broader urban problem framework." The foundation agreed that it would not be yet another tentacle of Anglo—and then elected Harry as First Chairman. Jan Steyn, a former Supreme Court judge, became Executive Director. Steyn called the new organization "the arm and voice of the private sector, applying its resources [more than ten million dollars] to help achieve the growth, prosperity, peace and stability that all South Africans seek." Translation: the black majority was at the gates, and the white minority must change direction, flee the country, or perish.

The Urban Foundation helped persuade the government to introduce a 99-year leasehold scheme, permitting a form of African home ownership in formerly all-white areas. It offered loan grants to African white-collar workers, became active in job training and literacy programs and preschool and public education. With the most honorable of intentions, however, these concessions seemed to be leftovers from the banquet table. So the Foundation, against all white tradition, endorsed a limited form of power sharing—"community councils," groups that would be the political voice of the townships.

The industrialists were not exactly gratified by the response. A township newsletter angrily questioned their motives. The Urban Foundation, it said, had no intention of reaching out to the vast numbers of poor. It was only trying to include the few who already belonged to the middle class, "giving them a few crumbs of equal rights in the hope that they will be a moderating influence on the mass of people, and that they will suppress antagonism toward big business." A black critic accused the Foundation of "propping up apartheid," since only legal residents could participate in the councils, thereby excluding thousands of squatters. White critics on the left accused Harry of "pushing on an open door."

They had a point. In the wake of the worst recession in 40 years, almost every segment of white society had been calling for a new South Africa. One group of prominent Afrikaaner businessmen actually sent a memorandum to the Prime Minister stressing "the need to ensure a stable, contented, urbanized black community in our metropolitan and urbanized areas" and calling for a permanent end to the Africans' "frustration and indignity." Faced with local as well as international criticism, Vorster made some adjustments. To begin with, he allowed photographers to take pictures of him at a state banquet flanked by Malawi women. "I did it in the interests of South Africa," he stated for all to hear, "and, if it is necessary for the interests of South Africa, I would do it again."

For the first time he allowed certain hotels and restaurants an "international" status, permitting them to receive black guests. Whites Only signs in Johannesburg parks came down. The tightly controlled separation of the races was relaxed in government buildings: "natives" and "Europeans" could take the revolutionary step of buying postage stamps from the same window.

Almost all of these changes were cosmetic. Vorster's liberalized hotel rules, for example, turned out to be another plank of petty apartheid. Only black visitors who held foreign passports could use *all* facilities. Other blacks could not drink in the bars. Similarly, blacks who were not residents of the hotel could be served liquor only if they were having a meal on the premises or attending a conference.

Watching the backstage and onstage shuffling, an Afrikaaner historian divided white South Africa into two camps, *verkrampte* (reactionary) and *verligte* (enlightened); there was no question about which group was in charge. The *verkrampte* included a lot more than right-wing officeholders and neo-Nazi fringe groups. On an overseas tour the executive secretary of the white Mine Workers Union expressed the views of his membership. "You have to know a black," he told a *New York Times* reporter. "He wants someone to be his boss. They can't think quickly. You can take a baboon and learn him to play a tune on the piano, but it's impossible for himself to use his own mind to go on to the next step."

For all of Vorster's integrated window dressing and relaxed public statements, he was squarely in the *verkrampte* camp. The Prime Minister refused to confront the *verligte* Harry personally, and he remained deeply suspicious of any Oppenheimer social work. "Efforts to use business organizations to bring about basic change in government policy will fail," he warned in one speech, adding darkly that liberal establishments like the Urban Foundation might be the cause of "unnecessary friction between the government and the private sector." The results of that friction could mean anything from taxes to takeovers.

South Africa's power game seemed to exhaust everybody but Harry. The bantam figure walked with a new bounce; the lined face broke out in frequent smiles. Silence became his strategy. Instead of rising to the bait he offered no response to the Afrikaaner overlords or the African underlings. Privately he told his colleagues that they could expect no help from Vorster and that they would receive "neither gratitude nor praise from black politicians or workers." On the contrary, he was to say, "such advances are likely to be met by new demands, heightened unrest and the open expression of hostility."

As always, Harry knew exactly what face to present to what faction. All but the extreme left conceded that he was more liberal than the rulers in Pretoria, and therefore someone to cultivate. At the same time, with the exception of the fascist fringe, every rightist could take comfort in the recently published biography, *Oppenheimer and Son*. The author, Anthony Hocking, had remarked, evidently with his subject's approval, that HFO "had never subscribed to the view that apartheid was morally wrong. In his view it was at root an honest attempt to cope with overwhelming racial problems."

In this way Harry was able to retain allies of almost every persuasion and color. Most of his enemies were in the government, men who regarded any Oppenheimer cause as either radical or selfish. They resolved to outlast him. How much longer could a man in his seventies stay on top of the pyramid? Time, they agreed, was on their side.

♦   ♦   ♦

As a diplomatic officer, Eschel Rhoodie had observed demonstrations against his country in New York, The Hague, and Sydney. It was more than a loyal public servant could endure. He determined that South Africa required "a drastic program of psychological and propaganda warfare."

Rhoodie found a sympathetic listener in Vorster. Pretoria's reputation had never been worse. Almost every day brought new charges of racism and brutality. Almost every member of the United Nations had turned its back on South Africa, and the International Olympic Committee barred South African athletes from its games. The economy stagnated as, one by one, the border countries turned from white rule to independent black republics. The white government of Rhodesia, the last remnant of Victorian imperialism, was soon to retire from the scene. Vorster needed some magic, and this 38-year-old seemed to be the man to work it.

Rhoodie, placed in the Department of Information, got carte blanche and a budget of more than $25 million. He set to work with great energy and profound secrecy. At home he established a jingoistic newspaper. *The Citizen* had two liabilities. In the first place its Afrikaaner "owner" was only a front. The paper's operating capital, thoroughly laundered in a Swiss bank account, came from public funds. In the second place, *The Citizen*'s attempts at journalism made it an international joke. Editors never bothered to separate news and opinion. Local troubles were buried on inside pages; other news made the front page. When a riot occurred in Cape Town, for example, the lead headline read "Stop the Blood." It referred to an account of seal-slaughtering in the Atlantic.

Rhoodie expected a circulation of 150,000. He never got more than a third of that number, and advertisers soon bailed out. This was the first of many fiascos. In England, Rhoodie set up a clandestine operation called "Operation Bowler Hat" that vainly sought to purchase the *Daily Express* and *The Guardian*. Other employees of the Department of Information established the pro-apartheid Committee for Fairness; the fairness, as British reporters acidly observed, meant South Africa's return to world sport. In the United States, South African funds were secretly used to acquire *The Sacramento Union* in California; an attempt to buy *The Washington Star* fell through. Rhoodie also acquired a 50 percent interest in an international television news agency, hoping to pump it full of upbeat stories on South Africa.

Along the way, Information officials lived well—a bit too well. They purchased property in London, Miami, and Cannes, arranged expensive holidays for themselves and their clients, and financed some dubious business ventures, all on taxpayers' money. The Information scandal began to unravel in February 1978, when the Auditor General buried a report criticizing unnamed officials for indulging themselves overseas. The English-language press got hold of the report and ran with it. Damaging new details emerged every week.

In a downhill process familiar to Americans, the Prime Minister was eventually destroyed not so much for what he had permitted, but for trying to cover it up. Like Richard Nixon six years before, Vorster began by dismissing aides—Rhoodie went in June—and ended by resigning in disgrace.

In the last days the only thing the government could produce was irony. Seeking to improve their country's image, the hidden persuaders kept pushing it deeper into the mud. And their employers, the *verkrampte* politicians who saw themselves as the custodians of South Africa well into the next century, watched their cause go under before the 1970s ran out.

Vorster's replacement was the pragmatic P. W. Botha, a former Minister of Defense who quickly distanced himself from the Vorster ministry. Botha's rallying cry was "adapt or die," and early on he shocked his constituency by telling them, "A white monopoly is untenable in the Africa of today. . . . A meaningful division of power is needed between all race groups. . . . Apartheid is a recipe for permanent conflict." The inhabitants of Soweto appeared to be just as astonished when he showed up in the black township to tell them "we are all South Africans."

As if this were not enough, he took his whole cabinet to meet Harry Oppenheimer, along with the country's other English-speaking industrialists. "We have our differences," Botha openly admitted, "but we are creating reciprocal channels to plan national strategy." It was the first time a Prime Minister had personally greeted Harry in thirteen years. Afterward one of the papers burbled, "The Anglo-Boer war is finally over." Essentially this was correct. An armistice had been declared in the battle of white versus white. The war against those of darker hue would continue, under other names and guises.

Botha oversaw that fight without ever acknowledging it. He continued to speak placating words to Africans. At the same time, under his administration the government embarked on a massive military buildup. It was intended to frighten and discourage the black nations without and the black agitators within. Defense took up more than 20 percent of the national budget. Every young white male was subject to two years' compulsory service in uniform. Army, navy, and airmen were supplemented by a well-armed police force. Much of their equipment and ordnance came from ARMSCOR, a state corporation that manufactured guns, bombs, fighter aircraft, missiles, and napalm.

A superabundance of equipment and personnel ensured peace without tranquillity. Police patrolled the ghettos as brutally as they wished. More than ever, whites lived behind physical and social barriers, deliberately reinforcing their ignorance of how blacks lived. If they read about the townships it was usually in a crime story. Sighs were sighed and tongues clucked; it was a shame, but what could one do? Better to leave things to private charities and the government. They knew best.

A report for the United Nations Children's Fund showed how little had changed since the harshest days of Verwoerd. "The impact on children's minds and values of the physical violence that they witness and experience, not least at the hands of the police, is a matter of grave concern," it said, underlining yet again "the widespread disorganization of family life due to the migratory labor system." It went on to deplore the powerlessness felt by so many black South African men, a futility that often manifested itself in domestic violence. The resulting incidents were, as always, lamented by the whites, who shook their heads and went on about their lives, thus ensuring that the cycle would continue.

All the while the government grew hungry for more sophisticated arms. The Soviets kept supplying the radical nations to the north, and Botha's representatives went shopping for countermeasures. Despite the U.N. embargo they found arms dealers everywhere: the United States, Taiwan, Europe, the Middle East. In these transactions, P. W. Botha and HFO found themselves curiously related, like men involved with the same woman. Neither of them would ever be comfortable with Israel, and neither of them could do without her.

19

BOILER ROOM FOLLIES

THE AFRIKAANERS and the Jews had never really made up their minds about each other. Every Boer child knew of the Great Trek and heard it compared to the one the Israelites took through the desert. Yet ever since the days of Alfred Beit and Barney Barnato, Afrikaaner newspapers had pictured Jews as Hoggenheimers or radicals.

The emergence of the Purified Nationalists coincided with the rise of the Third Reich, and their leaders appropriated the Nazi vocabulary. To them, prosperous Hebrews were those three most dreaded words in Afrikaaner demonology, "English-Jewish capitalists." Those not so well off were "international Communists and white niggers."

Even so, no matter what the administration, no matter how hateful the Afrikaaner rhetoric, Jews lived more or less undisturbed. Most of them had come from European countries with long histories of ghettos and pogroms; they knew something of oppression and racism. And here they were, privileged citizens of a wealthy nation, enjoying every possible freedom merely because of the color of their skin.

World War II rearranged the pieces on the board. The tough old campaigner Jan Smuts had backed the winning side, and while he held office anti-Semitism was unacceptable. When the Nationalists assumed power in 1948, however, *Judenhetze* came back into style. Ordinances were passed to foster "Christian Nationalism"; in the rural towns there was talk of abolishing *shehitah*, Jewish ritual slaughter. Like many anti-Semites, the hard-right Nationalists encouraged Zionism. *The Transvaaler*, an Afrikaaner newspaper, allowed that it would "grant the Jew his ideals in Palestine, but, at the same time, [we] desire an increasing exodus of Jews thither and not their increase here."

This may have been why South Africa rushed to recognize the Jewish state upon its creation in 1948. But it does not explain Prime Minister Daniel Malan's visit in 1953. That was prompted by cold politics. Malan, the most fundamental of the fundamentalists, saw that wonders could be worked by emphasizing the similarities instead of the differences between Pretoria and Tel Aviv. Both states, he pointed out, were essentially European countries surrounded by indigenous and hostile peoples. And both saw themselves as latter-day Spartas driven by national will and military force.

An entente cordiale began, only to falter in the early 1960s, when Israel reached out to the black African states, publicly criticized apartheid, and voted in the U.N. to impose sanctions on South Africa. Pretoria reacted by refusing to allow Jewish donations to Israel. Currency-export privileges were withdrawn, the Finance Minister gruffly explained, because Israel had "slapped South Africa in the face and ganged up with her enemies."

The malaise continued until the 1967 war. Israel's astonishing six-day victory over her Arab neighbors announced a new order. Those African states aligned with Moscow and the Arab bloc denounced the Jewish state as an imperialist aggressor. As they receded, South Africa drew closer. It studied Israel's military tactics, cultivated friendships in Tel Aviv, and allowed South African Jews to transfer some $20 million to Israel. The South African Foundation discussed expansion of trade with Israel. After the 1973 Yom Kippur War, 22 African nations did more than condemn Israel; they severed ties with her. That left only Lesotho, Malawi, Mauritius, and Swaziland. Significantly, all four also had close diplomatic and financial relations with South Africa.

In 1975 the U.N. General Assembly passed Resolution 3379, labeling Zionism a form of "racism and racial discrimination." The resolution also spoke of "the unholy alliance between South African racism and Zionism." Thus the two condemned nations were driven, not altogether unwillingly, into each other's arms. Prime Minister John Vorster, who had once been jailed for pro-Nazi activities, flew to Israel in 1976. His was truly a red-carpet tour; when the El Al plane touched down, a crimson rug was rolled to the door. At a state banquet Yitzhak Rabin toasted his guest: "We here follow with sympathy your own historic efforts to achieve detente on your continent." (Africa was also Israel's continent, a fact that was not stressed by the Prime Minister.) In return, Vorster did extraordinary things, for a one-time supporter of the Third Reich. He laid a wreath at Yad Vashem, the Holocaust memorial, visited religious sites, and climbed to the fortress of Masada.

Near the end of his trip Vorster told reporters that his country and Mr. Rabin's would exchange information and encourage the "development of trade, scientific and industrial cooperation and joint projects using South African raw material and Israeli manpower." The sale and manufacture of weapons lay in the future. At the time, the most significant raw material was diamonds.

The Jewish connection with precious stones had a long history, dating back to the Middle Ages. But it was only in recent times that the Middle East had become a significant part of the Oppenheimer empire. Shortly before World War II, a young Zionist named Zvi Rosenberg had fled the Nazis and emigrated to Palestine. There he set up his own small business, receiving stones from associates in Antwerp and sending back cut and polished jewels.

Rosenberg found that most of his fellow immigrants were socialists. They wanted nothing to do with emblems of conspicuous consumption, and they gave him and his diamonds a wide berth. Oved Ben Ami, mayor of Natanya, was an exception. A tireless fundraiser and advocate of immigration, he had built his little marshland village into a sizeable town. Its location was ideal: midway between Tel Aviv and Haifa, with constant sun and appealing beaches. It housed an intelligent and energetic work force. The missing element was industry; who would employ all these people?

Ben Ami persuaded Rosenberg to relocate in Natanya; other diamond polishers followed, and they hired trainees and apprentices. The mayor conceived a great vision of Natanya as a world-class diamond cutting center. As he saw it, the worse the news, the better for his dream. When German troops overran the Lowlands in 1940, he lobbied the mayors of Antwerp and Amsterdam, urging them to allow their Jewish diamond cutters passage to Palestine.

He pushed on to London, presenting his case to Otto Oppenheimer, Ernest's brother. Perhaps as a fellow Jew, he could persuade De Beers to send some stones in the direction of Palestine? The executive put the mayor off with a few palliative words: "I will be your ambassador." Otto was not being conciliatory for religious reasons. Ben Ami had been pulling the few strings he had, making his case at the Colonial Office; there was the distinct possibility the agitated little visitor might stir up trouble, inducing British authorities to take a closer look at the empire in wartime. The Oppenheimers were not anxious to have any government poking about their secrets. If placating Ben Ami would get him back to Palestine and out of the Colonial Office, De Beers would grant his wish. Soon a trickle of *melees*—mid-sized diamonds —began making its way to Natanya.

As the war progressed the rivulet became a headstream. Antwerp and Amsterdam fell. Jews were swallowed up in the Holocaust. By default Palestine grew into the diamond cutting center of the wartime world. By VJ Day an accounting showed that De Beers had shipped more than $100 million worth of stones to Palestine. Some 6,000 refugees had been trained as cutters.

After the war, dealers expected De Beers to abandon Antwerp for Natanya. It was not to be. Belgian companies still controlled major diamond mines in the Congo, and their home country had to be courted. In 1946 Antwerp experienced a renaissance of diamond cutting, even as Palestine suffered from cutbacks. In three years the flow of diamonds to Natanya dipped by as much as 70 percent.

Then, with the creation of Israel, came the great turnaround. Besides agriculture, the new nation had only one other industry, the manufacture of diamonds. Everything would be done to keep it viable. At very favorable rates, Israeli banks advanced credit to the country's diamond dealers. Armed with cash, these dealers went to De Beers's Belgian clients, bought uncut stones, and brought them back to Israel for cutting and polishing. From there the diamonds went out to the retail industry. The postwar boom lifted diamond prices, and Israel rose with the tide. Business charts tell the rest of the story. In 1949 the Israeli diamond industry produced 76,000 carats and employed 800 people. By 1968 production had risen to 1,472,000 carats and put 10,450 people to work. The empire reexamined its policies. Had Israel reassumed control of the *melee* market? Very well then, De Beers would send its *melees* directly to Natanya.

In Israel confidence built upon success, and success encouraged arrogance. No longer satisfied with *melees* alone, Israeli dealers entered the market for larger diamonds. Their credit was fully backed by the government, and they easily outbid foreign competitors. By 1975 more than 20,000 workers were employed in Israel's cutting and polishing factories. Diamonds accounted for nearly 40 percent of the country's non-agricultural exports. Meanwhile Antwerp's diamond business suffered from a sharp recession. Factories closed, throwing more than 25 percent of the cutters out of work. From his view atop the pyramid, Harry Oppenheimer did not like what he saw.

A group of De Beers executives headed to Tel Aviv, led by Anthony Oppenheimer, the son of Ernest's nephew Phillip. No one raised his voice; these were British gentlemen. Soft though the delivery was, however, the message came harsh and clear. The organization wanted a cease-fire in the undeclared war between Israel and Belgium. For the diamond industry, such conflict meant bad human relations and bad public relations. It was to stop immediately. To ensure a balance of trade, De Beers would diminish the flow of diamonds to Israel by 20 percent effective immediately.

The threat backfired. When Israeli diamond manufacturers and dealers learned about the 20 percent cut they started their own stockpile, journeying to Europe, America, and Africa in search of uncut diamonds. To maintain the flow of stones, some Israelis paid other dealers a markup of 100 percent.

At the International Hotel in Liberia, I.D.B. enjoyed a new life; smugglers sold their goods to Israeli buyers with no questions asked. Israeli banks underwrote 80 percent of all these diamond purchases, licit and otherwise. By De Beers's calculations, the Israeli stockpile stood at six million carats in 1977. The next year the store of diamonds grew at about half a million carats per month. At that pace, sometime in 1979 Israel would have more diamonds than De Beers in London. Then Israel could withhold stones or flood the market, controlling the prices however and whenever it chose.

When HFO felt threatened, not even the Rothschilds could move with greater effect. He knew that Barclays Discount Bank in Israel and the Union Bank of Israel backed more than half of the Israeli diamond purchases. Some time before, with the extraordinary prescience that marked every aspect of his career, Harry had joined the board of Barclays International Bank. In addition, one of De Beers's managing directors, E.J.G. Dawes, had conveniently been elected to the board of the Union Bank. The two men, it was said, served amiably, never forcing an issue or making a demand. Until now.

Without prior notice, De Beers began what one executive called The Blunt Instrument and another, The Billion Dollar Squeeze Play. A "temporary" surcharge of 40 percent would be imposed on all diamond buyers. How long was temporary? The cartel would decide. Overnight, diamonds became a deliberately overpriced commodity, prohibitive to buy, and probably difficult to sell. Israeli banks had extended more than $850 million in credit—nearly a third of Israel's foreign exchange—to the diamond industry. After the announcement of the surcharge, they demanded higher interest rates and more collateral. As they did, the empire opened combat on its second front. Forty clients who had been doing business with the Israelis received their death sentences. They were no longer welcome at "sights," where De Beers's finest uncut stones were sold. The other dealers got the message.

Deprived of ready loans, unable to rely on their old sources, the Israelis grew desperate. In order to survive they needed diamonds, but not diamonds that were marked up 40 percent. There was nothing left to do but reach into the stockpile that had so displeased the empire. Israel's major dealers had large reserves, and they came through this period chastened but whole. Some 350 smaller businesses declared bankruptcy. By 1980 the silent war was over. The empire had won; the Israelis would never threaten De Beers again. Ever afterward, diamond men would refer to the hard time of 1978–1980 as the *bren* —the burn. One ruined dealer described the battle from a soldier's point of view: "The generals in Johannesburg and London decided that they would rather burn down than build up. They could have negotiated, or even demanded. But no—they firebombed. De Beers didn't want a democracy, they wanted a theocracy. When the *bren* happened people said, 'Who does Oppenheimer think he is, God?' Today they know."

In case they doubted it, Harry showed the world—or at least his part of it—that a little ostentation never hurt anyone. For Bridget's sixtieth birthday he threw her a bash. Some 450 invitations were mailed out bearing her racing colors of yellow and black. The guests praised the music extravagantly; they said they had never heard anything like it in South Africa. Indeed they hadn't. It came from Peter Duchin's band, flown in from the United States for the occasion.

✦   ✦   ✦

IN THE LATE 1970s a small advertisement appeared in the Employment section of *The New York Times*: "Telephone pros . . . experienced only . . . sell investment quality diamonds." Successful applicants were expected to work in "boiler rooms," dialing number after number in harshly illuminated cubicles, trolling their wares until a customer wriggled on the line. Salespersons read from a series of scripts, each carefully worked out to the last inflection and enticement.

One read: "LET'S FACE IT THERE ARE NOT many commodities you can invest in, use and enjoy and 10 years later get back more than you paid for them, AM I RIGHT MR. ——? (wait for answer and continue). NOW I AM GOING TO RECOMMEND WE START WITH THE $2,480 PACKAGE. BASED ON A 23 PERCENT A YEAR INCREASE IN VALUE, WHICH IS A CONSERVATIVE ESTIMATE, THESE STONES WILL BE WORTH AT LEAST DOUBLE IN THE NEXT FIVE YEARS. . . . NOW WHERE SHALL I SEND THE CONFIRMATIONS?"

Diamonds had become the latest telephone hustle, supplanting Canadian mining stocks, silver coins, and London commodity options. *Jeweler's Circular–Keystone*, a wary trade publication, was among the first to notice an infestation of confidence men who "came in to hustle common folk blinded by visions of big easy money."

One of the early hustlers, Tel-Aviv Diamond Investment, Ltd., had no connections with Israel. It was run out of Scottsdale, Arizona, by one Rayburne Martin until his arrest for a long list of misdemeanors, including embezzlement and violation of security laws. Martin was found hanging in his cell on August 11, 1978, by the Scottsdale police. The management of Tel-Aviv went on with business as usual, operating under the instructions of Martin's widow.

Another boiler-room operation, De Beers Diamond Investment Ltd., had no connection whatever with *the* De Beers, but declined to share that information with its customers. Nor did it mention that one of its executives, Harold S. McClintock, had been charged by the Securities and Exchange Commission with selling unregistered stock.

Diamond Selection, Ltd., never vouchsafed the fact that its general manager, Eric Smith, operated a business in Toronto until the Ontario Securities Commission suspended his license in 1974. Nor were customers of International Diamond Corp. told about its former marketing director, Bernhard Dohrmann, who had received a jail sentence for securities fraud in 1976. Richard Neuberger of Kimberlite Diamond Resources Co. failed to notify his customers that he had abandoned his previous company, Neuberger Securities, after an injunction for fraud.

"Diamond selling was the con of choice," one of the marketers recalled. "We could count on two necessary ingredients from our pigeons, greed and ignorance. Doctors made our best customers, but there were plenty of others, people who wanted to make a fast buck and who had no time to do research. And we did have an unbeatable line: 'Just look how much diamonds have gone up in the last few years.' "

That they had, sometimes phenomenally. The *Circular–Keystone* reported that in 1972 a retail jeweler paid a New York gem supplier $1,775 for a one carat VVS (Very, Very Slightly Flawed) diamond. In 1978 the same jewel would cost him at least $7,650. Such diamonds outraced the inflation rate and outperformed blue chip stocks. Other diamonds looked just as promising to the untrained eye. These were the hustlers' jewels, stones offering the investor maximum risks at prohibitive prices.

From the early 1970s, amateur investors had been entering the diamond market as wolves and exiting as badly fleeced sheep. Few could tell whether the jewels they bought had the right combination of what diamontiers call The Four C's: carat, cut, color, and clarity. Carat pertains to the weight—one carat is 200 milligrams. Cut refers to the way a diamond is proportioned and faceted to bring out its internal "fire." Color and clarity are graded according to a system devised by the Gemological Institute of America. Color grades run from D, colorless, down toward the end of the alphabet, where stones get progressively yellower. Customarily, investment grade ends at H, a diamond that appears white to the untrained eye—but not to the jeweler with a loupe and a concentrated light. Clarity refers to the microscopic flaws and scratches on the diamond's surface and interior. These can affect the diffusion and refraction—the brilliant flash—that has given diamonds their traditional appeal. Clarity grades go from F (Flawless) and IF (Internally Flawless) through VVS, with subdivisions 1 and 2, and VSI (Very Slight Inclusions), all the way down to SI (Slightly Imperfect) and, at rock bottom, I (Imperfect).

But knowing all this was no guarantee of a good investment. Only specialists could tell high-quality diamonds from ordinary ones. And even the experts made mistakes, sometimes innocently, sometimes not. A classic example of failed expectations came in the late 1970s, when Elizabeth Taylor put the former "No Name" diamond up for sale. She and her husband, Richard Burton, had bought the 69.42 carat diamond in 1969 for the high price of $1,100,000 (the transfer from seller to buyer was actually made in a plane over the Mediterranean, to avoid sales tax).

A decade later, married to Senator John Warner, she let it be known that her famous gem was up for sale. Asking price: four million dollars. The insurance company demanded a huge fee to protect the stone against theft; to underwrite the premiums, Taylor charged each prospective buyer $2,000 per view.

No offers came in. The asking price dipped, and dipped again. The oversize diamond was purchased in 1980 by a New York diamond dealer, after much hesitation. The reported price: two million dollars. An impressive sum, until the accountants did their reckoning. Given the insurance costs over ten years and factoring in inflation, Miss Taylor had actually taken a loss.

Her case paralleled the experience of Colonel Jean-Bedel Bokassa of the Central African Republic. Bokassa had also acquired a large diamond—after first acquiring the Republic in a coup. Once in office, the colonel named himself Emperor and threatened to nationalize the country's biggest diamond mine. To avoid a takeover, the owners agreed to share their profits with the newly named Central African Empire. But this was not enough. Word came from an imperial messenger: a "very large diamond" should be presented "voluntarily" to the Imperial Majesty by Albert Jolis, whose family owned the mine.

Jolis could hardly refuse. On the other hand, mines in the country produced no such jewels. Would an expensive bauble have to be bought on the open market, then presented to the Emperor as if it were home-grown? Jolis thought not. One of his men had recently turned up an immense, 70 carat chunk of industrial diamond: bort, normally used for grit. At the current value of $2 per carat the stone was worth, at most, $140. Jolis knew that, his assistants knew it, and virtually every professional diamond assayer in Africa knew it. Bokassa, however, was a professional Emperor.

Jolis arranged to have the bort polished and a hole drilled on its surface. A quarter-carat jewel was set in the tiny excavation, and the whole ensemble mounted in a large ring. The Emperor received his present with appropriate ceremony. See, he was informed, the shape of the "black diamond" resembles the contours of Africa itself. And behold! The twinkling little diamond represents the capital of your Central African Empire.

Bokassa delightedly accepted the gift, said by his court to be worth half a million dollars. For two years he flashed the diamond before a parade of visiting dignitaries. Finally, in 1979, the French government tired of propping up the petty dictator and sent in paratroopers to enforce a bloodless coup. Emperor, entourage, and ring were flown under guard to a premature retirement on the Ivory Coast. There, in the benign sunshine, Bokassa continued to display his treasure to all who would look upon it. Asked about the black diamond, Jolis stated the real situation of all diamonds everywhere: The Emperor's new ring was "priceless—as long as he doesn't try to sell it."

♦　♦　♦

IN THE SUMMER of 1981, the South African Master Cutters Association noticed a letup in the supply of diamonds. To some it was a mystery. Not to Eddie Myers, chairman of the Association. "De Beers," he noted drily, "is holding back all the important stones." The organization gave out the word that it was "enlarging its inventories," a euphemism for hoarding. More than $1 billion in diamonds were being kept in safes, more than double the amount two years back. De Beers, in fact, had not curtailed its production this drastically since the 1930s, when Sir Ernest ruthlessly closed all the mines, faced down the government and the workers, and saved the cartel, he believed, for all time.

Now his son considered another diamond mine shutdown. "These," Harry commented grimly, "are the worst times that I can remember since the Depression." He failed to mention a prime cause of the bad times: De Beers itself. The cartel had made a series of missteps. Once the business with Israel had been settled, the surcharge was dropped, but shortly afterward De Beers boosted its prices by 30 percent. This cost to dealers was passed on to consumers. Demand for diamonds remained high through this period, and De Beers saw fit to announce yet another price hike of 12 percent.

By 1980 diamond prices were 140 percent higher than they had been five years before, even though the demand had not kept pace. The value of an individual jewel may depend on the four C's; but the value of diamonds in general depends on one S: scarcity. In order to support its overheated price structure, the empire had to keep the precious stones rare, taking them out of circulation by buying its own diamonds back from dealers and producers. De Beers's inventory went up from some $500 million to about $940 million. Having bought the stones, it had to store them; at these exorbitant prices, the cartel had no customers to take the diamonds off its hands.

With demand sliding, Harry ordered suppliers to trim diamond production. At the same time, he emphasized his long-standing belief in advertising and promotion. The Oppenheimer faith was carried on in the United States where, a De Beers marketing manager claimed, "millions of women [were] trying to decide what to buy a man instead of a tie or a shirt." $400,000 worth of commercials backed him up, delivering Diamonds Are Forever messages during the televised wedding of Prince Charles and Lady Diana. The United States, however, was suffering from double-digit inflation. Consumers did not rise to the bait.

A major dealer appraised the situation: "Diamonds are in trouble, no question about it. Look at what's happened in the last year. From Africa to Australia to America, everything is going downhill."

The plunge continued. In 1981 sales dropped to about half of what they had been the year before, when De Beers had made a profit of $1.1 billion. If there was any demand at all it was for smaller and smaller diamonds. In 1981 the average engagement ring diamond weighed .29 carats; five years before, the average stone was 25 percent bigger. About one third of all the pieces of diamond jewelry sold in the United States now cost less than $300. The average engagement ring cost $700.

In 1982, *Fortune* printed its annual list of the 500 largest corporations outside the States. "The startling thing about De Beers," the magazine commented, "is that it has fallen so far so fast." Since the previous year, the company had dropped from 169th to 339th, the most precipitous tumble of any on the list. "No wonder speculation has grown that diamonds have lost their place as both a luxury and an eternally wise investment, and that De Beers, after 50 years of domination, has lost its grip."

By then the investment market in diamonds had totally collapsed. Tracking wholesale prices, the Diamond Registry suggested that the rapacious seekers of 200 and 300 percent appreciation had run into a brick wall. Top-grade diamonds had lost two thirds of their value within two years.

In 1982 the investigative reporter Edward Jay Epstein published all the bad news in one volume. He concluded his closely researched and often brilliant book, *The Rise and Fall of Diamonds*, with a long list of negative disclosures about De Beers's labor and business practices. He defined diamonds as "an artificially maintained illusion of value now in danger of total collapse," and predicted the "coming crash of 1983." In American, Soviet, and Japanese laboratories, technicians had never given up on the idea of synthetic diamonds, Epstein asserted. Their methods improved by the month, and several scientists envisioned a time, not far off, when jewels fit for a fiancée would be manufactured in a hydraulic press. "If this occurs," Epstein predicted, "the diamond craze of the twentieth century, like [Holland's] tulipmania of the eighteenth, might disappear overnight."

De Beers had enough current problems without worrying about some future dystopia. Northern Mines in Western Australia had just unearthed its own large repositories of diamonds. They were found, in a fresh touch of irony, near the town of Kimberley, named many years before in honor of the South African city. As De Beers tried to gain control of Northern, Australia's opposition Labour Party spoke out against incursions from the country of apartheid. Once informed of the situation, the general public announced its dislike of *any* foreigners moving in on local industry. However friendly the Australian Prime Minister, Malcolm Fraser, may have felt toward HFO, he had no choice; Fraser informed Parliament that his government would oppose any and all attempts by De Beers—or its subsidiaries—to gain a foothold. There was no advantage to "arrangements which only serve to strengthen a South African monopoly."

After all its swagger and threats, black Africa at last seemed ready to walk away from South African companies. Zaire's President Mobutu, dissatisfied with the low sales of diamonds and with De Beers's 20 percent sales and sorting commission, refused to renew his nation's contract. Zaire would go it alone, taking its chances on the world market. Namibia and Botswana seemed at the breaking point with De Beers.

Epstein foresaw "the coming crash of 1983" because by then the Australian gems would be cascading onto the market, joined by stones from all the renegade countries of Africa anxious to break the De Beers stranglehold. "Under these circumstances," he wrote, "the diamond invention will disintegrate and be remembered only as a historical curiosity, as brilliant in its way as the glittering, brittle, little stones that it once made so valuable."

Naturally Harry Oppenheimer would hear none of this. The mine in Australia was, after all, "not a major thing." Zaire would be brought around. Japan had possibilities. In 1967 only six per cent of its brides-to-be had been given diamond engagement rings; now, two out of three received them. N. W. Ayer planned to push large stones, stressing their glamour and rarity. "A diamond of a carat or more," one ad would burble: "There's only one in a million." Another would show a discreetly undraped model, presumably on a nude beach in France, wearing only a solitaire diamond necklace. The copy line: "She can't flaunt a fur on the Côte d'Azur."

And if everything else failed, there was always De Beers's saving virtue: patience. The company held about $3 billion in assets outside the diamond business. Some 38 percent of it was invested in its sister company, Anglo-American, diversified into gold and steel, real estate and insurance. As a cartel, De Beers was forbidden to set up offices in America. Anglo however, had no monopoly on gold or any other resource, and it could make its moves anywhere in the 50 states. One acquisition showed just how far the empire had extended. Before July 1981, Salomon Bros. was America's largest private investment bank, as well as the world's largest bond-trading firm. That summer, after a weekend session, the 62 Salomon partners agreed to merge with Philbro, a company owned by Anglo.

How did an American concern fold so quickly into the Oppenheimer empire? Rhodes had shown the way: every man has his price. It had simply gone up in the twentieth century. Technically, Salomon Bros. partners were millionaires. But the money was legally frozen in the firm's capital fund. Suppose, it was suggested to them, that Philbro bought the company for $300 million? A way would then be found to make the partners millionaires in life, instead of on paper. Each partner would be guaranteed an average of $2.7 million, tax free, *plus* an average of $3.2 million in bonds. The seven-man executive committee would be entitled to about $11 million each. The partners took a weekend at the Tarrytown Conference Center, 30 miles from their headquarters, to consider the offer. The outcome was never in doubt. Having announced the decision, the managing partner, John Gutfreund, received a standing ovation. He might have given himself one: he stood to gain $32 million. If any of the partners worried about the implications of foreign takeovers, apartheid, or any other moral dilemma, their discussions passed unrecorded. One of them expressed the general sentiment by echoing Brer Rabbit: "Any time someone wants to stick me in a room and give me millions of dollars, 'please don't throw me in the briar patch.' " By the mid-1980s the briar patch was filled with rich men, and the Oppenheimers were given their solid stake in Philbro-Salomon. All the while, *Fortune* and Edward Epstein had been up too close; they had seen the difficulties of De Beers and not the calculations of the empire. For all the *Sturm und Drang*, there would be no loss of grip, no crash of 1983. There would only be profits and plans for expansion.

20

BUT NEVER JAM
TODAY

"CRIME IS ONE THING: no security forces can guarantee a foolproof system. And what the hell, De Beers has learned to live with a certain amount of theft. It can even add to the romance of diamonds—stealing the idol's eye and all that.

"But *revolution*; this is another matter entirely."

The New York dealer's outburst was one of many in the De Beers network, and their loud concerns were but a faint echo of the rumblings heard in the boardrooms of London and Johannesburg. In the 1980s, three maverick firms in London and Antwerp agreed to purchase Zaire's entire diamond output for the next five years, and they would pay more than the cartel's going rate. A cutting factory was to be set up within the country, and President Mobutu planned to modernize a big 50-year-old diamond mine at Miba.

The Oppenheimers had spent too many years and too many millions to allow desertions from the ranks. An example would have to be made of Mobutu. Almost immediately after Zaire's apostasy, one of that country's best customers, the Industrial Diamond Company of London, noticed a new attitude from the cartel. "We were approached," said its founder, Pincas Rothem, "by a dealer we know is associated with De Beers and offered a huge quantity of the kind of diamonds Zaire produces."

Having flooded the market with stones, De Beers opened a second front in this newest diamond war. Zaire had always been plagued with I.D.B. But the smugglers had never been able to get good prices for their stones. Now dealers were conveniently placed across the border in Brazzaville in the Congo. For illicit goods they paid a premium of 50 percent above the going price, no questions asked. Demand for Zaire's legitimate diamonds fell away to almost nothing. Two years after Mobutu made his bold announcement, he surrendered. Zaire would once again market its diamonds through De Beers.

Harry was not one to crow over the defeated. He took a regal, more-in-sorrow-than-in-anger tone: "I can't pretend that we are pleased that anybody breaks away. . . . I think you will find that over the period ahead people who looked at the thing carefully may come to the conclusion that the Zaire experiment should be looked upon as a warning rather than as an example."

Australia, however, was not Africa. On a distant continent De Beers had to conduct a very different sort of war. And a more urgent one: Harry's advisors predicted that the mine at Argyle would yield millions upon millions of carats; indeed, it might prove to be the world's richest source. Granted, the Australian stones were not first quality—60 percent were fit only for industrial use. Still, for symbolic as well as financial reasons, Argyle could not be allowed to operate outside the Oppenheimer network.

Harry, always a close student of Rhodes, knew precisely what route to take. Argyle was controlled by three companies: Ashton Mining, 38.2 percent; Rio Tinto Zinc, 56.8 percent; Northern Mining, 5 percent. Years before, Anglo had managed to acquire a 4 percent stake in RTZ, and recently it had shoehorned one of its directors, Sidney Spiro, onto the board. The parent company of Ashton Mining was Malaysian Mining. Anglo owned a substantial minority interest in that company as well. Only Northern flourished outside the empire, and since its share of the mine was so small, that company might be circumvented.

With its personnel located in the proper boardrooms, De Beers lobbied the government and the press. Influential Australian journalists were invited on an all-expenses-paid trip to South Africa, and presently their readers were treated to feature stories about the glamour and lore of famous jewels. Australia's Deputy Prime Minister reappraised the De Beers setup; it was, he said, the only organization fit for merchandizing Argyle's great cache. And the Australian Labour Party's treasurer, who used to warn that Australia's diamonds were going to be "raped by South Africans," changed his mind. In thinking it over, he decided that there was "no real commercial alternative" to De Beers's Central Selling Organization.

At about this time Harry, now in his early seventies, began edging toward retirement. Outsiders naturally regarded Nicky Oppenheimer as the heir apparent. The staff at De Beers and Anglo knew better. In his late twenties, Nicky presented a puzzling figure. He piloted his own helicopter and sported a beard (several old friends referred to him jovially as The Cuban); among the company elite, that made him as odd as a Vaal River prospector at a black-tie dinner. Yet he kept away from any hint of the spotlight and shied from interviews. His public speeches seemed more dutiful than heartfelt—hardly the stuff of top management. The business journals paused to consider some other candidates for the top job. Most speculation centered around Harry's longtime assistant, Julian Ogilvie Thompson. At 44, Thompson had every prerequisite. His father had been South Africa's Chief Justice in the early 1970s. Julian had won a Rhodes Scholarship and, after coming down from Oxford, joined Anglo's London office in 1956. He spent the obligatory period sorting diamonds at De Beers, then moved rapidly upward to become Harry's personal assistant before transferring to the company's finance division in 1961. His marriage was as impeccable as his bloodlines; Viscount Hampden, Julian's father-in-law, was managing director of the merchant bankers Lazard Bros., a trusted Oppenheimer ally since the days of Sir Ernest.

Superficially Julian Ogilvie Thompson was nothing like his leader. Harry was short, Julian well over six feet tall. Harry could be almost offhand as he spoke; Julian paused between words, squeezing the last nuance out of each phrase, arranging and rearranging the objects on his desk in geometric patterns. Harry wore no jewelry; Julian was known to display the occasional diamond stickpin. Harry liked a certain fashionable informality now and then; Julian was the scourge of secretaries who dared to show up in pantsuits. Harry saw to it that there was nothing between him and his listener; Julian had a habit of speaking with a cigar stub stuck firmly in the right corner of his mouth.

But underneath the mannerisms both men had similar outlooks and attributes. JOT, as he came to be called in sedulous imitation of HFO, hewed closely to the chairman's belief that economic growth, rather than mandated change, held the answer to South Africa's difficulties.

"Peaceful, evolutionary reform in a constructive sense," as he put it in words indistinguishable from HFO's. "Power sharing, yes," went the corporate line, "One-man, one-vote, no." Along with these political tenets came full faith in the cartel as the only way to run the diamond business. Harry could feel secure with this man nearby—and he was nearby. Seldom did HFO make a move without JOT at his side, and this access to greatness made it easy for Ogilvie Thompson to fend off any competitors for the chairmanship once Harry stepped down.

As one of the world's richest men, HFO was entitled to more than a single alter ego. Gavin Walter Hamilton Relly represented Harry's Anglo-American side. Here was yet another Rhodes scholar—an unwritten requirement for Anglo's most promising men in the 1970s and 1980s. After coming down from Trinity College, he had signed onto the staff of South Africa's Opposition cabinet minister, Sir de Villiers Graaff. During that time Relly came to the attention of another Opposition member, a Mr. Harry Oppenheimer of Kimberley. "He said he'd like me to come up and help him with his politics," the executive remembered, "but it gradually veered off and became a business liaison thing." That led to a job as private secretary to Sir Ernest, and later to Harry. Relly went to Anglo in 1949 and ascended rapidly, developing gold fields, running a coal-mining operation, helping to plan steel and vanadium projects. In 1958, at the age of 32, he became a corporate manager. International businessmen came to know him when he headed Anglo-American's North American division, based in Toronto.

Relly, who went three quarters of the way toward the Oppenheimer style (he signed himself G.W.H. Relly), developed a style of bemused affluence. In one breath he would speak fondly of salmon trips to Scotland or Patagonia; in the next he would deprecate his ability to catch anything. He was well aware that people considered his smile puckish and that he seemed about as threatening as a favorite uncle. It was all part of a design. Asked about the ideal image of the Anglo-American executive he could have described himself: "I think it is to be much tougher than one looks."

That he was. So were they all in the Oppenheimer empire, taking their cues from Ogilvie Thompson, assuming command at De Beers, and Relly, taking charge at Anglo. In December 1982, with these men in place, Harry felt confident enough to step down as chairman and director of Anglo-American. He delivered his farewell address outside 44 Main Street, Johannesburg. All 3,300 staff members were in attendance, from six-figure executives to black messengers. So impressed was the government that it waived the Riotous Assembly Act for this last hurrah.

The retirement that Harry called "a matter of sadness, but not a matter of regret" meant that he would relinquish the chairmanship of Anglo-American, as well as the seat on the board of directors he had occupied for 48 years. The King of Diamonds planned to indulge himself in horse breeding and acquisitions for his library. "I'm certainly going to be reading the papers," he said with a forced chuckle.

But at the age of 74 Harry was not quite ready to walk into the sunset. The empire needed its father figure. And besides, he nourished hopes of an improved relationship between the empire and the government; after all, he pointed out, "at one time they thought I had horns and a tail." To these ends he would stay on as chairman of the companies that controlled the two largest blocks of Anglo-American shares: Oppenheimer & Son, and De Beers Consolidated Mines. For the present, Harry's son would have to be content as head of the Central Selling Organization in London, overseeing the diamond business that his father saw as "a cross between mining and selling works of art." Was this a way of shunting Nicky to a career of paperwork and carats, making way at last for the first non-Oppenheimer regime? Or was Harry waiting for his diffident boy to bare his teeth?

While the world waited for an answer, Ogilvie Thompson enforced his own position at De Beers. Asked about his political views, he described them as differing "little, if at all, from those espoused with such clarity and eloquence by Harry Oppenheimer." At Anglo, Gavin Relly weighed in. He announced himself to be, like Harry Oppenheimer, "not in favor of one-man, one-vote in South Africa." The country's "extremely un-homogeneous society" needed some vague constitutional arrangement, rather than universal suffrage. To let everyone cast a ballot "would simply be a formula for unadulterated chaos at this point in time in our history."

Three fears underlay the empire's party line. First was the anxiety about Marxist influence at work in Angola and Ethiopia. Here was an enemy that could take various shapes and forms. It might be an external foe, gathering at the borders; or it might be a fifth column, seducing the black mind from within. "South African security men," observed *New York Times* journalist Joseph Lelyveld, tirelessly promoted "the ancient allegation that the miniscule, antediluvian Communist Party, which has dutifully followed Moscow's line on Czechoslovakia, Poland, and Afghanistan, dominates Umkhonto we Sizwe ("Spear of the Nation"), the underground's military arm."

The second fear had a firmer base in reality. As Pretoria watched, the independent African states dissolved in red ink and social chaos. Would their problems infect South Africa? The white government thought so, and the pessimists at De Beers and Anglo agreed. To them, one-man one-vote could easily bring South Africa down and spell the end of empire. They watched their neighbors and made up grim scenarios. The reality turned out to be just as dire. By the end of the decade, some 51 independent states experienced 21 assassinations and at least 72 wrenching changes of leadership, most of them effected by violent coup or military takeover. Sixteen radical socialist states showed no inclination to embrace a free market economy; and 41 had a gross national product of less than $1,000 per capita, less than half that of South Africa.

The third fear was aroused with the phrase, "the coming apocalypse," accompanied by relevant statistics. South Africa was about 26 percent Caucasian. Asians and coloreds constituted another 20 percent. Almost all of the remaining population was black. According to demographers, by the year 2000 blacks would outnumber the other races by a three-to-one ratio. Universal suffrage would mean black domination, followed by frantic upheaval and unpayable debt. The country would go back to tribal wars and sere earth. The status quo had to remain: apartheid yesterday, today, and tomorrow.

Yet there were plenty of whites who turned away from this retrograde policy. Most of the European elite and many of the younger generation of Afrikaaners spoke out against the government. They were sickened by the Nazi-like flag of the Purified Nationalists, and they had wearied of swimming against the moral tide. Even those who disliked Nelson Mandela and all he stood for knew that the old ways were obsolete. It was one thing to condemn the ANC and rail against the Organization of African States; the will of the world was too great an opponent.

Over the objections of President Ronald Reagan, a Democratic Congress was already preparing a comprehensive Anti-Apartheid Act, imposing punitive sanctions against South Africa. If it passed, United States investments and loans would be canceled, along with landing rights for South African Airways. American universities were finding it expedient to divest themselves of their holdings in South Africa. Wary of controversy and stockholders' revolt, a long list of companies started to withdraw from the country, including General Electric, General Motors, IBM, Coca-Cola, and Warner Communications.

Margaret Thatcher took up the fallen banner of the Reagan administration. She attacked the strategy of sanctions. In her opinion they would distress the very people they were supposed to help. Oliver Tambo, the ANC's president in exile, was unmoved by Mrs. Thatcher's sudden concern for the blacks of South Africa. Addressing a group of Commonwealth businessmen, diplomats, and churchmen he replied, "When you say that you don't want sanctions because they would hurt us most, you're not honest. You don't want to hurt your trade—which you think depends on apartheid."

Without a country or an office, Tambo acquired more allies than the British Prime Minister. The European Economic Community prepared a series of moves: no selling of gold krugerrands in member countries, no imports of South African coal. Some member countries demanded far greater restrictions, and Sweden and Denmark imposed a total trade ban.

HFO, Alan Paton, and many other prominent South African liberals found themselves in rare agreement with the Thatcher forces. They believed that sanctions would force Pretoria back to the siege mentality of the *laager*, prolonging apartheid and impoverishing the black community. In Soweto a street speaker put the well-meaning whites in their places. "Whatever pain comes as a result of sanctions, it is our pain, not theirs," he proclaimed. "It is what we choose, not them." Desmond Tutu, black Anglican Archbishop of Cape Town, added his voice. He believed that sanctions would eventually bring down the government: "When the ladder falls over, it is those at the top who get hurt the most."

With Harry out of public view and the new leaders only beginning to take root, the empire made one of its rare blunders. *The Rand Daily Mail*, South Africa's liberal English-language newspaper, had once regarded HFO as something of a savior. An editorial had praised his "brilliant talents" as a businessman and pleaded for him to reenter Parliament, in "the wider interests of the country." Mary Oppenheimer had written a gossip column in its pages. The paper had been in agreement with Harry's United Party, steadfastly opposing apartheid.

Harry returned the favors. When Pretoria threatened to take over some of the most outspoken anti-administration newspapers, Anglo set up a trust for the *Mail*, effectively keeping it free of government control. The paper retained its editorial independence, and Harry's image as rescuer remained intact. But in the late 1970s the paper began to lose advertising revenue to television. Personnel were forced out; policies altered. A problem arose because of the paper's large black readership. According to an ousted editor, management "believed it gave the paper 'a split image.' They held back circulation in the townships and pressed the editors to go for more white women readers." As the executive most directly involved, Harry's ex-son-in-law, Gordon Waddell, found himself besieged by other journalists. Were the rumors true? they wanted to know. Would the *Mail* abandon its policy of backing Harry's Progressive Party? Waddell assured them that it would not. What he did not say was that Anglo planned to put the paper to sleep.

On March 15, 1985, the *Mail*'s last editor, Rex Gibson, called in his staff: "When one has bad news to tell, it is best to tell it quickly. *The Rand Daily Mail* will close on 30 April." Questioned by a journalist, Waddell blamed it all on economics. The Progressives, he explained, "are more interested in politics. In this office, Ma'am, we're more concerned about the bottom line." Perhaps Harry came closer to the truth when he stated that the *Mail* was "addressing itself to too distant a future." The day after it closed, the *Mail* was replaced by *Business Day*, the "national newspaper for decision makers." It goes without saying that the decision makers were white.

To blacks, particularly black journalists, the whole process seemed a calculated and hypocritical decision. Was profit the true motive? Or had the *Mail*'s long career of muckraking been a cause of embarrassment at a time when the West was considering sanctions against Pretoria? The Society of Black Journalists had no doubt. A formal statement said that the group was "dismayed at the role played in this by Anglo-American. Anglo is a company which claims a record as having a social conscience and which, in an effort to stem the tide of disinvestment moves, is telling the world it is in the forefront of reform. . . . Anglo has exercised its power as a monopoly with devastating destructiveness."

The Black Media Workers Association called the closing "a stunning victory for the Nationalist government which schemed and plotted for a quarter of a century to silence or at least muffle the voice of the *Mail.*"

Whatever the motives of the Oppenheimer empire, its action could only be considered a public relations calamity. The savings were negligible, the loss of reputation incalculable. Three years after the "retirement," people began to wonder if Harry's age was finally showing. He had worked so diligently to make South Africa palatable to outsiders, to erect causeways between the hard-liners of Pretoria and the black leadership. And then, almost casually, he had allowed one of those causeways to be destroyed. With the *Mail* went a portion of his credibility. Years later a black leader asked, "If Waddell, one of the more liberal Anglo men, was to go for profits instead of ideals, what could we reasonably expect from HFO? Talk. Well-meaning oratory. Promises." That eminent Victorian Lewis Carroll had mocked just such situations. In Wonderland the White Queen tells Alice, "The rule is, jam tomorrow, and jam yesterday—but never jam today."

♦　　♦　　♦

THE SOUTH AFRICA of the 1980s was not the country that Cecil Rhodes had envisioned—or Ernest Oppenheimer, or Harry. Everything had changed: the skyline, the leadership, the natives, even the power elite. At Anglo, a new and very different generation of Oxonians was coming up. In a rare, playful mood Harry had once looked at his emerging young executives and observed, "A major job for the chairman of Anglo-American is to keep a proper balance between what I call the monkeys and the do-gooders. Because without the monkeys the do-gooders never succeed. And without the do-gooders any success the monkeys bring about tends to be a bit second rate. Of course, the ideal man for the Anglo-American Corporation is the idealist monkey."

And now those idealist monkeys were taking hold: university men who knew all about the appalling conditions in the mines. They studied black culture, read protest literature, went to see the new plays of Athol Fugard. The small, fervent group was not yet a force at De Beers and Anglo; the empire could have gotten rid of them. But the young executives were too bright and promising. One way or another, they had to be accommodated. The question was how.

As Relly and Ogilvie Thompson considered the problem, P. W. Botha gave them—and the idealist monkeys—reason to hope. The prime minister had just composed a major policy statement, and word circulated that its message would put Pretoria back in the world community. The South African press predicted that Botha's upcoming talk would amount to a "Rubicon speech," comparable to Julius Caesar's famous crossing of the river to his imperial destiny.

Anticlimactic was the most flattering description of the events of August 15, 1985. Botha addressed the television cameras of some 33 countries and, in a finger-wagging polemic, warned the world not to "push us too far." Nelson Mandela would not be released from prison; there would be no new reforms. This president was not prepared to lead "white South Africans and other minority groups to abdication and suicide."

Botha's message reassured his National partisans—and repelled just about everyone else. The international monetary community panicked, and within two weeks the rand plunged from an already depressed 52 United States cents to under 33 cents. Condemnations appeared in the press of almost every country, and each night major news programs made a point of showing government violence and suppression in the townships. Pretoria reacted exactly as the liberals had predicted; instead of going after the causes of misery and violence, the government attacked the press. Late in the year a cameraman filmed policemen opening fire on a group of stone-throwing blacks, killing three. Botha castigated foreign correspondents for "paying blacks to incite unrest" and barred all camera teams from "sensitive" areas.

Harry kept on hoping for a quiet retirement. But he knew that

Botha's policies were destroying South Africa's economy, and that the empire had to act. First he sent Anglo executives to speak informally with representatives of the ANC. Then on September 13, even though he was known to be "twitchy" about it, HFO stood aside as Gavin Relly, accompanied by a small group of South African businessmen, flew to Zambia for an extraordinary meeting with Tambo himself. At the ANC president's side was his director of information, Thabo Mkei, whose father, Govan, was in prison with Nelson Mandela. Botha found out about the flight and exploded: the white men were publicly denounced as "disloyal." Relly and the others went right ahead with their plans. In their view, accommodating this government would be worse than defying it.

Zambian President Kenneth Kaunda chaired the meeting, held at a hunting lodge in Mfuwe, Zambia's game park. As elephants ponderously hosed themselves down in a nearby river, he began: "Things that bring men together come from God; the things that divide us are man-made." The blacks wore suits and ties, the whites had open collars and slacks. One of those whites later commented on the role reversals: "If you'd been asked to say which were the businessmen and which were the revolutionaries, you'd have got it the wrong way round."

The smiling faces, the easy "call me Oliver" and "call me Gavin" relationship, the unprecedented six-hour dialogue could not disguise the differences of opinion. The whites, for example, spoke of the need for constitutional guarantees in a multiracial society; the ANC, opposed to any racial qualifications, stood for the protection of all rights without mention of black or white or colored. The ANC charter of 1955 had called for a black government to nationalize some major corporations. "They represent tremendous wealth," Tambo pointed out, "in the midst of unspeakable poverty." This socialist idea was of course anathema to Anglo and De Beers, and to the directors of every other publicly held company. Nevertheless Relly listened to Tambo calmly, keeping his voice steady and conciliatory. Indeed, there were times when Anglo's top executive seemed almost revolutionary himself, talking in favor of Mandela's unconditional release, integrated education, and immediate reforms of the apartheid system. On the big question of universal suffrage, however, neither side capitulated; then again, neither side had the power to change the laws that kept them apart. In the end the colloquy was more important for having occurred than for anything that was said.

His interest in the meeting, Relly later recalled, "was entirely to develop a judgement about the importance of this crummy Marxism which they purported to advocate. I'm less concerned about who runs South Africa than I am about the form of economic system which prevails." He concluded that "the leadership of the ANC would be more interested in a viable and vibrant South African economy than they would be in the Marxian form of economy. . . . They were people who can be talked to and I am not so rigid about my own point of view that I am not capable of being talked to either."

The idea of De Beers and Anglo courting black friends in high places was appalling to the Afrikaaner right and astonishing to the press. Relly had been regarded as more conservative and cautious than Harry, and here he was making up to the African National Congress, as if he wanted to establish the company credentials in case of a black takeover. Taking stock in *The Guardian*, the South African journalist Stanley Uys observed: "Capitalism has now entered the fight for its survival."

But that was not the only battle taking place in South Africa. Throughout the townships, blacks accused of collaborating with the white government were being "necklaced"—tires placed around their necks, soaked in gasoline and set afire. At Christmastime 1985, a bomb killed five shoppers. Cars were blown up as they drove over land mines. Tambo disavowed some of the more outrageous murders, but he refused to condemn bloodshed on principle. "It was *because* of the violence," he insisted, that Relly had come to talk. But Relly, appalled by the terror tactics and public outrages, was no longer the friendly Gavin. He now claimed that in Zambia he had been misled by Mr. Tambo.

Extremists had always defined racial cooperation as the trade name for treason; these latest outrages were exactly what they had prophesied. The Afrikaaner right felt justified in representing blacks as primitives in Western garb, circling around the wagons for the kill; what chance would whites have in a government of shamans and their feral children? A spokesman for the Purified National Party argued even against Botha's slight attempts to modify apartheid. "We can't pay our debts," he reminded South Africans. "We are sitting on an inflation rate of 16 percent, people are going bankrupt at an unheard-of rate, unemployment is increasing. The basic cause of all this is that the government started with equality." For its part the black left, in inflammatory I-told-you-so rhetoric, described whites as Nazis advancing their genocidal program; what opportunities could poor people have in a nation of outlaws pretending to be statesmen?

Not many could believe in the future of South Africa anymore. As the sanctions began to bite, Botha tried a second Rubicon speech, attempting to win back the West. This time he acknowledged that apartheid was "outdated," called for an end to the Pass Law for Africans, and offered to include black leaders in a new "statutory council" with himself as chairman. This was more like it, Relly decided. The speech had "brought South Africa back into the mainstream of western thinking." Or so it seemed as the rand climbed up to 45 cents.

To the majority of blacks, however, Botha's promises were a hoax. Their lives continued as barren and despairing as before. The townships continued to erupt. Within black South Africa horrific power struggles took place, secretly encouraged by the white authorities. The Zulu-based Inkatha movement, led by Chief Mangosuthu Buthelezi, had been tolerated by the government for understandable reasons: the chief praised the capitalist system and opposed sanctions. Leaders of the ANC spoke out against his positions. Members of Inkatha answered back with great fury. Bloody encounters followed. They amounted to a black civil war, and during the unrest in one township, police turned up a cache of Soviet-made AK-47 rifles. Here was fresh evidence, they said, that Moscow pulled the strings of native insurgents. Botha declared a new state of emergency and ordered the roundup of known activists.

Once again, South Africa appeared on the front pages of major newspapers all over the world. In the House of Commons, Britain's former Prime Minister Ted Heath offered a contemptuous summary: "The South African government believe . . . that they can always use the Communist threat as the argument with which to handle Washington and Whitehall. The irony of the situation is that the longer South Africa continues its present policy, the more it drives its black population into Communist hands and the more it is encouraging the other black states in Africa to move towards a Communist outlook."

The sectarian conflicts, the battle of government and empire, began to wear down the whites. Most of them just talked about going away. But hundreds packed up their belongings and moved to new lives in foreign countries. The Nationalists dismissed their actions as making "the chicken run" and tried to disregard the exodus. But one man was too celebrated to ignore. In 1987, at the age of 49, Gordon Waddell called it quits and relocated in England. The *Mail* controversy may have played a part in his exit; as a man of liberal sympathies he could not have been happy with his role as imperial executioner. But mainly he was disturbed by the pace of social progress and doubtful about the future of free enterprise in South Africa. Only a short time before, he had startled some directors of Anglo by standing up in his shirtsleeves and banging a ham hand on the table. "Well, gentlemen," he demanded, "which one of you wants this company to be remembered as the I. G. Farben of Apartheid?" A chill went down the backs of some executives: with the use of slave labor, Farben had become the industrial core of the Third Reich.

Minutes of that meeting leaked to the black community. It was unmoved by the warning about Nazis. "All very well for Waddell to talk," a trade unionist complained, "but he's no different from the others. Where are [Anglo's] black directors? Where are its black managers? There aren't any." He was not quite accurate. Anglo had six mining houses with 100 managers. Two of them were black.

21

THE MOST
DANGEROUS AGE

OLIVER TWIST first encounters Fagin in a region of blackened alleys and gaslit incubators of crime: "In its filthy shops, are exposed for sale huge bunches of second-hand silk handkerchiefs, of all sizes and patterns; for here reside the traders who purchase them from pick-pockets. . . . It is an emporium of petty larceny: visited at early morning, and setting-in of dusk, by silent merchants, who traffic in dark back-parlors, and who go as strangely as they come. Here, the clothesman and the rag merchant display their goods, as sign-boards to the petty thief; here, stores of old iron and bones, and heaps of mildewy fragments of woolen-stuff and linen, rust and rot in the grimy cellars."

On the same turf, a century later, the thieves' carnival has given way to the headquarters of Oppenheimer empire. Much has been made of this by the enemies of HFO and his companies. They say Holborn is a fitting center for De Beers and Anglo, that nothing has really changed since Dickens's day. Except that now the larceny is grand.

Until the late 1980s Harry's defenders could parry these attacks with examples of sound business practices and good works. If one could judge a man by the enemies he acquired, Oppenheimer's credentials were impressive. The violent wing of the ANC condemned mining capitalists out of hand. Meanwhile the extremist *Afrikaaner Weerstandsbeweging* (Resistance Movement), assailed Harry from the far side of politics. Led by the ex-policeman Eugene Terre'Blanche, the AWB pledged to stop multiracialism and end "spiritual and economic enslavement by Anglo-Jewish money."

Harry's reputation did not rest on ill will alone. One way or another

357

his companies did business in almost every country. Politicians went out of their way to greet the celebrated contradiction in terms: a liberal businessman from South Africa. Employees respected the chairman emeritus. Stockholders adored him. When his practices came under attack—a frequent occurrence in the 1980s—Harry seldom responded. He left that to his friends. They always gave way a little, conceding that the interlocking directorates *did* seem rather murky. But this, they pointed out, was only to protect them from unreasonable taxes and predatory takeovers. Yes, they allowed, the diamond monopoly *was* an almost airtight construction violating all known rules of fair competition; indeed, some OPEC members went around citing it as their platonic ideal. Yet the syndicate's "victims" were its loudest advocates. "Oppenheimer runs a cartel," as one Israeli dealer pointed out. "But diggers, dealers, cutters, name me anybody who fails to benefit from it. From diamonds everybody makes a good living. De Beers is tough, always has been, no question about it. But bring in competition and diamonds are dead. A year from now we would all be pushing carts instead of selling dreams."

That was exactly what the empire wanted the world to believe, and its public relations staffs worked overtime to promote the image of benign power. "Harry's boys" stubbed their toes now and then, went the line. No executive was infallible. Yet in the end, when the accountants got through, the empire was just a shade larger, its planners a bit more confident, its shareholders a bit more secure.

In fact, the empire was deeply and secretly troubled. The bad times had begun with the catastrophes at Charter Consolidated. One of Harry's assistants defined the concept of Charter in the era of global economies: It was "to be a company outside of South African exchange controls which would have the financial and technological clout to undertake major mining business around the world." In short, a new way of extending the Oppenheimer empire across two oceans.

In the 1970s Charter had undertaken three major efforts. One, the Cleveland Potash company, began work in North Yorkshire. Then, with the permission of the government of Mauritania, Charter invested heavily in a copper mining enterprise, using "Torco," a smelting process developed by Anglo-American. A third project, a copper mine in the

Congo, operated under a consortium led by Charter and the Congolese government.

One by one they fell apart. The Torco process, which had looked so efficient on paper, failed to work in the dust and hundred-degree heat of the Mauritanian desert. The loss: over $30 million. Then the Congolese mining operation met with trouble. Copper prices receded on the international market just as inflation forced up the price of materials and labor. Engineers predicted a final cost of $800 million. Charter pulled out and cut its losses at $230 million. More bad news came from Cleveland Potash. Serpentine seams of the chemical were difficult and expensive to trace, and the price of potash steadily weakened on the international market. After spending some $27 million, Charter decided that this effort, too, was expendable. The losses mounted up, and the market analysts made unflattering notes.

The failure of all three projects was followed by another disagreeable incident. Hoping to recoup its losses, Charter made a bid for a British-based mining equipment company, Anderson Strathclyde. The Monopolies and Mergers Commission looked into the bid. In the past, De Beers and Anglo American had been able to live with their reputations of arrogance and rapacity, for even the empire's most hostile takeovers had resulted in stronger managements and larger dividends for the stockholders. But that no longer held true, and the Commission was quick to recognize the new reality. "Judging by the financial record of its mining and industrial subsidiaries," read its report, "and disturbing incidents of its attitude towards the management of acquisitions, little confidence should be placed in the suitability of Charter for the control of Anderson Strathclyde."

That judgment did not stand, not in the face of the empire's political and financial influence. Pressure was brought to bear, and for a price of £95 million, Charter got its wish. However, the folk wisdom of Africa and Europe—that one should not want anything too much because the gods might grant it—was about to be illustrated. By the mid-1980s Strathclyde's profits had been cut in half. In 1988–1989 the company was in arrears by more than £3 million. This time market analysts published their findings. In August 1989, Shearson Lehman Hutton told its customers, "As an entity, Charter seems to have outlived its role and has not yet succeeded in finding a new one." It was not the sort of report card HFO was used to receiving, and it marked the beginning of De Beers's and Anglo's most dangerous age.

◆　◆　◆

WHEN CHARTER STUMBLED, money managers felt a tremor. After the Gold Fields fiasco, entire financial markets shuddered. For the first time, the empire had not privately miscalculated, it had failed before the world.

The acquisition had seemed preordained, and almost everyone expected it to occur without incident. After all, Consolidated Gold Fields and De Beers shared the same father, Cecil Rhodes; bringing them together would practically be a family affair. Back in 1887, while he was managing the diamond business, the Colossus had founded Gold Fields of South Africa. Since then the company name had changed to Consolidated Gold Fields, and its fortunes had passed through many hands. What bothered Harry, a century later, was that the hands were not his.

As a producer of precious metal Gold Fields was second only to Anglo, and far more efficient than its giant rival. Anglo's operating costs ran at about $302 per ounce versus $177 for Gold Fields. But there were more compelling reasons to acquire the company. Under the leadership of its Chairman, Lord Erroll, Gold Fields reached into Australia, New Guinea, and most remarkably, into the mines of California, Nevada, and New Mexico. Diversification, the reach outside the limits of South Africa, had been one of Harry's keenest desires. Here was a corporation with just such assets. Would it resist a takeover, or was it ripe for the plucking? Late in 1980 the Anglo boys rubbed their hands and got ready for harvest time.

According to British tradition, a company had to be officially notified by anyone purchasing 5 percent or more of its outstanding stock. But suppose six "independent corporations" were to acquire, say, 4.9 percent each? One was De Beers Holdings, a wholly owned subsidiary of De Beers. A second was the Central Selling Organization. Third came Chajo Properties, a subsidiary of Rosmic, itself an offshoot of E. Oppenheimer & Son. Other companies weighed in: Welsburg, FEW Properties, Brent Ltd. All were part of the Oppenheimer empire. Working swiftly through various agents, they purchased outstanding shares in a matter of hours.

Actually, some of the corporations went over the 5 percent limit. But by then their mission had been accomplished: Anglo held more than one quarter of Gold Fields, upsetting Lord Erroll—and the British government. A subsequent investigation by the Department of Trade and Industry traced all six companies back to the Oppenheimer empire. A scheme had been formulated, the Department found, "with the express intention of avoiding the disclosure provisions of the Companies Acts."

In Harry's opinion the violations had been strictly unintentional. Admittedly a "dawn raid," as the financial papers called it, was an unpleasant thing. But where had De Beers or Anglo violated the law? Search as it might, the government could find no prosecutable offense. Harry and his companies were off the hook.

Refreshed by yet another triumph, HFO flew off to London bearing a statuette of Cecil Rhodes. In the spirit of reconciliation, Harry presented it to Lord Erroll. The fraternal spirit failed to take hold. Erroll demanded a halt to the empire's march, and after unpleasant and protracted negotiations a cold announcement came from De Beers and Anglo-American. The companies "have made it clear that there is no immediate intention on their behalf or any of their associates to increase their existing holding and that in any case it would not be their intention to increase their combined holding in [Gold Fields] beyond 29.9 per cent in the future."

The operative word was "immediate." Eight years later, Anglo was ready for its next move. By then the lord was accompanied by a commoner, chief executive officer Rudolph Agnew. The new, Australian-born chairman was 45, quite young for such a large job and very alert to threats. Agnew was a second-generation gold man —his father had been a mining engineer who helped run Gold Fields in the 1930s; Rudolph himself had been with the company since 1957.

He was known as a canny and volatile manager. On several occasions, for example, he ignited the paper in his wastebasket; the point of this exercise, he told astonished colleagues, was to see how long it took before people took alarm. The record was 18 minutes. His assistants needed far less time to see how badly things were going in 1988.

To maintain a semblance of fairness, Gold Fields and Anglo arranged what Agnew resentfully called "the corporate equivalent of an exchange of prisoners." Julian Ogilvie Thompson and another Anglo man, Neil Clarke, sat on the board of Gold Fields. In return, Agnew was welcomed onto the board of Anglo-American. The arrangement was supposed to provide a method of checks and balances: with executives sitting on each others' boards, neither company could make plans without the other's knowledge. But that was not the way things actually worked. "I joined the board," Agnew was to recall, "in the mistaken belief that it was a significant body. I soon discovered it was a total waste of time. All the decisions that matter were taken elsewhere." Elsewhere, in this case, meant other Anglo-American nerve centers, located in cities such as Johannesburg.

An atmosphere of mutual hostility settled over everything. Gold Fields's financial chief, Anthony Hitchens, was to remember that "the mistrust was extraordinary. If Anglo did X, we would do Y. I couldn't understand the attitude of my colleagues towards Anglo. I came to the company free of all the hang-ups about Anglo American and the religion of gold. I couldn't see what the other directors were getting at, when they kept warning me about Anglo. Before long, I did."

When Hitchens learned to distrust Anglo, it was too late to do anything about it. After months of total secrecy, the truth leaked out: Oppenheimer was going to attempt a hostile takeover of Gold Fields's properties in England and America. That would be done through a branch of the empire called Minorco, based in Luxembourg. The company had replaced Charter as the main overseas investor for Oppenheimer funds, and it was now in the hunt for cash. Minorco found all it needed on Wall Street. The financial community was astonished in September 1987, when Anglo sold off a prize possession, Salomon Bros., the largest investment trading house in New York.

Analysts warned that their timing was off, that Anglo desperately required this foothold in the United States, that the bull market had yet to reach its peak. Harry's men ignored the advice. The official sale occurred just a month before the stock market crash that reduced Salomon Bros. to a shell. Anglo was not among the mourners. It had gained a profit of $1.4 billion by selling prematurely. The money was allocated for the Gold Fields takeover.

Minorco management had the look of winners. Two of its board members enjoyed direct connections to Harry. Hank Slack was Mary's third and final husband. Sensitive to the charges of nepotism, he worked overtime to be more than just HFO's lucky son-in-law. Shuttling between the States, London, and Johannesburg, Slack was forever supervising company business and overbooking himself in the process. The word around Anglo was that he needed two secretaries: the first to arrange his schedule, the second to untangle it. Another board member, Roger Phillimore, was Harry's godson. "There's nothing special about being one," Roger once said, in an unconvincing act of self-deprecation. "I think I am one of 96." Just so, but none of the others had gone so far at Minorco.

With all their connections, both men suffered a great liability. They were South Africans at a time when their home country was battered by sanctions and labeled a moral pariah at the United Nations. In order to make the world forget Minorco's Johannesburg connections, the company had to be given a tweed suit and an English accent. Thus a rare outsider, Sir Michael Edwardes, received an appointment to the board. The former head of England's largest car manufacturer, British Leyland, would lead the raid on Gold Fields.

Under his direction, Minorco's merchant bankers, Morgan Grenfell, began to speak in schoolboy code: Achilles for Minorco, Hector for Gold Fields. This was a peculiar choice of myths: Achilles did indeed destroy Hector. But after that, Achilles himself was slain, by a wound in the heel—his one vulnerable part. Was that tale prophetic? Not according to the gods at Anglo. Hank Slack confidently bought an estate in New Jersey; the new, expanded Minorco would need a good man in the United States.

On the morning of September 21, 1988, Minorco launched a bid of £13.06 for each outstanding share of Gold Fields stock, then selling at £10.75. The stock markets rang with takeover rumors. Sir Michael Edwardes attempted to head off the critics in the financial press who saw him as Harry's English butler. Edwardes had taken this job, he insisted, with the understanding that the South African Anglo would have nothing to do with the Luxembourg-based Minorco. In a speech he piously looked toward the unification of Europe, with one currency and justice for all, and suggested that Minorco be considered a "pan-European" enterprise: "We're almost living in 1992 already."

On the other side of the battlefield Rudolph Agnew prepared his counter-attack. He opened with the anti-apartheid maneuver. No one should be deceived, he said, by this "Luxembourg shell which was a front for South Africa." The press was reminded that for all of Harry's vaunted liberalism, when a strike threatened to cripple Anglo's gold mines, 40,000 workers were dismissed.

Harry responded hotly. "I find it insufferable to be attacked on grounds of South African connections," he fumed, "particularly by a group which has been very active in South Africa and which has certainly not been in the forefront of opposition to the apartheid policy."

Harry was correct. The Gold Fields portfolio represented the largest private British investment in that country. Most of the money was used in mine development, and most of those mines ruthlessly exploited their workers. Gold Fields South Africa funded and housed one of the largest private armies in the country, complete with dogs, armored vehicles, and its own patented rubber bullets. According to a Granada TV documentary, GFSA had been viciously opposed to the principle of miners' unions. To intimidate their employees the company had used every means from propaganda to guns. In one company video, a well-dressed African sat behind a desk advising the viewer; images of unemployment lines and underfed families went by. The speaker winked at the camera. "Do nothing foolish. Plenty of people want your job."

Taking their cue from HFO, Minorco forces kept smearing the opponent's history and management. Gold Fields replied by shooting over Minorco's head at South Africa itself. The Reagan administration was warned against the masters of apartheid: through its corporations, South Africa was not merely after the gold market. It wanted to control Gold Fields's production of titanium and zircon, vital raw materials for America's defensive weapons.

Gold Fields also hammered away at the private sector. Before the time of sanctions, workers at the American Aggregates Corporation in Greenville, Ohio, might have had trouble finding Johannesburg on the map. By 1989, the laborers had learned where South Africa was and what a takeover might mean to their incomes. Should Minorco acquire the Gold Fields affiliate, they were told, United States restrictions against South African companies would immediately apply. That might put hundreds on the unemployment line.

"We're beginning to appreciate that the fight against apartheid is not confined to South Africa," said Ohio's executive assistant for economic development. "Deals made in Johannesburg, Luxembourg or London have a direct impact on a small town like Greenville."

An angry Julian Ogilvie Thompson raised the heat. At Minorco's annual meeting he called attention to the "world-wide orchestrated program of villification and abuse against Minorco, Anglo-American, De Beers, Harry Oppenheimer." Of all the accusations, perhaps most offensive was the ancient and unproven rumor that De Beers had sold diamonds to the Third Reich.

In the confusion of battle each side committed its own public relations blunders. Minorco was frantic to prove that its management was not fronting for the South African government, that it was, in fact, composed of hands-on mining guys. To that end, the company ordered a special ad to run in the local papers. Edwardes and Phillimore would be seen at a pithead complete with pickaxes, hard hats, and miners' helmets. For the picture Edwardes removed his glasses, and Phillimore his watch. The trouble was, the "mine" was in a London studio, the axes were props, and the grease on their faces was shoe polish. After a sober look at the result, executives ordered the negatives destroyed and the ad canceled.

Gold Fields offered a video portraying itself as the victim of South African predators. A telephone hotline was set up to answer requests. On the first day the wire was accidentally crossed with an AIDS information jingle, warning the caller against "sleeping around."

Throughout the winter, fierce skirmishes went on with all the modern weapons of war: advertising, legal briefs, threats, whispering campaigns. Neither side could claim a clean victory or a final defeat; neither side showed the slightest inclination to call a truce. Minorco finally broke through the lines on February 2, 1989. That was the day Britain's Monopolies and Mergers Commission published its conclusion: "We do not believe, as it was suggested to us, that the proposed merger would operate against the public interest on account of the characteristics of the Anglo-American group, or Minorco's South African associations in general."

Certain of victory, Roger Phillimore sent each of his advisors a case of champagne. No bubbly poured at Gold Fields. Agnew vainly protested that the Commission's message was "do not, for God's sake, look to the authorities for protection." The MMC decision was "absurd . . . like the Mad Hatter's tea party."

There was still the U.S. to contend with, but the British financial press, quick to nose any shift in the wind, predicted an early victory for Minorco. "It is hard to imagine," said *The Daily Telegraph*, "that even the averagely arrogant American court will stand in Minorco's way now that its assault on Gold Fields has been blessed by the Monopolies Commission."

As many foreign observers have painfully learned, American courts are not as predictable as the ones at home. Transcripts of the official hearing, before Judge Michael Mukasey of the New York District Court, show a scrupulous weighing of both sides. The court cites the plaintiff's claims that if Minorco gets its talons on Gold Fields, the empire would be in a position to control more than 20% of the world's gold market. It is "significant that De Beers, one of the protagonists in this takeover, has apparently sought to monopolize the world supply of diamonds."

In fairness, the court notes Minorco's counter-argument: Minorco could not control the price of gold in South Africa even if it wanted to. Only the government has such power.

But this is not the whole truth. The court notes that Anglo "has far more control over price and output than Minorco concedes. . . . The [South African] government essentially acts as a mere conduit through which defendants obtain the market price for their gold. Thus, even accepting defendant's argument that mining companies have no control over output, they can affect price by restricting output outside South Africa in order to increase the world price for gold and reap greater profits from the South African mines."

The most telling blow comes in a paragraph examining Minorco's "argument that it is an investing company, not a mining company, and thus that Anglo and De Beers's commanding share of the market cannot be imputed to it.

"Anglo and De Beers, which together own over 60% of Minorco, own outright most of their mining concerns. In addition, Anglo owns

39.8% of, and has effective control over, the affairs of another large South African gold mining house, JCI. Moreover, plaintiffs have presented substantial affidavits and other evidence demonstrating that the entire group is controlled by Harry Oppenheimer through Central Holdings.

"Minorco's argument is thus without merit."

Insiders were not as surprised as the journalists when Judge Mukasey delivered his official opinion on May 16. Just after noon the terse message appeared on screens all over Wall Street: *US Judge refuses to lift injunction barring Minorco from Gold Fields takeover.* The impossible had happened, after all. The empire had lost.

Rudolph Agnew could not find it in his heart to be magnanimous. "What we proved in New York," he concluded, "was that South African control is just not acceptable in large areas of the world." But there was more to the defeat than geopolitics. De Beers and Anglo had miscalculated the situation, and now the entire world knew that the powerful, intimidating empire was vulnerable after all.

Once the judgment came down, Minorco's takeover plans were finished. And the debacle was not complete. Gold Fields eventually went to another bidder, Hanson, for a much lower price than the South Africans had offered. A London market analyst wrote to his clients that "Agnew should have announced the terms of an agreed bid for Gold Fields at London Zoo. There are some shareholders who would have liked to have put Mr Agnew behind bars for agreeing to a bid which offered them less than Minorco."

Agnew exhibited no remorse for shortchanging the shareholders— or for spending more than £30 million of their money in order to put down the South Africans. For him it had been a matter of principle: "History shows that companies that fall under the influence of Anglo-American either conform or are rejected in a brutal way."

In the end Hanson proved to be more peremptory than the South Africans. Under new management, the Gold Fields office closed down and all 85 employees were let go, along with most of the company directors. For his efforts Agnew received a pink slip and a generous pension. Julian Ogilvie Thompson, who compared the outcome to the last scene of *Othello*, all motiveless malignity, looked on sadly with his nose pressed against the window. JOT had put in a very modest request:

could the statuette of Rhodes be returned to Minorco? Even this was refused. The Colossus stayed behind to decorate some functionary's desk with a history he would not understand, shiny and emptied of meaning, like the Oppenheimers' dreams of gold.

♦   ♦   ♦

YET IN THESE WORST OF TIMES for Anglo, the Oppenheimer empire seemed to have one unlimited consolation: De Beers. If gold meant treachery and disappointment, diamonds signified safety: as the 1990s began, the cartel maintained its control over some 90 percent of the world's supply. Every year millions of women would become engaged and duly receive their rings. And every year would see the purchase of anniversary rings, tiaras, baguettes, necklaces. . . . As the diamond dealers liked to say of their wares, "Nobody needs them, everybody wants them." And then suddenly, for the first time since the days of Sir Ernest, the question was *whose* diamonds everybody wanted. That 90 percent was slipping away fast to 85 percent, then 80 percent. De Beers was in danger of losing its chokehold on the market.

The trouble had begun in post-revolutionary Angola, where isolated parts of the country now fended for themselves, without law or license. The most volatile area was the malarial jungle marking the border with Zaire. Here, along the diamond-rich banks of the Cuango River, some 30,000 *garimpieros*—prospectors—freely roamed, beyond the reaches of the cartel. The *garimpieros* quarried precious stones and carried them off to clandestine trading houses in Luanda, the nation's capital city. From there, the diamonds made their way to the diamond market at Antwerp.

In a grotesque replay of nineteenth-century New Rush, a town called Canfunfo had risen up to house these fortune hunters. From 1990 to 1992, its population mushroomed from 5,000 to 40,000. In Canfunfo, money and power were the sole criteria for measuring a man. Power meant weapons, and the most successful prospectors acquired some unusual ordnance. That was why the government so seldom flew its planes near the area; they could be shot down by missiles. As for money, it was not merely spent, it was flaunted everywhere. Local policemen received frequent payments of $2,000 for looking the other way. Luxurious Range Rovers with tinted windows became the vehicles

of choice—in a territory of rutted and unpaved roads, Mercedes and
BMWs were out of the question. The vehicles constantly hauled in the
most advanced refrigerators, television sets, and VCRs. There was no
telephone service, and the dealers preferred it that way. The less the
outside world learned of Canfunfo the better.

But De Beers knew all about the town. Early in 1992 a graphic
demonstration had taken place at its headquarters on Charterhouse
Street. Along one wall, eight mounds of raw diamonds greeted the
eye. Along another wall, four somewhat smaller mounds had been set
out in contrast. The first row represented the quantity of diamonds
smuggled out of Angola in just four months. They were worth $40
million. The second row stood for Angolese diamonds legally mined
during the same period. With one glance, the executives took in the
dimensions of their predicament: De Beers was receiving less than a
third of the Angolan output, and the cartel could do nothing until the
political situation was resolved.

Canfunfo could not have arisen at a worse time: De Beers stood
ready to open its newest mine, Venetia, in the northern Transvaal.
Venetia would yield gems worth some $400 million a year. Who would
purchase those diamonds? In flush years the company could look to
North America, Germany, and Japan. But at the moment all three
regions suffered from severe recessions.

There was worse to come. Since the 1950s, when diamonds were
discovered in Yakutia, a remote province in northeastern Siberia, the
U.S.S.R. had enjoyed a sub rosa arrangement with De Beers. After
years of dealing under the table, both sides arrived at an open agreement
in 1990. For the next five years the cartel would provide a billion-
dollar trade loan to the U.S.S.R., the money to be paid back in diamonds. Even Michael Spriggs of Warburgs, De Beers's brokers, had
to acknowledge that it was "a marvelous deal from the Russians' point
of view." Yet there was no other way; in order to maintain the legend
of diamond scarcity, the Yakutian stones had to be acquired and stored.
The transaction amounted to an act of faith. Every month, men from
Moscow handed over a cardboard box full of uncut jewels. Was it 100
percent of the crop? 90 percent? 80 percent? Might Russia be stockpiling its own stones for some future emergency? The empire could
not be sure.

As if that arrangement were not uncomfortable enough, the dissolution of the Soviet Union brought more complications. Now there were two separate entities to negotiate with: Russia, which controlled the flow of jewels, and Yakutia, which unearthed them. Both were in desperate need of foreign currency; uncut Yakutian stones began to appear in European markets, and polished ones turned up in Japan. Eventually the two states agreed to form a company to mine and sort the diamonds—Moscow would stay in control of the flow, but revenues from some 25 percent of the production would go back to Yakutia. The relations between the two remained uneasy, however, and in the fall of 1992 Harry and Nicky Oppenheimer found it necessary to visit Moscow. Officially they came to open an office; the real purpose of their journey was to convince the Russians to stay in the syndicate. Father and son worked out an agreement—for the moment. They knew that if the former Soviet Union continued to deteriorate, if ethnic strife were to erode the new governments, all bets would be off. A temporary guarantee was all that anyone could ask, even the Oppenheimers.

Until 1992, the notion of De Beers going hat in hand to one of its producers would have been unthinkable. Almost as unthinkable as De Beers in the role of loser. Yet loser it was in the 1990s, forced to pay out cash and take in diamonds. How many diamonds, only the highest officers in the empire knew for certain. But insiders estimate that at least $4.8 billion in uncut stones were purchased, and that did not include the Angolan stones. Given current market conditions, consumers would not buy more than $3.5 billion worth of jewels. The gap between these sums added up to an almost insurmountable debt.

As a result, in August 1992, JOT announced that De Beers was cutting its dividend and curtailing production. The stock went from $28 a share to about $18, and with it went the legend of Oppenheimer invulnerability. Another legend went as well: the cherished company line that if De Beers was a cartel, it was a cartel that benefited everyone, from the miner who unearthed the diamond all the way up to the fiancée who received it. The fact was that the miner would be laid off, the wholesalers would have to cut profits, the retailers would close stores, and the consumers would be the victims of a scheme to keep genuine diamonds artificially rare.

To allay fears in and out of the industry, De Beers sent forth a message from W. J. Lear, its Director of Communications. The company had "healthy cash balances of $759 million" and a "$5 billion-plus portfolio of investments outside the diamond industry."

As far as stockpiles were concerned, Lear went on, at the beginning of the 1990s, "they were just over $3 billion, equivalent to about three-quarters of that year's sales. In the last recession they reached over one-and-a-third times 1982 sales."

But in the intervening decade there had been cataclysmic social and economic changes. Lear failed to mention them. Russia was not the same, nor Europe, nor the United States, nor, of course, South Africa. James Picton, a Johannesburg economist who specializes in the diamond industry, had these changes in mind when he made his appraisal: "Ten years ago I said, 'Of course De Beers can hold the line.' This time I don't think there's any 'of course' about it. I do think they will hold the line. But at what price?" No one knew, least of all Harry Frederick Oppenheimer.

♦   ♦   ♦

WHILE ANGLO-AMERICAN TENDS to its wounds and De Beers confronts its narrowing list of options, Harry remains in Johannesburg, waiting for history. When the tension grows unbearable, his library at Brenthurst provides an ideal retreat. It sits like a monastery in the Middle Ages, isolated from the city's violent surroundings. The library's guarded rooms and hallways are meant for the connoisseur and scholar of Africana; in these hushed precincts, "The Bridge" seems as incongruous as a scream.

Painted by the Australian artist Leonard French, the 12′ × 6′ mural displays a vivid palette of enamel colors. But its subject, like all subjects in South Africa, comes down to a matter of black and white. On a burning wooden bridge two white armies converge to fight and kill each other. Their shouting lips are the mouths of cannons. Below, blacks march inexorably toward the onlooker. A large painted "rip" in the canvas divides the images on the left from those on the right.

When the library opened in 1982 Alan Paton, the octogenarian author of *Cry, the Beloved Country*, mentioned the art work in his address. "The meaning is painful to me," he said in a cloudy voice.

"Mr. French's painting is a forecast of the cataclysm, and the irony of this painting is that if it is true, there will be no libraries left in which such a painting could be displayed." For Harry, "The Bridge" has another, less oppressive message. Protected from harm by all the wealth of Brenthurst, it suggests that the empire is big enough to envelop anything—even the apocalypse.

And perhaps it is. Reflecting on the enormous number of carats De Beers had bought to shore up the cartel, company director Tim Capon noted, "We were able to put our hands in our pockets. Not many companies could have gone out and bought that much at the drop of a hat." Not *any* companies would be closer to the truth. Even now, the riches of the Oppenheimer empire—in excess of $21 billion— exceed the gross national product of a great many small nations. Its 1,300 companies testify to the growing diversity of the empire, and its nerve centers have subtly shifted to the Continent and to England, where Nicholas Oppenheimer spends at least half of every year. Although denials are offered from time to time, he is preparing to assume the crown and the robe. Other Anglo and De Beers executives have tremendous salaries and responsibilities. But they are not of royal blood. "My son," Harry remarks, "will provide the continuity of family."

The official word at Anglo categorizes three generations of Oppenheimers: Ernest, "the great entrepreneur"; Harry, "the philosopher king"; Nicholas ("call me Nicky"), "the man of action." Not for him the Byron first editions and the scholarly pursuits. "I am much more of a Philistine," he says, freely acknowledging a preference for cricket, squash, and shooting. For a time, the son and grandson of Jewish converts to Christianity drove in a little Renault with the bumper sticker "Jesus Saves." Now he prefers to pilot his own helicopter, chopping off to meetings in Antwerp or flying above English traffic.

Office-seeking holds little appeal; by his own admission he is just "not very good at pressing the flesh." Nicky has become only a bit more political since the days when he conceded that he should have met more African leaders: "I've never been one for meeting black people just because they were black."

He is much less patient than his father, whose eyes would lose their focus when he was bored by a speaker, but who would never express his ennui in so many words. At meetings, Nicholas will brusquely interrupt a discussion to impose his authority. Even so, he seeks the advice of others just as his grandfather and father did. To do so, in his view, reflects "a certain African ethos." As tribesmen discuss matters in a *kraal*, Anglo officials make most of their decisions by consensus. "This has always been our way," he says, in the tone of a man shoring up the fragments of tradition against the ruinous future.

The ruin, if it comes, is certain to be more figurative than literal. Should South Africa dissolve into another Lebanon, the Oppenheimers would simply relocate and live out their lives in the manner of White Russians who escaped before the revolution could seize their properties. Deprived of the mines, the Oppenheimers would still be supremely prosperous managers of a varied portfolio.

But the family has no intention of presiding over the dissolution of its empire. The Oppenheimers have endured threats to their lives, outlived a global depression and two world wars, survived Afrikaaner terror, United Nations denunciations, miners' strikes, revolutionaries, sanctions, failed lawsuits, black consciousness. They have heard themselves called slavers in modern dress, ascending on backs of Africans; they have also received awards for sharing their wealth with African employees and for welcoming blacks into the fold of Anglo management. All along, they have multiplied their billions by keeping straight faces as they dealt with Communist enemies, African nations, and critics around the world. The sanctions are lifting, and the deals are likely to go on well into the twenty-first century and perhaps a lot longer than that. "I'm a South African," Nicky is quick to assert. "That's my home, and that's where I will wind up." And the line does not end with him. Behind Nicky is his 22-year-old son, Jonathan, effectively treading the family path from Harrow and Oxford to De Beers and beyond.

Barring the low road to Beirut, Nicky will soon settle in at 44 Main Street, Johannesburg, seated beneath the portraits of Sir Ernest at one end of the room and Harry at the other. Outside the office that awaits the king, the protestors move through the townships and the city streets. Their advocates take up the cause on every continent, holding up placards demanding justice and equality, making speeches that transfix the listener with eloquence and righteousness. Gold shines on their watches and bracelets and rings; diamonds wink on their fingers. The ironies continue to mount, as they have since that distant afternoon when Erasmus Stephanus Jacobs picked up the *mooi klip* and held the cornerstone of empire in his innocent hand.

NOTES

       INTRODUCTION

7 *I belong to a generation:* David Koskoff, *The Diamond World*, New York, 1981, 61.

8 *People buy diamonds:* Ken Anderson, *And So They Talked*, Cape Town, 1963; see also Anthony Hocking, *Oppenheimer and Son*, Johannesburg, 1973.

8-11 History of diamonds: George Fredrick Kunz, *The Curious Lore of Precious Stones*, New York, 1989; see also Max Bauer, *Precious Stones*, London, 1904; E. W. Streeter, *The Great Diamonds of the World*, London, 1882; Diamond J. R. Sutton, *Diamond*, London, 1928; Sir Richard Burton, *Explorations of the Mountains of Brazil*, London, 1869.

I. A FOCUS OF HUMAN PASSION

15 *In a fit of absence of mind:* Brian Gardner, *The African Dream*, New York, 1970, 57.

16 *Her Majesty possesses not:* F. Boyle, *To the Cape for Diamonds*, London, 1873.

16 *In the glare of the strong sun:* Emily Hahn, *Diamond*, New York, 1956, 20; see also Marian Robertson, *Diamond Fever*, Cape Town, 1974.

17 *Hateren en tateren:* Charles Berlitz, *Native Tongues*, New York, 1982, 91.

17 *In blue cloth jackets:* Henry Gibbs, *Background to Bitterness*, New York, 1955, 37.

19 *Bound on a cross:* Ibid., 27, 28.

20 *His neighbor's smoke:* Rudyard Kipling, *The Voortrekker*, in *Rudyard Kipling's Verse*, Definitive Edition, New York, 1939, 556.

20 *Not so much the freeing:* Mark Strage, *Cape to Cairo*, New York, 1973, 27.

20 *We leave this country:* Gardner, 20.

21 *Would note the date:* Reader's Digest Illustrated History of South Africa, New York, 1988, 119.

22 *Down to the tenth degree:* Geoffrey Wheatcroft, *The Randlords*, New York, 1986, 21.

22 *I wish the black sympathizers:* H.A.C. Cairns, *Prelude to Imperialism*, London, 1965, 204.

23 *From end to end:* Olive Schreiner, *The Story of an African Farm*, New York, 1927, 29.

24 *A dozen of beer:* Brian Roberts, *Kimberley, Turbulent City*, Cape Town, 1976, 6.

24 *Stranger things have come to pass:* M. Robertson, 40.

25 *If a proper search were made:* Ibid., 117.

25 *I made a very lengthy examination:* Controversy in *Geological Magazine*, London, January and May 1869.

26 *A lazy man:* M. Robertson, 175.

27 *Gentlemen, this is the rock:* Oswald Doughty, *Early Diamond Days*, London, 1963, 3.

27 *At times we travelers:* George Beet, *Grand Old Days of the Diamond Fields*, Cape Town, 1931, 12–14.

29 *The Jews have got ahead:* M. Robertson, 225.

30 *A mutual regard:* Doughty, 6.

30 *Fancy sleeping:* The Friend, Bloemfontein, August 1870.

32 *Before we were out of sight:* M. Robertson, 43; see also Beet manuscript, Kimberley Library.

33 *Fleet, I want to see you:* Hedley Chilvers, *The Story of De Beers*, London, 1940, 23, 24; Beet, *Grand Old Days*, 75–77.

33 *Sick of standing:* Doughty, 15.

34 *Rabbis, rebels, rogues:* Louis Cohen, *Reminiscences of Kimberley*, London, 1911, 74–75.

34 *We should have asked six million:* John Angove, *In the Early Days*, Johannesburg, 1910; see also Gardner Williams, *The Diamond Mines of South Africa*, London, 1903.

2. DEEPER INTO THE EARTH

35 *Criers swinging bells:* Williams, 210–217; see also Charles Payton, *The Diamond Diggings of South Africa*, London, 1872.

37 *Large ostrich feathers:* Doughty, 42.

38 *Ultimately, the erring one:* Cohen, 41, 42.

38 Spider fights: Angove, 44, 45; see also *Diamond News*, Kimberley, 1872.

39 *Over-and-under tables:* Angove, 44.

40 *Just fancy: The Friend*, Bloemfontein, September 21, 1871.

40 *Merely the trunk:* J. S. Matthews, *Incwadi Yami*, London, 1887.

40 *A Dutchman buys an old claim:* Doughty, 77.

41 *Discovered a large diamond: Harper's Magazine*, February 1873.

42 Pass Laws: William Worger, *South Africa's City of Diamonds*, New Haven, 1987, 114–115.

43 *The blacks, on the whole: Harper's*, February 1873.

44 *Threatened with closer proximity: Diamond News*, Kimberley, July 20, 1872.

45 *This time last year: Diamond Field Keepsake*, 1873.

45 *Never has an eye:* Williams, 127.

46 *Must receive:* J. B. Currey, "Half a Century in South Africa," manuscript, South African Library, Cape Town; Roberts, *Kimberley*, 115.

47 *Started as a timber merchant:* Altheus Williams, *Some Dreams Come True*, Cape Town, 1948; Cohen.

50 *As old and verdant: Life, Sport and Drama*, Johannesburg, 1921–1922; Roberts, *Kimberley*, 21; see also Stanley Jackson, *The Great Barnato*, London, 1970.

50 *If anybody wants to steal: Diamond News*, November 26, 1872.

51 *It occupied nearly two months:* Roberts, *Kimberley*, 90, 91; see also Harry Raymond, *B.I. Barnato*, London, 1897.

52 Barnato as peddler: Ivor Herbert, *The Diamond Diggers*, London, 1971, 45, 46.

3. THE BOY-MEN

53 *It resembles me:* Jackson.

54 *Decidedly unscrupulous:* Cohen, 217, 225.

55 *Introduction enough:* Brian Roberts, *The Diamond Magnates*, New York, 1971, 61.

56 *When I heard the words: Winning Post*, July 18, 1908.

56 *Look in that gentleman's boot:* G. H. Wilson, *Gone Down the Years*, Cape Town, 1947.

56 *'Ow the dogs do 'owl:* Louis Hermann, *A History of the Jews in South Africa*, Cape Town, 1935, 228; Cohen, 335.

57 *Haply that I am black:* Jackson, 44.

58 *Externally, the two young men:* G. Williams, 274–275.

59 *Vulgar megalomaniac:* Hannah Arendt, *Origins of Totalitarianism*, New York, 1958, 214–215.

60 *I am left in charge:* Robert I. Rotberg, *The Founder*, New York, 1988, 48.

60 *You cannot understand:* Ibid., 52.

61 *It was never an easy matter:* Guy McDonald, "Rhodes in Natal," *Cape Argus*, June 6, 1936.

61 *I am a boy:* Rotberg, 64.

62 *Desperate to grow up:* Tim Jeal, *The Boy-Man*, New York, 1990, 353.

62 *Works just like Stilton:* Strage, 34.

63 *Every man has his price:* Brian Roberts, *Cecil Rhodes*, London, 1987, 36.

63 *Going up to Oxford:* Felix Gross, *Rhodes of Africa*, London, 1956, 20.

64 *Fifty-fifty chance:* Sarah Gertrude Millin, *Rhodes*, London, 1933, 35.

64 *I shall pass:* Rotberg, 89.

64 *There is a destiny:* J. G. Lockhart and C. M. Woodhouse, *Cecil Rhodes*, New York, 1963, 49, 50; John Ruskin, *Lectures in Art*, Oxford, 1870.

65 *A season of mental anguish:* Winwood Reade, *The Martyrdom of Man*, New York, 1874.

65 *A creepy book:* Gross, 25.

65 *It often strikes a man*, et seq.: Wheatcroft, 140, 141; John Flint, *Cecil Rhodes*, Boston, 1974, 248–252; Gross, 61, 62.

4. "WE HAD BETTER JOIN HANDS"

67 *A robust, well-built man:* Leo Weinthal, *Memories, Mines and Millions*, London, 1929, 76.

67 *Sour-faced and green:* Cohen, 92, 93.

67 *His immunity: Cape Times*, October 31, 1929.

68 *I brought up all my boys:* Eric Rosenthal, *Other Men's Millions*, Cape Town, n.d., 191; Roberts, *Magnates*, 18.

68 *Diamond Merchant:* Roberts, *Kimberley*, 102.

68 *His duty in that state: Diamond News*, June 5, 1872.

68 *The pliant whip: Diamond News*, October 3, 1872.

69 *Such claimholders:* Roberts, *Magnates*, 103, 104.

69 *Mr. Whittlestaff:* Anthony Trollope, *An Old Man's Love*, London, 1884.

70 *To "do" South Africa:* Trollope, *South Africa*, reprinted New York, 1987, Vols. 1 and 2; see also V. L. Allen, *The History of Black Mineworkers in South Africa*, Vol. 1, Johannesburg, 1992.

70 *Crusty, quarrelsome:* W. H. Auden, *Forewords and Afterwords*, New York, 1973, 159, 263.

70 *Whipping every one of his boys:* Lionel Phillips, *Some Reminiscences*, London, 1924, 43.

71 *Unroofed, but covered:* Doughty, 199.

72 *Could not the police:* Worger, 100, 122.

73 *Real savages:* Phillips, 43.

73 *Too much kindness:* Doughty, 201.

77 *I was one of the poor Beits:* Frank Harris, *My Life and Loves*, New York, 1970, 752.

77 *I am in favor of conversion:* Paul Johnson, *The History of the Jews*, New York, 1987, 392.

78 *I just did my work:* Harris, 753.

79 *Of all the men:* Phillips, 87; see also Thelma Gutsche, *No Ordinary Woman*, Cape Town, 1966.

79 *That's funny:* Rotberg, 113, 114.

79 *A commercial Viking:* William Plomer, *Cecil Rhodes*, London, 1933, 12.

80 Comparisons of Beit and Rhodes: Harris, 752, 753.

5. A VEHICLE FOR PLUNDER

81 *For the mere sake:* Worger, 168.

81 *A file of ten men: Diamond News*, December 12, 1878.

82 *Fermenting and bubbling:* Worger, 152.

82 *A full fledged Town Councillor: Diamond News*, April 5, 1878.

82 *Although he looked: Winning Post*, April 11, 1908.

83 *I am no Negrophilist: Independent*, May 15, 1881.

84 *My ancestors:* Gross, 69, 70.

84 *From the day of my arrival:* Leander Starr, *Personal Reminiscences of Mr. Rhodes*, London, 1897, 391–413; Rotberg, 127.

84 *I knew a chap: Winning Post*, May 2, 1908.

85 *If word about smallpox:* Hans Sauer, *Ex Africa*, London, 1937, 72–92; Matthews, 108–111; Rotberg, 18.

85 *The natives directed:* David Harris, *Pioneer, Soldier and Politician*, London, 1931, 96.

86 *Strangely altered: Winning Post*, April 10, 1909.

87 *It was astonishing:* Matthews, 247, 248.

87 *There is every chance:* Phyllis Lewsen, ed., *Selections from the Correspondence of J. X. Merriman*, Cape Town, 1960, Rhodes letter, February 16, 1880.

88 *As for the moneyed men:* J.S. Little, *South Africa: A Sketch Book*, London, 1887, 43.

88 *Kaffirs were bribed: Winning Post*, March 24, 1906; see also Colin Newbury, *The Diamond Ring*, London, 1989.

89 *Compounding of natives:* Wheatcroft, 96; S. Ransome, *The Engineer in South Africa*, London, 1903, 66.

89 *Only put it to yourself:* John Smalberger, "IDB and the Mining Compound System in the 1880s," *The South African Journal of Economics*, 1974, 398–414; see also Louise Vescelius-Sheldon, *An I.D.B. in South Africa*, New York, 1888.

90 *Would not submit: Dutoitspan Herald*, April 5, 1884.

90 *Don't fire on us:* Worger, 184–187.

91 *I doubt if any young fellow: Winning Post*, October 3, 1908.

91 *We are not here: Diamond Field Advertiser*, November 7, 1882.

92 *The departure of hordes:* Robert V. Turrell, *Capital and Labor on the Kimberley Diamond Fields 1871–1890*, London, 1987, 178.

93 *He explained: Diamond Field Advertiser*, March 24, April 3, 21, 28, May 8, 1885.

94 *I am a good friend:* Roberts, *Magnates*, 148.

94 *The fact is that this mania:* Lewsen, Vol 1.

95 *Rhodes is the same:* Roberts, *Magnates*, 178.

96 *The Transvaal Navy: Diamond Field Advertiser*, July 8, 1887.

6. VANITY AND DEPRAVITY

97 *Rolling in his chair:* Lockhart, 79.

98 *What a sad affair:* Rotberg, 105.

98 Gordon and Rhodes: Lord Elton, *General Gordon*, London, 1954, 303–309; Rotberg, 144; Lockhart, 77, 78.

99 Pickering and Rhodes: Sir Lewis Mitchell, *The Life of the Right Hon. Cecil John Rhodes*, London, 1910, Vol. I; Roberts, *Magnates*, 129.

100–1 Pickering's illness and death: Ian Colvin, *The Life of Jameson*, London, 1922; Roberts, *Magnates*, 250–254.

102 *Well, Mr. Rhodes:* Gardner Williams, 287.

102 *Looking as fit:* Turrell, 216.

102 *You can go and offer:* "Vindex" (Rev. John Verschoyle), *Cecil Rhodes, His Political Life and Speeches,* London, 1900, 750.

103 *I'll tell you what:* Ibid.

104 *Rhodes only beat me:* Jackson, 78.

104 *It took Barnato's experts:* Roberts, *Magnates*, 198–199.

104 *Aren't those just dreams:* Lockhart, 120.

105 *You've had your whim:* Basil Williams, *Cecil Rhodes*, London, 1921.

105 *If anybody laughed:* Turrell, 227.

106 *Can do anything:* Michel; Raymond, 44–48.

107 *We will now commit: Independent*, June 5, 1888.

107 *The reduction:* Chilvers, 68.

108 *Monastery of labor:* Wheatcroft, 109.

108 *Stripped perfectly naked:* Matthews, 221–222.

109 *Nothing in the external:* Lord Randolph Churchill, *Men, Mines and Animals in South Africa*, London, 1892.

110 *The existence and domination:* Millin, 104.

111 *Events hurried on:* Rotberg, 341, 342.

111 *The excitement: Independent*, February 7, 1891.

111 *Influence of powerful monopolists: Independent*, February 24, 1891.

112 Argus vs. Americus: *Independent*, February, March 1891.

112 Henry Ward: Chilvers, 100, 101.

113 *How can I hate:* Frederick Ponsonby, *Recollections of Three Reigns*, London, 1951, 31.

113 *A few paying gold reefs: Reader's Digest History*, 218.

113 *The iron way: Fortnightly Review*, 1886; Strage, 52.

7. LYING IN STATE

115 Rhodes's racial policies: Rotberg, Ch. 17; Vindex; see also C. W. de Kiewiet, *The Imperial Factor in South Africa*, 1937, and *A History of South Africa*, London, 1941.

117 *The soldiers numbered:* T. M. Thomas, *Eleven Years in South Africa*, London, 1872.

118 *As far as I know: The Memoirs of Paul Kruger*, London, 1902, vol. I; also Howard C. Hillegas, *Oom Paul's People*, New York, 1899.

119 *Do not talk to me:* Weinthal.

119 *Inconvenient emissaries:* Millin.

121 *If gold is found:* Stuart Cloete, *Against These Three*, Cambridge, Mass., 1945, 219.

121–22 Umshete and Babjaan's visit: Strage, 65, 66; see also Friederich Posselt, *Lobengula the Scatterer*, Rhodesia, 1945; Gustav S. Preller, *Lobengula*, Johannesburg, 1963.

123 *The King never lies:* Jameson letter to Howard Pim, 1890, Rhodes House Library, Oxford.

123 *When at last:* Williams, 150.

123 *Has anyone else:* Plomer, 64.

123 *The fragile peace:* Lockhart, Chapter 21; Gross.

124 *Whatever happens:* Hilaire Belloc, "The Modern Traveler," in *Complete Verse of H. Belloc*, London, 1988, 165.

125 *These filibustering:* Hesketh Pearson, *Labby*, London, 1936.

126 *What have you been doing:* Lockhart, 279. Variants of this dialogue occur in almost every Rhodes biography, including Plomer, Williams, and Millin.

126 *Return address as Hell:* Lewsen, Vol. III, 42–43; see also Charles van Onselen, *New Nineveh, New Tyre*, Johannesburg, 1982, Vol 2.

127 *Thieves and murderers:* Lockhart, 291.

127 *Take a tortoise: English Historical Review*, 1957, LXXIII, 292–293.

127 *Ten financial houses:* T. V. Bulpin, *Storm Over the Transvaal*, Cape Town, 1955.

128 *An Afrikander:* Cohen.

129 *Our general scheme: The Autobiography of John Hays Hammond*, New York, 1935. The Jameson Raid and its aftermath has provoked scores of books, pamphlets, and doctoral theses. A list of cross references would tend to obfuscate, rather than clarify, the incident. Rhodes's

earlier biographers tried to put the best possible face on the Raid: Howard Hensman, *Cecil John Rhodes* (London, 1901) is typical. He insists that Rhodes's antagonists have "failed to show that he hoped or expected to reap the slightest personal gain from the revolution in Johannesburg." Later biographers have shown a higher regard for the truth; Lockhart, Plomer, Williams, and Roberts (*Rhodes*) especially have compiled damning evidence, and Rotberg has provided the last word. The most complete account can be found in Jean van der Poel, *The Jameson Raid* (London, 1951) and in Elizabeth Pakenham, *Jameson's Raid* (Johannesburg, 1958). An antique but valuable account is Edmund Garret and E. J. Edwards, *The Story of an African Crisis* (New York, 1897). See also Colvin; A. Geoffrey Blainey, "Lost Causes of the Jameson Raid," *Economic History Review* XLVIII, 1965; and John Hays Hammond and Alleyne Ireland, *The Liberal Party and The Truth about the Jameson Raid* (Boston, 1918).

132 *How did you ever:* Cloete.

132 *You are no gentleman:* Jackson, 120.

133 *Wrong! Is it wrong?:* London *Times*, January 4, 1897.

134 *In times of political adversity: Eastern Province Herald*, June 1, 1896.

134 *A mere vulgar promoter:* Pearson.

134 *Lying in State:* Marquess of Crewe, *Lord Rosebery*, New York, 1931, 441.

134 *What is there in South Africa:* Wheatcroft, 189.

135 *In Memoriam: Westminster Gazette*, July 1897.

136 Barnato's descent: Jackson; Raymond.

137 *I suppose you thought:* Lockhart, 382; Gross, 362.

8. EXIT RHODES, ENTER HOGGENHEIMER

139 *Ruin or disgrace:* Jackson, 236.

140 *If that is your final decision:* Stanhope Joel, *Ace of Diamonds*, London, 1958, 76.

142 *When you've shouted:* Rudyard Kipling, "The Absent-Minded Beggar," *Kipling's Verse*, 457.

142 *Trembled to think:* David Harris, 153.

143 *I do not know:* Michell, Vol II.

144 *Borne with this man:* Altheus Gardner, 201.

144 *Superior calculating intellect:* C. Holme, Ed., *Immigrants and Minorities in British Society*, "A. Hobson and the Jews," London, 1978; Wheatcroft, 205.

144 *Johannesburg is essentially: Manchester Guardian*, September 28, 1889.

145 *Mr. Rhodes and his associates:* S. Koss, Ed., *The Pro Boers*, London, 1973, 94.

145 *A hell full:* Ibid., 55–57.

145 *We also know:* Hilaire Belloc, "Verses to a Lord," *Complete Verse*, 151.

146 *Aquiline features:* Plomer, 17.

146 *Why, you seem:* Olive Schreiner, *Trooper Peter Halket of Mashonaland*, Johannesburg, 1897.

148 *It was necessary:* Brian Roberts, *Cecil Rhodes and the Princess*, London, 1969, 312.

149 *Without religion: Natal Witness*, May 3, 1902.

149 *The world is nearly:* Gardner, 207.

149 *Dreamer devout:* Rudyard Kipling, "The Burial." *Kipling's Verse*, 209.

150 *What a legacy of hate:* Eric Rosenthal, *Gold! Gold! Gold!*, London, 1970, 331–335.

151 *Born under the British:* Wheatcroft, 213.

152 *Two hordes:* Dan H. Laurence, Ed., *The Letters of George Bernard Shaw*, 1985, Volume 2, 122.

152 *When driving through the park:* Hahn, 105, 106; see also Murray and Elzabe Schoonraad, *Companion to South African Cartoonists*, Johannesburg, 1989. The inventor of the Hoggenheimer caricature, Daniel C. Boonzaier, was the exceptionally skilled political cartoonist of *The South African News*, where he first published his symbol of the beaky, grasping capitalist. Accused of anti-Semitism, he replied with a drawing, "Die Evolusie van Hoggenheimer" (The Evolution of Hoggenheimer), attempting to demonstrate that the character had derived from ancient caricatures of Dutch, French, English, and German, as well as Jewish, plutocrats. But this was disingenuous; when *The Girl from Kay's* came to South Africa, the audience knew very well what Hoggenheimer was intended to represent. *The Star* commented, "By all accounts the English comedian . . . delighted audiences with his portrayal of the wealthy Jewish financier of Park Lane." Hoggenheimer later entered South Africa's public domain, and at least six other artists made full use of Hoggenheimer as the overdressed capitalist with hook nose and voracious appetites.

153 *A young German Jew:* Anthony Hocking, *Oppenheimer and Son*, Johannesburg, 1973; Edward Jessup, *Ernest Oppenheimer, A Study in Power*, London, 1979; see also Sir Theodore Gregory, *Ernest Oppenheimer and the Economic Development of South Africa*, Cape Town, 1962; *South Africa's Hall of Fame*, Johannesburg, 1960; "Sir Ernest Oppenheimer, A Portrait by his Son" *Optima*, September 1967.

9. THE SPECTRE, THE SCAM, AND SATYAGRAHA

159 Prinsloo and Cullinan: Herbert, 95–97; Jessup, 44; see also Eric Rosenthal, *Here Are Diamonds*, Johannesburg, 1950.

159 *Whenever you hear:* Rhodes speeches, Chilvers.

160 Oats and the Premier: Jessup, 45.

161 Ernest and May: Hocking, 34–39; Jessup, 48, 49.

162 I thought of only one thing: Seymour Fort, *Alfred Beit*, London, 1932.

162 *First let me into:* G.A.L. Green, *An Editor Looks Back*, Cape Town, 1947, 122; Roberts, *Magnates*, 286–289.

165 *They roar with laughter:* Gutsche, 224.

165 *Just like something in Balzac:* George Painter, *Proust*, Volume II, 1965, 98–104.

165 *We are having:* Green, 122.

165–66 Death of Alfred Beit: Michell; Fort.

167 *They were the unhappiest:* P. Tennyson Cole, *Vanity Varnished*, London, 1931, 175.

167 *Milner's kindergarten:* Lionel Curtis, *With Milner in South Africa*, London, 1951; C. W. de Kiewiet, *A History of South Africa*, London, 1941; Cecil Headlam, Ed., *The Milner Papers: South Africa*, London, 1931.

168–70 Chinese coolies: Peter Richardson, *Chinese Mine Labor on the Transvaal*, London, 1982; Neame, 160, 161; A. P. Cartwright, *Gold Paved the Way*, London, 1967, 106, 107; Phyllis Lewsen, *John X. Merriman*, 278; Curtis; Wheatcroft, 223–226. A sort of apologia for Milner's "coolie" policy may be found in Cartwright's *The Corner House*, London, 1965, 183, 184.

170–71 *Will affect our competitors:* Jessup, 55.

173 *Satyagraha:* Erik H. Erikson, *Gandhi's Truth*, New York, 1969, 204–216.

173–74 Ernest Oppenheimer as Mayor: Hocking.

173–75 Hicks vs. Ernest Oppenheimer: *Diamond Field Advertiser*, September, May 1914; Hocking, Ch. 3.

10. MONKEYING ABOUT WITH THE CAPITAL

176 *A soldier who disdains:* Louis Cohen, *Reminiscences*; see also Richard West, *The Diamonds and the Necklace*, London, 1989, 150–153.

178 *Wickedly suborning: South Africa*, February 28, 1914; Brian Roberts, *Magnates*, New York, 1972, 297–299.

178 *If we only had a half-dozen:* Hocking, 69.

179 *I want to be a director:* Jessup, 78.

180 *Baying for blood and gold:* Hocking, 71.

180 *On consideration:* Jessup, 93.

181 Lionel Phillips: Lionel Phillips, *Some Reminiscences*, Johannesburg, 1986, 11–28.

183 *What about "African American":* Sir Theodore Gregory, *Ernest Oppenheimer and the Economic Development of Southern Africa*, Cape Town, 1962, 88.

184 *Galway Castle: African World*, London, January 23, 1933; Hocking, 82–85.

186 *I naturally suffered:* V. I. Lenin, *Imperialism*, reprinted New York, 1980; Lewis Feuer, *Imperialism and the Anti-Imperialist Mind*, New York, 1986, 10, 74.

186 *There will be no performance:* J. S. Hobson, "For Whom Are We Fighting?" pamphlet, London, 1899.

187 *Some readers may think:* Leonard Thompson, *A History of South Africa*, New Haven, 1989, 165; Sol Plaatje, *Native Life in South Africa*, New York, 1969, 2, 3.

188 *If anyone had told us: Reader's Digest History*, 292.

190 *Except on the battlefields:* Anthony Sampson, *Black and Gold*, London, 1987, 70, 71; Brian Lapping, *Apartheid, a History*, New York, 1989, 52.

191 *Like all solicitors: Reader's Digest History*, 288, 289.

11. A SIDE ENTRANCE TO DE BEERS

193 *From the conversations:* Jessup, 112.

194 *To make a Jew a peer:* Frederick Morton, *The Rothschilds*, New York, 1983, 168.

194 *A leading part: African World*, London, January 8, 1921; Hocking, 91, 92.

195 *Disposition of peers:* Winston Churchill to Bonar Law, January 2, 1921.

195 *A general strike:* Phillips, 172–174; *Reader's Digest History*, 304.

196–97 Cohen in Johannesburg: Louis Cohen, *Memories of Johannesburg*, London, 1924.

197 *The Chamber of Mines:* F. Addington Symonds, *The Johannesburg Story*, London, 1953, 189, 199.

198 *The character of the revolt:* L. E. Neame, *City Built on Gold*, London, 1960, 220, 221.

198–99 Smuts in Cape Town: Symonds, 193, 194.

201 *Robinson's talent:* B. Roberts, 230, 231; Wheatcroft, 300, 301.

204 *I have the honor:* Jessup, 125, 126.

205 *The biggest name:* Hocking, Ch. 5.

12. THE DEATH OF HOPE

208 *Into the bush:* Hocking, 147, 148.

209 *I am not going to be pointed out:* Speech to diamond conference, June 30, 1931; David Pallister, Sarah Stewart, and Ian Lepper, *South Africa Inc.*, New Haven, 1988, 65.

210 *We have the spectacle:* South Africa Parliamentary reports, 1924–1934; Hocking, 154–159.

214 *I feel very tired: Cape Argus*, Cape Town, February 6, 1934; Hocking, 165.

215 *Ernest received the news:* Pallister et al. , 64. Ernest Oppenheimer's conversion was the subject of intense speculation in his own lifetime and remains so today. His grandson Nicky has privately claimed that he has no Jewish relatives, which would seem to indicate that at various times all five Oppenheimer brothers and their spouses converted from Judaism to Christianity without, perhaps, going through Sir Ernest's spiritual crisis. Although the retail diamond industry is almost exclusively Jewish, De Beers has remarkably few Jewish executives. Nonetheless, after some unpleasant intervals the family enjoys excellent relations with Israel and with thousands of Jewish diamontiers in America and Europe. It may well be, as one

47th Street broker says, "We Jews make better soldiers, so we prefer to be on the front lines. De Beers makes better generals. We don't need affirmative action here. Let it be." See also Murray Schumach, *The Diamond People*, New York, 1981, especially Chapter 3, "Why Diamonds Are Jewish."

217 *Apartness: Reader's Digest History*, 318.

220 *He who betrays the Bond:* Ivor Wilkins and Hans Strydom, *The Broederbond*, London, 1979, 97–107; Allister Sparks, *The Mind of South Africa*, New York, 1990, 171.

220 *In the style of Adolf Hitler: Reader's Digest History*, 336–339.

222–23 Luckoff's parting sermon: René Kraus, *Old Master*, London, 1944, 381.

223 *With more and more colleagues:* Hocking, 179–182.

13. CLEAVING A DIAMOND WITH A BUTTER KNIFE

225 *To show you how much:* Oppenheimer Correspondence, Brenthurst Library, Johannesburg; Hocking, 198, 199.

226 *Anyone might have imagined:* Gregory, 473.

227–28 *Artificially created fear:* Jessup, 216.

228–29 *With a dignified silence: Time*, February 12, 1945.

228 *The diamond section:* Edward Jay Epstein, *The Rise and Fall of Diamonds*, New York 1982, 90.

229 *Ruthless in stamping it out:* Ibid., 91, 92.

231 *Colored men: Reader's Digest History*, 352.

231 *All the achievements:* Jessup, 301; Ken Luckhardt and Brenda Wall, *Organize or Starve!*, London, 1980, 69.

232 *Pay special attention:* Gregory, 573, 574.

232 *The compound system:* Lapping, 85.

232 *Appropriate action:* Jonathan Ball, *Bullion Johannesburg*, Johannesburg, 1986, 375; Lapping, 85.

234 *Through the inventions:* Hocking, 232.

234 *Utterly impractical:* Martin Meredith, *In the Name of Apartheid*, London, 1988, 46, 47.

235 *Either that of integration:* Lapping, 96, 97.

236 *Sir Ernest Oppenheimer:* Alan Paton, *Cry, the Beloved Country*, New York, 1956, 171.

237 *My old comrades:* Hocking, 240; J. C. Smuts, *Jan Christian Smuts*, London, 307–398.

238 *Arguing with the honorable member:* Hocking, 247–249.

240 *The sale of uranium:* John Gunther, *Inside Africa*, New York, 1955, 553.

241 *As things stand:* Hocking, 254.

14. GETTING AWAY WITH IT

242 Williamson: Isobel and Florence McHugh, *The Diamond Seeker*, London, 1959.

243 *They only want me:* Hocking, 256.

244 *A quarrel suddenly flared:* H. F. Burgess, *Diamonds Unlimited*, London, 1960.

244–45 Williamson and Oppenheimer: Koskoff, 107–109.

246 *Sir Percy, They Presume:* Ian Fleming, *The Diamond Smugglers*, New York, 1957, 6.

248 *Dishonesty has been accepted:* Ibid., 103.

249 *Fiction's frequently sublime:* Hocking, 288.

249–58 Accounts of Brenthurst robbery: Dennis Craig and Brian Parkes, *Drama in Diamonds*, Cape Town, 1956, and author interviews.

15. CROWNING THE NEW KING

259 *High reputation:* Jessup, 316, 317.

260 *Grand Apartheid:* Meredith, 71; Lapping, 105; *Reader's Digest History*, 376.

261 *This extraordinary progress:* Jessup, 264, 265.

261 *We must maintain:* Hocking, 310, 321, 322.

262 *In the morning:* Rev. Trevor Huddleston, *Naught For Your Comfort*, London, 1956.

263 *What a sad figure:* Alexander Steward, *You Are Wrong, Father Huddleston*, London, 1957.

263 *How can you give:* Margaret Friend, *Without Fear or Favor*, Cape Town, 1958, 68, 69.

265 *Anyone who has visited:* Hocking, 325–327.

265 *It was the smoke:* Emily Hahn, *Diamond*, New York, 1956, 149.

266 *Diamonds were my first love:* Ibid., 172.

267 *What's going on?:* "Suid-Afrika se Magtigte Sakeman," *Die Burger*, May 1957; Hocking, 331–337.

269 *I am smoking:* Epstein, 116.

272–74 *Synthetic diamonds:* Eric Bruton, *Diamonds*, London, 1981, 426, 427; Epstein, Ch. 17; Hocking, Ch. 10.

274 My father's death: Hocking, 343–346.

276 *I just saw brains:* Sparks, 233; see also *Optima*, Johannesburg, Vol. 24, 216; Laurie Flynn, *Studded with Diamonds and Gold*, 197, 198; Gail M. Gerhart, *Black Power in South Africa*, Berkeley, 1978, Ch. 7, "Sharpeville and Quiescence."

276 *A planned demonstration:* Thompson, 211.

277 *The Oppenheimer group:* Hocking, 370.

16. A NASTY SORT OF SURVIVAL

282 *Humane policies:* William Minter, *King Solomon's Mines Revisited*, London, 1986, 200.

282 *No arts; no letters:* Hocking, 377–399; see also Adrian Leftwich, Ed., *South Africa, Economic Growth and Political Change*, London, 1974.

285 *Mr. Bond:* Ian Fleming, *Goldfinger*, New York, 1989, 184.

286 *If you find:* Forbes, June 15, 1973.

286–87 Verwoerd assassination: Lapping, 149, 150.

288 *No stone is to be left:* Ibid., 154, 155; see also Herbert Adam and Hermann Gilomiee, *Ethnic Power Mobilized*, New Haven, 1979, 201, 202.

289 *Suppression of Communism:* Paul Johnson, *Modern Times*, New York, 1986, 514–517.

290 *Not very happy:* Hocking, 386.

293 *I realize I am living: Melbourne Herald*, April 23, 1970.

293 *If business men outside:* Hocking, 435; see also Stephen Gelb, Ed., *South Africa's Economic Crisis*, London, 1991, 19, 20.

17. FUNIGALO AND FLASH FRED

296 *I am not one of those:* Hocking, 361; see also *Forbes*, July 1973; Duncan Innes, *Anglo-American and the Rise of Modern South Africa*, London, 1984, 188–219.

297 *We did have occasionally:* Pallister et al., 45.

299 *I am happy on the mine:* Ernest Cole, *House of Bondage*, New York, 1967, 22.

300 *However they leave:* Ibid., 24; see also Ann Seidman, *The Roots of Crisis in South Africa*, Johannesburg, 1985.

301 *It's not easy:* Hocking, 390; see also Peter Randall, *Little England on the Veld*, Johannesburg, 1982.

304 *Although I don't think:* Hocking, 443–445.

305 *So pure:* Ian Fleming, *Diamonds Are Forever*, New York, 1959, 14.

306–11 Kamil hijacking: Fred Kamil, *The Diamond Underworld*, London, 1979; Hocking, 446–460; and author interviews.

18. UNDER ANGLO EVERY ONE

312 *We are justified:* Hocking, 468–472.

313 *South Africa's oldest industry:* Forbes, June 15, 1973.

314 *A wild feverish city:* Malcolm Muggeridge, *The Infernal Grove*, London, 1983, 160.

314 *Where have all the houses gone:* Hocking, 461.

316 *The time has come:* Ibid., 464.

316 *Once you get:* Forbes, June 15, 1973.

317 *Conspiracy . . . to suppress:* Epstein, 209–211.

319 *Evil Marxists:* Reader's Digest History, 435–438.

320 *After the events:* New York Times, June 2, 1976.

320–22 Soweto uprising: Meredith, 143–148; John Kane-Berman, *Soweto: Black Revolt, White Reaction*, London, 1978; Jeremy Brickhill, *Whirlwind Before the Storm*, London, 1980; Reader's Digest History, 440–447.

322 *Not to be dominated: The Progressive Party of South Africa 1950–1981*, Thesis, Balliol College, Oxford; Pallister et al., 103.

324 *Verkrampte* and *verligte:* Meredith, 167.

324 *Neither gratitude nor praise:* Chairman's Annual Statement, 1981.

324–25 *Had never subscribed:* Hocking, 427.

325 *A drastic program:* Eschel Roodie, *The Real Information Scandal*, Johannesburg, 1983; Reader's Digest History, 449; see also Graham Leach, *South Africa*, London, 1987, 41, 105.

326 *Adapt or die:* Meredith, 171.

19. BOILER ROOM FOLLIES

329 *Grant the Jew his ideals: Transvaaler*, December 1, 1946.

330 *Slapped South Africa:* Jane Hunger, *Israeli Foreign Policy*, London, 1987, 25.

331 *We here follow: Jerusalem Post*, April 13, 1976.

331 *Development of trade:* "Hands Across South Africa." *South African Digest*, April 23, 1976.

332 *I will be your ambassador:* Epstein, 176.

334 *The generals in Johannesburg:* Author interview, October 3, 1991.

335 *LET'S FACE IT: Forbes*, September 18, 1978.

336 *Diamond selling was the con:* Author interview, November 21, 1991.

337 *No offers came in:* Epstein, 238, 239.

338 *The Emperor's new ring:* Ibid., 242.

338 *De Beers is holding back: New York Times*, September 16, 1981.

339 *These are the worst times: Fortune*, September 6, 1982.

340 *An artificially maintained illusion:* Epstein, 267.

341 *She can't flaunt a fur: Fortune*, September 6, 1982.

20. BUT NEVER JAM TODAY

343 *Crime is one thing:* Author interview, May 12, 1991.

343 *We were approached: Independent*, October 14, 1992.

344 *I can't pretend: Financial Times*, March 9, 1983.

346 *I think it is to be much tougher: New York Times*, November 18, 1985.

347 *At one time they thought: Financial Times*, January 31, 1983.

347 *Little, if at all: Financial Times*, December 28, 1984.

347 *Not in favor: New York Times*, November 18, 1985.

348 *The ancient allegation:* Joseph Lelyveld, *Move Your Shadow*, New York, 1985, 332.

349 *When you say that you don't want sanctions: Reader's Digest History*, 483.

350 Waddell and the *Daily Mail:* Pallister et al., 145; *Financial Times*, January 24, 1987; author interviews.

350 *Believed it gave the paper: Finance Week,* April 25–May 1, 1985.

350 *More interested in politics:* Pallister, et al., 272.

350 *Addressing itself: Washington Post*, June 24, 1990.

351 *Dismayed at the role: Rand Daily Mail*, March 16, 1985.

353 *Things that bring men together:* Pallister, et al., 275–279.

353 *If you'd been asked:* Sampson, 194.

354 *Capitalism has now entered: The Guardian*, October 7, 1985.

354 *We can't pay our debts:* Sampson, 225.

355 *The South African government believe:* Record of British House of Commons, July 16, 1986.

356 *Well, gentlemen: Los Angeles Times*, July 9, 1990.

21. THE MOST DANGEROUS AGE

357 *Spiritual and economic enslavement:* Sampson, 234; *Weekly Mail*, May 2, 1986; see also Sparks, 325, 343.

358 *Oppenheimer runs a cartel:* Author interview, February 9, 1991.

358 *To be a company outside:* Bill Jamieson, *Goldstrike!*, London, 1990, 52; see also *Forbes*, September 16, 1991.

359 *Judging by the financial record:* Monopolies Commission Report: Minorco and Consolidated Gold Fields, February 1989.

359 *As an entity:* Shearson Lehman Hutton Analyst's Report, August 1989.

360 *Anglo's operating costs: Business Week*, October 3, 1988.

361 *With the express intention:* Jamieson, 61–69. Dockets 88–7932, 88–7944, U.S. Court of Appeals, Consolidated Gold Fields v. Minorco, Argued Dec. 20, 1988. Decided March 22, 1989.

361–67 Jamieson, *Gold Strike!* and author interviews. *Goldstrike!* is the most succinct history of the Gold Fields debacle and is indispensable for historians of the empire's recent past. To be fair, though, it should be tempered with a small volume: Clem Sunter, *The World and South Africa in the 90's* (Cape Town, 1987). Sunter, a high-ranking Oppenheimer executive, takes note of the risks inherent in South Africa's changeover to a truly representative government. In the main, however, he is sanguine about the nation's future. A closing paragraph sounds the cautiously upbeat message: "In the summer of 1787, there was a nation which was in danger of falling apart. Then fifty-five men assembled at a convention and drew up a document: The place was Philadelphia and the nation was America. That event was not predictable—it was made to happen by great men. The same can happen here." An opposing view is expressed in Minter, a biting criticism of South Africa's white capitalists and their legacy.

371 *The meaning is painful:* Jamieson, 2.

371 *I am much more of a Philistine: Optima*, Vol. 36, No. 3; *Business Week*, May 2, 1983.

INDEX

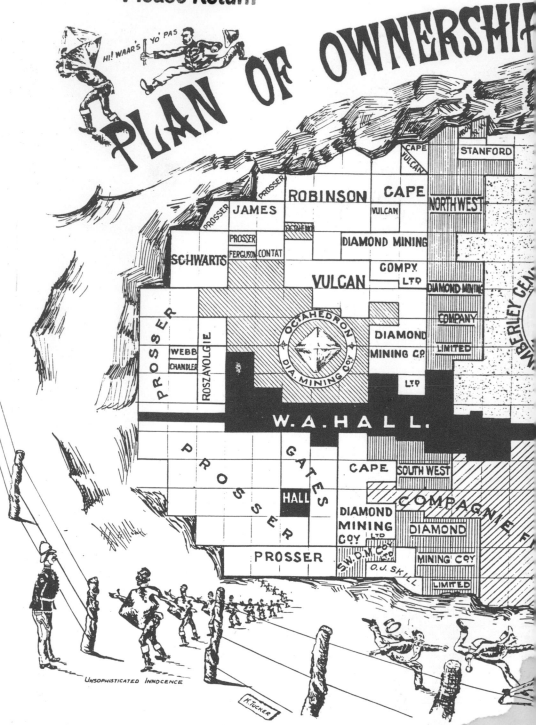

PLAN OF OWNERSHIP

HI! WAAR'S YO' PAS

STANFORD

CAPE VULCAN

ROBINSON   CAPE

PROSSER   VULCAN   NORTHWEST

PROSSER   JAMES

OCTAHEDRON   DIAMOND MINING

PROSSER

SCHWARTS   FERGUSON CONTAT   COMPY. LTD

VULCAN   DIAMOND MINING

PROSSER   DIAMOND

WEBB   ROSZAVOLGIE   OCTAHEDRON   MINING C.P.   COMPANY

CHANDLER   DIA. MINING CO.   LIMITED

LTD

W. A. HALL.

PROSSER   GATES   CAPE   SOUTH WEST

COMPAGNIE

HALL   DIAMOND

DIAMOND   MINING   DIAMOND

PROSSER   COY. LTD   MINING COY

S.W.D.M.CO. LTD   O.J. SKILL   LIMITED

UNSOPHISTICATED INNOCENCE

K. TUCKER

KIMBERLEY CEN